Praise for

JUSTICE FOR ANIMALS

"The most important book on animal ethics written to date, *Justice for Animals* is a brilliant and remarkably comprehensive exploration of the ethical issues connected with human treatment of nonhumans. A milestone in the field."

—Thomas I. White, author of *In Defense of Dolphins*

"With urgent clarity, Martha Nussbaum explains why we must and how we can take responsibility for the multispecies world that is our reality. *Justice for Animals* is a celebration of the human potential for love and mutuality and a song of hope, as much as it is a steely eyed analysis of our callous dominance of the nonhuman world."

—Amy Linch, Penn State University

"Martha Nussbaum's work has changed the humanities, but in this book her focus is startling, born of an ardent love for her late daughter and for all animals on Earth."

—Jeremy Bendik-Keymer, Case Western
Reserve University, and Senior Research Fellow,
Earth System Governance Project

"Martha Nussbaum takes an honest look at how animals may survive in a human-dominated world and lays out a plan of action to help creatures great and small in important and critical ways."

—Dr. Denise Herzing, founder and Research Director of
the Wild Dolphin Project

"A provocative book. Nussbaum lays out a foundation for the political rights of animals and asks what creating a world where animals could be our friends would look like. An essential read for anyone interested in what we owe to our fellow creatures."

—Nicolas Delon, Associate Professor of Philosophy and Environmental Studies, New College of Florida

"The morality of the human-animal relation urgently needs updating. We can't wish for a more insightful and compassionate guide than philosopher Martha Nussbaum. She urges us to look beyond pain and pleasure and to consider all animals, not just those that resemble us. Each species' specific needs and capabilities offer a guide of how they should be treated."

—Frans de Waal, author of *Different: Gender Through the Eyes of a Primatologist*

"A thought-provoking guide to ethical coexistence with the diverse creatures of Earth."

—*Kirkus Reviews*

"This trenchant and masterful blend of political analysis, philosophical study, and call to action is a must-read."

—*Publishers Weekly* (starred review)

"Here, as in other works, her arguments are thorough, elegantly written, and compelling—so finely tuned that Aristotle himself would need to be in top form to engage her on the subject. . . . Sure to become a classic of ethics."

—Matthew Scully, *National Review*

"Brilliant and accessible work. . . . All readers, not only readers already committed to animal rights, ought to read Nussbaum's new book."

—Ross Collin, *Chicago Review of Books*

"Nussbaum's writing is energetic and direct, full of stories and anecdotes. The book is pleasingly constructive . . . it is a virtue of this book that the mind of the author is so clearly on display."

—Dale Jamieson, *Science*

ALSO BY MARTHA C. NUSSBAUM

*The Monarchy of Fear: A Philosopher Looks
at Our Political Crisis* (2018)

Aristotle's De Motu Animalium (1978)

*The Fragility of Goodness: Luck and Ethics
in Greek Tragedy and Philosophy* (1986)

Love's Knowledge: Essays on Philosophy and Literature (1990)

*The Therapy of Desire: Theory and Practice
in Hellenistic Ethics* (1994)

Poetic Justice: The Literary Imagination and Public Life (1995)

*Cultivating Humanity: A Classical Defense
of Reform in Liberal Education* (1997)

Sex and Social Justice (1999)

Women and Human Development: The Capabilities Approach (2000)

Upheavals of Thought: The Intelligence of Emotions (2001)

Hiding from Humanity: Disgust, Shame, and the Law (2004)

Frontiers of Justice: Disability, Nationality, Species Membership (2006)

JUSTICE

FOR

ANIMALS

Our Collective Responsibility

MARTHA C.
NUSSBAUM

SIMON & SCHUSTER PAPERBACKS

New York   London   Toronto   Sydney   New Delhi

An Imprint of Simon & Schuster, Inc.
1230 Avenue of the Americas
New York, NY 10020

First Simon & Schuster trade paperback edition January 2024

SIMON & SCHUSTER PAPERBACKS and colophon are
registered trademarks of Simon & Schuster, Inc.

Simon & Schuster: Celebrating 100 Years of Publishing in 2024

For information about special discounts for bulk purchases,
please contact Simon & Schuster Special Sales
at 1-866-506-1949 or business@simonandschuster.com.

The Simon & Schuster Speakers Bureau can bring authors to your live event.
For more information or to book an event, contact the
Simon & Schuster Speakers Bureau at 1-866-248-3049 or
visit our website at www.simonspeakers.com.

Interior design by Ruth Lee-Mui

Manufactured in the United States of America

1   3   5   7   9   10   8   6   4   2

Library of Congress Cataloging-in-Publication Data has been applied for.

ISBN 978-1-9821-0250-0
ISBN 978-1-9821-0251-7 (pbk)
ISBN 978-1-9821-0252-4 (ebook)

To the memory of Rachel,
and to all the whales

Contents

Introduction

Animals are in trouble all over the world.[1] Our world is dominated by humans everywhere: on land, in the seas, and in the air. No non-human animal escapes human domination. Much of the time, that domination inflicts wrongful injury on animals: whether through the barbarous cruelties of the factory meat industry, through poaching and game hunting, through habitat destruction, through pollution of the air and the seas, or through neglect of the companion animals that people purport to love.

In a way, this problem is age-old. Both Western and non-Western philosophical traditions have deplored human cruelty to animals for around two millennia. The Hindu emperor Ashoka (c. 304–232 BCE), a convert to Buddhism, wrote about his efforts to give up meat and to forgo all practices that harmed animals. In Greece the Platonist philosophers Plutarch (46–119 CE) and Porphyry (c. 234–305 CE) wrote detailed treatises deploring human cruelty to animals, describing their keen intelligence and their capacity for social life, and urging humans to change their diet and their way of life. But by and large these voices have fallen on deaf ears, even in the supposedly moral realm of the philosophers, and most humans have continued to treat most animals like objects, whose suffering does not matter—although they sometimes make an exception for companion animals. Meanwhile, countless animals have suffered cruelty, deprivation, and neglect.

Today, we have, then, a long-overdue ethical debt: to listen to arguments we have refused to hear, to care for what we have obtusely ignored, and to act on the knowledge of our bad practices that we can so easily attain. But today we have reasons humans never had before to do something about human wrongs to animals. First, human domination has increased exponentially in the past two centuries. In Porphyry's world, animals suffered when they were killed for meat, but up to that point they lived pretty decent lives. There was no factory meat industry that, today, breeds these animals as if they were just meat already, confining them in horrible conditions, cramped and isolated, until they die before ever having decently lived. Animals were long hunted in the wild, but for the most part their habitats were not taken over for human dwellings or invaded by poachers seeking to make money from the murder of an intelligent being, an elephant or a rhinoceros. In the seas, humans have always fished for food, and whales have long been hunted for their commercial value. But the sea was not full of plastic trash that entices animals to dine on it, and then chokes them to death. Nor did companies drilling for undersea oil create noise pollution everywhere (drilling, air bombs used to chart the ocean's floor), making life increasingly difficult for social creatures whose sense of hearing is their primary mode of communication. Birds were shot for food, but those who escaped did not choke on air pollution or crash fatally into urban skyscrapers, whose lights entice them. In short: the scope of human cruelty and neglect was relatively narrow. Today new forms of animal cruelty turn up all the time—without even being recognized as cruelty, since their impact on the lives of intelligent beings is barely considered. So we have not just the overdue debt of the past, but a new moral debt that has increased a thousandfold and is continually increasing.

Because the reach of human cruelty has expanded, so too has the involvement of virtually all people in it. Even people who do not consume meat produced by the factory farming industry are likely to have used single-use plastic items, to use fossil fuels mined beneath the ocean and polluting the air, to dwell in areas in which elephants and bears once roamed, or to live in high-rise buildings that spell death for migratory birds. The extent of our own implication in practices that harm animals should make every person with a conscience consider what we can all do to change this situation. Pinning guilt is less important than accepting the fact that humanity as a whole has a collective duty to face and solve these problems.

So far, I have not spoken of the extinction of animal species, because this is a book about loss and deprivation suffered by individual creatures, each of whom matters. Species as such do not suffer loss. However, extinction never takes place without massive suffering of individual creatures: the hunger of a polar bear, starving on an ice floc, unable to cross the sea to hunt; the sadness of an orphan elephant, deprived of care and community as the species dwindles rapidly; the mass extinctions of songbird species as a result of unbreathable air, a horrible death. When human practices hound species toward extinction, member animals always suffer greatly and live squashed and thwarted lives. Besides, the species themselves matter for creating diverse ecosystems in which animals can live well (see further in chapter 5).

Extinctions would take place even without human intervention. Even in such cases we might have reasons to intervene to stop them, because of the importance of biodiversity. But scientists agree that today's extinctions are between one thousand and ten thousand times higher than the natural extinction rate.[2] (Our uncertainty is huge, because we are very ignorant of how many species there actually are, particularly where fish and insects are concerned.) Worldwide, approximately one-quarter of the world's mammals and over 40 percent of amphibians are currently threatened with extinction.[3] These include several species of bear, the Asian elephant (endangered), the African elephant (threatened), the tiger, six species of whale, the gray wolf, and so many more. All in all, more than 370 animal species are either endangered or threatened, using the criteria of the US Endangered Species Act, not including birds, and a separate list of similar length for birds. Asian songbirds are virtually extinct in the wild, on account of the lucrative trade in these luxury items.[4] And many other species of birds have recently become extinct.[5] Meanwhile, the international treaty called CITES that is supposed to protect birds (and many other creatures) is toothless and unenforced.[6] The story of this book is not that story of mass extinction, but the sufferings of individual creatures that take place against this background of human indifference to biodiversity.

There is a further reason why the ethical evasion of the past must end now. Today we know far more about animal lives than we did even fifty years ago. We know much too much for the glib excuses of the past to be offered without shame. Porphyry and Plutarch (and Aristotle before them) knew a lot about animal intelligence and sensitivity. But somehow humans find ways of "forgetting" what the science of the past has plainly revealed, and for many centuries most people, including most philosophers, thought animals were "brute beasts," automata without a subjective sense of the world, without emotions, without society, and perhaps even without the feeling of pain.

Recent decades, however, have seen an explosion of high-level research covering all areas of the animal world. One of the great pleasures of writing this book has been that of immersion in this research. We now know more not only about animals long closely studied—primates and companion animals—but also about animals who are difficult to study—marine mammals, whales, fish, birds, reptiles, and cephalopods.

What do we know? We know—not just by observation, but by carefully designed experimental work—that all vertebrates and many invertebrates feel pain subjectively, and have, more generally, a subjectively felt view of the world: the world looks like something to them. We know that all of these animals experience at least some emotions (fear being the most ubiquitous), and that many experience emotions like compassion and grief that involve more complex "takes" on a situation. We know that animals as different as dolphins and crows can solve complicated problems and learn to use tools to solve them. We know that animals have complex forms of social organization and social behavior. More recently, we have been learning that these social groups are not simply places where a rote inherited repertory is acted out, but places of complicated social learning. Species as different as whales, dogs, and many types of birds clearly transmit key parts of the species' repertoire to their young socially, not just genetically.

I'll be using this research a lot in this book. What are its implications for ethics? Huge, clearly. We can no longer draw the usual line between our own species and "the beasts," a line meant to distinguish intelligence, emotion, and sentience from the dense life of a "brute beast." Nor can we even draw a line between a group of animals we already recognize as sort of "like us"—apes, elephants, whales, dogs—and others who are supposed to be unintelligent. Intelligence takes multiple and fascinating forms in the real world, and birds, evolving by a very different path from humans, have converged on many similar abilities. Even an invertebrate such as the octopus has surprising capacities for intelligent perception: an octopus can recognize individual humans, and can solve complex problems, guiding one of its arms through a maze to obtain food using only its eyes.[7] Once we recognize all this we can hardly be unchanged in our ethical thinking. To put a "brute beast" in a cage seems no more wrong than putting a rock in a terrarium. But that is not what we are doing. We are deforming the existence of intelligent and complexly sentient forms of life. Each of these animals strives for a flourishing life, and each has abilities, social and individual, that equip it to negotiate a decent life in a world that gives animals difficult challenges. What humans are doing is to thwart this striving—and this seems wrong. (In chapter 1, I will develop this ethical intuition into a rudimentary idea of justice.)

But even though the time has come to recognize our ethical responsibility to the other animals, we have few intellectual tools to effect meaningful change. The third reason why we must confront what we are doing to animals now, today, is that we have built a world in which two of humanity's best tools for progress, law and political theory, have, so far, no or little help to offer us. Law, as this book will show—both domestic and international—has quite a lot to say about the lives of companion animals, but very little to say about any other animals. Nor do animals in most nations have what lawyers call "standing": that is, the status to bring a legal claim if they are wronged. Of course, animals cannot themselves bring a legal claim, but neither can most humans, including children, people with cognitive disabilities—and, to tell the truth, almost everybody, since people have little knowledge of the law. All of us need a lawyer to press our claims. But all the humans I have mentioned—including people with lifelong cognitive disabilities—count, and can bring a legal claim, assisted by an able advocate. The way we have designed the world's legal systems, animals do not have this simple privilege. They do not count.

Law is built by humans using the theories they have. When those theories were racist, laws were racist. When theories of sex and gender excluded women, so too did law. And there is no denying that most political thought by humans the world over has been human-centered, excluding animals. Even the theories that purport to offer help in the struggle against abuse are deeply defective, built on an inadequate picture of animal lives and animal striving. As a philosopher and political theorist who is also deeply immersed in law and law teaching, I hope to change things with this book, offering a philosophical theory that is based on an accurate view of animal lives and that gives good advice to the law.

I've said it is crucial to get things right, basing theory on an accurate view (supported by the best current science) of a diverse range of animal lives, looking at how animals strive to flourish, and how they are thwarted by various human practices. Let me begin, then, by inviting you to consider these five animals, chosen to represent the zones of the world in which harm to animals happens: land, sea, domestic meat farming, air, and domestic companionship.

My examples will be only the smallest sample of what can befall an animal, and only a sampling of animal kinds. I will describe the animal going about its own life, flourishing, and then the animal brought to grief by wrongful human treatment.

Because non-human animals are so often treated as things, not individual sentient beings, and because one aspect of that thing-like treatment has been the refusal of a proper name, scientists today insist on giving proper names to the individual animals they study. I follow this practice here, taking names from both fact and fiction.

In all my cases except that of Lupa, who had experienced both bad times and good, the animals were flourishing when I (or others) observed and described them. My second description is hypothetical, but based on all-too-common calamities in the lives of animals of these kinds.

THE MOTHER ELEPHANT: VIRGINIA'S STORY

Virginia is a sensitive female elephant in Kenya, described (and named) by elephant scientist Joyce Poole in her memoir, *Coming of Age with Elephants*.[8] Virginia has large amber eyes. When she hears music she likes, she stands very still and her lids droop. Joyce Poole spends her days with the whole matriarchal group, and finds that Virginia—smaller than the older matriarch, Victoria—has a particular fondness for Joyce's singing, "Amazing Grace" being a favorite. Often, however, Virginia is on the move, covering huge tracts of grassland, her huge feet padding noiselessly across the floor of Kenya's Amboseli National Park. Her new baby elephant walks beneath her belly, sheltered by that enormous maternal frame. (Elephants are wonderful mothers, highly protective of their young, and even known to sacrifice their lives to save young elephants from danger.)

Now consider something that might happen, that does often happen. Virginia lies on her side, dead, her tusks and trunk hacked off by a machete or hacksaw, her face a bloody red hole. (The ivory trade flourishes despite many attempts to curb it. And the market for animal trophies, such as tails and trunks, thrives with few impediments: it is not even illegal to import such trophies into the United States.) The other females gather around her and try vainly to lift her body with their trunks. Eventually, giving up the effort, they sprinkle earth and grass upon her body.[9] The baby elephant is missing—taken, very likely, to sell to some zoo in the US that is not too particular about origins.[10]

THE HUMPBACK WHALE: HAL'S STORY

Hal Whitehead is a great whale scientist, especially focused on whale song,[11] so I have given his name to a humpback whale who is proficient at singing, one of a group I observed from a whale-watching boat near the

Great Barrier Reef in Australia. Our small boat cuts through the choppy surf. In the distance, several pods of humpback whales appear, breaching and slapping their tails and flukes. Their huge backs gleam in the sun. One of them is Hal. Over the boat's motor we hear the whales singing, the patterns of sound too complex for our ears to chart them, although we know that humpback whale song has a complicated melodic structure and enormous variety, and is constantly changing—sometimes, apparently, out of sheer fashion and interest in novelty. A variant that originates here may make its way to Hawaii in a year's time, as whales imitate one another. The sound is beautiful to us, and profoundly mysterious.

Now look at Hal: washed up, dead, on a beach in the Philippines.[12] His once healthy frame is emaciated. Inside, researchers find eighty-eight pounds of plastic trash, including bags, cups, and other single-use items. (Another whale who similarly choked on plastic was found to contain, among the refuse, a pair of flip-flops.) Hal has starved to death. Plastic gives whales a sensation of fullness but no nutrition. Eventually there is no room for real food to enter. Some of the plastic in Hal's stomach had been there so long that it had calcified, turned into a plastic brick. He will not sing again.

THE SOW: THE STORY OF EMPRESS OF BLANDINGS

Because I know of no real-life pig who is treated well, I choose a life-inspired fiction. No fictional pig is more imperious and more striking than Empress of Blandings in the novels of P. G. Wodehouse, a noble black Berkshire sow in superb condition, who wins many medals. Because Wodehouse was a famous animal lover and advocate, his fictional description is known to be based on loving observation. Empress of Blandings is enormous. Cared for as a favorite companion on the estate of Blandings Castle, she loves her trough, where appetizing food is always offered her by her human caretaker, Cyril Wellbeloved. When Wellbeloved has to go to jail for a short time for drunken and disorderly conduct, however, she begins to pine and loses her appetite. Her human family, especially the very pig-focused Lord Emsworth, worry helplessly about her well-being, tempting her with various treats, but in vain. By a stroke of good fortune, James Belford turns up at Blandings, and his skill in hog-calling, learned during a period of work on a farm in Nebraska, brings the Empress back to her usual good spirits. She eats with gusto, making "a sort of gulpy, gurgly, plobby, squishy, wofflesome sound" that delights Lord Emsworth. Shortly thereafter she takes her first silver medal at the eighty-seventh Shropshire Agricultural Show, in the Fat Pigs class.[13]

Now imagine a different life for the Empress: instead of flourishing among the kindly people and fostering surroundings of Blandings Castle, and the gentle world of P. G. Wodehouse, where all beings are treated with love and humor, the Empress has the bad fate to be living on a hog farm in Iowa in the early twenty-first century.[14] Newly pregnant, she has been thrust into a "gestation crate," a narrow metal enclosure the size of her body, with no bedding, floored with slats of concrete or metal to allow waste to descend into sewage "lagoons" below. She cannot walk or turn around, and she cannot even lie down. No kind hog-caller speaks to her; no pig-loving humans admire and love her; no other pigs or other farm animals greet her. She is just a thing, a breeding machine. Most of the approximately 6 million sows in the US are on factory farms, and these crates are used in most states, though banned in nine states and in several countries.[15] Gestation crates cause loss of muscle and bone mass from lack of exercise. Crates force pigs to defecate where they live, which pigs, very clean animals, detest. And crates deprive these social animals of all society.[16]

THE FINCH: JEAN-PIERRE'S STORY

Jean-Pierre Rampal, the great flautist (1922–2000), recorded many works in which the sound of a bird's warble is scored for the flute, so I have named my proficient finch, to whom I listen on the website of the Cornell Lab of Ornithology, after him. Jean-Pierre is a male house finch.[17] He has bright red feathers just above his beak, and then the color shades to red-gray on the back of his head. Below his beak, red shades to pink and white, and then to striped gray in the underbelly. His wings are striped gray and white. He sings a rapid warbling composed of short notes, ending with an upward or downward slur.[18] Jean-Pierre is compelling to look at: such delicate gradations of color in his plumage, so active and intelligent as he socializes with other birds—and, above all, entrancing to hear as he spins his complicated warbling compositions. He never tires of singing.

Now look at Jean-Pierre: after gasping for air with a compromised respiratory system, he lies dead on the ground beneath the tree on which he once sang so fluidly. Thousands of small migratory birds (finches, sparrows, warblers, species that make up 86 percent of North America's land bird species) are believed to die every year from the effects of air pollution. Ozone damages the respiratory systems of birds, and also harms the plants that attract the insects birds consume. In this case there is some good news: programs to reduce ozone pollution under the Clean Air Act have also helped birds. It is estimated that these programs have averted the loss of 1.5 billion birds over forty years, nearly 20 percent of bird life in the US today. It was, however, too little, too late for Jean-Pierre. Like Hal, he won't sing again.

THE DOG: LUPA'S STORY

Lupa is a formerly abused dog who lived wild for a while and then found a happy home with Princeton professors George Pitcher and Ed Cone, as described in Pitcher's *The Dogs Who Came to Stay*.[19] Lupa runs rapidly across the Princeton golf course, off leash, outstripping her companion, philosopher George Pitcher, and his houseguest, me—but not outstripping her young son Remus, who bounds ahead of her following a scent, then circles back to join her. She is a thickset dog of medium size, part German shepherd, part unknown; he is slender and small, with a shorter coat, the shepherd traits less pronounced. Both dogs have gleaming coats, and play happily. Although Lupa is very shy with me, she shows great affection to George—and Remus is affectionate and playful with us both. Both dogs are clearly flourishing, in a symbiotic life that includes George, his partner Ed, one another, and various visiting animals and humans.

In this case, the bad story is in the past. Lupa was a wild dog for some time, before George and Ed found her when she chose the underside of a shed on their property to deliver a litter of puppies. She was not in good condition: life in the wild is hard for dogs. And her life before that could be read in her fearful responses. Certain things always frightened her, even much later: a raised hand, a phone call made from a particular telephone on the ground floor. All new humans had to prove themselves with Lupa over a long period of time, and few met the test. She preferred to retreat beneath the grand piano. Both cruelty and neglect were clearly etched in her memory. Remus, by contrast, knew only the good life.

I could have told stories of so many other types of animals: cats, horses, dairy cows, chickens, dolphins, every type of large land mammal. We'll hear more about the octopus, about birds of all sorts, about fish. And I might have imagined different obstacles for the animals I did "profile": for elephants, hunger due to shrinking habitat, as humans encroach on elephant lands; for whales, disturbance of ordinary life by marine noise, including the sonar program of the US Navy, which disrupts migration and breeding patterns; for farm animals, the whole set of institutions and practices that is the factory farm industry; for birds, being shot at by recreational hunters; for dogs, birth and early life in a puppy mill, with all its attendant diseases, or being bred for fighting, or just being bored from lack of exercise and attention. The tales of brutality and neglect go on and on.

A contrast between flourishing lives and impeded lives is a core idea of this book. It is at the very heart of the concept of justice, or so I will argue in chapter 1. And thinking well about this contrast is a key to developing a good theory of justice for animals. What is wrong with the three leading theories on this topic, I'll argue, is that they do not pay attention to this contrast and the diverse ways it turns up in the diverse lives animals lead. I will be developing a new theoretical basis for thinking about justice and injustice to animals, one based on the ability of the animal to lead its own characteristic form of life, and I will argue that because it makes the contrast between flourishing lives and impeded lives central, it is able to overcome challenges that other theories cannot. Theories direct action, and bad theories direct action badly. I think that the dominant theories in this area are defective, and that mine will direct action better.

But for me this book is a work of love and, now, of what I might call constructive mourning—attempting to carry forward the commitments of a person the world has tragically lost. My daughter, Rachel Nussbaum, was my mentor and inspiration as I began, relatively late in life, to take a keen interest in the plight of non-human animals. After a PhD and a short teaching career in German intellectual history, she decided to follow her passion for animals to law school, and was lucky to be at the University of Washington, whose law school has a curriculum full of courses in animal law and related topics. Meanwhile, she and her husband lived in Seattle, close to places well suited for watching the whales and orcas that were her greatest passion. She was even luckier to get her ideal job, as a lawyer with the animal legal organization Friends of Animals, working in the wildlife division in Denver, headed by the wonderful animal law expert Michael Harris. For five years she worked on the legal problems of wild animals, including elephants trafficked into US zoos, wild horses threatened with culling by ranchers, endangered bisons, and so many others. She worked on briefs. She testified before state legislatures considering pro-animal laws.

And she talked to her mother, getting her to share her own passion and commitment for wild animals. Her dedication to improving the lives of abused and suffering creatures was intense, and beautiful. It continues to inspire me. We began to write a series of co-authored articles about the legal status of marine mammals and about more general issues concerning wild animal–human relations. (I supplied the philosophical theory, pushing my Capabilities Approach in a new direction. She supplied the facts and the law.[20])

Rachel died in December 2019, at the age of forty-seven, of a drug-resistant fungal infection following a successful organ transplant. It turned out that the donor organ had a structural defect that caused it to "seed" infection and pump it into the body. The defect could not be seen until the autopsy. Because it was clear that for some reason the donor organ was not doing the job, she was scheduled for retransplant. An organ was found, and she was just about to be wheeled to the OR when a fungal infection was discovered. It proved drug-resistant. The time from the initial transplant to her death was only five months. During that time, her husband, Gerd Wichert, and I saw her in the hospital virtually every day, except that she encouraged me to go to London to present our final collaborative paper to the Human Development and Capability Association, at a time when she was doing really well and about to be sent home. She talked to her HDCA friends on a transatlantic call and was happily looking forward to joining them the following year. And throughout those days we had many talks about the animals we loved. Fortunately it was before COVID, so her father and her boss from Friends of Animals could join Gerd and me to be with her on frequent visits, and all of us were with her on her last day.

As long as I live I will see the sparkle in her green eyes and her subversive smile. We were a study in contrasts, I with curly blond hair, she with a black almost-buzz cut, I with femmy colorful dresses, she with all-black pantsuits; but so deeply our hearts were allied.

This is not a book about that tragedy. This book is different: it looks forward, attempting to further the causes she loved, with a theory she knew about and supported. This theory, a version of my Capabilities Approach, measures justice by asking whether people (or, in this case, sentient animals) have been enabled by laws and institutions to live a decently flourishing life, as defined by a list of opportunities for choice and activity that the creature has (or lacks), in its political and legal context. Rachel had even lectured on the Capabilities Approach at Denver University, near her workplace. She had read the brief foray into animal issues, using the Capabilities Approach, that I wrote in my 2006 book, *Frontiers of Justice*. We often discussed the project of this book, and I even showed her some drafts, particularly the chapter on wild animals. And our co-authored work figures extensively in it, particularly in the chapter on law and the chapter on human-animal friendship. So I feel that she is speaking through me and I am channeling the voice I loved.

The Roman philosopher and statesman Cicero, whose daughter, Tullia, died when just a bit younger than Rachel, expressed his profound grief and mourning by planning, in what turned out to be the last years of his life, to build a shrine to her memory. I hope that a book that keeps Rachel's commitments alive in the world and prompts others to follow them may be even a better expression of love and grief than that shrine—since it will exemplify her values and communicate them all over the world.

What is the Capabilities Approach (CA), and why would lawyers passionate about animal justice care about it?[21] It is easy to say what it is not. The CA does not rank animals by likeness to humans or seek special privileges for those deemed most "like us," as do some other popular theoretical approaches. The CA has concern for the finch and the pig as much as the whale and the elephant. And it argues that the human form of life is simply irrelevant when we think about what each type of animal needs and deserves. What is relevant is *their own* forms of life. Just as humans seek to be able to enjoy the characteristic goods of a human life, so a finch seeks a finch's life and the whale a whale's life. (And for each, room for individual differentiation is a part of the life they seek.) We should extend ourselves and learn, not lazily picture animals as lesser humans, seeking a life sort of like our own. According to the CA, each sentient creature (capable of having a subjective point of view on the world and feeling pain and pleasure) should have the opportunity to flourish in the form of life characteristic for that creature.

Nor does the CA care only about pain and pleasure, as does the most prominent approach to animal justice today, based on the classical Utilitarianism of the eighteenth-century British philosopher Jeremy Bentham and brought up to date by contemporary Australian philosopher Peter Singer. Pain is very very important, and one of the great sources of injustice and harm in animal lives. But it is not the only thing. Animals also need social interactions, often with a large group of fellow species members. They need plenty of room to move around. They need play and stimulation. We should certainly prevent non-beneficial pain, but we should also think about the other aspects of a flourishing animal life. We would not opt for a pain-free life if it meant forfeiting love, friendship, activity, and the other things we have reason to care about. Animals are equally plural in their concerns. Defective theories give defective advice.

The large story this book tells is the story of why we need a new theory to direct politics and law as we try to meet our ethical responsibilities to the five animals I described, and so many others—and why the CA is the best template for ethical and political intervention into the practices that blight and thwart these lives.

I begin, in chapter 1, by talking about what justice means, and about some faculties we humans have that enable us to grasp and respond to injustice. My next three chapters investigate three defective theories that are currently used in law and philosophy: a human-centered theory that I call the "So Like Us" approach, which tries to aid creatures who seem very similar to human beings (and those alone); the Utilitarian theory of Jeremy Bentham, J. S. Mill, Henry Sidgwick, and Peter Singer, which focuses on pleasure and pain and reduces other aspects of an animal's life to quantities of pleasure and pain (though Mill diverges from the others here); and the Kantian approach of philosopher Christine Korsgaard, which makes great strides forward in respecting the dignity of animal lives, but, I claim, comes up short in some key respects.

In two central chapters, 5 and 6, I then lay out my own theory, and argue that animals have rights, that is, entitlements based on justice to decently flourishing lives. I show what that means in terms of my own theory. I then discuss the key concept of sentience, giving my reasons for saying that justice applies only to animals that have a point of view on the world, and not to those that do not, nor to plants.

Chapter 7 asks whether death is always a harm to an animal, revisiting the perennial philosophical question of whether we are harmed by death. Chapter 8 examines "tragic conflicts" between two ethically important duties—a problem we often encounter in promoting the good of animals—and asks how we might approach them so as to mitigate the harm we may temporarily have to do to solve knotty problems, such as those posed by animal experimentation.

Chapters 9 and 10 then look at the two major types of animals in our world: animals who live with and near us, and "wild animals"—who are not, I believe, really wild after all, in the sense that all animals live in spaces dominated by human beings, but they did not evolve to be symbiotic with humans. In each case I ask what the CA suggests about how law and policy should deal with these animal lives.

Chapter 11 turns to the key goal of friendship between humans and other animals, showing how there can be such friendships—even with "wild" animals—and claiming that the ideal of friendship will help us think well about the tasks before us. And finally, chapter 12 turns to law—existing laws, both domestic and international, with their many defects—asking what resources we have in law that could be used to forge a better path.

We humans can and must do better. Law can and must do better. Now, I believe, is the time of a great awakening: to our kinship with a world of remarkable intelligent creatures, and to real accountability for our treatment of them. Toward a justice that is genuinely global, including all sentient beings. I hope this book will help direct that awakening, giving it moral urgency and theoretical structure, and inspiring new people to take up the cause of justice for animals—just as Rachel's passion for marine mammals made me curious, willing to embark on a difficult voyage that has proven more rewarding than any other journey in my life, apart from the journey of motherhood.

1

BRUTALITY AND NEGLECT

Injustice in Animal Lives

Animals suffer injustice at our hands. The project of this entire book is to make good on that statement and to recommend a powerful theoretical strategy to diagnose injustice and suggest appropriate remedies: a version of my Capabilities Approach.

In this chapter, I will begin by looking, first, at our everyday pre-philosophical idea of injustice, which involves, I think, the idea that someone is striving to get something reasonably significant, and has been blocked by someone else—wrongfully, whether by malice or by negligence.

That idea already puts us on the track of my Capabilities Approach, because that approach focuses on meaningful activities and on the conditions that make it possible for a creature to pursue those without damage or blockage. In other words, to lead a flourishing life. Unlike other approaches that focus narrowly on pain as the primary bad thing, this approach will focus on many different types of meaningful activity (including movement, communication, social bonding, and play), any of which can be blocked by the interference of others, and on many types of wrongful blocking activity, whether by malice or by negligence.

In this chapter, I will first compare animals flourishing with animals thwarted in their striving, in order to prepare for a rudimentary account of justice and injustice. Next I will look at our ordinary pre-philosophical idea of injustice, to demonstrate how the animals in my examples have suffered unjust treatment. Then, after developing the idea of wrongful obstruction of significant activity, I will investigate three abilities all readers of this book have, which commend animals to our attention and care: wonder, compassion, and outrage. These three emotions are also resources: suitably developed and cultivated, they help us better understand the larger ethical and philosophical framework of animal rights.

Those who doubt that animals deserve justice at our hands, and have the right to demand it, must wait until the statement of my theory in chapter 5 to see my full argument on this crucial issue, since different theories give different answers to that question. But to put my essential point very briefly: all animals, both human and non-human, live on this fragile planet, on which we depend for everything that matters. We didn't choose to be here. We found ourselves here. We humans think that because we found ourselves here this gives us the right to use the planet to sustain ourselves and to take parts of it as our property. But we deny other animals the same right, although their situation is exactly the same. They too found themselves here and have to try to live as best they can. By what right do we deny them the right to use the planet in order to live, in just the way that we claim that right? Typically, no argument at all is offered for that denial. I believe that any reason supporting our own claim to use the planet to survive and flourish is a reason for animals to have the same right.[1]

First, however, we need to have a working conception of justice and injustice. That is the project of this chapter.

Before we can begin, we need some examples: cases that inspire wonder at the complexity and impressive activities of an animal, and painful compassion, combined with action-directed outrage, at what has become of that animal in a world of human brutality and neglect.

ANIMALS FLOURISHING, ANIMALS THWARTED

My introduction acquainted you with five particular animals, trying to live but encountering various types of blockage and frustration. I described, first, the flourishing activity of the animal going about its characteristic life, and, then, the same animal brought to grief by human mistreatment.

Virginia, the mother elephant, was enjoying free movement and social life with her female group, along with the small baby elephants that the group raises communally. Then she was attacked and killed by poachers, her face hacked open for her ivory, and her baby was taken from the group to be sold to a zoo that would not give it a flourishing life.

Hal, the humpback whale, enjoyed free movement, social interaction with his whale group, and singing. And then, having ingested plastic trash, he starved from a blocked digestive tract and was washed up on the shore.

Empress of Blandings had a happy life at Blandings Castle, well-fed and cared for by people who loved pigs and understood their distinctive personalities and needs. She encountered a very different life on a pig farm in Iowa, confined to a gestation crate, forced to eat near her own feces, deprived of all social life and free movement.

Jean-Pierre used to fly freely, sing wonderful warbles, and enjoyed social interaction with other finches. But air pollution finished him off.

Lupa's is the one story that moves from pain to happiness and from injustice to flourishing. Formerly beaten by a cruel human, then a stray foraging on the streets, she then found a long and happy life with humans who treated her with kindness, love, and respect, gave her excellent medical care and plenty of exercise, and adopted her puppy Remus as well (finding good homes for the other siblings), so that she had canine as well as human company.

These are but five stories, among the millions that are there to be told. Tales of brutality and neglect go on and on. But they give us the material we need to delve into the ideas of justice and injustice. In all these stories we see a flourishing life—and, significantly, all these stories involve free movement, social life, and the expression of abilities typical of each species. By contrast, we then see these abilities thwarted, these movements blocked, these social exchanges rendered impossible.

The contrast between flourishing lives and impeded lives is the core intuitive idea of this book. Not every impediment, however, counts as an injustice that we should address. Let us turn, then, to that question.

JUSTICE: THE BASIC INTUITIVE IDEA

What is it to suffer injustice? When are the damages of life not just harms but also wrongs for which we ought to hold somebody accountable, and remediate if possible, prevent for the future, if not?

Here I'm going down to the bedrock intuitions of my theory, where it is really very hard to give further reasons. Let me try, however, to articulate the basic ideas, since they will guide us in what follows. What is it for a creature to suffer injustice and to have entitlements based on justice?

Let's imagine an animal: since even a hypothetical generic animal needs a name, let's call her Susan. Susan is going about her life, planning, acting, relating, pursuing all the things that matter to an animal of Susan's sort. Susan uses her senses and thoughts. She reaches out for things, desiring them. She moves toward them, and tries to get them. Along the way, Susan encounters obstacles to her efforts. Some of them are trivial: they block projects that are side issues and not central to her life. Among the more serious obstacles, some derive from physical limitations that seem to be nobody's fault: Susan is stricken by illness; a major storm wrecks her dwelling. So far, it appears that Susan has not suffered injustice, though she has suffered harms, some smaller and some larger.

Suppose, however, that Susan is blocked by another creature, or by a situation set up by another creature. Still, Susan may not have suffered injustice, if the other creature did nothing wrong—was just going about her own business and happened to collide or compete with Susan. She took some food Susan was reaching for. Or: her justifiable defense of her life and that of her family entailed fighting off and harming Susan.

But suppose Susan's dwelling was deliberately ruined by another creature who was capable of knowing better and doing better. Suppose Susan was deliberately imprisoned and killed, along with thousands of her fellow species members. Such is the lot of most of the world's chickens and many of its pigs and calves. Suppose, like Empress of Blandings, Susan was locked in a metal cage and made to defecate through slats into a foul-smelling lagoon, meanwhile becoming diseased through lack of exercise. Suppose, like Virginia, her face was hacked to a bloody pulp with a machete to satisfy the ivory market, an illegal global crime syndicate. Suppose, like Lupa, she was beaten by someone who claimed to be her owner. Now we're in the domain of injustice, because now Susan's efforts are blocked by interference that appears wrongful. If Susan were a human, we would quickly conclude that injustice is involved.

The cases of Hal and Jean-Pierre seem different, because there is no deliberate act that inflicted the harm. If Hal had been harpooned (a gruesome practice no longer permitted by the International Whaling Commission, but practiced anyway by Japan, who seceded from that group over the issue), then we could quickly agree that the wrongdoing was deliberate. Even if Hal had been thwarted by the sonar program developed in good faith by the US Navy—even then, as we'll see further in chapter 5, a US court has halted the program for wrongfully interfering with the activities of whales.[2] So if the navy went ahead in defiance of the court, they would be committing a deliberate wrong. But Hal the beached whale choked by human garbage is more complicated. Sure, we humans might have been a bit thoughtless about where all that plastic trash would end up, but does that rise to the level of negligence? And who bears the liability? Even if we are not to blame this time, what about the future? Now that we have seen the beached whale, are we on notice that we will be blameworthy the next time—even if the garbage is out there, and the seas very difficult to clean?[3]

Jean-Pierre choked by air pollution is similarly difficult: the by-products of our industrial life do harm to many species, including our own, but at what point does this rise to the level of wrongful damage? And who is to blame? Our legal system (especially the Clean Air Act) has been wrestling with this for humans, but actionable protections for pollution under the Migratory Bird Treaty Act are a politically contested issue (see chapter 12).

However, if Susan were Hal, her friends would point out that there are already laws on the books preventing harm to marine mammals, and this harm, if not malicious, was clearly foreseeable and negligent, even if it cannot be pinned on a single wrongdoer. The seas are lamentably badly regulated, but it is in principle possible that this sort of trash dumping could be regulated by law, if nations would cooperate. Air pollution too has been curtailed by laws, and a violator of these laws, even a negligent rather than a deliberate violator, is acting wrongfully. Are birds different? Time and politics will give the answer, but I know what I think.

Injustice, then, involves striving on Susan's part, to get something at least reasonably significant to her life; and it involves not just harm but also wrongdoing by someone else, whether by a deliberate act or by negligence.

So far, it seems that the victim of injustice need not be human, but can be a non-human animal. Injustice depends on the action taken against a sentient being, not on the type of being: Susan might be a human, a pig, an elephant. (In chapter 6, I'll ask whether all animals can suffer injustice, or only some, and define that boundary further.) In most cases of deliberate wrongdoing, the perpetrator is human, because humans are capable of deliberate malevolent intent in a way that few animals are. However, we'll later see that humans are actually not the only ethical creatures, nor the only creatures to whom duties can be assigned. This will be important later in constructing a convincing theory of a multispecies community.

Sometimes things that appear to be accidents involve injustice when we look into them further, because they involve culpable negligence. This is well-known in the human world. You get stricken by a disease for which there is a known vaccine, but your doctor told you that vaccines are harmful. You have a terrible automobile accident because of a manufacturer's error. You get poisoned by tainted produce because of faulty inspections. The whole landscape of tort liability opens before us. In the COVID-19 pandemic there has been a yet more complicated and murky set of connections between suffering and blame. How many people would not have lost their lives had testing been more efficiently arranged and lockdowns more thorough? (Lots, as the case of New Zealand shows.) How many would not have died even so, had they not been afflicted all their lives by diseases and disabilities associated with poverty, such as diabetes and malnutrition? Is there fault there, and, if so, whose? And who's to blame for people who do not get life-saving vaccinations because of misinformation? The person, for gullibility and lack of concern for science? The purveyors of the misinformation? Both? And so forth. Whenever there are people in charge, or who ought to be in charge, and wherever there are media that ought to aspire to truth and reliability, damages begin to look like wrongs: they ought to have foreseen the harm, and they could then have averted it, given their power. Hal's case looks like this, and Jean-Pierre's too.

Sometimes, too, there seems to be negligence somewhere, but it is difficult to pin it down. For example, what about the harms creatures suffer in "Nature," when humans are on the scene and could help? When elephants starve because of a drought that kills the vegetation they eat? (Human use of the surrounding land is probably a major cause of that drought.) When animals are crippled by a disease that we know how to cure? (A tiger in Chicago's Brookfield Zoo had successful hip replacement surgery. A tiger in a nature preserve overseen and monitored by humans but still "wild" might or might not have surgical intervention.) And what about predation? Should we attempt to stop a pack of wild dogs from killing and eating a deer, when we can do so, knowing that we would almost certainly stop a companion dog or cat from engaging in similar aggression?

It is very hard, then, to figure out when there is injustice, and by whom. But the general intuition should be emerging more clearly: injustice centrally involves *significant striving* blocked by not just *harm* but also *wrongful thwarting*, whether negligent or deliberate. Often, thwarting includes the infliction of pain, which impedes almost every ordinary activity of an organism (perceiving, eating, moving, loving).

Just suppose for now that you are convinced that animals can suffer not just harm but injustice, understood as wrongful thwarting. In what follows I will be giving you reasons why you should think this, although I hope that these examples already strike a chord with you.

Humans and human ways of life are everywhere: on land, squeezing the habitats of large mammals and using water the animals need; in the air, changing the flight patterns of birds and the very air they breathe; in the seas, changing, in countless ways, the habitats of mammals and fish. The pervasiveness of human power makes human responsibility spread into domains we previously thought of as just "wild" and "Nature." Where does justice begin and end?

This book will not deal with every hard case, but it will try to show a way of thinking about animal flourishing and what impedes it that can help us deal with the hard cases better than other rival theories. I will argue that we humans are all collectively responsible for supporting the most essential life-activities of the creatures with whom we share this planet, both by stopping our wrongful interference with so many of these activities and also by protecting habitats so that all sentient creatures (all those who have a point of view on the world, for whom things matter)—a group that includes all vertebrates and many invertebrates—have a decent shot at a flourishing life. These opportunities to choose significant activities are what I mean by "capabilities." So: we should all be supporting the Central Capabilities of our fellow animals.

WONDER, COMPASSION, OUTRAGE: OPENING THE SOUL'S EYES

I have tried to describe these cases in such a way as to awaken a sense that wrong has been done. To say it once more: this is the project of this entire book, since I am attempting to persuade you that many human actions toward animals are forms of wrongful thwarting. Everyone knows that the actions of humans cause animals a lot of suffering and many other impediments, but many people don't admit that this is wrong. We have a right to carry on as we are doing, although perhaps it would be nice to be somewhat more compassionate. Even John Rawls, the twentieth century's greatest philosopher of justice, held that it was virtuous to treat animals with compassion, but that they could not be treated justly or unjustly.

Later, when I lay out my own theory, I will present my argument that animals have rights. But before people are likely to care about a philosophical argument, they need to be motivated to care. What equipment do we humans have that might help us get there? Some people are already in loving relationships with some animals; that love can be a starting point for a more inclusive concern. But existing loves by themselves may fall short, because people love what they know, and, all too often, not all the millions of animals that they don't know—just as loving parents of human children are not always motivated to try to end child hunger and child sexual abuse all over the world. What else can we call to our assistance? What emotions have the potential to carry us beyond our daily context?

My descriptions have attempted to awaken a sense of ethically attuned *wonder* that might lead to an ethically directed *compassion* when the animal's striving is wrongfully thwarted, and a forward-looking *outrage* that says: "This is unacceptable. It must not happen again." As it will turn out, all of these moral emotions are closely linked to my Capabilities Approach, because all of them help us to see the world in the way in which my approach will ultimately depict it: as a world of remarkably diverse forms of animal striving that seem significant and worth supporting. Wonder arrests our attention, informing us of the importance and value of what we see and hear. Compassion alerts us to the suffering of others and its significance. And outrage, which I will later call Transition-Anger, *turns* us from simply reacting toward remaking the future, directing us to take remedial action. Let us pause, then, to investigate these emotions.

When we see Hal leaping into the sun, and hear his mysterious song;

when we see Virginia walking softly across the grass, her baby beneath her belly, and hear her booming trumpet; when we see Empress of Blandings happily feeding, and hear her "plobby, squishy, wofflesome" sound (the invented words themselves express loving attention); when we see Jean-Pierre on a bough, with his bright multicolored feathers, and hear his complex warble; when we see Lupa bounding across the golf course and hear her panting as she returns after a good gallop—in all these cases we are apt to feel an emotion that I will call wonder. It is akin to awe, both being strong emotions responding to something impressive and mysterious, but wonder is more active than awe, more connected to curiosity.[4]

As Aristotle said long ago: wonder involves first being impressed by something, brought up short, and then being motivated to try to figure out what is going on behind the sights and sounds that impress us. He links wonder closely to the recognition of sentient life. When his students apparently resisted learning about animals and their faculties, thinking that animals are too humble, and not divine like the heavenly stars, he told them that in all of nature you can find wonderful forms of organized functioning. And then he told a story: some wise people from far away came to visit the philosopher Heraclitus. They probably expected to find the sage on a lofty seat surrounded by worshipful students. Instead they found him "at the hearth." (Scholars think that the phrase very likely means the privy.) He said, "Come in, don't be afraid. There are gods here too."[5]

Most emotions are closely connected to our own personal well-being. Fear, grief, anger, jealousy, envy, pride—all make reference to the self and how the self's attachments are doing in the world. I have used the word "eudaimonistic" to describe this characteristic of emotions: they relate their object to the self, and the self's conception of well-being.[6] Wonder is different: it takes us out of ourselves and toward the other. It seems to be non-eudaimonistic, having nothing to do with our own personal search for well-being. It is connected to our original joy at life itself. It is at the furthest remove from narcissism or pride, and closer to play. Wonder is childlike, it is our humanity at play in a world of remarkable beings.

Wonder, then, is not always solemn. I think the very invention of words like "plobby" and "wofflesome" is a form of comic wonder, a child-like play with language expressing joy at the way a noble pig eats. (Wodehouse, as I said, was a famous lover of animals.)

We have wonder in the presence of many things. (It's hard to know what the best preposition is: wonder "at" or "about"? Philosopher Jeremy Bendik-Keymer suggests "over" is better, because it's slower, more deliberative.) But in Aristotle's conception, and I will borrow and extend it, wonder is especially closely connected to our awareness of movement and sentience. We see and hear these creatures moving and doing all these things, and we imagine that something is going on inside: it's not sheer random motion, but directed somehow by an inner awareness, by a someone. Wonder is connected to our perception of striving: we see that creatures have a purpose, that the world is meaningful to them in some ways we don't fully understand, and we are curious about that: What is the world for them? Why do they move? What are they trying to get? We interpret the movement as meaningful, and that leads us to imagine a sentient life within.

Really, this is what happens when we meet other human beings. Our senses give us only an outer shape, and then it is our curiosity, our imagination, that makes the leap to imagining that the world looks like something to that other shape, that it is another sentient being, not an automaton.[7] In chapter 6, I will argue that in fact our grounds for ascribing sentience to a range of animals are the same as our grounds for positing "other minds" when we meet such humanoid shapes. Sometimes we may turn out to be mistaken: we think something is going on inside when it is really a very clever machine. Or, we take the movements of some animals to be meaningful when, on further inspection, we find that evidence does not support ascribing sentience to them: that is what I say about most insects. But in many cases, further inspection will support the ascription of sentience, a point of view on the world.

How is wonder linked to ethical concern? Aristotle himself did not make the link. Unlike many other ancient Greek thinkers, he appears not to have pursued his reflections about wonder into the ethical domain. He has nothing to say (or nothing that survives) about the moral case for vegetarianism, or about other issues of humane animal treatment. And yet, if we feel wonder looking at the complex activity and striving of an animal, that wonder at least suggests the idea that it is worthwhile for that being to persist and flourish as the kind of thing it is.[8] This idea is at least closely related to an ethical judgment that it is wrong when the flourishing of a creature is blocked by the harmful agency of another. That more complex idea lies at the heart of the Capabilities Approach. Wonder, like love, is epistemic: it leads us out of ourselves and awakens a nascent ethical concern.

How do we develop wonder? I think small children typically have great curiosity about animal lives, linked to a powerful concern. They often develop their imaginations by seeing animals up close. But they may also develop their ideas through picture books, through films, through TV documentaries, and, more problematically, by visits to a zoo or theme park. (I'll discuss the problems these present in chapter 10.) In our world there are many excellent ways of awakening and nurturing wonder in children—although parents need to ask whether what the film shows is correct, and whether it contains inaccurate stereotypes of animal behavior—as they would for any other film their children see. I think wonder begins very naturally. Our main problem is not that we don't get started, it is that daily life, competition, and clutter overwhelm the mind's eye and make us forget what we once saw.

Wonder is not the only emotion evoked by my contrasting scenarios. If your attention has been gripped by the good scenario, your response to the bad scenario is likely to be one of both outrage—such things should not happen—and a painful compassion. I'll return to the outrage later. Let's now think about compassion. When we feel pain at the significant suffering of another creature, that emotion has, Aristotle thought, three elements—and I've added a fourth.[9] First, you have to think that the suffering is important, not trivial. I've built this into the stories, showing how much of the animal's life is blighted by what has happened. Second, you have to think that the animal herself is not to blame for her bad predicament. That too is evident in the stories, and it contrasts with cases where we may withhold compassion because we think the animal's behavior was malicious. (We also withhold compassion in cases where an animal's aggression threatens our life, as I'll argue later, talking about a self-defense principle that can sometimes justify harming an animal. In many of these cases it is wrong to blame the animal: rats are just living their ratty lives, and so forth; but the potentially dangerous nature of the behavior may justify us in withholding compassion.) Third, says Aristotle, we have to have a kind of fellow feeling with the sufferer: we must think that our own possibilities are *similar* to hers. In earlier work I rejected this, saying that we do not always have to believe in similar possibilities in order to have compassion, and I offered the case of non-human animals to illustrate this. I now think that this was both right and wrong. Right, because when we are drawn outside of ourselves to have concern for a whale or a pig, it is crucial that we see the alienness of that form of life. We don't, or at least shouldn't, care because we imagine the whale to be very like us, as I'll argue further later. But balancing that sense of alienness, I now think, is a sense of a larger generic similarity. We are all animals, thrown into this world together, striving to get the things we need, and often thwarted in the attempt. We are all Animalia, and that family likeness is important in making sense of our experience.

Crucially, our sense of similarity should not be the sort depicted in the traditional *scala naturae* or "ladder of nature": the idea that animal species are arranged in a linear hierarchy with humans at the top, closest to the divine. I'll reject that idea in chapter 2. It is just not a good guide to the world we find if we study animals seriously. Animal abilities are remarkable and complex, and on many parameters many animals do better than humans. In the end, the whole idea of a single ranking is of little use. Here, then, I am definitely not saying that we should give the whale high marks because it seems more like humans than does a dog or a pig. We should, however, notice something generically similar about all of these creatures: the world looks like something to them, and, reacting to what they perceive, they move forward to get what they want. It was on this basis that Aristotle, in *De Motu Animalium*, felt able to propose what he called a "common explanation" of animal motion.[10]

Similarity is seductive, potentially leading to error. It can cause us to neglect, and perhaps not even to see, the amazing diversity and otherness of animal life. It can also lead us to suspend critical faculties, ascribing sentience to creatures when the evidence does not support it. But a sense of a common fate in this world, linking us with animals in a family relationship, is amply justified and epistemically valuable. If we combine the sense of similarity with wonder, which motivates curiosity and alerts us to difference and surprising otherness, we are less likely to be misled.

And there is a fourth element: we need to believe that the suffering being matters, is part of our circle of concern. In my books on emotion I call this the *eudaimonistic* element, but perhaps that is too narrow: a creature can be moved into our circle of concern without our thinking that the creature's well-being is part of our own flourishing. Wonder moves many creatures into our circle of concern without being self-referential: our concern is directed to the other as other, and not even as an intrinsically valuable part of our own life (as a relative or friend might be).

The point of including this fourth element is that we know of many catastrophes in the world, and many injustices. But only some move us. Our attention needs to be arrested, and our thought about ends and goals needs to be modified. Sometimes the modification is fleeting. You hear about people who died in a flood, and you are moved—but then you quickly forget about it, and go about your life unchanged. So for a lasting compassion to take root, the imagination must, in some durable way, move the creature closer, make it a part of our world of goals and projects.

Compassion by itself already prompts helping behavior, as the experiments of the great psychologist C. Daniel Batson have shown.[11] But it may often prove a weak, or at least an incomplete, motivator. Its message is: These things are bad, and it would be good for them to be made better. It motivates behavior that helps the victim. But, focused as it is on the victim's suffering, it does not fully react to the wrongfulness of the perpetrator's actions, which are the causes of suffering. (To make his task conceptually simpler, most of Batson's experiments concern suffering without wrongdoing: for example, a student who has broken her leg and needs help getting to her classes.) So compassion by itself does not lead us to stop the damager from doing further damage. For this we need another emotion, which, so far, I have called "outrage." Now I must explain further.

Outrage is a form of anger. But anger, as philosophers have defined it for centuries, is partly a retributive emotion. It reacts to perceived wrongful damage, but it also projects a satisfying tit-for-tat sort of payback. For Aristotle and all the philosophers in the Western tradition who follow him (and also Buddhist and Hindu Indian philosophers) the wish for payback is a conceptual part of anger. I have argued elsewhere that this payback idea is no use to anyone: it is an empty fantasy to think that pain in the present can atone for or fix the past.[12] For example, killing a murderer does not restore the victim to life, although many families of victims seek capital punishment as if it did somehow atone for or annul the damages of crime. Retributive anger often motivates us to actions that are not only aggressive but also counterproductive. People who approach a divorce negotiation in a retributive "payback" spirit, seeking to pile on the misery for the "bad" spouse, often make the world a lot worse, not only for children and friends, but also for themselves.

There is, however, a type of anger that is free from retributive payback wishes—an exceptional type not noticed by these philosophical definitions. This species of anger turns to face forward, and its aim is to create a better future. For that reason I call it Transition-Anger, and from now on I use that invented term, because no ordinary-language term, such as "outrage" or "indignation," makes it crystal clear that this is an anger without the retributive wish. A good way of imagining this type of anger is to think about parents and children. Children do bad things, and parents are outraged. But they typically do not seek retributive payback, and certainly not a punishment that obeys the *lex talionis*, "an eye for an eye." They focus on how to make the future better: how to make the bad behavior stop, and to get their child to behave differently in the future. The entire content of Transition-Anger is: "How unacceptable, how outrageous, this is. It must not happen from now on."

Transition-Anger sometimes seeks punishment of wrongful conduct—but not because punishment is a form of payback or retribution. We may also punish in order to deter people from engaging in that sort of conduct in the future: either deterring the same person from committing another similar crime ("specific deterrence") or deterring other people from imitating the bad act ("general deterrence"). And we may punish, too, in order to reform the perpetrator and in order to educate the next generation, making a statement that this sort of behavior is not what they should emulate. In the process we also make an expressive statement of our values as a society. All of this the proponent of Transition-Anger embraces.

Transition-Anger is the third emotion we need. It is, I think, usually useless and even self-indulgent to bemoan our guilty past or to heap coals of fire on the bad actors (in this case, all of us). What is needed is a new attitude to the future: let's stop this. There is work to be done. Let's do things differently. Outrage directs us to a project that is both oppositional—going up against the wrongful actors, committed to stopping them (sometimes by punishments, criminal or civil)—and also constructive. Let's find a better way to do things. We can't go on like this any longer.

This book is about a large human injustice, but it would be of no use if it simply inspired readers to study human injustice, frowning at ourselves in a mirror. In the end, ethical thought has to become practical, or it is idle. These are very hard problems, but there are many things that can be done to move us closer to justice, and each reader can find some place to dig in, some job to do, that will shoulder one small part of our huge collective responsibility.

Wonder arrests our attention and draws us out of ourselves, inspiring curiosity about an alien world. Compassion links us to the suffering animal in a powerful emotional experience. Transition-Anger prepares us for action.

But there is one more thing we need: an adequate theory to direct our efforts. I'll now show, in my next three chapters, that three prominent theories of animal justice (or animal ethics, since they don't all use the word "justice") have serious flaws that make them inadequate guides to our future constructive efforts—although I'll also identify points of convergence with my own theory, showing that, and how, people of good will from "the other camp" can join in a common effort.

The next four chapters will study the major theoretical alternatives. In chapter 2, I'll study an influential approach that focuses on winning protections for a limited range of animals on account of their likeness to human beings: the "So Like Us" approach. I'll argue that this theory is too narrow—unworthy of the alienness and sheer diversity of animal lives—and is counterproductive as a strategy to help wronged animals. In chapter 3, I'll study the approach of the British Utilitarians, who focused on pain and pleasure as universal norms guiding the lives of all sentient beings. This approach has many advantages, but in the end its defects are too large and numerous for it to be a fully adequate guide. In chapter 4, I'll turn to the best philosophical theory of animal lives in the recent literature, worthy of a full chapter in itself: the approach of Christine Korsgaard in her recent book *Fellow Creatures*. Korsgaard bases her philosophical theory on materials drawn from Immanuel Kant, but she is keenly sensitive to the defects of Kant's actual views about animals. Her own views are far more interesting, and her complex view, which includes a way of valuing the opportunity of each creature to lead its own life, converges at many points with the approach that I recommend. And yet, I'll argue, its debt to a view that privileges reason and moral choice over all other abilities, in thinking about law and citizenship, proves a handicap in developing a fully adequate approach to law and public policy.

Finally, in chapter 5, we reach the approach that I myself recommend: my version of the Capabilities Approach (CA), originally developed to guide international development agencies working with human populations, but well suited to provide a good basis for animal entitlements as well. This theory will take us back to the themes of this chapter. The CA has links to wonder, being built on a recognition of a wide diversity of animal forms of life, and a diversity that is "horizontal" rather than "vertical"—not establishing a ladder or hierarchy, though recognizing some generic commonalities. It also has links to compassion, focused as it is on the need of each animal to have conditions in which it can live, move, perceive, act in its own characteristic way. When these conditions are blocked, compassion is warranted. And so too, often (if the blocking is wrongful) is Transition-Anger. When we see wrongful thwarting, that is no time to sob and wring our hands. It is a time to say, "No more!"

2

THE *SCALA NATURAE* AND
THE "SO LIKE US" APPROACH

Let's now turn to the central question of this book: What theoretical approach to injustice in animal lives is best to direct serious thought about those lives, and especially matters of law and policy? We humans are undoubtedly in control of the world at this point, and we are the makers of laws. But although law is made by us, it is not only for and about us. Laws and policies regulate how other creatures get to pursue their own goals, and give or foreclose opportunities for flourishing. So far, humans have done this job in a very haphazard way, where other animals are concerned. We need to do better. And for that we need to think theoretically, choosing approaches that fit with what we know about the world of nature and also with what ethical argument tells us about our responsibilities.

In this chapter, I'll study an influential approach that focuses on winning protections for a limited range of animals on account of their likeness to human beings: the "So Like Us" approach, which has become very influential in US law and policy through the work of legal scholar and activist Steven Wise. This theory is too narrow, unworthy of the alienness and sheer diversity of animal lives. And it is counterproductive as a strategy to expand animal entitlements.

Wise chooses his approach pragmatically, in order, he hopes, to appeal to judges who have had an average Western education. So it seems important to begin by summarizing, briefly, where the inadequacies of Western philosophy (and religion) have left us. This history contains some excellent approaches to animal lives, but these have on the whole lacked influence, while the dominant views in the West have been those that deny the moral significance of animal abilities and animal lives.

THE HISTORY OF WESTERN PHILOSOPHY AND THE *SCALA NATURAE*

Most people in Euro-American cultures, over the course of many centuries, have absorbed a particular picture of nature: nature is a ladder, with lower rungs and higher rungs, reaching toward the divine. On the topmost rung is the human being, closer to the divine than any other living being in virtue of having reason and language—as well as an ability to understand, if not necessarily to abide by, moral distinctions of right and wrong.

It is not as if creatures or their species can actually *climb* this ladder: the medieval picture of the *scala naturae* long antecedes the theory of evolution, and even evolution does not permit creatures to guide their own evolution in an aspirational manner. The context of the *scala naturae* is a world of species believed to be fixed and immutable. It is a ladder, then, that nobody ever climbs, one whose only purpose is to indicate permanent superiority and inferiority.

Not all religions and worldviews have held that humans are a superior species. Buddhism and Hinduism have more generous views of the world of nature.[1] Under the influence of Hindu traditions, an Indian court has even ruled that circus animals are "persons" covered by the meaning of that word in the Indian constitution (see chapter 12).[2] Many Hindus are strict vegetarians, and any Indian airline today standardly offers two choices, "veg" or "non-veg." Buddhism even more strictly bans the abuse of all animals: it focuses on the kinship of all life and the primacy of suffering, which is the common property of all sentient beings. Buddhist ethics is in many ways close to the views of the British Utilitarians, whom we will meet in the following chapter, and who gave the modern Western animal rights movement its impetus. The belief that ethical sensitivity to our treatment of animals is a recent invention is a sign of ignorance of other world traditions.

As British philosopher Richard Sorabji has shown, even in the Western tradition the humans-on-top view was not held by all the ancient Greco-Roman schools of philosophy, most of whom refused to draw a sharp line between humans and other animals, and some of whom strictly prohibited meat eating, along with all infliction of pain on animals.[3] (Sorabji, a leading historian of ancient Greco-Roman thought, tells his readers that the motivation for his project came from his family's Indian origins, which introduced him to attitudes about animals more generous than those on which he was brought up in England.) Some pre-Socratic Greek thinkers insisted on vegetarianism, including both Pythagoras (and his school) in the sixth century BCE and Empedocles in the fifth. They cited the kinship of all nature as their reason, holding that animals and even plants contain living and sentient souls. Plato (d. 347 BCE) believed in the transmigration of souls from one species to another. Although he did not address animal ethics in detail in the dialogues that survive to us, his works provided the basis for later writings that powerfully defended vegetarianism. And Aristotle, to whom the *scala naturae* is most often ascribed, insisted throughout his writings on natural philosophy and biology that each creature strives for flourishing in its own way. The goal or end of each is the life and flourishing of each, and no creature exists for the sake of other "higher" species. A few texts do suggest a different picture, but Aristotle had a relatively long life (384/3–322 BCE), and discovered the joy of studying animals only after a period of exile from Athens after Plato's death. There are many ways to think about the dissonant texts in Aristotle, without imputing to him an overall view of nature that is contradicted by so many statements in his biological works (which, unfortunately, few philosophers read).[4] As I mentioned in the introduction, the late work *On the Motion of Animals* offers a "common explanation" of the movements of animals of many different kinds toward their objects of desire, urging us to prefer this common explanation to one that treats humans as a species apart.[5] It's extremely important to distinguish Aristotle's actual writings from the use of them made during the Middle Ages to create the Christian form of Aristotelianism known as Scholasticism, which invented the *scala naturae* as we know it today.

During the Hellenistic era (the era that begins right around Aristotle's death), there was, however, a shift. Epicureans still seem to have had a generous and inclusive view of animals, and their texts often insist on similarities between humans and other sentient creatures. (The Roman Epicurean poet Lucretius, for example, writing in the first century BCE, gives a marvelous description of the dreams of animals, designed to show a similarity with humans in perceptual and desiderative capacities.) Holding that pleasure and pain are the only things good and bad for their own sake, Epicureans draw a tight link between humans and other sentient creatures, providing, much later, a source for Utilitarian ethics when it began to emerge in the eighteenth century. (Upper-class British thinkers were all brought up on the Greeks and Romans, which gave them a ready store of alternative views when the normative views of conventional religion began to be questioned.)

However, the ancient Greek and Roman Stoics, enormously influential both in antiquity and in the development of Christian ethics, did not agree with the Epicureans. They held that non-human animals were brutes, without thought or emotion, while humans are quasi-divine, and that on that account we can use animals as we wish. The Stoic school, from the late fourth century BCE to the early Roman empire (first two centuries CE), became culturally dominant, shaping everyday thought in profound ways. Stoicism later influenced Christianity—as did Judaism, which similarly held that the human being is special. Both were popularly understood to teach that the human, made in the image of God, is the only truly intelligent and spiritual being, and the only being to whom salvation is open.

Even then, there continued to be a vigorous debate within the ancient Greco-Roman world. The late Platonists Plutarch and Porphyry (see the introduction) wrote eloquent works that we can study today, defending the intelligence and sentience of animals and arguing for a meatless diet. Porphyry's *On Abstaining from Animal Flesh* is a marvelous work full of detailed and highly cogent arguments that should figure prominently in philosophy curricula, although few philosophers know anything about it. These views, however, were increasingly marginalized by the dominance of Christianity.

Like the Stoics, most Christian and Jewish thinkers sharply distinguished humans from all other animals, and in both religions the distinction has long been widely taken to justify using animals for our own human purposes.[6] The medieval codification of this division in the metaphor of the *scala naturae* seems slightly more generous than the Stoic view, in that it posits a gradual series of steps, with some animals higher up than others. In practice, however, the ladder metaphor gets interpreted in a Stoic way, to suggest a deep chasm between humans and all other animals. This chasm view continues to shape the ideas of philosophers nourished in the Judeo-Christian tradition.[7]

The idea of the ladder of nature is essentially a religious idea, whether in its Stoic form (where only humans partake in Zeus's rational plan for the universe) or in its Judeo-Christian form. It rests less on argument and observation than on a belief system that people are asked to accept as a framework for living without thoroughly testing it. The Stoics were rationalists, and they favored critical thinking; but in this crucial matter they did not test their beliefs by reason. Their opponents offered devastating refutations of their claims about the brutishness of animals. One representative and rather amusing example, used by ancient skeptics to criticize their Stoic opponents, concerns a fictional dog, imagined to belong to Chrysippus himself, the most important of the Stoic philosophers. This dog is chasing a rabbit, and arrives at a threefold fork in the road. He sniffs down path A, then sniffs down path B—and, getting negative sniff feedback from paths A and B, he does not pause to sniff down path C, but dashes down it without sniffing, as if convinced that the rabbit must have taken path C. The Stoics' opponents want to show that Chrysippus's own dog refutes the contention that animals are brutes, for this dog has mastered the disjunctive syllogism: either A or B or C; not A; not B; therefore C![8] It isn't just a joke, as dog lovers will know.

Even though Stoicism was very influential in Rome, Romans who were strongly influenced by Stoic doctrines in other respects did not fully accept their view about the brutishness of all animals. They were inconsistent and selective, but they did see surprising evidence of animal sentience and complexity. In 55 BCE, the Roman leader Pompey staged a combat between humans and elephants.[9] Surrounded in the arena, the animals perceived that they had no hope of escape.[10] According to Pliny, they then "entreated the crowd, trying to win their compassion with indescribable gestures, bewailing their plight with a sort of lamentation."[11] The audience, moved to pity and protest by their plight, rose to curse Pompey—feeling, writes the philosopher and statesman Cicero, who was present, that the elephants had a relation of commonality (*societas*) with the human race.[12]

The Stoic and Judeo-Christian belief in animal brutishness is not simply untested and untestable, it derives from a type of religion that is anthropocentric and anthropomorphic, according to which God, imagined as rather like us, only better, using speech, reasoning, and language, makes us special, like God, and then values us because we are godlike.

Even though both the ladder and the chasm became central tenets of mainstream Judeo-Christian religion as practiced, we should pause here to point to some ways in which they are in tension with deeper features of those religions. First, to imagine God (God the Father, in the Christian case) as human in form is regarded by both Jews and many Christians as idolatrous. But further: both religions hold that God created all the species, and took delight in the whole of creation as "good." The Genesis story encourages wonder at the beauty and variety of living creation.[13]

Later, when Noah and his family enter the Ark before the flood, they are asked by God to take pairs, male and female, from each animal species, including birds, as if all species deserve preservation and respect.[14] The post-flood covenant is made between God and "you and every living creature that is with you, for everlasting generations."[15] We do not find in the Torah (the five books of Moses) any sign that the animals were created to be food and prey for humans. The dominant idea in both stories is one of wonder and at least a limited sort of respect.

It is true that in Genesis 1:26–8, God gives humans "sway" over the other living creatures. And the word translated as "sway" (in other translations, "dominion"), *radah*, does connote a type of rule: as scholar and translator Robert Alter argues, a very strong form of rule or mastery. But we usually believe that good rulers are those who take care of those they rule, not those who treat them like property and inflict torments on them. And since in the story humans are regents for God, taking charge of a creation God loved and thought good, surely the way humans ought to "rule" is by exercising intelligent and sensitive stewardship. Moreover, the gift of "sway" is contrasted with God's gift of plants as "food" for both humans and other animals. In verses 29 and 30, God says: "Look, I have given you every seed-bearing plant on the face of all the earth and every tree that has fruit bearing seed, yours they will be for food. And to all the beasts of the earth and to all the fowl of the heavens and to all that crawls on the earth, which has the breath of life within it, the green plants for food."[16] This passage strongly suggests that vegetarianism was the norm before the fall and that meat eating may thus be an expression of our fallen nature. In the Garden of Eden, it seems that even animals are not carnivores. What is absolutely clear is that "sway" is not best read as entitlement to plunder and abuse animal creation. In short, the Judeo-Christian tradition is more respectful of animals than popular belief and practice often allege.

A marvelous book drawing out the implications of this idea, and juxtaposing it with the reality of our current brutal practices, is *Dominion* by Matthew Scully.[17] Scully is a conservative and a Republican speechwriter, especially for President George W. Bush. The aim of his eloquent book is to make a case for compassionate stewardship. His vivid account of some of the cruelest practices Americans currently engage in toward animals includes a gruesome description of the factory farming industry, a mordant satire of the hypocritical self-justifications of the Safari Club, as they promote wild-animal hunts by talking in spiritual terms, and a deft send-up of philosophers who pontificate on the "sacredness" of fox hunting. (The late Roger Scruton comes in for justified mockery.[18]) Along the way, Scully studies both biblical texts and the writings of later Christian thinkers who decry cruelty and inhumanity to animals, and some of whom object to all killing. Scully's main goal is to show that the hideous and wanton cruelty of current practices is a creation of human greed and has no justification in authentic Christianity. It's a fine contribution, shattering complacency, whether or not one is religious in the Judeo-Christian way.

The philosophical schools of Greco-Roman antiquity and the canonical texts of Judaism and Christianity arose in a world in which everyone assumed that the species were fixed. Darwin's theory of evolution caused an enormous upheaval in many quarters in the US, and still does, because it tells us that humans were not created directly as such by a special act of God, but that our species attained its characteristics over eons of time, in a gradual transformation out of primate ancestors. The close historical kinship the theory establishes between humans and non-human animals has often been found repugnant, partly because it seems to deny God's special creation of human beings, and partly because any close association of our species with apes has struck many people as disgusting. Teaching the theory of evolution was made illegal at various times and in various places in the US for these reasons—most famously in the Tennessee law called the Butler Act that gave rise to the Scopes Trial in 1925.[19] Today, although teaching evolution is not illegal anywhere in the US, fourteen states require the simultaneous teaching of "creation science" as an alternative view, despite the fact that "creation science" and its relative "intelligent design" have been rejected by the scientific community: they just aren't science, whatever other insight they may offer. But in reality, although Darwin's theory—which by now is thoroughly established in its general outlines—is at odds with a fully literal reading of the Book of Genesis, so too is all received science about the age of the earth, as Clarence Darrow memorably showed when he questioned William Jennings Bryan on the witness stand at the Scopes Trial. Bryan believed in a literal calculation of the age of the earth based on the ages of the prophets in Genesis, which put the date of the creation at 4004 BCE, a preposterous date from the point of view of archaeology. Few if any Americans today would join Bryan in that belief. But then, metaphorical reading must take over at some point, and the only question is, at what point. Darwin's theory is not incompatible with the idea that humans have a special place and receive special concern from God. But for a religious Darwinian, that special stature has to be investigated with proper humility: What precisely is it that sets humans off from other creations historically related to us? Don't we perhaps have special duties as well as privileges?

The Western tradition is more complicated than we sometimes think. At this point, it is natural for a sensitive Darwinian who still likes the idea of the *scala naturae* to ask whether apes and other creatures "high" on the ladder somehow share in our specialness. If we somehow climbed past other apes to the top of nature's ladder, doesn't this also mean that they climbed almost as far up, and are therefore entitled to at least some special treatment in virtue of that likeness?

Enter the "So Like Us" approach.

THE "SO LIKE US" APPROACH: TRADING ON THE *SCALA NATURAE* TO MAKE PROGRESS

Why not begin where most Americans seem to be and try to nudge them in the direction of limited rights for a limited group of creatures? A prominent and influential approach to animal ethics and law, which I call the "So Like Us" approach, does just that. It seeks recognition of legal personhood, and some autonomy rights, for a specific set of animal species, on the grounds of their humanlike capacities. This approach is associated, above all, with activist and author Steven Wise.[20]

Wise is one of the most significant pioneers of animal law. His 2000 book, *Rattling the Cage*, took the field of animal ethics into law, with striking results.[21] His course on animal law at Harvard Law School was one of the first law school courses of its kind, maybe even the first. And, as the leading figure in the 2016 documentary *Unlocking the Cage*, shown at the Sundance festival, he eloquently describes to the film's many viewers the goals of the Nonhuman Rights Project, which he leads; the film follows his legal battles to win limited personhood rights for several chimpanzees being held in captivity.[22] Wise is a heroic pioneer, and he chooses his conceptual approach not because he thinks it ultimately the best, but because he thinks it can help make progress, here and now, for animals suffering from grave injustice. My criticisms of his approach are not in any way meant to detract from my admiration for Wise and his legal work.

Wise does not ground his view in our evolutionary historical kinship with apes, but rather on similarity itself; so it is compatible both with the original fixed *scala naturae* or with a modified Darwinian form. But he does not focus on evolutionary kinship or limit his concern to creatures who have a close evolutionary relationship with humans.

Wise's focus in the 2000 book was on chimpanzees and bonobos,[23] but by now he explicitly includes all four species of great apes, as well as elephants (presumably all three species) and whales and dolphins (presumably all species of both of those).[24] His argument rests heavily on claims about the similarity of these animals to human beings. They are, he says, self-conscious, they are self-directing, they have a theory of mind, they have culture, they are not "cabined by instinct," they are able to contemplate their own future. In general, they are "really really smart."[25] Centrally, he holds that they are "autonomous creatures" who, for that reason, should have "autonomous lives."[26]

Wise is not a philosopher, and he does not explain which of the concepts of autonomy used by philosophers he has in mind. Since he also says that he thinks of chimpanzees as at the level of a five-year-old human child, it is not clear that he really should ascribe autonomy to them, if that means, as it typically does, the ability to criticize one's desires in the light of some higher-order principles, or, as Kant famously held, the ability to free oneself from the influence of religion and culture.[27] Probably he means some less exacting form of self-directedness, such as the ability to choose among alternatives. (But many other species of animals choose among alternatives!) In any case, as both book and film repeatedly emphasize, Wise thinks these species of animals are very like humans, and he makes that likeness the basis for his crusade to win them some limited legal rights.[28]

By showing how like us these animals are, Wise hopes to demonstrate, he says in the film, that the line typically drawn in law between humans and animals is irrational and needs rethinking.[29] If we think that children and people with severe cognitive disabilities have some rights, albeit with some qualifications and limitations, and a need for guardianship, we should grant that these species of animals also have rights. It is irrational and inconsistent to treat all humans as persons, bearing rights, and to treat all animals as like things. At this point, Wise uses an analogy to slavery: just as law used to treat slaves as property, and we have now seen that this was morally heinous, so too we should realize that our current treatment of animals is morally heinous.[30] In the film the slavery analogy gets strong pushback from some of Wise's interlocutors, presumably because it can be read as suggesting, inappropriately, that African Americans are like chimps, which is not the idea he means to convey.[31] So he backs away from the analogy; but he does not back away from the core idea that we must make a transition in law from thinking of animals as things and property to seeing them as persons.[32] He repeatedly points out—a very good point—that corporations are given rights under law; the extension of rights to self-directing animals is an easier step than that![33]

As this last analogy shows, Wise is above all a lawyer. He is not so much trying to create the best philosophical theory of animal law as he is trying to argue animals into a better position, using the materials, legal and theoretical, at his disposal. Many people think that the extension of personhood to corporations was a big mistake, and for all we know Wise himself may think this. But he is arguing from precedent like a shrewd lawyer: we've already decided this, now we need to see its implications for the animal question. His focus on similarity is strategic more than philosophical: he is just trying to move the needle with judges, beginning from where they are. So to criticize his theory as a theory may be a bit churlish. Nonetheless, it is put forward as a good basis for public argument, and it persuades, insofar as it does, only to the extent that people believe it. So, with all due respect for Wise's clever legal strategizing, I will examine his view as a theoretical basis for the justification of (some) animal entitlements.

Throughout both book and film, Wise presents lots of evidence that the chosen species of animals have human-like abilities of many types.[34] His central rhetorical strategy in the film is to show us chimpanzees and other apes doing things that the viewer will immediately recognize as human-like: using sign language, giving displays of empathy when shown a film of humans displaying emotions, and so forth.[35]

Wise makes the shrewd guess that if he is to make progress on animal rights he will have to begin where the audience is. He calls this beginning "the first salvo in a strategic war" and also talks of "kicking the first door open."[36] So he clearly isn't indifferent to the wider project of winning rights of some type for all animals. And his close and determined attention to the capacities and deprivations of some species is commendable. Nonetheless, one might raise worries. The choice of a framework influences where we will be able to go. It is important to get the theory right for reasons of truth and understanding. And it is also important to get a strategy that starts us in the right direction, rather than pointing us down a blind alley.

What, then, might be some problems with Wise's strategy from the philosophical viewpoint? Most obviously, it validates and plays upon the unscientific and anthropocentric idea of the *scala naturae* with us at the top. Some animals get favorable treatment, but only because they are (almost) like us. The first door is opened, but then it is slammed shut behind us: nobody else gets included. Instead of the old line, we have a slightly different line, but it is not really all that different, and most of the animal world still lies outside in the dark domain of thinghood.

The image of the *scala naturae* is not drawn from looking at nature, and it does not correspond to what we see when we look at nature, if we can put aside our arrogance. What we see are thousands of different animal life-forms, all exhibiting a kind of ordered striving toward survival, flourishing, and reproduction. Life-forms don't line up to be graded on a single scale: they are just wonderfully different. If we want to play the rating game, let's play it fairly. We humans win the prize on the IQ and language parameters. And guess who invented those tests! But many animals are much stronger and swifter. Birds do vastly better on spatial perception and the ability to remember distant destinations. Most animals have a keener sense of smell. Our hearing is very limited: some animals (e.g., dogs) hear higher frequencies than we can and many (elephants, whales) hear lower frequencies.[37] We sing opera, birds sing amazing birdsong, whales sing whale songs. Is one "better"? To a lover of music that's like asking whether we should prefer Mozart or Wagner: they are so different that it is a silly waste of time to compare them on a single scale.

As for life-sustaining abilities: rats are far more successful reproducers and survivors; numerous animals from tube worms to bowhead whales have greater individual longevity. Shall we ask about moral abilities? Well, we pride ourselves there, but we humans engage in depths of deliberate cruelty and torture known to no other animal species, and we'll see later on that numerous animal species show capacities for friendship and love. Do we think we are the most beautiful? Jonathan Swift was persuasive when he depicted Gulliver, after years with the lovely horselike Houyhnhnms, finding the human shape and smell disgusting.[38] No other animal has such arrogance about its beauty. At the same time, no other animal hates itself and flees from itself.

In short, if we line up the abilities fairly, not prejudging in favor of the things we happen to be good at, many other animals "win" many different ratings games. But by this time the whole idea of the ratings game is likely to seem a bit silly and artificial. What seems truly interesting is to study the sheer differentness and distinctiveness of each form of life. Anthropocentrism, then, begins to be revealed as a phony sort of arrogance. How great we are! If only all creatures were like us, well, some are, a little bit. Rather than unsettling our thinking in a way that might truly lead to a revolutionary embrace of animal lives, Wise just keeps the old thinking and the old line in place, and simply shifts several species to the other side. Again: this might be a shrewd strategy when addressing judges with limited imaginations; but in the end a defective theory is likely to have defective long-term results.

The *scala naturae* is potentially dangerous in other ways as well. It discourages useful self-criticism. It leads to ugly projects in which humans imagine transcending their animal bodies by casting aspersions on the smells and fluids of the body.[39] These projects are often accompanied by attempts to subordinate some other group of human beings, on the grounds that they are the true animals.[40] Bad smell, contaminating physicality, and hypersexuality are imputed to some relatively powerless subgroup, as an excuse for violent types of subordination. One may trace these ideas in US racism, in the Indian caste hierarchy, in misogyny everywhere, in homophobia, in prejudice against aging people.[41] Wise's strategy does nothing to undermine these baneful human practices; it risks reinforcing them with its line drawing. When what we need is a wholly new way of seeing our bodies, it gives us the same old way, with a few minor adjustments.

Meanwhile, Wise's approach cuts most of the animal kingdom adrift with no help from his interventions. He clearly doesn't want this result, but it's hard to know what his theory yields for the terrible suffering of pigs and chickens, for the loss of habitat by polar bears and dozens of other wild animals. Or rather, it is not hard to know what he offers, but all too easy: he offers nothing. A wholly new approach would need to be invented once we move outside the special sphere of the species who are so like us. It's pretty clear that in the long run Wise wants to come up with some approach or other to deal with these cases, but he gives us no idea what that new approach would be, or how it could later be reconciled with the thoroughgoing anthropocentrism of his starting point. What is lacking is wonder at the diversity of nature, love of its many distinctive forms of life.

There is a further disturbing consequence of the "So Like Us" approach: it leads to a focus on artificial performances that are not really characteristic of the species as it lives its life in the wild. Thus, *Unlocking the Cage* spends a good deal of time on sign language, and it is true, and impressive, that chimpanzees, bonobos, and gorillas can learn sign language.[42] But they don't use it when they are not living among humans. Although dolphins occasionally carry human-learned behavior with them back into the wild and teach it to other dolphins,[43] I am not aware of any case in which apes have done the same thing. It just isn't useful to them. And although Wise might have demonstrated the empathy and emotion of apes and elephants in many types of behavior that they engage in with their own species, as Frans de Waal has done for decades,[44] he instead dwells, in the film, on an example of empathy that is conveyed through the use of sign language.[45] A gorilla watches a movie in which a human child is saying goodbye to its family, and makes the signs for sad and so forth. Again, using sign language to indicate emotion is something apes do for and to humans, not something they do among themselves—although among themselves they have, as de Waal repeatedly shows, plenty of ways of communicating emotion.[46] And why did it have to be a movie about humans? Wise presumably likes the sign language–empathy example because it helps him establish likeness to us. But it is a pet trick. It becomes very hard, in fact, to understand the rationale by which Wise condemns some taught ape tricks, such as an ape doing karate kicks, and yet loves and foregrounds the language tricks. Both are similar, it seems to me (assuming the karate was taught through positive reinforcement and not cruelty): parlor tricks that show something about the animal, but not something that lies at the heart of its form of life. Whether it is ethical to teach such tricks can be debated, and I'm sure Wise would defend the language trick for what it teaches us. But that's just it: what it teaches *us*, not what it does for and in the animal life.

Wise argues that we need to begin by focusing on only a few rights for a few species, because people will be terrified if the door is open to all sorts of rights for all sorts of creatures. We'll later see, however, that giving animals some political voice can be done in a way that is sensible and acceptable as a long-range goal. People appreciate consistency and theoretical integrity. Sooner or later, people will wake up to the fact that Wise is playing bait and switch: likeness to humans for some creatures, some other as yet unannounced rationale for other creatures.

Wise is a skillful lawyer. In a case by now famous, in which he tried to get two chimps declared persons in order to win their transfer to an animal sanctuary, he and his Nonhuman Rights Project had a limited success. Although the New York Supreme Court rejected Wise's argument by a 5–0 vote, one judge was clearly moved by Wise's argument. In a striking concurring opinion, Judge Eugene Fahey wrote: "Does an intelligent nonhuman animal who thinks and plans and appreciates life as human beings do have the right to the protection of the law against arbitrary cruelties and enforced detentions visited on him or her? This is not merely a definitional question, but a deep dilemma of ethics and policy that demands our attention."[47] So Wise is right to think his approach can move the needle. But so too can the Capabilities Approach—and in theoretically more coherent and pertinent ways.

A MODIFIED *SCALA NATURAE*: WHITE'S "ALIEN INTELLIGENCE"

Before we move beyond the *scala naturae*, it is worth spending time with a splendid philosophical book that not only describes in loving detail the form of life of a particular type of animal, but also advances an ethical/policy approach that is considerably more nuanced and careful than that of Wise, avoiding at least some of the pitfalls of Wise's anthropocentrism. The book is *In Defense of Dolphins: The New Moral Frontier* by Thomas I. White.[48] White is a philosopher, and his book is written with impressive conceptual and argumentative care. He also knows a huge amount about dolphins, on the basis of both personal observation and exhaustive read-ing of the scientific literature. He is a clear and vivid writer, capable of communicating well with a large public. His aim is ultimately similar to that of Wise, though limited to one species: to convince readers that dol-phins have sophisticated cognitive and emotional lives, to convince them, further, that the standard philosophical/legal concept of "person" fits dol-phins just as well as it does humans, and that, for this reason, it is im-portant to treat dolphins not as things or property, but as selves, each an individual end in itself, worthy of the Kantian status of having a "dignity" rather than only a "price." His specific goals are to end tuna-fishing prac-tices that injure and kill dolphins and to cause people to rethink radically the practice of keeping dolphins in captivity. I'll discuss the latter complex topic in chapter 10, so for now I focus on White's general approach.

Like Wise, White uses a familiar philosophical concept of personhood that includes: self-consciousness, a sense of self (shown by the ability to pass the "mirror test"[49]), "advanced" cognitive and emotional capacities,[50] the ability to control behavior in the light of one's goals, the ability to choose "freely" among alternative actions, and the ability to recognize other per-sons and to treat them appropriately.[51] Much of the book is spent convincing readers that dolphins have all of these capacities, and it is clear that White wants readers to treat dolphins differently *because* they have these "ad-vanced" capacities. So his approach is vulnerable to many of the criticisms that I have addressed to Wise. In particular, White moves far too quickly from the correct claim that a creature's form of life determines what can be a harm for that creature to the apparent conclusion that non-persons are things and property who cannot really be harmed in significant respects.[52] White is a Kantian, and he gives these personhood attributes central nor-mative significance in conferring "moral status."

In the end, then, White's view is subtly different from that of Wise. Wise simply appeals to similarity: These animals are like us. Personhood and autonomy are important just because we have them and for no inde-pendent reason. White goes further, ascribing independent value to par-ticular capacities humans have, and then arguing that dolphins possess these. His view is less straightforwardly narcissistic than that of Wise, though it is limited in similar ways. We need a longer argument to rebut his claim that these capacities are more important than others: we need to show that the right way to evaluate capacities is to look at their role in a creature's overall form of life. Some human capacities would not suit the lives of birds, just as some remarkable bird capacities would not be useful in a human life. I will pursue that argument fully in chapter 5. For now, we can see that White's narrowness concerns not just his evaluation of animal lives but also his view of how we ought to evaluate ourselves: we ought to be proud because we possess these remarkable traits. This view in the end seems blinkered and arrogant in much the same way as that of Wise.

Still, White's book makes three significant improvements over Wise's paradigm, which he criticizes in some of the ways I have, for focusing too much on language and on artificial performance.[53] First, although he thinks that his approach, focusing on similarity and personhood, is a good one to meet the public where it is, and that it is sufficient to jus-tify large changes in our treatment of dolphins, a justification that "even the most anthropocentric humans" would accept, he repeatedly denies that it is the only basis for ethical concern for non-human animals.[54] For example: "I want to make it clear from the outset that I am not claiming that personhood is the sole, or necessarily the most important ground for nonhumans to have moral standing."[55] There are passages in the book where he doesn't fully stick to this, where, carried away by his Kantian enthusiasm for self-consciousness and choice, he suggests that without the traits of personhood a being can be counted as a thing with no dignity. But his official position is that he has taken no stand on sufficient condi-tions for moral standing.

Second, woven through White's argument for dolphin personhood is a fascinating account of their "alien intelligence." Whereas Wise focuses on ape performances that are human-like, even when they play no signifi-cant role in normal ape lives, White is sensitive to the many ways in which dolphins, while intelligent, are utterly different, their intelligence "alien" to our own. Describing dolphin faculties and forms of life in great detail,

White makes us see how even perception and consciousness are realized in very different ways in human and dolphin lives—as is really not surprising, given that they adapted to life in the water and we adapted to life on land. Dolphins do much more by sound than by sight, for example. And they have a remarkable ability to "echolocate," to "read" an object through sonar-like clicks. Echolocation allows dolphins not only to chart the outsides of a thing, it also permits them to perceive the insides. (In one remarkable case, a dolphin knew that its trainer was pregnant before the trainer herself knew this!) A lovely section of the book imagines how humans are likely to appear from a dolphin viewpoint: similar, but also strangely lacking in some essential faculties. This wonder at the complexity and strangeness of other forms of life is what Wise's approach sorely lacks.

Sometimes White's emphasis on dolphin alienness goes too far. For example, he keeps saying that dolphins are highly social creatures, whereas humans, at least lots of or most humans, are solitary individuals. He points to studies that ask people to self-characterize: some people mention relationships, many don't.[56] But what people say on a survey is not all that helpful in understanding what really guides their actions. In this era of the coronavirus we are all reminded of how deeply social humans really are, as even when physical proximity is denied, we email, phone, and Zoom chat—or even, in one local Chicago instance, have a public wedding in a park using appropriate six-foot "social distancing." Some people may have thought that being able to do without others is manly, or strong; but that is not to say that, when they really are forced to be solitary, they don't hate it.[57]

Be that as it may, the third, and in some ways most important, manner in which White qualifies his claims for personhood is his frank admission that the entire category of "personhood"—even when envisaged in a way that makes room for dolphin social instincts and alien intelligence—may be inappropriately anthropocentric.[58]

At the end of the day, however, White's capacity for wonder goes only so far. He is able to be curious about and impressed with an alien mode of doing something we humans do, but he does not venture into the wholly different worlds of creatures whose separate evolutionary path leads them to abilities and forms of intelligence far more alien to us—birds and fish, above all. Dolphins have a neuroanatomy very comparable to ours, and their intelligence, while alien, is not all that alien. Birds, by "convergent evolution," have developed remarkable abilities (see chapter 6), but in a way that looks much more totally alien and in many respects mysterious. Because of this preference for likeness over strangeness, he still leaves in place a linear conception of nature, where some human-like "persons" are at the top of some ladder—rather than exploding the whole idea of linearity in favor of the rich and amazing world we are actually in.

I am delighted to report that White has recently shifted his view, and now recommends the Capabilities Approach (see Conclusion).

BEYOND THE *SCALA NATURAE*: WONDERFUL AND ALIEN LIVES

White's book asks us to see the world through the eyes of a creature very different from ourselves, with genuine curiosity and a sense of wonder about its surprising form of life. That is a remarkable contribution to ethics, and it's what I think we should be doing across the whole of the animal world. He wraps up his comparison by urging us to ask, when thinking of how to treat a creature, what that creature's basic needs are, and how these are realized in its characteristic form of life. Only then can we decide, he says, whether a contemplated form of treatment (zoo captivity for dolphins, for example) is or is not appropriate.[59] These are exactly the questions my own approach urges us to ask about all sentient animals. White's account is fascinating and moving, but simply too narrow. In the end, I do not think White has given us any good reasons to confine that inquiry to creatures who are very like us. Personhood, however broadened, is objectionably anthropocentric.

Admittedly, it's a lot easier to ask and answer such questions concerning creatures who are rather similar to us, however alien in some respects.

But the difficulty of pressing this question further should not deter us from making the attempt, with the sort of humility, curiosity, and devotion to fact that White exhibits. The epistemic problem does not resolve our normative question of the best procedure and framework. If it's possible to imagine how odd human perception looks to a dolphin, it should be possible to think hard and resourcefully about how the world looks to birds, to all mammals, even to fish.

Of course, any linguistic account is a distortion. But we're familiar with that problem from our own studies of infant cognition, or our attempts to talk verbally about a pictorial or musical experience. But for better or worse, language is the medium for philosophical and scientific inquiry, so the "stammering translation" (words used by composer Gustav Mahler of his own attempts to describe his music in words) must be made. It's not clear why it can't be made across the whole animal world, if we are careful, humble, and resourceful.

We have now investigated a theoretical conception of animal rights and justice that is not only influential, but that also corresponds more than the others to the unexamined thoughts that most people raised in Western cultures are likely to have. The conception is blinkered. It ranks and rates beings without curiosity and with considerable unjustified narcissism. Let's now turn to a view that issued a powerful challenge to this one, emphasizing the commonality of all animals in our shared vulnerability to pain.

3

THE UTILITARIANS

Pleasure and Pain

In the late eighteenth century, the great British Utilitarian philosopher Jeremy Bentham (1748–1832) issued a clarion call. Comparing our current treatment of other animals to slavery, he said the right question to ask about animals is not "'Can they reason?' but 'Can they suffer?'" For Bentham, pleasure and pain are the key ethical facts, to which all the others are reducible. And, for Bentham, pleasure is unitary, varying only in quantity (intensity and duration), not in quality. The aim of a rational politics should be to maximize the net balance of pleasure over pain in the universe.

Nor was Bentham the only Utilitarian to focus on the suffering of animals. His pupil and successor John Stuart Mill (1806–1873) did significant work on this question, though his overall view diverged from Bentham's in crucial respects; he left his fortune to the Society for the Prevention of Cruelty to Animals. The distinguished Victorian philosopher Henry Sidgwick (1838–1900), returning to Bentham's views and rejecting Mill's critique, developed the philosophical aspects of Bentham's views far more rigorously, though without a particular focus on animals. And in our time, Utilitarian Peter Singer (b. 1946), a close follower of Bentham's and Sidgwick's ideas, has been among the leading thinkers to tackle the issue of cruelty to animals, in his famous book *Animal Liberation*[1] and many academic writings.

In this chapter, I examine the Utilitarians' powerful approach to animal welfare—with admiration and a good deal of sympathetic agreement, but also with significant criticisms.

The Utilitarian approach deserves enormous respect for its keen sensitivity to animal suffering. It looks like the opposite of the "So Like Us" approach, which I criticized in my previous chapter, and in one way it is, in its assault on human species arrogance. In another way, however, the two approaches share a defect. They both fail to grasp that the world of animal lives is one of surprising variety and diversity. Careful attention reveals neither a "ladder" nor a single homogeneous nature, but, instead, great complexity in the interlocking activities that comprise every animal way of life. Both approaches fail, that is, in *wonder*, in open-eyed curiosity. The first approach is willing to see only one template, the human one; the second, which we might call the "least common denominator view," acknowledges only one aspect of animal lives.

BENTHAM'S FOOTNOTE

Bentham famously held that the salient ethical facts, and the only salient ethical facts, are pleasure and pain. He strongly insisted that pleasures and pains do not vary along any qualitative dimension, but only along several dimensions of quantity (of which duration and intensity are the most important). The goal of each individual sentient being is, and ought to be,[2] the maximization of net pleasure. The goal of a rational society ought to be the maximization of net pleasure for all of society's members. That, and nothing else, is what happiness is.

Which members? Rather late in his *Principles of Morals and Legislation*, Bentham gets around to that all-important question.[3] Ethics and law, he urges, ought to be concerned with all living beings who are "susceptible of happiness," understood on his terms. These are "of two sorts": First, "human beings, who are styled persons."[4] Second, "other animals, which, on account of their interest having been neglected by the insensibility of the ancient jurists, stand degraded into the class of *things*."[5] Bentham, then, rejects the conventional distinction between (human) persons and things; he rejects the demotion of animals to the latter category, and with it, apparently, the idea that they are property. He does not assert that other animals are persons, but the passage clearly suggests that whatever the right rubric is, it is one that includes humans and animals together. He then attaches at this point a famous footnote. Often quoted in part, it deserves quotation in full:

> Under the Gentoo and Mahometan religions, the interests of the rest of the animal creation seem to have met with some attention. Why have they not, universally, with as much as those of human creatures, allowance made for the difference in point of sensibility? Because the laws that are have been the work of mutual fear; a sentiment which the less rational animals have not had the same means as man has of turning to account. Why *ought* they not? No reason can be given. If the being eaten were all, there is very good reason why we should be suffered to eat such of them as we like to eat: we are the better for it, and they are never the worse. They have none of those long-protracted anticipations of future misery which we have. The death they suffer in our hands commonly is, and always may be, a speedier, and by that means a less painful one, than that which would await them in the inevitable course of nature. If the being killed were all, there is very good reason why we should be suffered to kill such as molest us: we should be the worse for their living, and they are never the worse for being dead. But is there any reason why we should be suffered to torment them? Not any that I can see. Are there any why we should *not* be suffered to torment them? Yes, several. [Bentham here refers to another manuscript of his.] The day has been, I grieve it to say in many places it is not yet past, in which the greater

part of the species, under the denomination of slaves, have been treated
by the law exactly upon the same footing as, in England for example,
the inferior races of animals are still. The day *may* come, when the rest
of the animal creation may acquire those rights which never could have
been withholden from them but by the hand of tyranny. The French
have already discovered that the blackness of skin is no reason why a
human being should be abandoned without redress to the caprice of a
tormentor. It may come one day to be recognized, that the number of
legs, the villosity of the skin, or the termination of the *os sacrum*, are
reasons equally insufficient for abandoning a sensitive being to the same
fate. What else is it that should trace the insuperable line? Is it the faculty
of reason, or perhaps, the faculty of discourse? But a full-grown horse or
dog is beyond comparison a more rational, as well as a more conversable
animal, than an infant of a day, or a week, or even a month old. But suppose the case were otherwise, what would it avail? the question is not,
Can they *reason*? nor, Can they *talk*? but, Can they *suffer*?[6]

Bentham insists, shockingly, that animals ought to be treated together
with humans under law (whether under the rubric of personhood or, more
likely, under some new concept highlighting shared vulnerability). They
should not be treated as things or property, and their interests should be
treated with as much attention as those of humans, "allowance made for
the difference in point of sensibility."[7] Lest that qualification seems to take
away most of what he has said, he tells us quite clearly what it means: similar interests should be treated similarly, but something that is irrelevant to
the interests of a creature should not matter in thinking about its needs.
Elsewhere he announces this precept: each to count for one, and none for
more than one.

Here and in other texts, Bentham does admit a difference with respect
to the permissibility of killing. Other animals, because of the different nature of their minds, do not (he believes) have similar interests in not being
killed, because they cannot foresee and anticipate their own death. They
live in the present moment: so a painless death is not a wrong to them. I

agree with a part of this principle, but deny that it applies to most animals. Bentham also insists, rightly, that other animals are, like humans, subject to a self-defense principle: we may use deadly force if they threaten to cause us grievous harm. These claims will concern us in chapter 7. But the main thing is that where interests are similar, attention by law should be similar, and this means that we must not deliberately or negligently inflict pain on animals, any more than we are permitted to do so to humans. Even though elsewhere Bentham disparages the idea of rights, he here asserts it: animals have rights against cruel treatment, whether or not law has recognized these rights.

Bentham next confronts an imaginary interlocutor who advocates some version of the *scala naturae*, pointing to bodily differences as signs of a difference in moral status. Bentham first points out that in the case of slavery we now reject the idea that a bodily difference creates a "line" in nature. So too, he predicts, we will ultimately come to reject the idea that the bodily traits of non-human animals constitute such a "line." The interlocutor now is imagined to refer to "reason" and "discourse" as the real justifications for tracing such a "line" between us and them, a "line" that supposedly makes cruel treatment permissible. Bentham first denies the existence of any such sharp line: some animals reason better than some humans. But then he makes his real reply: it doesn't matter. The salient moral fact is not the capacity for reasoning, but the capacity for suffering.

Bentham's interest in animals was genuine, as numerous remarks gathered by his devoted editor, John Bowring (1792–1872), attest. He expressed a fondness for a wide range of animals, including cats, donkeys, pigs, and mice. He cultivated a friendship with a pig, who used to follow him around on his walks. A cat whom he named Reverend John Langborn used to eat macaroni at the table with him. He loved to have mice play in his study and eat crumbs from his lap. "I love everything that has four legs," he wrote. He used to recall with dismay the cruelties that he himself had inflicted on animals as a child, and the salutary effect that his uncle's reproaches had on him.[8] Clearly Bentham was not on the most extreme fringe of Victorian animal rights concern: other thinkers defended a total ban on the use of animals for food or clothing.[9] But he defended the limits of his argument (see chapter 7), and repeatedly asserted that where interests are similar, legal concern too should be similar. To most of Bentham's audience these claims were radical. The Christian prelate William Whewell was one strong critic of this radicalism, and Mill elegantly rebuts his critique, as we will see.

BENTHAM'S ANTI-VICTORIAN RADICALISM

But Bentham was more radical still. As has become clear only recently, with the publication of works that were not published during his lifetime, he boldly questioned British morality's puritanical hatred of bodily pleasure and our human animality, attitudes that helped produce the Victorian disdain for animals that he rejects. Since we too should question our frequently negative attitudes to our own animality, this context is of great importance today.

Especially in the book *Not Paul, but Jesus*, a radical rereading of Christian ethics, published only in 2013,[10] Bentham proclaims the equal worth of all pleasures and all pains, regardless of their source, and attacks the whole idea that some pleasures are "high" and others "low." He insists that Jesus was not averse to sexual pleasure, and that it is only the hypocrisy of the dominant group that has decreed that only marital sex is good and other types of sex are bad, deserving criminal punishment. He makes a remarkable and powerful set of arguments in favor of decriminalizing same-sex conduct and giving women greater sexual autonomy. Above all, Bentham urges his reader to drop the hatred of bodies that animates so much of Victorian culture.

From his vantage point we may see a large truth: much of humanity's denigration of other animals is inspired by self-loathing and fear. Because our own animal nature troubles, disgusts, and frightens us, we call that part of ourselves base, and project a similar contempt and loathing onto the rest of the animal kingdom—and also onto subordinate groups whom we irrationally deem more animal than we are. Puritanism and contempt for the other animal reinforce one another, and speciesism and other evils such as racism, sexism, and homophobia may have a common source.

Bentham, then, did more than ask for better treatment for animals: he traced our ill-treatment to its source, asking us to question ourselves in a courageous way.

DIFFICULTIES: QUALITY, ACTIVITY, IDENTITY

Utilitarianism is bracingly radical, and its ideas have been crucial to much recent progress in limiting human cruelty to animals. Suffering is one very large fact in animal lives. Utilitarians are right about that, and courageous when they emphasize it—although Bentham is probably thinking above all about physical suffering and not mental anguish, so he does not insist, as he should have, that animals are psychologically complex and capable of mental torment and frustration. Bentham's profound assault on Victorian attitudes makes his arguments important for the contemporary defender of animal rights, whether or not we agree with his specific proposals.

But in several ways the view is too simple.

First of all, Bentham offers no account of pleasure and pain; he does not even recognize that there is a philosophical question about this, as Mill notes, and he certainly does not show that all pleasures and pains are homogeneous in quality. The philosophers of ancient Greece and Rome had vigorous debates about what pleasure actually is: Is it a feeling? Is it a way of being active (without stress or impediment)? Or, perhaps most plausibly, is it a feeling that is very closely linked to activity, so closely that we can't pry it apart from the activity and measure it on its own? The pleasure of eating a delicious meal seems very different from the pleasure of holding a beloved child, and both are different from the pleasure of learning and studying—and so forth. Aristotle convincingly said that pleasure is something that "supervenes" on the activity, "like the bloom on the cheek" of a healthy young person. In other words, it is very closely linked to the activity: you can't get it without pursuing that activity. But if this is true, the entire project of maximizing net pleasure is in trouble from the start.

Moreover, once we recognize these qualitative differences, it looks as if we need to figure out which pleasures are worth fostering: the idea that all are equally worthwhile is dubious. Many people find pleasure in cruelty; others in amassing limitless wealth. Perhaps these are not the pleasures that someone concerned with creating a decent society should favor. This issue is huge when we think of human-animal relationships. For all of recorded history, many if not most human beings have found pleasure in domination over the other animals, and in many practices, from factory farming to the fur industry, that force animals to lead miserable lives. If all those pleasures count as positives in the social calculus, it will be difficult for the Utilitarian to argue convincingly that those practices ought to cease. But why on earth should they count as positives? We can respect Bentham's reason for ignoring these questions—he is eager to undermine a specific Victorian hierarchy of pleasures. But we must still insist that he has ignored a fundamental question.

Even if we put aside that basic question for a moment, the Benthamite calculus has further problems. The social goal, for Bentham, is an aggregate, either a total or an average. The *distribution* of pleasure and pain is not taken into account. Good aggregate results can be produced in a variety of ways, some involving great misery for those at the bottom of the social scale. Bentham's theory has no way of devoting special attention to the least well off, whose status is of immense importance for a person concerned with equal or even adequate opportunities for flourishing. The aggregation problem is even more worrisome if the goal is understood to be total rather than average pleasure: for this goal could justify bringing into the world creatures, of whatever species, whose lives are extremely miserable, just so long as those lives exhibit a slim net balance of pleasure over pain. (Might this not be true of many animal lives created by the food industry?)

Another way to see the problem with Utilitarian aggregation has been subtly raised by Christine Korsgaard, who contends, plausibly, that in aggregating, Utilitarians neglect the salience of individual lives.[11] Bentham appears to say that what is important is the amount of pleasure in society. Individual creatures matter only as containers of pleasures or satisfactions. If we can replace one individual with another who can hold a tiny bit more pleasure, we ought to do so. Society, in short, is not held accountable to individual sentient beings at all. The view does not respect them. They are like vessels into which a greater or lesser amount of pleasure may be poured, but the fact that it is *them*, each one a creature who has just one life to live, does not matter at all. Perhaps a Utilitarian view can be fashioned that defeats this objection: I think Mill's does. It is clear, however, that Bentham has not even contemplated this objection, far less addressed it.

A different issue arises when we consider the ability of all animals to adapt to substandard conditions. Sometimes people learn not to be pained by indignities and deprivations, through the process known as "adaptation" and the creation of "adaptive preferences."[12] Some adaptation is benign: as we grow up, we stop feeling upset because we can't fly, and we adjust to our bipedal state. But some adaptation reflects the pernicious tyranny of social custom. Women in sexist societies often learn not to want things that society denies them, such as higher education, sexual autonomy, and full political participation. Animals have this problem too: thus, animals raised in zoos from birth may not feel pain and dissatisfaction about their lack of free movement or social company, since they have never experienced these things, and since, like women, they are rewarded by their keepers for docility and punished for protest and aggression.

Beyond this, Bentham's account gives us a very narrow account of what is important in animal (including human animal) lives: just pleasure (seen as a qualitatively homogeneous feeling) and the avoidance of pain. Thus there is no room for the special value of free movement, of companionship and relationships with other members of one's kind, of sensory stimulation, of a pleasing and suitable habitat. In this failing, Benthamism converges with the "So Like Us" approach: both refuse to consider fully, and positively value, the many complex forms of life that animals actually lead. Pleasure and pain simply are not the only relevant issues when evaluating an animal's chances to flourish.

There is also an issue about activity. Bentham, as we said, thinks of pleasure as a feeling. That feeling is typically produced by an activity: the pleasure of eating is produced by eating, the pleasures of friendship by friendship. But of course, it might be produced in some other way, and in Bentham's conception, unlike Aristotle's, the pleasure and the activity are not closely linked. However, activity is important to living creatures. Philosopher Robert Nozick imagines an "experience machine": hooked up to that machine you would have the impression that you were eating, talking to your friends, and so forth, and you would have the enjoyment related to those pursuits—but without doing anything at all.[13] Nozick bets that most people would reject the experience machine, since being the author of their own actions is important to them, not just the experiences they have. The same is true of animals. Most animals like doing things; being the author of their actions matters to them. The Utilitarian approach has a hard time accounting for this.[14]

We should retain Utilitarianism's courageous focus on suffering and its equally courageous acknowledgment of extensive commonality between humans and other animals. We should also retain in some form Bentham's radical assault on Victorian elitism and prudery about bodily pleasure. But the Utilitarian who wants to reformulate the view so as to defeat this long list of objections has a lot of work to do.

BENTHAM'S FOLLOWERS: SIDGWICK AND SINGER

Victorian philosopher Henry Sidgwick was a remarkably insightful and rigorous philosopher, whose monumental *The Methods of Ethics*[15] repays close study by all who are interested in well-being, whether they agree with Utilitarian ideas or not. His careful defense of Utilitarianism against many criticisms (including those of J. S. Mill, which I'll discuss in the following section) does far more than Bentham to show the view's philosophical strength. And Sidgwick was, like Bentham, an activist, a pioneer in women's higher education who, with his wife, Eleanor, founded Newnham College, Cambridge, one of the first places in Britain to offer university degrees to women.[16] I do not consider his ideas in detail for three reasons. First, Sidgwick never adequately responds to the critiques I have made of Bentham's theory, and never even considers most of them. Second, Sidgwick never discusses animals and their entitlements, although scattered remarks suggest that he understood his theory to apply to them. Third, the most distinguished of Bentham's direct heirs, Peter Singer, is a major theorist of animal rights, as Sidgwick was not. Because he is also an expert on Sidgwick's philosophy, and views this as the basis for his own ideas, we can study Sidgwickian Benthamism by considering Singer.[17]

Peter Singer is without a doubt one of the most important figures in the history of the movement for animal rights. *Animal Liberation*, with its vivid writing and clear arguments, issued a clarion call to the world. Unlike Bentham, who tucked his key observations into a footnote in a book on criminal punishment, and unlike Mill, who confined his observations on that issue to a reply in a journal, Singer addressed the general public head-on, with all the horrors of human treatment of animals. Singer is also a sophisticated philosopher, who deals resourcefully with objections to his views.[18] Although what he says will not satisfy everyone, he says something, where Bentham said virtually nothing.

Like Bentham, Singer is resolutely opposed to a ranking of some lives as more valuable than others. He argues in detail against speciesism, but since I have already given my own arguments on this point I have no need to present his. Like Bentham, he insists that all interests must be treated equally. The principle of equal consideration does not dictate that all creatures must be treated alike, since creatures' interests may differ. It dictates that similar interests must be treated similarly. This is a major point of convergence between Singer's Benthamism and my own view.

Singer is an activist who seeks intellectual convergence in order to further the cause. He draws attention to the fact that in popular writing such as *Animal Liberation* he does not presuppose agreement on his version of Utilitarianism, but argues in a way that people with other related views might agree with.[19] I believe convergence is an important issue, and will discuss it in chapter 5 and in my conclusion. However, he and I also agree that it is important to get the philosophical view right!

There are two further points of convergence between Singer's view and mine. One is his insistence that sentience, or conscious awareness, marks an important dividing line in nature, and that animals without it (he discusses the cases I'll puzzle over in chapter 6), as well as plants, are not proper objects of ethical concern in a theory of justice, although they may be proper objects of other types of concern.

The other (partial) convergence concerns the wrongness of killing. Like Bentham, Singer believes that it is permissible to kill a creature who lives entirely in the present moment. However, he has an implausible account of that group, which, for him, includes most animals.[20] I agree with something like this principle in chapter 7, but with a very different account of which creatures (very few) actually do live in the present moment.

So much for Singer's agreement with Bentham. When we reach the details of Singer's view, however, significant divergences begin to appear.

Bentham appears to regard pleasure and pain as objective facts in the world, which a scientist might measure. That is how he was read by Sidgwick, whom Singer will later emulate. But in the earlier parts of his career, Singer focused not on the facts of pleasure and pain but on people's subjective preferences, and his version of the Utilitarian goal was the maximization of the net satisfaction of preferences.

Although this view seems, and is, different from Bentham's, it is vulnerable to all the objections I have made against Bentham. First, distribution is not salient in Singer's calculus. He has to rely on its turning out that diminishing cruelty to animals does in fact contribute to maximize net preference-satisfaction. This is tricky, because for Bentham, and presumably for Singer, intensity is an important dimension in the measurement of experience, and it is difficult to rule out that humans derive very intense satisfactions from meat eating, thus possibly counterbalancing the pains of many animals. The calculus is utterly obscure at this point, and not very useful. Nor, my second objection, does Singer recognize qualitative differences among satisfactions. He is like Bentham and Sidgwick, and unlike Mill, in his determination to have a single calculus.

As for adaptive preferences, I do not know of any discussion of these by Singer, but he would presumably dig in and say that a satisfaction is a satisfaction, regardless of the process that led to it. The special value of agency is, once again, something about which he does not comment (no reply to that aspect of Nozick, for example[21]), but he would presumably say that the experience machine is just fine, if it really works to satisfy preferences. Singer does comment on the container/replaceability argument, as I mentioned, but not in a way that would satisfy Korsgaard, the original objector.

In any case, by now Singer has dropped the insistence that pleasure is subjective and has shifted to a view like that of Sidgwick and Bentham: pleasure is a measurable fact in the world.[22]

Overall, then, Singer's arguments have greater philosophical sophistication than Bentham's, but similar problems. They make a giant step beyond the traditional "So Like Us" approach. But, following Mill's lead, we can and should do better.

CAN MILL SOLVE THESE PROBLEMS?

Bentham's distinguished heir, John Stuart Mill, made a great deal of progress on most of these issues. Because, like Bentham, he could not hold an academic position, or even obtain an academic degree, on account of his atheism,[23] and because, unlike Bentham, he was not independently wealthy, Mill had to earn a living, partly through a day job with the British East India Company and partly through journalistic writing. In consequence, Mill's published works are sometimes brief and cryptic. One wishes he had developed many of these points at greater length. But he gives us promising materials to build with—although they were explicitly rejected by Sidgwick and are often simply ignored by contemporary Utilitarians.[24]

First, Mill insists that pleasures differ in quality as well as in quantity. He also emphasized the value of agency, and connected it to a creature's dignity. He emphasizes the importance of specific items, such as health, dignity, friendship, and self-cultivation. He seems to have thought that these valuable things, when realized, are typically accompanied by pleasure, but he speaks as if the pleasure gets its value from the activity to which it is linked, rather than the other way around. He makes it very clear that satisfaction all by itself is insufficient for a flourishing life: activity, and the specific quality of an activity, matter greatly. In short, he has a picture of well-being similar to Aristotle's idea of multidimensional flourishing, or *eudaimonia*. And he is also sensitive to the fact that in a corrupt society people's pleasures might not be reliable indicators of value. In his important writings on women's equality, particularly *The Subjection of Women*, he insists that women's desires and preferences have been warped and twisted by male domination: women learn to be fearful and docile and to believe that being so is what makes them sexually attractive. Thus the "masters of women" have "enslaved" women's minds. He thus anticipates recent critics of Utilitarianism who write about "adaptive preferences."

Moreover, Mill clearly cares greatly about the distribution of utility in society. He insists in "Utilitarianism" that ideas of justice and rights must provide a floor beneath which law will not permit citizens to be pushed, even for overall welfare. In his political writings he is a social democrat, favoring a strong role for government in securing adequate education to all, protecting good working conditions, and extending the franchise. (As a member of Parliament, he introduced the first legislative proposal in Britain to open the vote to women, in 1872.) He also recommended laws against domestic violence and rape within marriage. He insists that in the "present imperfect state of society" there is a large gap between what people think will produce flourishing and what will really produce flourishing lives for all. He hopes that this problem will ultimately be addressed by educational enlightenment, but in the meantime law must take the lead.

Crucially, Mill addresses the "container" problem, albeit only in his correspondence. When asked by a friend how, exactly, happiness is aggregated across lives, his response is that we do so simply by counting the number of people who have happy lives (presumably happy up to some reasonable threshold): "I merely meant in this particular sentence to argue that since A's happiness is a good, B's is a good, C's a good, etc., the sum of all these goods must be a good."[25] Although we might wish for more extensive theoretical discussion, it seems that his view is determined to treat each creature's life as a separate source of value.

In a lot of his writings Mill speaks only of human beings and human society. But it is perfectly clear that he intended his ideas to extend to other animals and their flourishing. Although he never spelled out his own ideas about the philosophical basis for animal rights in detail, he does make his basic position extremely clear in an article known as the "Reply to Whewell."

William Whewell was a Christian cleric and intellectual who defended a version of the "ladder of nature," holding that humans occupy a unique place at the top of creation. He published a very hostile account of Bentham's views, saying that it was a *reductio ad absurdum* of the Utilitarian calculus that it would require us to consider the pleasures and pains of animals as on a par with those of humans. Whewell said that, on the contrary, we should judge the worth of any being's pleasures by their likeness to ourselves, and we should view ourselves as bound by ties of "human brotherhood" to put human pleasures first, and not even to weigh in the same calculus the pleasures of other animals. In a lengthy journal article, Mill replied with scathing wit and devastating logic, refuting him on a number of issues, including this one.

Mill insists that perceptions of likeness are contingent and highly manipulable. In the US South, he observes, the pleasures and pains of Black men are regarded as totally unlike those of white men. Five centuries ago, the pleasures and pains of the feudal nobility were viewed as in no way

comparable to those of serfs. According to Whewell, it would be right
for the dominant group in each case to refuse to consider the pleasures
and pains of the subordinate group in the same calculus. But these views
are "superstitions of selfishness."[26] For Mill, by contrast, we must always
ask: "Granted that any practice causes more pain to animals than it gives
pleasure to man: is that practice moral or immoral? And if, exactly in
proportion as human beings raise their heads out of the slough of selfishness, they do not with one voice answer 'immoral,' let the morality of the
principle of utility be for ever condemned."[27]

Mill's principle is vague, and in this passage he does not tell us how
he would reshape Bentham's calculus to include his own insights on the
question of qualitative differences, the crucial threshold of rights and justice, the adaptive preferences issue, and the thorny issue of how to aggregate pleasures. We have to do that work for him, but it can be done. My
positive proposal in chapter 5 will be highly Millian in spirit.

On one important issue, however, we must turn away from Mill. In
place of Bentham's radical democratization of pleasure, Mill reimports
the familiar Victorian distinction between "higher pleasures" and "lower
pleasures." Worse still, he illustrated the latter with an animal example:
the "pig satisfied." Mill's residual puritanism about bodily pleasure is definitely not helpful in getting the right idea of our kinship with the other
animals and the right wholehearted acknowledgment of that kinship. He
might have kept qualitative distinctions without going back to the conventional hierarchy, simply saying, with Aristotle, that each activity comes
with its own associated distinctive pleasure.

So one might say that my Capabilities Approach will articulate what
Mill would have said about animals had he been less afflicted by Victorian
prudery and shame!

ONWARD FROM BENTHAM'S CALCULUS

The Utilitarians were, and are, ethical heroes. They saw and heard what
others refused to see and hear, and they had not just compassion, which

might be uneven, but also a principled determination to treat all sentient creatures alike. The shortcomings of Utilitarianism should lead us to seek an approach that shares Bentham's courageous emphasis on suffering as a common bond among all animals, and on sentience as a salient dividing line in nature, marking off those creatures that can be treated justly or unjustly—but that goes beyond Bentham in attending to the whole form of life of each kind of animal, and the many different aspects of animal flourishing and animal deprivation. In this effort, Mill's critique of Bentham will be very important, and I agree with much of it: the importance of each being's dignity; the importance of activities as well as states; and the need to recognize an irreducible plurality of important values. Mill, however, lacked Bentham's radical zeal to rehabilitate the body and its pleasures. For this reason we need to keep Bentham in mind as well as Mill as we try to make progress.

My approach will be like Utilitarianism in taking all sentient beings' interests to have equal weight and in taking sentience to mark a very important boundary. But although pain is very important, and ending gratuitous pain is an urgent goal, animals are agents, and their lives have other relevant aspects: dignity, social capacity, curiosity, play, planning, and free movement among others. Their flourishing is best conceived in terms of opportunities for choice of activities, not just states of satisfaction. Let us, then, learn from the Utilitarians, but move onward.

4

CHRISTINE KORSGAARD'S
KANTIAN APPROACH

KANT, DIGNITY, AND ENDS

I have rejected approaches that set humans on a pedestal, judging animals worth caring about only to the extent that they resemble us. I have also rejected Bentham's form of Utilitarianism, demanding a view that respects the dignity of each sentient creature and that values animals as agents, not just containers of satisfaction. Now we move to a third theoretical approach that is much closer to my own, overlapping with it in many ways: Christine Korsgaard's approach based on the thought of Immanuel Kant, and in particular Kant's idea that we must always treat creatures (for Kant, only humans, for Korsgaard all sentient animals) as ends, not simply as means to our own ends. This is the most significant philosophical book on animal rights in recent years, worth engaging with just on account of its sheer quality. But it is also important to understand why the approach, impressive though it is, comes up short, not doing full justice to animal agency and the complexity of animal lives.

Immanuel Kant (1724–1804) was Bentham's contemporary, and

another major architect of the liberal Enlightenment. Both wanted more human choice and less arbitrary authority in society. Both, opposing the domination of authoritarian religion and custom, sought public policies accountable only to human reason. Both were bold internationalists, seeking cooperation among nations and criticizing colonialism. Both opposed slavery and the slave trade.[1]

Nonetheless, they also differed in fundamental ways. Bentham thought pleasure and pain the only relevant normative facts; Kant ascribed no moral worth to pleasure as such, focusing instead on the dignity of the human ability for ethical choice.[2] They also differed in their practical conclusions, in ways connected to that fundamental difference. While Bentham understood that sexual norms were often ways of subordinating powerless groups, including women and people who desired same-sex relationships, and sought the right for all to find pleasure in their own preferred way, Kant seems to have had little or no interest in the equality of women and held severe conventional views about sexual impropriety (even holding that masturbation is worse than rape!). He was utterly contemptuous of pleasure and desire. While Bentham was keenly aware of the suffering of animals at human hands, thinking of this, too, as an unacceptable type of "tyranny," Kant thought animals, lacking the capacity for ethical choice, were utterly lacking in dignity, and concluded that humans may use them "as we please."[3]

Through his generous concern with suffering and his skeptical unmasking of all forms of domination, Bentham corrects (so to speak, since he probably did not read him) some of Kant's worst failings. But matters are not simple, because we can also say the same thing in reverse. Whereas Bentham, obsessively focused on aggregation, lacks a sense of the inviolability and dignity of the individual creature, Kant puts that dignity right at the heart of his moral philosophy (for humans only), holding that the basic form of wrongdoing is to treat a human being as simply a means rather than an end. Each, it seems, has things to teach us that we may apply to the lives and the sufferings of animals, if we are careful to avoid the errors of both.[4]

In this chapter, I will argue that the lover of animals has a lot to learn from thinking about Kant, but that we must think critically about what a Kantian approach offers us. I do so by focusing on the work of Christine Korsgaard, one of Kant's most distinguished interpreters and heirs, and also one of our most compelling contemporary philosophers. Korsgaard is also an animal lover and one of our best thinkers about animal selves and animal rights. Despite her awareness that Kant himself has little respect for animals, she has long believed that Kant's ethical outlook contains materials that we can use to construct a view of animal rights, and she has worked out her views in two important publications: her 2004 Tanner Lectures, titled "Fellow Creatures: Kantian Ethics and Our Duties to Animals,"[5] and her 2018 book, *Fellow Creatures: Our Obligations to the Other Animals*.[6] As the similar titles suggest, the two works are very close in argument; the book, far longer, develops out of the lectures. Nonetheless, there are significant differences that warrant sequential treatment.

While I do not agree with everything in Korsgaard's 2018 book, I regard it as a major philosophical achievement, and I urge all readers of this book to read it too, since I cover only some of its rich and important discussions.

Korsgaard is a Kantian, but she also has learned a lot from Aristotle. (Her Harvard PhD dissertation was on both Kant and Aristotle.[7]) Aristotle—of whom I'll say much more in describing my own view—was keenly interested in commonalities between humans and other animals, holding that all animals move toward their goals using cognitive faculties (perception, imagination, and desire) and forms of desire and emotion, seeking to maintain their characteristic form of life. Korsgaard considers these insights important. From Aristotle she draws an understanding of how sentient creatures of all sorts strive to achieve their ends, and to live in accordance with the type of functioning peculiar to each species. These are insights missing in Kant,[8] and Korsgaard uses an Aristotelian understanding of how animals (including humans) strive to attain their ends to open up a space in Kant's relentlessly anthropocentric ethics within which a lover of animals may begin to do justice to animals and their strivings.

But then why stick to Kant? Because of his insight into the inviolable dignity of the individual creature, an insight Aristotle never articulates.

I agree with Korsgaard that any good approach to animal justice needs both an Aristotelian element and a Kantian element. Aristotle lacks the notion of dignity, and of being treated as an end in oneself. We need these ideas. Korsgaard and I combine the Aristotelian and Kantian elements in significantly different ways, but we end up with many of the same conclusions. This chapter, then, will be both a study of a rival view and, at the same time, a prelude to the approach that I favor.

KANT ON THE TREATMENT OF ANIMALS

For Kant, the key fact about human beings is our capacity for ethical reasoning and choice, our ability to bind ourselves by laws of our own creation. This capacity seemed to him of priceless worth, whereas other animal capacities had no worth. In the conclusion of his *Critique of Practical Reason*, he makes this famous observation: "Two things fill the mind with ever new and increasing admiration and awe, the more often and steadily one reflects on them: *the starry heavens above me and the moral law within me*."[9] Our respect and awe before this capacity is for him the basic starting point for ethics.

Kant thought there could be other morally rational beings: angels for example. But in our daily world, humans are alone. Like the Stoics, he denied that animals had any share in the capacity for moral legislation: they were just creatures of instinct and desire, which, in and of themselves, have no moral worth. Because of our unique (in this world) capacity for self-legislation, we are "utterly different in rank and dignity from *things*, such as irrational animals, which we can dispose of as we please."[10]

Kant articulates the normative consequences of human dignity in the four formulations of his famous "Categorical Imperative."[11] "Categorical" is contrasted with "hypothetical." A hypothetical imperative tells you to do action A if you want to get B: it is contingent on your prior aim. A categorical imperative is binding in all situations and no matter what you want or feel. The Categorical Imperative is probably best regarded as a way of testing the principle of a person's proposed action, to see whether it passes ethical muster. Does it, then, embody the sort of law that we ought to be giving to ourselves as we prepare to act?

Much has been written about Kant's different formulations of the Categorical Imperative, and much of it is irrelevant to our purposes here. I am in strong agreement with Korsgaard that Kant's central idea is best captured in the second formulation, the Formula of Humanity or Formula of the End-in-Itself:[12] "So act that you use humanity, in your own person as well as in the person of any other, always at the same time as an end, never merely as a means."[13] The key idea, then, is that of treating a creature not (or not only) as an instrument of your own ends, an object of your purposes, but always as a being whose interests matter intrinsically, just because the creature who has them matters intrinsically. Of course, one might use a creature as both a means and an end; for example, employing a worker to get things done for you while treating the worker with respect and genuine concern. The Kantian insists that any such instrumental use of a creature should be limited by the dominant idea that you value the creature for itself and seek to respect its pursuit of its own ends. This is an idea that laws and constitutions all over the world build into the framework of nations as a way of circumscribing what majorities may and may not do.

Kant illustrates this formula (like his others) with reference to four examples. The clearest one is the deceptive promise: Making a deceptive promise for personal gain is obviously a way of treating another person as a means, so the Categorical Imperative vetoes such conduct. The existence of deception shows that you are not sufficiently respecting that person as a choice maker. We can understand from this case that treating humanity as an end requires us not to exploit others through coercion or fraud.

But Kant thinks that we also have duties to ourselves. So he argues, through another example, that people who live for pleasure, not developing their talents, are also showing a lack of respect for their own moral faculties, and treating them as means to enjoyment. It is not totally clear that Kant is correct. Perhaps in a very extreme case the person's pursuit of pleasure may completely destroy their capacity for choice, and that extreme case could be objectionable. But often such arguments are used as a screen for puritanism, and Kant is not immune to that objection.

Using a further example, Kant argues that people in comfortable circumstances who do nothing at all to aid the needy are, in effect, treating them as nothing but means—since they would eagerly accept aid themselves if they were needy. This idea is interesting, but needs much more development than Kant gives it. It is likely that at times comfortable people exploit others who are less well off, relying on them as servants of their own interests rather than respecting them as ends. But it takes care to articulate the conditions under which that criticism would be justified.[14]

Another way of seeing what is at stake in respect for humanity is to think about what the world would be like if we made our own principle a universal law. This Formula of Universal Law, Kant's first formulation of the Categorical Imperative, is intended to be closely connected with the Formula of Humanity and to give us another way of understanding it. Kant believes a central form of moral error is that of making a special case of ourselves, giving ourselves exemptions from rules that we impose on others. Universalizing our principle reveals the self-dealing involved in such conduct, helping us to see its exploitative aspect. The false promiser does not want everyone to be able to make false promises: for then the institution of promising would cease to exist, and she is relying on the institution to promote herself at the expense of others. Kant also thinks that the lazy pleasure seeker could not possibly will a world in which everyone was lazy and lived for pleasure, since nobody would do the things essential to making the world stable and worth living in. In short, she is a parasite on the labors of others. The person who won't help others, again, could not possibly will the whole world to be like that, because nobody would help her if she needed help. Once again, then, she exploits others.

Kant's basic idea, then, is one of respecting each human being as a creature of intrinsic worth and autonomy, a maker of choices like ourselves, and not subordinating their ends to ours. Let's now see how that principle might work if applied to our dealings with other animals.

If we humans were to test the principles of our actions toward other animals, thinking of ourselves as sharing the world of nature with them, very little would pass the scrutiny of the Categorical Imperative. Humans reason that it is fine to imprison pigs in gestation crates—but would be appalled if their own children were taken from them and thrust into a painful and degrading form of confinement.[15] Humans think it fine to commit acts of painful and often lethal aggression against animals, but we do not tolerate the aggression of other animals against humans. Humans typically do not think it important to help animals who are in need—although we rely on animals to supply us with all sorts of things we need, without even asking consent. And humans do not reflect that one of our duties to ourselves might be to develop our capacities for wonder and awe at the lives of animals. In most of our conduct toward other animals, then, we use them as things, as means—and we also fail to will that we ourselves become different. So the Categorical Imperative appears to have rich critical resources for our current treatment of animals—if animals get included in our deliberation in the first place.

Kant, however, does not think any of these thoughts, because he has already drawn a line in the sand, between creatures of self-given ethical law and creatures of instinct, and has ruled without further ado that the latter deserve no ethical consideration at all. In his essay "Conjectures on the Beginnings of Human History," Kant describes as a crucial stage in human progress the stage at which human reason raises "man completely above animal society." Humans realize that they are "the true *end of* nature." At that point, their relationship to animals is transformed: the human being "no longer regarded them as fellow creatures, but as means and instruments to be used at will for the attainment of whatever ends he pleased."[16]

Somewhat surprisingly, however, Kant does forbid the cruel treatment of animals: not because they are ends in themselves, but for a very different reason. Adopting a common eighteenth-century view, Kant claims that cruel treatment of animals makes human beings callous and more likely to be cruel toward humans. One famous illustration of this view is the artist William Hogarth's *The Four Stages of Cruelty* (1751): the little boy, Tom Nero, begins by torturing a dog, then, as an adult, progresses to beating a horse, and then to robbery and the brutal murder of a woman. Finally, he is executed by hanging, and his body is dissected by medical students. Referring to these engravings in his *Lectures on Ethics*, Kant says they should be "an impressive lesson to children."[17]

Kant thought these psychological laws sufficient to rule out cruelty, which for him included many of the acts that Bentham also forbids: recreational hunting and fishing, sports like bearbaiting and cockfighting. Kant thinks we may kill animals (and, presumably, eat them), but that we must do this painlessly. We may make animals work, but must not overstrain them. And we must not do medical experiments on animals for the sake of "mere speculation," whenever we could learn what we want to know in some other way. He also criticizes the practice of killing animals when they are too old to be useful.[18] More generally, he holds that animals inspire in us many feelings, such as compassion, gratitude, and love, which are useful and should be strengthened—*because they help us behave well to human beings.*[19] None of this, however, is for the sake of the animals. In effect, they are being used as means to human moral self-cultivation. We owe these duties not to the animals, but to ourselves.

As Korsgaard argues, Kant's position is unstable. He wants us to see animals as similar to ourselves in many ways, and to have toward them a range of genuine feelings: to love them, not just to treat them as if we did. But then, if we do love animals, don't we want to treat them well for their own sake, not for the sake of our own improvement? As she says: "There is surely some tension between loving a creature for his or her own sake, and seeing that love as a way to 'preserve a natural disposition that is very serviceable to morality in our relations with other people.'"[20]

Korsgaard is convinced that a Kantian can, and should, do better.

KORSGAARD'S FIRST KANTIAN VIEW OF ANIMAL RIGHTS

For Korsgaard as for Kant, we humans are the only creatures who can be obligated and *have* duties, on account of our possession of the capacity for ethical reflection and choice. Korsgaard, however, sees that this fact does not imply that we are the only creatures who can be the *objects* of duties, creatures to whom duties are owed. Kant assumes that these two ways in which something can be an end in itself pick out the same class of beings, namely all and only human beings. Korsgaard points out that a being may be an end in itself in the first sense—a cat, for example, may be a creature whom we are obligated to treat with respect, even though the cat lacks the capacity for ethical legislation that she thinks crucial for being an end in the second, ethical lawmaking, sense.[21]

Korsgaard's conception of animal nature is not Kantian, but Aristotelian, as mine too will be: she sees animals, including the animal nature of human beings, as self-maintaining systems who pursue a good and who matter to themselves. She gives a fine account of the way in which we may see animals as, in that sense, intelligent—as having a sense of self and a picture of their own good, and thus as having interests whose fulfillment matters to them. We human beings are like that too, she argues, and if we are honest we will see that our lives are in that sense not different from other animal lives. However, in her view, there remains a split: we humans have another separate part, the part that performs ethical reflection and choice. So in reality, her view is not mine, as we'll see: I believe all our capacities are parts of our animal nature.

When a human being chooses and "legislates," she does so, according to Kant and Korsgaard, in virtue of a moral capacity that no other animal has. This does not mean, however, that all human legislation is *for* and *about* the autonomous will. Much of ethics, in fact, has to do with the interests and pursuits characteristic of the capacities that Korsgaard thinks belong to our animal nature: we think ethically about how to fulfill our bodily needs, desires, and other projects. When we do make laws for ourselves with regard to the (legitimate) fulfillment of our animal needs and desires, it is simply inconsistent, and bad faith, Korsgaard argues, to fail to include within the domain of these laws the other beings who—like cats, dogs, and all sorts of other fellow creatures—are similar to us in having such needs and desires. Just as a maxim cannot pass Kant's test if it singles out a group of humans, or a single human, for special treatment and omits other humans similarly situated, so too it cannot truly pass Kant's test, as Korsgaard reinterprets it, if it cuts the animal part of human life from the animal lives of our fellow creatures. Jane is obligated to take steps to protect her bodily health; but then, she is inconsistent if she does not take steps to protect the health of her cat, her dog, and other animals who also have animal projects.

Korsgaard's conception of duties to animals combines two elements that it seems an adequate view ought to combine: that is, it has a Kantian part and an Aristotelian part. It says that we should treat animals as ends in themselves, beings whose ends matter in themselves, not just as instruments of human ends. And it also conceives of animal lives, including our own, as rich self-maintaining systems involving complex varieties of intelligence. So far so good, although the split between animal nature and rational nature is worrisome.

I have saved until last a part of Korsgaard's conception that lies at its very heart. We humans, she insists, are the creators of value. Value does not exist in the world to be discovered or seen; it comes into being through the work of our autonomous wills. Our ends are not good in themselves; they are good only relatively to our own interests. We take our interest in something "to confer a kind of value upon it," making it worthy of choice. That, in turn, means that we are according a kind of value to ourselves, including not only our rational nature but also our animal nature. Animals matter because of their kinship to (the animal nature of) a creature who matters, and that creature matters because it has conferred value on itself.

To me this is simply too indirect. What seems wonderful about an animal life—say, the life of a cat—is its own active pursuit of ends, so our wonder and awe before such a life is quite different from our response to the Grand Canyon or the Pacific Ocean: it is a response to the worth or dignity of an active being who is striving to attain its good. Because they are active sentient beings pursuing a system of goals, animals can be impeded in their pursuit by human interference. This quality of active, striving agency suggests that animals are not only objects of wonder but also subjects of justice, an idea that I'll develop further in chapters 5 and 6.

Wonder suggests to us that animals matter directly, for their own sake—not because of some similarity they have to ourselves. Wonder turns us outward toward the cat, not inward toward ourselves. Korsgaard does not exactly make the value of animals derivative from the value of human beings. Instead, her picture is that when we ascribe value to ourselves, we ascribe value to the members of a species of a genus, and then it is bad faith, having once done that, to deny that the members of other species of that genus, insofar as they are similar, possess that same action-guiding value. However, there still seems to be a strange indirectness about that route to animal value. It is only because we have similar animal natures ourselves, and confer value on that nature, that we are also bound in consistency to confer value on animal lives. Had we had a very different nature, let's say that of an android, we would have no reason to value animal lives. And, so far as I can see, the rational beings recognized by Kant who are not animal (angels, God) have no reason to value the lives of animals.

This seems wrong: animals matter because of what *they* are, not because of kinship to ourselves. Even if there were no such kinship, they would still matter for what they are, and their striving would be worthy of support. To put it differently, for Korsgaard, it's in effect an accident that animals matter: we just happen to be pretty much like them. But I think that the value of animal lives ought to come from within those lives. Value comes in many varieties in the world, and each distinctive sort is valuable because of the sort it is, not because of its likeness to ourselves. [22]

In short: Korsgaard avoids most of the errors of the "So Like Us" approach, but in the end she ties herself to a version of it: the value of animals is derivative from likeness to humanity.

That is my first objection to Korsgaard. Now let us turn to the split between the rational and the animal. Korsgaard makes a very compelling case for recognizing in animals a range of types of awareness; even those who can't pass the mirror test are held to have a point of view on the world, and ends that matter to them. All this seems just right. So, while one might have expected that a Kantian view would draw a too-sharp line between the human and the animal, up to a point that seems not to be true of Korsgaard's view. The rabbit's own goals, she says, are the only ones pertinent to the rabbit. However, in the end she does draw too sharp a line.

Korsgaard says that humans are the only truly moral animals, the only ones that have a full-fledged capacity to stand back from our ends, test them, and consider whether to adopt them. She does, however, say of children and people with mental disabilities that they too are rational beings in the ethical sense, it's just that they reason badly. If she once makes that move, I do not see how she can avoid extending at least a part of that ethical rationality to many if not most animals. Because this problem persists in Korsgaard's book, I will develop my objection fully in my next section, arguing that our moral nature is actually one part of our animal nature, not something apart from it.

In short, Korsgaard has pushed Kant to the limit in giving her extremely sensitive and appealing picture of how Kant and Aristotle may cooperate, but there is really no way, without departing from Kant more radically, to acknowledge that our moral capacities are themselves animal capacities, part and parcel of an animal nature. Chapter 2 reminded us that any conception that doesn't acknowledge this is in ethical peril, courting a danger of self-splitting and self-contempt (so often linked with contempt for women, for people with disabilities, for anything that reminds us too keenly of the animal side of ourselves). Although Korsgaard heads off this peril sagely wherever it manifests itself, she still doesn't altogether get rid of it; it is still lurking, in the very idea that we are somehow, in being moral, above the world of nature.

FELLOW CREATURES: FURTHER
DEVELOPMENT OF THE KANTIAN VIEW

Fellow Creatures is an important book, with eloquent arguments on most issues of importance to animal lovers. And it issues an exhilarating challenge to those who are not already animal lovers but simply want to follow reasoned argument where it leads. I focus only on its main line of argument here, and I will make some criticisms. In chapter 5, however, developing my own view, I will simply take over from Korsgaard an argument about law and the grounding of rights that she develops in two articles separate from the book.

Korsgaard does not expect her readers to be familiar with the details of her earlier lectures. She consequently just develops her view, without pointing out the respects in which her view has evolved. The reader is left to figure this out for herself, and since the differences are often subtle, I characterize them with considerable caution.

Korsgaard now develops what I've called the Aristotelian side of her view much more fully, and relies on it much more centrally. All animals, both human and non-human, she insists, are functional systems striving for a good that is their own, intrinsic to their form of life. All animals are made of fragile materials, but they are always replenishing themselves, and also trying to reproduce their kind. And all animals are perceivers, with the capacity to represent the world to themselves. Moreover, their perceiving is evaluative, so that, seeing some things as good for them and others as harmful, they are drawn to some things and away from others. All of this, she says, is not just a fact about animals, it is part of the very concept of what it is to be an animal (as distinct from a rock, an immortal god, or even a plant).

All animals, then, want and ascribe value to the ends for which they strive. A rabbit values the food, the freedom from danger, and the reproductive opportunities that are part of its way of life. Humans mistakenly try to rank the ends of different creatures absolutely, to say that some ends some creatures strive for are more important than others. (She alludes, in effect, to the *scala naturae* and other views like it.) But this is not a coherent position: all value, all importance, is importance *for* someone. There is nowhere we can stand from which we can ask coherently which creatures are more important: all value is "tethered." For a rabbit, the goals of human beings do not matter at all: everything that matters is summed up in its own set of goals and ends. At death, the rabbit will lose the whole world. It is a necessary truth that for a creature who functions in this way, life is a good for her.

All animals also have death and senescence built into their form of life, but not in the same way: they do not seek out these things, these things are not part of their good.[23]

And if we think we are the only creatures who have consciousness, or a self, we are wrong: all animals experience the effects of the world on their condition.[24] All animals locate themselves relationally in the world. And animals have a variety of ways of experiencing themselves in relation to the world, pain and sense-perception above all. Having an animal self involves just that awareness and that point of view on the world.

All of this, Korsgaard notes, we can understand using the standpoint of empathy. The fact that we so rarely use empathy in this way, preferring to think of animals as unfeeling brutes, is a defect of ethical perception, and a species of a more general moral error in human life. "It is the perpetual temptation, especially of the safe and privileged, to harbor the thought that those less fortunate than ourselves are also simpler beings to whom misfortune probably does not matter as much, or in the same vivid way, as it would if the same things were happening to us."[25]

When we pursue our ends, we treat ourselves as ends in ourselves: we resist being used as tools of other people's purposes. But that is what any animal does too, and this way of valuing our ends is just our way of being an animal.[26] All animals confer absolute value on their ends. For Korsgaard, this suffices for the conclusion that animals are ends in themselves in Kant's sense, meaning that they have, each of them, a dignity, not just a price, like property. Treating animals as nothing but means violates that dignity.[27] Treating an animal as an end means valuing what is good for it for the sake of that creature, not for your sake or for the sake of some absolute untethered value.[28] We can understand, if we try, what is good for a rabbit, and treating a rabbit as an end means valuing those things (life, food, safety) for that rabbit because they matter to the rabbit. Just as each human being's right to pursue her own ends is limited by the rights of every other human being, so too our right to pursue our ends is limited (or should be) by our empathetic understanding of the good of other animals. In short, the claim of the other animals to the standing of ends in themselves has the same ultimate foundation as our own claim does, the same ultimate foundation as all morality—the self-affirming nature of life itself.[29] And a further reason to keep animals near us is that they are good for us: they remind us of "the all-important thing we share with them: the sheer joy and terror of conscious existence."[30]

All of this seems just right, and by emphasizing these (Aristotelian) facts, Korsgaard makes a significant improvement over the argument in the Tanner Lectures. In the lectures she seemed to say that we ought to value animals because we perceive that they are like us, and I questioned that move. Now it is much clearer that the perception of similarity between ourselves and other animals is only heuristic, helping us understand the sorts of creatures they are, rather than the ground of their claim on us. Their claim on us and our claims on one another have exactly the same source. The view seems no longer open to my objection that if we had been different, like robots, we would have no reason to care about other animals. Our moral reasons would be just the same: because animals pursue a good and confer value on it, for that reason alone we ought to treat them as ends in themselves. It would just be harder for us to come to an empathetic understanding of their lives. So far, Korsgaard and I are in complete agreement.

A large difference, however, emerges from the fact that Korsgaard insists, here as in the lectures, that all value is a human creation. It does not exist "out there" to be discovered. So when we value the lives of animals it is because we confer value upon those lives, as we do upon our own. Korsgaard's reasons for her view are Kantian: our reason is limited in scope, and

does not entitle us to make claims that go outside the bounds of our experience. My full reply to her on this point will come in chapter 5. Briefly,
it is that this controversial metaphysical position is not necessary for her
conclusion about the worth of animal lives, and is actually inappropriate
if what we are pursuing is the creation of good political principles that can
unite people of different religious and metaphysical views. If we are seeking political principles, as I think we both are, we must endeavor to construct a political and legal view that can ultimately be acceptable to people
holding many different metaphysical and secular conceptions of the ultimate sources of value. And this means that we must not attempt to justify
a fully comprehensive ethical view, saying what we think on all questions
of ultimate metaphysics. I'll elaborate on this further in chapter 5, describing my own view. Korsgaard never says whether she is creating a basis for
political principles and laws, but it seems that this must be what she is
doing, not just creating her own preferred ethical-metaphysical view: she
ultimately wants to end up with good laws. She should not, then, include
divisive metaphysical elements that are not necessary to make the case for
animal rights. This is one large disagreement I have with Korsgaard, and
is a further objection to her project, even as modified.

INSTINCT, CULTURE, CHOICE: AGAINST THE KANTIAN DICHOTOMY

I had two objections to Korsgaard's first view of animal rights. One objection—that she valued animals only because of an accidental similarity to
ourselves—has been removed by the book's subtle analysis. The second
objection, however, remains. Korsgaard continues to draw a very sharp
line between humans and all other animals in the area of moral capacity. The world, she says, comes to animals as already practically interpreted: objects appear to the animal as to-be-fled, to-be-pursued, etc. It
is inherited instinct that makes these demarcations. Animals are highly
intelligent, and intelligence enables them to learn from experience, increasing the range and success of instinct. But they are tethered, still, to

their instincts, and all their "choices" are dictated by instinct and are not really choices. For this reason, she concludes, they can never be more than "passive citizens." By this Korsgaard seems to mean that they can never take part in the sort of ethical reciprocity that is essential to make good political choices. We can see what their good is, and take account of it. But they cannot modify their view of their good, choose to inhibit inappropriate behaviors, or enter into any type of dialogue about norms. All of this would be an essential part of active citizenship.

(Moral) rationality is different: it is a capacity to analyze the grounds of our actions, to "ask whether the potential reasons for our beliefs and actions are good ones, and to adjust our beliefs and actions according to the answers we get."[31] Intelligence looks outward at the world and its connections. Rationality, by contrast, looks inward at the workings of our minds and asks normative questions about the connections it finds.[32] This capacity for normative self-government, she insists, is something that other animals completely lack. Their instinctive action isn't always mechanical, and can be flexible, but is governed by teleological perception. We humans, by contrast, test and evaluate our reasons. Seeing our actions as having their source in ourselves, we evaluate ourselves. Our very self-conception is normative or evaluative.[33]

Korsgaard grants that self-evaluative emotions such as pride and shame appear to exist in animal lives, but she judges these as close calls, not the real thing, refusing to concede that other animals evaluate themselves—although she admits that this is an empirical question.[34] She also finds two further differences. Humans, she says, have a conception of their species, and of their lives as part of the larger life of the human kind.[35] And humans can ask what the world looks like to another center of self, whether of the same or a different species.[36] No other animal, she insists, can do that: animals see the world always from the point of view of their own interests.

Once again, where Korsgaard sees a sharp binary division, I believe that we really find a continuum. When a dog heroically saves a drowning child; when mother elephants risk, and sometimes lose, their lives to try to save a baby elephant who has wandered onto a railroad track;[37] when wild dogs distribute meat to disabled dogs who are unable to keep up with the pack,[38] they are performing acts of altruism and treating other creatures as ends, usually inhibiting selfish desires to do so.[39] Chimpanzees, gorillas, and bonobos are by now famous for their many types of altruistic behavior, through the path-breaking work of Frans de Waal.[40] And few who live with a dog could deny their keen responses to the distress of companion humans, or their willingness to take personal risk to come to the aid of a human or, sometimes, another animal.

No doubt this behavior has its basis in instinct, but here we should make two points. First, our own moral behavior is also based on our instinctual evolutionary endowment: an inherited tendency to assist others has helped humans to survive and flourish. Second, both humans and other animals need teaching to develop their instincts in an appropriate way. We see this cultural element in animal behavior clearly when we live with animals: dogs who are not appropriately trained behave lawlessly, and can even be schooled into dangerous aggression (as when pit bulls, who can be loving and cooperative, are trained, instead, to attack). Dogs who are well trained internalize norms pertinent to their conduct.

The same is true for many wild animals. Scientists have now observed that when elephant communities are savaged by poaching, leaving babies with no maternal group to raise them, lawless and what we could call pathological behavior results—the expected result of an absence of love and appropriate teaching. Sadly, we see this in other species too: for example, orcas ripped from their pod to be entertainers in marine theme parks (see chapter 10). And we now know that primates who have been abused as children become abusers, just as humans do. Experiments by primatologist Dario Maestripieri with rhesus macaques involve exchanging animal children: an abusive mother monkey is given the child of a decent mother to raise, and the child of the abusive mother is given to the decent mother. The experiment shows conclusively that behavior follows environment, not genes: the abusive mother makes her foster child an abuser, and the decent mother raises a decent child.[41]

The extent to which animal behavior is determined by culture rather than instinct will be different in different species, and we need to learn much more about this question. But the role of culture is turning out to be greater than we used to think, more or less everywhere. In one particularly rigorous exploration of the "genes/culture" question in a large group of mammals, biologists Hal Whitehead and Luke Rendell have conclusively shown that many aspects of the lives of whales and dolphins are formed by teaching within a group, rather than by instinct.[42] Another excellent probing of this distinction is Carl Safina's *Becoming Wild: How Animal Cultures Raise Families, Create Beauty, and Achieve Peace*.[43] Safina is not a researcher, but his knowledge of the pertinent research is deep, and he accompanies the researchers during their work. Studying three species—sperm whales, macaws, and chimpanzees—he displays the huge role of social learning in all three. All have social mechanisms for teaching young members appropriate norms, thus developing instinctual endowments in a direction that promotes group and individual welfare. And isn't that really what all good parents are trying to do?

And who do we think we are? is the logical next question. We are not angels or aliens from a special rationality planet. Because we are also partly creatures of instinct, we too need to learn to inhibit inappropriate behaviors and to learn pro-social behaviors. When that doesn't happen, we see excess and narcissism of many types. So the difference, if there is one, seems to be one of degree rather than kind. Few humans are perfect Kantians: that is the whole point of Kant's highly aspirational ethic. Human social teaching is highly variable and produces a large amount of social dysfunction. As Korsgaard herself grants in a response to de Waal, when things go wrong they can go very, very wrong: humans are capable of distortions and perversities unknown in the rest of the animal world.[44]

Sometimes animals give us lessons in ethics, especially by displaying a capacity for unconditional love and devotion, when human love is so frequently corrupted by self-seeking. We can find many such cases in real life, but let's consider a fictional case based on the author's real-life observations: the love of the dog Rollo for Effi in Theodor Fontane's tragic novel *Effi Briest* (1895). Effi, married by her parents at the age of sixteen to a decent but solemn man in his forties, deprived of fun and friendship, falls into an affair, which she soon breaks off, believing her marriage can improve. And it does improve, with the birth of a child and the husband's decision to move to Berlin to give Effi more fun and friendship. But after eight years of happy life, the husband discovers evidence of the long-ago affair. Although he loves her and forgives her in his heart, he feels compelled by social codes to repudiate and shun her, and to fight a duel with the lover (whom he kills). Her parents too feel compelled to shun her. In her last days, as she withers and dies, only the Newfoundland dog Rollo cares for her, forgoing food and pleasure. Only he mourns by her grave. Her father suggests to her mother that perhaps animals know something important that humans do not know—and the novel ends on that question. What Rollo failed to know was a bunch of repressive social conventions that branded Effi as a "fallen woman." What he did know was love, a point Fontane, a keen observer of animals, makes often in his work.

As for Korsgaard's claim that animals lack a capacity to see the world from the point of view of another, this capacity for perspectival thought belongs to many species, including dogs, many primates, elephants, dolphins, many birds, and very likely many others, as we'll see in chapter 6. Primate scientist Barbara Smuts describes the way her companion dog, Safi, was so attuned to Barbara's moods that she was aware of a severe depression in the offing, even when Barbara herself had not yet become conscious of it. Safi's worry showed Barbara that there was something to worry about. This is not unusual when people treat animals with respect and intimacy.[45] Moreover, the fact that we don't understand the languages in which other animals communicate their thoughts (see chapter 6) should not make us think there are no thoughts there. Someday our understanding of these communication systems may improve. In the meantime, we should (as Korsgaard herself suggests) use empathy and just imagine how the world might look to an animal we are trying to understand.

Korsgaard claims that other animals are not capable of seeing themselves as members of a species, and that this too is a severe ethical limitation. Well, the first question is whether an acute consciousness of one's human species membership and a tendency to define oneself in terms of the destiny of "humankind" is a virtue or a vice. I tend to think that it is more vice than virtue, all too often a way of cutting ourselves off from other sentient beings. I think it would be a good thing if human beings could think, instead, of a shared project of inhabiting this globe with justice and kindness. But even the sense of species membership is not unique. Elephants grieve when they see elephant bones, even when the bones are not connected to their own group. Very likely, as our knowledge increases, we will find many other examples of this sort.

What does all this mean for the type of citizenship that animals can exercise? We should grant, first, that all animals make demands. They give indications of what their flourishing requires, if we are attentive enough to decipher them. That already, for me, is a way in which animals should be understood as active, rather than "passive," citizens. But most animals also exhibit the capacity to learn to conform their behavior to norms, and this capacity is crucial for creating a shared multispecies society. The ways in which this will matter for laws and rules will vary considerably with the species, and I discuss this in more detail in my chapters on companion animals and wild animals. What animals cannot be expected to do is to take part in parliamentary procedures, the drafting of laws, voting, bringing lawsuits, and so forth. If one thinks that these things lie at the heart of citizenship, one will doubt that animals can be active citizens. But I think that this is too narrow: taking part, somehow, in shaping the conditions that govern our shared existence on this planet is the core of citizenship, and animals are fully capable of that, although they will need human surrogates to draft the statutes, bring the lawsuits, and so forth, on their behalf.

Kant's whole enterprise involves an attempt to raise humanity up above the animal kingdom. He puts us on a par with the angels, or rather represents us as fallen angels. So there is no way that Kant himself would accept the idea that our moral capacities are part and parcel of our animal nature, that we are, however good and deep we may sometimes be, nothing more

glorious and nothing less glorious than a unique sort of animal. Korsgaard is in an uncomfortable position—unable to agree with Kant that the
other creatures are not ends, and valuable, but also unable to give up the
Kantian idea that there is something truly unique, and uniquely wonderful, about our own capacities, something that sets us apart from the rest
of nature, though not above it. Her position would not be uncomfortable
if she simply said: this is the human form of life, and to some extent it
is different from other forms of life. All lives are uniquely wonderful in
their own way. But she clearly wants to make larger claims for human
moral rationality, and remains a Kantian in that respect—although she
does not need these claims to make her argument for animal rights, and
these claims confuse the reader, moving her uncomfortably close to the
views I rejected in chapter 2.

For me, the right way forward is to see these capacities for what they
are: a special and wonderful type of animal nature, one among the many
wonderful types of animal natures, all different in myriad ways. And instead of seeing morality as something that sets us apart from our fellow
creatures, we should see it as a thread that connects us to them. Awareness
of this commonality should deepen our curiosity and leaven our understanding.

Korsgaard's view and mine have many similarities, and her view is
sufficient to ground a rich ethical and political concern for other animals.
Its practical conclusions dovetail with mine in most respects. And in the
next chapter we'll see that there is one part of the Kantian view that my
Capabilities Approach can happily take over: an attractive account of the
basis of animal rights and the function of law.

If readers remain more attached to human specialness than I am (*not*
superiority, which Korsgaard repudiates), her view may be an attractive
one to cling to. It makes a lot of progress beyond the "So Like Us" approach and even the Utilitarian view (though perhaps it is not superior to
Mill's form). But the reader tempted to cling to Korsgaard's view should
remember that it does have the disadvantage of making large—and, I
would say, unnecessary—metaphysical claims. That is a disagreement

with Korsgaard that I have already identified, and which I'll pursue further in articulating my own view. If readers of chapter 5 agree with me
that such claims are unsuitable for the framing of shared political principles, that will give them a further reason to reject Korsgaard's view.

Korsgaard's Kantian arguments have illuminated the concept of respecting another individual creature's dignity, a concept I found sorely
lacking in Utilitarianism. This is where people concerned with animals
can learn a great deal from Kant. For me, however, her arguments still split
human animals off from the world of nature, in a way that is not necessary
for most of her own ethical-political project. She and I can converge in accepting the deep insight that animals are ends. And I believe that for the
purpose of framing political principles she could deemphasize her claims
about human moral specialness. At that point we would overlap almost
completely. It is time, then, to turn to the Capabilities Approach.

5

THE CAPABILITIES APPROACH

Forms of Life and Respecting the Creatures Who Live Them

What are people actually able to do and to be? That very basic question is the starting point for my own approach, the Capabilities Approach (CA).

This approach argues that a society is even minimally just only if it secures to each individual citizen a minimum threshold amount of a list of Central Capabilities, which are defined as *substantial freedoms*, or opportunities for choice and action in areas of life that people in general have reason to value. Capabilities are core entitlements, closely comparable to a list of fundamental rights. But the Capabilities Approach emphasizes that the goal is not simply high-sounding words on paper. It is to make people really able to select that activity if they want to. So it emphasizes *material empowerment* more than do many rights-based approaches. Like rights-based approaches, however, it leaves spaces for individual freedom: someone who has all the basic opportunities or entitlements spelled out in the list of capabilities is not required to act on them. The choice to act is left up to them.

Although the CA is a theory of political justice, and uses theoretical language, it focuses on getting close to the real efforts of people, seeing

citizens as active striving beings seeking a flourishing life that they themselves create.

Essentially, then, the CA is about giving striving creatures a chance
to flourish. For the capability theorist, a chance to flourish means not
just avoiding pain, but a list of positive opportunities, which we'll later
encounter in the Capabilities List: being able to enjoy good health, to protect one's bodily integrity, to develop and enjoy the use of one's senses
and imagination, the opportunity to plan a life, to have a variety of social
affiliations, to play and have pleasure, to have relationships with other
species and the world of nature, and to control, in key ways, one's own
environment. This emphasis on flourishing and on a wide plurality of key
opportunities is what makes it so suitable as a basis for a theory of animal
justice, as well as human justice.

In this theory as in Korsgaard's Kantian theory, each individual creature is seen as having a dignity that law and politics must respect, treating that individual as an end, not simply as a means. Unlike Korsgaard's
theory, however, the CA does not single out human moral powers as more
crucial for political choice than other aspects of animal living, and it sees
all human powers as parts of the equipment of a mortal and vulnerable animal who deserves a fair shake in life—as do all sentient animals. (Chapter
6 deals with the key issue of what sentience is and which animals have it.)

The job of this chapter is to flesh out that brief capsule summary,
showing how the CA can be extended to cover the issues of justice we've
seen in animal lives.[1] I'll try to persuade you that it goes beyond its rivals
in addressing the diversity and complexity of the animal world and providing a sound ethical basis for politics and law in the area of justice for
animals. Because the approach has previously been worked out within the
world of human life, as a theoretical tool for development economics and,
further, as a basis for an account of minimal justice and constitutional
entitlements, I must begin with the human background, before showing
what it offers as we think about justice for all sentient animals, and how it
must be reshaped to make it adequate to that task.

THE CAPABILITIES APPROACH IN THE HUMAN WORLD

For many years I have worked with an international group of economists and philosophers to refine and promote the CA.[2] Its original architect is the Nobel Prize–winning economist and philosopher Amartya Sen, a citizen of India who lives and teaches in the United States. In 1985, I began to collaborate with Sen, eventually taking the approach in a somewhat different direction.[3] An international organization, the Human Development and Capability Association,[4] launched in 2004, brings together scholars and policy makers from all over the world to pursue the various versions of the approach, through annual meetings, seminars, and a journal. We have lots of differences and arguments; Sen's ideas, for example, are subtly different from mine. In this section I'll introduce the approach in general terms, then turn to my own version.

Economics is about people's lives, and development economics is supposed to be about improving those lives. That's what the word "development" means. But for many years the dominant approaches to policy in development economics were obtuse in human terms. They measured a nation's or region's success in terms of gross domestic product per capita, without probing more deeply to see how growth does or does not improve individual people's lives, in areas of central human importance. As the late Mahbub ul Haq—the Pakistani economist who inaugurated the Human Development Reports of the United Nations Development Programme— wrote in the first of those reports, in 1990: "The real wealth of a nation is its people. And the purpose of development is to create an enabling environment for people to enjoy long, healthy, and creative lives. This simple but powerful truth is too often forgotten in the pursuit of material and financial wealth."[5]

What is wrong with measuring a nation's progress by GDP averaged over the population? Of course, it's good to promote growth other things equal. But this figure is an average. It tells us nothing about distribution, and may conceal large inequalities in basic life-chances between

individuals and groups. Each person has only one life to live, and people are not likely to feel consoled for having a life full of impediments
and deprivations when they are told that their nation (or state) is doing
very nicely on average. All over the world, human beings—like the other
animals—are striving to live, and live well, to attain lives worthy of their
innate human dignity. Each is an individual, and each should be considered as an end, none as only a means to the ends of others. (Here the CA
converges with Kant.)

The GDP approach also neglects the plurality and qualitative heterogeneity of the different parts of a human life. Health, bodily integrity,
education, access to political participation, leisure time, relationships of
respect and non-humiliation—these and other elements of life are all important, and a greater quantity of one of them does not atone for the absence of another. People are striving for a life that is plural and diverse,
and governments need to pay attention to the different ends people have
reason to value, which are not reducible to a single metric. Growth sometimes improves all these important things, but by no means always and by
no means evenly.

One step up in terms of adequacy, we find another economic approach to development, one that is based on economic Utilitarianism.
Economic Utilitarianism standardly strives to maximize the satisfaction
of people's preferences (usually average, rather than total, satisfaction).
This approach has four defects, when we hold it up against people's actual
strivings. These defects may be briefly stated, since we have met them
already in chapter 3.

First, like the GDP approach, it is an average, neglecting inequalities
in distribution. So it can give high marks to nations that tolerate huge
inequalities.

Second, again like GDP, it neglects the plural activities that people
strive to attain, treating activities as sources of a homogeneous state of
satisfaction.

Third, the Utilitarian approach masks inequality in yet a further
way. Under conditions of deprivation, people often form "adaptive

preferences," preferences tailored to the low-level people believe they can attain (see chapter 3). This pernicious dynamic may cause people to feel satisfied with subordination, once it becomes habitual: thus the Utilitarian approach can be the ally of an unjust status quo. This problem is particularly acute when women are raised to feel that higher education, or political participation, are not "for" them. Cut off from these things, they may report satisfaction with their situation. At times, as research by Sen has shown, they even report satisfaction with a weak and malnourished health status, believing that women are naturally weaker and that they are doing all right "for a woman."[6]

Finally, the Utilitarian calculus values a *state* of pleasure or satisfaction, not, ultimately, the activities that produce it. As we saw, this devaluation of activities (captured in Robert Nozick's "experience machine" thought experiment, which we met in chapter 3) wrongly downgrades the value that really *doing* something has for people. The experience machine is surefire, removing chance, while human activity is full of chance reversals and possibilities of frustration. Nonetheless, people want to be doers and strivers—attaining satisfaction, if they do, as the outcome of an activity that is their own. Short-sighted development policies often aim to make people feel good rather than to empower them. Such policies usually show an inadequate respect for poor people, treating them only as vessels of satisfaction rather than full human beings actively shaping their lives.

In the highly bureaucratized world of human development policy, it is useful to focus on some real-life people struggling to flourish so that we can ask what they are trying to be and do, and what is impeding their flourishing. In earlier work, I focused on a poor woman named Vasanti, whom I met in 1998 at the Self-Employed Women's Association (SEWA) in Ahmedabad, Gujarat, in Western India. Vasanti, a victim of domestic violence, had left her husband and returned to her birth family, and was earning a tiny income from sewing while sleeping on the floor of what used to be her father's shop. She was then assisted by SEWA, taught to read, encouraged to take part in politics, and given a loan to get a better sewing machine, to increase her income.

Proponents of the dominant approach to development would say that Vasanti is doing very well, because Gujarat is a rich state, with a relatively high GDP per capita. What does that GDP average, however glorious, mean to Vasanti? It doesn't reach her life, and it doesn't solve her problems. Somewhere in Gujarat there is some increased wealth deriving from foreign investment, but she doesn't have it. To her, hearing that GDP per capita has increased nicely is like being told that somewhere in Gujarat there is a beautiful painting—only she can't look at it; or a table set with delicious food, only she can't have any. Insofar as she was doing better by the time I met her, it was no thanks to the government of Gujarat, but only because of the work of SEWA, a nongovernmental organization.

In his 1854 novel, *Hard Times*, Charles Dickens, insightfully critical of the development economics of his day, portrayed a classroom in which children were taught the growth-based approach to economic development that is still dominant today. Circus girl Sissy Jupe—who has only recently joined the class—is told that she is to imagine that the classroom is a nation, and in that nation there are "fifty millions of money." Now, says the teacher, "Girl number twenty" (in keeping with the emphasis on aggregation, students have numbers rather than names), "isn't this a prosperous nation, and a'n't you in a thriving state?" Sissy bursts into tears and runs out of the room. She tells her friend Louisa Gradgrind that she could not answer the question, "unless I knew who had got the money and whether any of it was mine. But that had nothing to do with it. It was not in the figures at all."[7]

Dickens was right: what we need in development policy is an approach that asks Sissy Jupe's question, an approach that defines achievement in terms of the opportunities of each person, regarding each as an end. Such an approach had better begin close to the ground, looking at life stories and the human meaning of policy changes for real people. Developing policies that are truly pertinent to a wide range of human situations means studying many stories like Vasanti's alongside the economic, legal, and scientific data, acquiring a trained sensitivity to diverse factors that affect the quality of a human life—asking, in each area, "What are people (and what is each person) actually able to do and to be?"

The Capabilities Approach asks, and answers, that very basic and very practical question. The word "capability" does not mean "skill." It means a real, substantive freedom, or opportunity to choose to act, in a specific area of life deemed valuable. To go into a little more terminological detail, I identify three different types of capabilities that all figure in my theory. First are *basic capabilities*: the innate equipment of people that enables them to pursue their ends. Second are *internal capabilities*, and these are like skills: developed traits, which usually require help from family and society, and which are ripe for activity, in propitious circumstances. Knowing how to read is an internal capability.[8] But circumstances are not always propitious: many people have the internal ability to speak their mind on issues of importance, but are unable to do so for fear of political repression. Most people are capable of religious belief and activity, but many the world over are unable to exercise their religion. So the third and most important type of capabilities are what I call *combined capabilities*, meaning internal capabilities plus suitable circumstances for actual choice of the associated activity.

In the (human) CA, each individual human being is an end, meaning that the goal of policy should be to protect and enhance the capabilities of each and every one, treating none as simply a means to the ends of others. The approach is a general theory, but it is always accountable to stories like Vasanti's, to people's real lives and strivings. In aggregating the data (for in any development theory one has to aggregate in some way, although aggregation always creates risks of using individuals as means to some desired end), special attention is devoted to the worst off, making sure that they are up to an adequate level. Each capability is treated as separate from all the others, not used as means to attain the others. (So the aim is not to maximize the totality of people's capabilities.) People may do well on one capability while doing badly on others. All are pertinent to the question of justice. Nor does the approach seek to maximize capability within each capability area. It aims, instead, at a high but reasonable *threshold* in each area.

There are often some particularly good intervention points, capabilities with fruitful consequences for other capabilities. A good policy maker will focus on them first, in order to raise the capability level across the board. In their excellent book *Disadvantage*,[9] Jonathan Wolff and Avner de-Shalit call these *fertile functionings*.[10] Thus, education is often an all-purpose capability enhancer, promoting employment opportunities, political participation, health, self-respect, and much more. The correlative bad situation is what Wolff and de-Shalit call *corrosive disadvantage*: a capability failure that has bad spillover effects across the board. In Vasanti's story, domestic violence was a corrosive disadvantage. It impaired bodily integrity, health, and emotional equanimity; through these it also impaired employment options, political participation, and affiliations with others. These concepts are valuable in thinking about the lives of animals too, and I'll return to them. By now we can see how much information users of this approach need in order to ask the right questions and make pertinent recommendations for law and policy.

To summarize where we are: the CA is a normative theory of development—a theory aimed at showing how to make things better—that focuses on getting close to the strivings of real people, and the impediments to these strivings, seeing people as active beings seeking a flourishing life that they themselves create.

FROM COMPARATIVE RANKING TO A MAP OF BASIC JUSTICE

When the CA was first developed, its purpose was to provide a new template for comparing one nation or region to others, a template that was people-sensitive rather than distant from real-life problems. In its use in the Human Development Reports, it already selected some opportunities rather than others, because of their perceived salience in people's lives. Education and health, for example, were emphasized, and Sen's writings have continually emphasized the importance of freedom of speech and freedom of the press. But there was no real list of the most important goals. There wasn't really a need for one, so long as the approach was being used merely comparatively.

The minute we begin to ask what a decently just society will provide to all its members, however, we need to get definite about content—in a humble and flexible way, but still making claims that could be enshrined in a nation's constitution, if it has a written constitution, or could be legally expressed in other ways if it does not. What does each and every person have a *right* to demand, as a matter of basic, minimal justice?

My formulation of this template for fundamental entitlements takes the form of a list of *Central Capabilities*, which, in the language of the theory, are *combined capabilities*.[11]

THE CENTRAL CAPABILITIES

1. **Life.** Being able to live to the end of a human life of normal length; not dying prematurely, or before one's life is so reduced as to be not worth living.

2. **Bodily Health.** Being able to have good health, including reproductive health; to be adequately nourished; to have adequate shelter.

3. **Bodily Integrity.** Being able to move freely from place to place; to be secure against violent assault, including sexual assault and domestic violence; having opportunities for sexual satisfaction and for choice in matters of reproduction.

4. **Senses, Imagination, and Thought.** Being able to use the senses, to imagine, think, and reason—and to do these things in a "truly human" way, a way informed and cultivated by an adequate education, including, but by no means limited to, literacy and basic mathematical and scientific training. Being able to use imagination and thought in connection with experiencing and producing works and events of one's own choice, religious, literary, musical, and so forth. Being able to use one's mind in ways protected by guarantees of freedom of expression with respect to both political and artistic speech, and freedom of religious exercise. Being able to have pleasurable experiences and to avoid non-beneficial pain.

5. **Emotions.** Being able to have attachments to things and people outside

ourselves; to love those who love and care for us, to grieve at their absence; in general, to love, to grieve, to experience longing, gratitude, and justified anger. Not having one's emotional development blighted by fear and anxiety. (Supporting this capability means supporting forms of human association that can be shown to be crucial in their development.)

6. **Practical Reason.** Being able to form a conception of the good and to engage in critical reflection about the planning of one's life. (This entails protection for the liberty of conscience and religious observance.)

7. **Affiliation.**

   a. Being able to live with and toward others, to recognize and show concern for other human beings, to engage in various forms of social interaction; to be able to imagine the situation of another. (Protecting this capability means protecting institutions that constitute and nourish such forms of affiliation, and also protecting the freedom of assembly and political speech.)

   b. Having the social bases of self-respect and non-humiliation; being able to be treated as a dignified being whose worth is equal to that of others. This entails provisions of nondiscrimination on the basis of race, sex, sexual orientation, ethnicity, caste, religion, national origin.

8. **Other Species.** Being able to live with concern for and in relation to animals, plants, and the world of nature.

9. **Play.** Being able to laugh, to play, to enjoy recreational activities.

10. **Control Over One's Environment.**

    a. **Political.** Being able to participate effectively in political choices that govern one's life; having the right of political participation, protections of free speech and association.

    b. **Material.** Being able to hold property (both land and movable goods), and having property rights on an equal basis with others; having the right to seek employment on an equal basis with others; having the freedom from unwarranted search and seizure. In work, being able to work as a human being, exercising practical reason, and entering into meaningful relationships of mutual recognition with other workers.

The idea is that these can be further specified in accordance with the particular needs and situation of each nation, as it works out a set of benchmarks of minimal justice that it can actually hope to deliver, if not immediately, then in a reasonable time. For that purpose, the nation's constitution must supply a *threshold* for each of these, whether in a written text or through incremental judicial interpretation. If the nation does not deliver a threshold amount of each and every one of these to each citizen, then it has fallen short of minimal justice, no matter how ample its provisions are in other areas. As with all constitutional lists of fundamental entitlements, the items are seen as qualitatively distinct and not replaceable, one with another. Thus, if someone complains that her freedom of speech is compromised, it is not a good reply to say, "But look at the ample education we provide!" (Some nations do make this reply, but it is a paper-thin excuse for tyranny.)

Why is the list a list of capabilities, rather than of actual functions? The whole point is that people should be enabled to act! However: people are all different in their choices. Some will not want to avail themselves of all the opportunities on the list. Some people have no interest in religion, and do not engage in religious activities. They would strenuously object to a constitution that suggested that all people have to engage in religion. But they are unlikely to object to the *opportunity*, because it is one that many other people do wish to use. Some people don't want leisure time, and choose to lead a workaholic life. Again, they don't want to be forced to loll around. But they do not object to the recognition that for most people leisure time is valuable. Making the list one of capabilities shows respect for the heterogeneity of people's life choices and for their freedom to choose different paths. (Occasionally, as with mandatory education for children, we are entitled to mandate functioning—on grounds of immaturity and with a view to mature choice.)

Number 8 on the list recognizes animals as important participants in relationships with humans, but it doesn't make them ends in themselves. This was a step that many people in the movement were not ready to take at that time, and even today few want to take the further steps that I have taken by now. So number 8 should be viewed as a halfway measure that commanded broad consensus at the time I formulated the list (some thirty years ago). We can and must do better!

But how on earth would we measure capabilities? The difficulty of this enterprise is one reason why development economics has often preferred the inadequate criterion of GDP per capita, which can at least be measured. But we should not begin from what we can measure right now and turn that into the most important thing. We should, instead, begin with the most important things, and figure out how to measure those. Many books and many meetings of the Human Development and Capability Association have been devoted to questions of measurement for each capability. And nations have found ways to use law to establish rough metrics in many of the areas that seem least tractable. Think of freedom of speech and freedom of religion. The way we can assess how these freedoms are faring in a nation is to look at the challenges brought on these constitutional grounds and see how these challenges have fared over the years. The US, for example, has an evolving understanding of these freedoms that has unfolded case by case, gradually demarcating the boundaries of the right.

One way of thinking about what all the items on the list have in common is that they all seem to be inherent in the intuitive idea we form of a life that is *worthy of human dignity*. The presumption of the list is that all people have inherent dignity, and what we want is that this dignity should be paid respect: people should get what they need in order to live lives worthy of their dignity. The idea of dignity is vague, and is very similar to the idea of deserving treatment as an end, not a means. We can't give it further content without connecting it to a network of political principles. But here as in the international human rights movement, it proves intuitively helpful: imagining people without a given opportunity, we feel that their dignity has been violated, and they have been used simply as means.[12] This emphasis on dignity is a link to the Kantian approach.[13] But it also links the theory to Mill's nuanced form of Utilitarianism.

This view makes each person an end, and in that way it is linked to classical liberalism. But liberalism of this type is not exclusively Western: the inherent dignity of each individual person is at the foundation of the Indian and South African constitutions, to name just two. These two nations have embraced the dignity of the individual in the course of throwing off unjust tyrannies that demeaned peoples and groups. They have said: each and every one of us matters, and we won't be subordinated. The view is anti-monarchical and anti-imperial, and opposed, as well, to hierarchies based upon gender and race.

Kant thought that only humans have dignity. Mill and I (with Korsgaard) beg to differ: all sentient animals have a dignity of their own, which deserves respect. They should not be treated as means, and the central question of this book is what that insight demands from law and policy.

People may often be able to get themselves up to the capability threshold by their own efforts, or the efforts of informal groups, even when the nation or state in which they live has done little or nothing to address their striving. Elites can usually arrange for adequate health care, or good education, for example, even in the absence of any public provision. Even Vasanti, a poor woman, did pretty well because of the good luck that one of the best women's NGOs in the world was right in her backyard. But this obviously isn't enough to make the nation or state a just one. The nation has ignored its people's needs, and elites have attained their goals by good luck, while others suffer. Securing the capabilities for all is a task for government, and my list, like a virtual constitution, is a list of fundamental tasks of government. Governments may often employ private organizations to attain their ends, but final accountability rests with the government: if it doesn't bring people up above the threshold, government must shoulder the blame. This doesn't mean that people always should rely on government to solve their problems. Sometimes they simply can't: government is corrupt, or hopelessly inefficient. But it does mean that the whole matter of justice depends on getting a stable political structure that is able, enough of the time, to deliver the capabilities to the people who chose and empowered it.

"POLITICAL LIBERALISM": AN IMPORTANT CONSTRAINT

The political principles built around the Capabilities List are one part of a nation's set of core political principles. But political principles must obey some restrictions, in order to be adequately respectful of human diversity and freedom. In his important book *Political Liberalism*, John Rawls has advanced an important argument with which I fully agree, and incorporate in my approach to justice for animals, as well as for humans.[14] Under conditions of freedom, he argues, people attach themselves to a wide range of "comprehensive doctrines" that give normative instructions for how one should live. Catholicism, Protestantism, Marxism, Utilitarianism, Buddhism—these are just a few of the comprehensive doctrines of value that exist in most societies. Any doctrine that is compatible with the basic idea of justice—with (as he sees it) proposing and accepting fair terms of cooperation—should be shown respect. But it isn't respectful to impose some overall doctrine of the good life, politically, on people who have their own ideas and are attached to them. Even when a nation does not constrain the freedom of people who think differently—as when a nation has an established church but allows wide freedom of religious belief and practice—the nation is still making a statement that its own view is the best, and subordinating other views. But of course a set of political principles has to have some definite ethical content. So what can be done?

The solution to the problem, Rawls urges (and I have long agreed), is to propose political principles that are, first, *narrow in scope*, not covering all areas of human concern (not talking, for example, about the possibility of life after death), and, second, *thin*, expressed in a neutral ethical language rather than in the metaphysical language of one group rather than another. (Thus, for example, the ethical language of *human dignity* would be preferred to the sectarian notion of *the soul*.)[15] If we manage things with restraint, the political principles can form what Rawls called a "module" that all citizens who hold different reasonable comprehensive doctrines ("reasonable" meaning willing to propose and accept fair terms of cooperation) can attach to their own doctrines, whatever they are. Eventually, it is hoped, the political principles will become the object of an "overlapping consensus" among the partisans of all those doctrines.[16] This may take a long time, but the proponent of the CA ought to be able to sketch a path by which people of differing views might ultimately come to agree on these core principles.

Not all proponents of the CA agree with this restriction, so it is important to be aware that it is a central part of my own view, not of all types of CA views. Without the restriction, a political view based on the CA could not, in my view, be sufficiently respectful of human difference and freedom.

Now the objection to Korsgaard that I postponed in chapter 4 can be made clearer. She takes no stand on Rawls's arguments, one way or another—somewhat oddly, for a student of Rawls who is fully aware of his book and its importance. She does not announce whether her own view aspires to be a political view, and yet it must be a political view, since she wants practical political consequences to flow from it, and eloquently defends the view that animals have rights that should be vindicated by law. And since she provides no rebuttal of Rawls's very cogent arguments against using comprehensive metaphysics in framing political principles, it seems fair to criticize her for grounding her view in a controversial metaphysical doctrine (see chapter 4).

The defender of a political doctrine based on the CA does need to reject some metaphysical views—namely, views that demean animals and announce that the worth of species is arranged in accordance with the *scala naturae*. Such views could not join the "overlapping consensus" without major modification of their claims. (Holders of such views would still have freedom to express them; but since the nation's constitution goes contrary to them, they could not bring their proposals up for a simple majority vote; they would need to amend the constitution.) But there is no need to decide between Korsgaard's view that all value is internal to a point of view and the position that animals have intrinsic worth (a view I hold). Both views are fully compatible with good political principles protecting animal rights.[17]

The CA, then, is a partial (not comprehensive) political (not comprehensively ethical) doctrine. Like Mill's view, it is a view that aims at a set of plural and distinct ends, these ends being viewed as not just good but also mandatory for a society wishing to lay claim to even minimal justice. Activities and opportunities for them are viewed as parts of the goal, not means to an end-state, such as satisfaction.

Because the ends of society are plural, the CA leaves room for conflict. And because these ends are mandatory, not just optional, any trade-offs that have to be made in a difficult situation are not just unfortunate, but also, often, tragic: if they push some citizens below the minimal threshold of justice, they involve a serious violation. Society must therefore think and work ahead to minimize such tragic conflicts. Chapter 8 will address this issue in the even more conflict-laden area of animal justice.

THE CA AS A BASIS FOR JUSTICE FOR ANIMALS

Human beings are vulnerable sentient animals, each trying to achieve a good life amid dangers and obstacles. Justice is about promoting the opportunity of each to flourish in accordance with the person's own choice, through the use of laws that both enable and restrain. People are often used as tools, but the CA holds that a nation is minimally just only when each person is treated as an end in some very important areas of life, their dignity respected. In thinking about what to put on the list, I have inevitably thought about opportunities that we can expect a large number of people to hold dear, and I have suggested that we focus on those that seem intuitively to be inherent in the idea of a life worthy of human dignity. But because the ends are opportunities, people with minority choices are also protected, in areas of central importance: thus the free exercise of religion protects both Roman Catholics, who are numerous, and members of small religions—as well as atheists and people who are indifferent to religion.

Why on earth would such an approach to the lives of other animals not be appropriate, for similar reasons? They too are vulnerable sentient animals. They too live amid a staggering, and today an increasing, number of dangers and obstacles, many of them of our making. They too have an inherent dignity that inspires respect and wonder. The fact that the dignity of a dolphin or an elephant is not precisely the same as human dignity—and that the dignity of an elephant is different from that of a dolphin—does not mean that there is not dignity there, that vague property that means, basically, deserving of end-like treatment rather than means-like use. Korsgaard was correct in her argument that the pursuit of valued goals by an animal, all by itself, entitles the striving animal to end-like treatment: it has a dignity, not just a price. We see that dignity intuitively when we watch dolphins swimming freely through the water in social groupings, echolocating their way around obstacles and leaping for joy; when we see a group of elephants caring communally for their young and attempting to rear them in safety, despite the ubiquity of man-made threats. Our sense of wonder is an epistemic faculty oriented to dignity: it says to us, "This is not just some rubbish, something I can use any way I like. This is a being who must be treated as an end." Why, then, should we think we are more important than they are, more deserving of basic legal protection?

I'll shortly provide an argument for the idea that animals have legally enforceable rights, but for now I want to lay out the basic ideas of the CA.

A CHARACTERISTIC FORM OF LIFE

Animals, like humans, have, each of them, a form of life that involves a set of important goals toward which they strive. For now, let's think of this form of life as a species form, though I'll complicate this later. In thinking about human beings, we thought about some things that are especially important for human beings trying to live. We can do the same thing for each type of animal, if we learn enough and look hard enough. Each animal is a teleological system directed toward a set of good ends centering around survival, reproduction, and, in most cases, social interaction.

What the CA thinks in the human case is that those strivings should not be thwarted. And (agreeing with Korsgaard) that it is arrogant, presumptuous, groundless, and just plain selfish to say that we matter more than they do. Each form of life is different. But each one is the right one for that type of being. If a magpie flourishes, it will be in the way characteristic of the life of that bird species. Being more like a human would not be good or pertinent for a magpie. We humans are similar to magpies, dolphins, and elephants in groping toward survival and flourishing in a mostly hostile world; we differ in the specific nature of the goods we seek.

The CA is basically about giving striving beings a decent chance to flourish. That is how it views the role of law and government. Humans will have to take the lead in making the laws and establishing the institutions of government, but there is no reason why humans should do this only *for* and *about* other humans. There is no good reason to say that only some sentient creatures matter. Each matters in its own way. The metric of likeness to humans makes no sense from the point of view of a horse or a whale. Nor is it useful for a fair-minded lawmaker, trying to help sentient creatures have a shot at living decent lives of the sort they seek. (In chapter 6, I'll argue that sentience—the ability to feel, to have a subjective perspective on the world—is a necessary basis for being a subject of justice, and I'll give my view about which creatures have that capacity.)

Nor, as I said in chapter 4, criticizing Korsgaard, is there any good reason why only humans should participate actively in legislation and institution-building. Animals do not speak human language, but they have a wide range of language-like ways of communicating about their situation (as we'll see further in chapter 6), and if we humans happen to be in the driver's seat politically, it should be our responsibility to attend to those voices, to figure out how animals are doing and what obstacles they face. We already do this for human beings who have disabilities that prevent them from participating in political life *in the usual way*: we give them guardians or "collaborators"[18] to whom they express their situation and who become adept readers of their needs. We should never say that nonverbal children are *passive citizens* or nonparticipants in political life:

they actively express themselves in many ways, and it is our responsibility to translate that into political action. Also, most ordinary citizens do not understand their legal rights and could not represent themselves in court or perform many of the other tasks of citizenship without representation. So too, I claim, with non-human animals.

At this point we must ask whether direct, nonrepresentational participation in politics is intrinsically valuable, or only instrumentally valuable. This is a debated point by users of the CA. I myself think it is instrumentally valuable: the important thing is being able to influence the conditions that govern one's own life by one's own agency. But this doesn't mean that every human citizen has to go to court, or organize political projects, or, even, vote—so long as there is someone who represents the person's demands in courts and legislatures, and votes on that person's behalf (as I have urged for people with severe cognitive disabilities). With animals, I think the solution need not and should not involve a proxy vote for every animal in every election. This would quickly become absurd. Rather, duly qualified animal "collaborators" should be charged with making policy on the animals' behalf, and bringing challenges to unjust arrangements in the courts. Chapters 9 and 10 will give many examples of how this can be done.

In attending to animal voices as quasi-guardians and listeners, we will not focus only on pleasure and pain. Just as, in thinking about Vasanti, the CA considered not only how and whether she felt pain or pleasure, but also her many other opportunities (or lack of opportunity) for types of valuable activity, so too the reductive Benthamite way of thinking about the good of a living thing seems wrong for non-human creatures. It has undeniable power because currently humans cause so much unnecessary pain to non-human creatures, and simply eliminating that would be great progress. But we need a map of the goal that is adequate to the complexity of animal lives. For other animals, as for us, avoiding pain is not all that matters. Social relationships, kinship, reproduction, free movement, play, and enjoyment, all these matter to most animals, and as we understand each specific form of life more adequately, we can make the list more complete.

To get the pertinent issues on the table, we need to listen to many

stories of animal lives, told by experts who have lived closely with a certain type of animal and studied those animals over long periods of time—
looking at shared goals, internal diversity, and prevalent problems and
obstacles. We would consider the stories about abused and neglected companion animals (for example the story of Lupa in my introduction). These
stories—which have many points of similarity with Vasanti's—give us
ideas about how law needs to promote the flourishing of companion animals, preventing cruelty, promoting nutrition, and, more generally, con-
veying models of reciprocity, respect, and friendship. We would consider
the stories scientists who have lived with wild animals tell about the animals with whom they work, and about the obstacles to their flourishing—
seeking both expertise and diversity in our sources, and attending to ways
in which different experts emphasize different points. This task, so exhilarating and so urgent, is potentially unending, as new knowledge turns up,
and problems and circumstances change. That, after all, is also true of our
study of the situation of humans in different parts of the world. The task
is long, but with companion animals we have been working this way for a
long time, holding public hearings and constructing humane laws. So we
know it can be done.

A Virtual Constitution

In the human case, the CA supplies a template for constitution-making.
The list has both content and a tentative threshold for each item. A nation
aiming at minimal justice can consult it, and also consult its own particular environment and history, and frame its own list with more locally
specific accounts of each of the major capabilities on the list. For two reasons, this approach to the other animals is not possible at present. First,
the other animals often roam across national borders, or occupy regions
of air and sea that are not the property of a single nation; so a national
constitution is not sufficient to protect migratory species. Second, there
is not anything like sufficient political will in most of the nations of the
world to enact any such protections any time soon.

The ideal outcome would be for all the nations of the world (listening astutely to the demands of animals and those who most knowledgeably represent them) to agree to a legally enforceable constitution for the various animal species, each with its own list of capabilities to be protected, and each supplied with a threshold level beneath which non-protection becomes injustice. Animals would then be protected no matter where they are, just as whales are (inadequately) protected all over the world by the IWC (International Whaling Commission, to be discussed in chapter 12). This constitution could then be supplemented by more specific nation-based laws for animals living within a given national jurisdiction, in a way tailored to those specific contexts. However, we know that humanity's halting steps toward international accountability for human injustice have not been terribly successful. Even in the human case, our best hope is with the laws of individual nations. If that is so for humans, it is far more so for animals. I will later discuss the role of international treaties and conventions, but for the most part, for the foreseeable future, animals must be protected by the laws of nations, states, and localities. That does not mean, however, that there is no use in having an international map of a destination.

Right now, therefore, the CA aims to supply a *virtual constitution* to which nations, states, and regions may look in trying to improve (or newly frame) their animal-protective laws. It is my hope that over time this virtual constitution can increasingly become the object of a Rawlsian political "overlapping consensus," both within each nation and across national boundaries. This will take time and work; so too does the task of framing and protecting human rights. Still, this flexible approach permits nations to stride boldly ahead without waiting to get a global consensus. (Later, I'll offer a legal argument about the basis for these animal entitlements.) The basic goal is that all animals would have the opportunity to live lives compatible with their dignity and striving, up to a reasonable threshold level of protection.

This virtual constitution, like the human version of the CA, is political and not metaphysical. Because its aim is to secure, over time, an overlapping consensus among all the fair-minded comprehensive doctrines of value, it will not make contentious metaphysical claims, and it will not cover every issue. Animal capabilities are not held to have intrinsic value, and claims of intrinsic value are not denied, either. My hope is that support for animal capabilities can come from many directions: from religious views that believe in human superiority for religious and metaphysical reasons, but are still willing to extend fair terms of cooperation to animals and to support their capabilities; from ecocentric views that really believe that ecosystems, not individuals, should be the primary focus of concern, but are willing, politically, to support animal capabilities as one crucial element in helping ecosystems to flourish; from Buddhist views that similarly deny the salience of the individual, but still recommend fair treatment of animal lives; from views like Korsgaard's, that remain agnostic about claims of intrinsic value; and from views like my own, which (ethically, though not in my political theory) think of animal lives as having intrinsic value.

Lists and Lives

Ideally we should learn enough to make a separate list for each type of creature, putting on the list the things that matter most when it comes to survival and flourishing. The list is really made by the animals themselves as they express their deepest concerns while they try to live. The people who can be trusted to record the unheard voices of animals are people who have lived with a given type of animal for years and with love and sensitivity, for example Barbara Smuts with baboons, Joyce Poole and Cynthia Moss with elephants, Luke Rendell and Hal Whitehead with whales, Peter Godfrey-Smith with octopuses, Frans de Waal with chimpanzees and bonobos, Janet Mann and Thomas White with dolphins. Ideally there should be a group of such people for each species, because any individual is fallible. These "collaborators" and listeners should know individual animals within the species in all their variety, and should be able to tell many stories like those of the individual animals mentioned in the introduction—about what obstacles each creature faces, and what interventions prove helpful.

One remarkable example of the basis for such a list is the Elephant Ethogram recently compiled by Joyce Poole and her fellow workers for the African savanna elephant. This remarkable database incorporates all our knowledge to date about the elephant form of life (for that species): communication, movement, and all characteristic activities.[19] Studying the ethogram, friends of elephants can then suggest the capabilities that seem most central, most important to protect.

My idea means a huge number of different lists, based on many different ethograms. However, I believe that if we focus on the large general rubrics of the CA list for humans, it offers good guidance as a starting point in virtually all cases. That should come as no surprise, since the CA list captures, in effect, the shared terrain of vulnerable, striving animality that each species inhabits in its own way. All strive for *life*; for *health*; for *bodily integrity*; for the opportunity to use whatever *senses*, *imagination*, and *thought* are characteristic for that kind of creature. *Practical reason* sounds, at first, too human to be a good guide, but really it isn't. All creatures want the opportunity to make some key choices about how their lives will go, to be the makers of plans and choices. *Affiliation* is crucial for all animals, though its types vary greatly. All seek to relate well to the world of nature around them, and this usually includes members of other species. *Play* and *fun* are not peculiar to humans, as researchers increasingly understand, but key aspects of animal sociability. And all animals seek types of control over their material and social environment. If there are other large rubrics pertinent to animal lives that the human list omits, I can't think of them now, but would be totally open to expanding the large rubrics of the list, if any should be convincingly brought forward.

People might worry that such a list is bound to be anthropomorphic, verging on some of the errors of the "So Like Us" approach. I understand this charge, but think it mistaken. The list was made up not by thinking of what is distinctively human, but by thinking in very general terms about animality—allowing for significant variations at the specific level, but insisting that at a general level we can find a common pattern. However, we must always be on our guard against obtuseness or self-privileging perception.

Sometimes the lists we frame will include items within the finer rubrics of the human list that appear at first blush not to matter to the lives of animals. Consider "freedom of association" and "freedom of speech." What are most zoos but means of denying freedom of association to animals? As for speech, animals express what they need and want in their own ways, often very sophisticated. Even under formal US law, freedom of speech pertains to many forms of expressive activity, not just to words on paper. Why then should this legal category not include the ways animals speak? It certainly could, if only animals had legal standing in the first place.[20] It's not that they don't speak, it's that we humans usually don't listen. Animals are not free to speak, however, when their complaints are ignored, when information about conditions in the factory farming industry are systematically screened from public view, when even human allies of the afflicted pigs and chickens are prevented by "ag-gag" laws (laws restricting reporting) from describing those conditions. Freedom of speech is hugely pertinent to animals, and it is important for exactly the reasons John Stuart Mill, a defender of animal rights, gave when he defended free speech in *On Liberty*: free speech gives information we need to make our society better; it challenges complacency and smugness; it brings forward unfashionable positions that deserve, indeed require, a hearing.

And what about "freedom of the press" and "political participation"? Animals do not write newspaper articles, but the free circulation of information about their predicament is a crucial part of their good, in this world where humans dominate all animal lives. In *Poverty and Famines*, Amartya Sen argued that a free press is an essential ingredient of staving off (human) famine, because there must be information out there to goad people into political action.[21] I would extend Sen's point: correct information about all the dire predicaments of animals today—habitat loss, torture in the meat industry, poaching, the filling of the seas with plastics—all of this information must get out there if action preventing terrible animal suffering is ever to be taken. To be sure, the articles and books and films will have to be made by humans. But they matter for and in the lives of the animals whose voices of complaint they record and whose intolerable conditions they display.

Much the same is true of political participation. Most animals, though often political enough within their own species group, have little interest in political participation in the human-dominated world, and are unaware of elections, assemblies, and offices. Nonetheless, what happens there matters hugely for them. In the human-dominated world, politics determines the rights and privileges of all denizens of a given place, and makes crucial decisions about matters of welfare, habitat, and so forth. So it matters that animals have a political say, which means, I believe, legal standing (the right to go to court as the plaintiff of an action) and some type of legal representation. Right now we allow surrogate representation for humans with cognitive disabilities, so the proposal involves nothing terribly surprising. Creatures who live in a place should have a say in how they live.

It might appear that it is only because we humans dominate the world and have created a lot of trouble for animals that freedom of the press and political participation matter for them. One would think this way if one thought that the world of nature without human interference is idyllic, or wonderful, or peaceable, or in some way good for animals. I do not think this, as chapter 10 will argue further. Even without our damaging interference, there would still be famines, floods, and other forms of climate disaster. I therefore think that even without our own bad behavior, we have strong reasons to make sure that the news of their predicaments gets out and that their voices have a say in how they live.

At the level of the concrete rubrics of the list, however, there will also be much divergence, and we should always be open to surprise and learning; thus each kind of animal has its own form of social organization, and even of sense-perception. Only painstaking and loving study will show what should be said.

Fertile Functionings, Corrosive Disadvantages

Because the approach I envisage is specific to each type of animal life, its demands are many and heterogeneous. But within each case, and even across many cases, there are likely to be capabilities that are particularly fertile, promoting good life across the board, and capability failures that are especially damaging. For all animals, subjection to arbitrary human violence is a corrosive disadvantage, whether it takes the form of whales' vulnerability to harpooning, elephants' vulnerability to poaching, pigs' confinement in "gestation crates," or a dog's vulnerability to the cruelty and neglect of an "owner." Another corrosive disadvantage across the board is environmental pollution, which causes lethal conditions, whether of air or water, for many species and depletes their habitats. So the opposite of these ills—bans on cruel practices and a dedication to environmental cleanup—will prove fertile, enhancing capabilities across the board for many animals.

Species Members Are Individuals

So far, I've spoken of a list for each species of animal. But for animals, as for humans, each individual creature should be treated as an end. And animals are individuals not just numerically (each one matters), but also qualitatively: each species member is subtly different, one from every other. People who live with companion animals know that the personalities and preferences of their companions are highly individual, and that what is good for one dog or one cat is not necessarily good for all. We usually fail to notice this variety in the case of animals with whom we don't live, but people who do live with a given type of animal recognize and emphasize these differences. Each baboon, each elephant, is a member of baboon (elephant) society, but each individual has a unique way of inhabiting that world. So too with every type of animal that we have been able to study carefully.[22] For biologists, the notion of species is rough; what they really work with are populations, made up out of individual creatures.

But if each individual is both separate from others (having its own life to live, not anyone else's) and qualitatively different in some ways from others, isn't it a mistake to frame the lists as centering around a species form of life? Isn't that to deny each animal's uniqueness? Isn't it obtuse, even objectifying, to speak of "the dolphin" and "the dolphin form of life," rather than to create a separate story, and list, for each individual dolphin—for example for Fungie, the beloved dolphin in Dingle Bay, Ireland, whose disappearance in October 2020 has caused widespread distress?[23] The inhabitants of Dingle came to know Fungie over the decades as a dolphin with a unique personality—quirky, oddly solitary for a dolphin, atypically social toward humans. Why wouldn't Fungie's uniqueness be obliterated by an approach based on the species?

Think again, however, about Vasanti. From an understanding of her unique story (and many other such stories), the founders of the CA built a general approach to quality of life and political justice, a set of human entitlements that seems to suit the human form of life, and that can be legalized with contextual refinement in each nation and region. Knowing lots of particulars helps us build toward the general, a set of constitutional entitlements.

But isn't this generality unfair to the particularity of real lives? Isn't it unfair or disrespectful to Vasanti, that particular woman, to use her as an input into a list of constitutional entitlements? No, for three reasons. First, the list is a list of capabilities, not mandatory functions. The opportunities it creates can be used by different people in different ways, or not used at all, if the person does not want to use them. Capabilities are entitlements, a type of rights.[24] People typically do not think that human rights reduce all humans to a cookie-cutter model: they are spaces within which varied individuals are free to choose. Second, in the ongoing process of judicial interpretation of rights, individual litigants, with all the particularity of their stories, will come forward to be heard. Any record of judicial interpretation of our Bill of Rights shows a continual back-and-forth between individual and general, as the individual tests the limits of the general text, and a new decision further specifies the general text for all. Third, if there really is something an individual deeply strives for that the list doesn't make room for, even at the level of general opportunities, changing the list of entitlements is always possible.

I think it's the same story with each kind of animal. We study communities belonging to a given species (and "species," as we recall, is a rough term for what's common to various populations, not a metaphysical entity). We frame a list. Then the qualitatively different species members can use those entitlements each in their own ways. Fungie is different from every other dolphin, but the capabilities that protect dolphins in general will also protect him, and be used by him in his unique way. He doesn't have to socialize with a large pod if he doesn't want to, and he is perfectly free to hang around the coast. And if one day he decides to go off in search of a larger pod, he is protected in that choice too. (That's one possibility for what happened to him, although, given his relatively advanced age, death is another possibility. An apparent 2021 sighting has encouraged those who care about him.) That's how the approach respects individual creatures: by creating protected spaces for them to seek flourishing, each in their own way. Through future judicial specification, the list will get refined. And if people who live with and care about that type of animal were to protest that the list is incomplete or mistaken, it can always be changed.

Part of the Good Might Be Interspecies

The human Capabilities List included among its rubrics "relations with other animals and the world of nature": in other words, a decent society should make good inter-species relationships available. There are some animals whose usual lives are pretty much wrapped up in the life of their kind. Dolphins and elephants do not seem to rely on robust relationships with other species as a crucial element in their good (although that's not to say that a friendship across the species barrier might not arise under suitable conditions). But there are other animals whose form of life is far more relational across the species barrier: dogs, cats, many horses, and farm animals. These animals cultivate relationships with one another, and they all seem to seek and need relationships with humans. Chapter 9 will study that whole issue. So this simply gets built into the list we would make for each type of creature, as a desideratum. Reliance on a species norm does not imprison a creature within its own species. As these relationships develop further over time, the lists can change to reflect that.

THE FOUR VIEWS COMPARED

The CA does not rank species in any sort of "ladder," or give prizes for likeness to us. Instead, it follows wonder and curiosity, discovering the varied and remarkable ways that animals strive for flourishing. It sees some commonalities in the ways animals move and live: all have some type of sense perception, all have faculties for delivering information about the environment, all nourish themselves, all reproduce, and all are social, albeit in many different ways. Unlike the "So Like Us" approach, the CA does not place special emphasis on a creature's ability to communicate using a human type of language (e.g., sign language). Instead, it studies the many ways creatures do in fact communicate, some more "language-like" than others, but all suited to the specific creature's context, body, and form of life. The very idea that a whale would be better off with human language seems very odd. Its physiology, its environment, and its needs are all so completely different. It's much more interesting to see what types of communication are really out there.

Needless to say, the CA cares a great deal about pain, a great evil for all sentient creatures. But there are bad things other than pain. Creatures can be deprived of free movement, of species-normal society, of the chance to play and use their faculties in a relaxed way—all without being subjected to bodily pain. Looking at capabilities rather than following Bentham, we see many axes of deprivation in an animal life, just as in Vasanti's human life. And the CA treats animals as agents, not as containers of pleasure and pain, in that way respecting them.

The CA is close to Korsgaard's Kantian view in many ways. It insists that all animals deserve respect for their dignity, that we can't rank one type of creature as more important than others, and that each creature deserves a shot at flourishing in its own way. But the CA sees animals as agents and potentially active, not "passive," citizens, communicating their needs to those willing to listen. And the CA also insists that nature does not show us Korsgaard's sharp division between following instinct and following ethically inflected selection and choice. Many, if not most, animals have culture, following instinct part of the time, but following learned behavior and making their own selections part of the time. Nor are the ethical faculties discontinuous in nature. Creatures of many types follow rules of conduct, often very other-regarding rules, and teach these rules to their young. Human rules may be more elaborate and more philosophical, but they are not utterly different in kind, and they have evolved, like animal rules, to suit the context of human life. Dogs, elephants, cheetahs, and many others choose to put the good of others over self, and this is not just instinct, it is partially culture. Despite my admiration for Korsgaard's book, and despite the fact that we are allies over a large terrain, I suggest that the CA is somewhat more adequate to our world and the animals in it, as well as our own animality. And by framing political principles in a non-metaphysical way, it shows a superior respect for plurality and difference.

Even though I believe the CA is more adequate to our world than the other three views, it is important to see that all four views converge in opposition to some of the worst practices in the human-animal relationship. Although Steven Wise does not comment on factory farming, confining his efforts to the cruel treatment of captive primates and elephants, he intentionally leaves the door open for an extension to other species in due course, and meanwhile I am happy to support his practical legal efforts.[25] Utilitarians have made powerful critiques of factory farming, the torture of animals in laboratories, and all the indignities documented by Peter Singer in *Animal Liberation*. Singer and I are political allies, though we differ philosophically. The same is true of Korsgaard: her view and mine are practical allies, differing more in specific ethical arguments than in political principles. What this convergence means is that we are well on our way to an "overlapping consensus" of the different views, where political principles are concerned. Even though I think the CA is the best source of political principles, the other theories can in due course latch onto it and build it into a revised version of their own view.

ENDANGERED INDIVIDUALS AND ENDANGERED SPECIES

The CA focuses on each individual animal, and makes the individual, whether human or non-human, the focus of its concern. The general idea behind this is that no individual or group of individuals ought to be used as property of others or means to the ends of others. Each individual is an end.

But what about the species? Some of the animal-protective legislation we see today is legislation protecting endangered species. Defending the CA requires defining its relationship to this movement. So: Does the CA support protecting endangered species? My answer is complicated.

First of all, as I said earlier, the notion of species is itself problematic.[26] Boundaries in nature are not as hard and fast as many biologists used to think, and scientists now work, for the most part, with the looser notion of "populations." Interbreeding doesn't mark a sharp divide. Still, the traditional notion of species is a rough cut, so to speak, which can be helpful if we remember its limitations.

But if we retain a working notion of species, we must still insist that a species does not, as such, have a good. Individual species members have a perceived good and reach out for it, and they are to be treated as ends. It would be just as wrong to treat individual creatures as mere means to the flourishing of their species as to treat them as means to the ends of other creatures. A species has no point of view on the world. It does not feel, or suffer, or perceive. "The whale" does not die from ingesting plastic, "the elephant" is not killed by poachers. It is individual whales and individual elephants who suffer and die. If a species were suddenly to become extinct, by just waving a wand, no individual creature would suffer, it seems, and no sentient being would be wronged. This observation suggests that while species preservation may have scientific or aesthetic value, it does not, as such, count as an end for the purposes of political justice.

However, species preservation has great instrumental value for the individual creatures who are ends in themselves. Biodiversity is usually good for creatures, and while the idea that nature is a lovely harmonious system is a myth, which I'll criticize in chapter 10, we know that the disappearance of a species, even of non-sentient creatures, can inflict harm on many sentient creatures, who need those species for a variety of purposes (as food, as pollination aids, as creatures who kill off dangerous parasites, as sustainers of a diverse and healthy habitat, and so forth). Usually, too, we are much too ignorant of these interconnections to be able to say, "This one can go without harming the individual creatures who remain." Moreover, creatures need diversity in the gene pool of their own species, if their young are not to suffer from diseases of inbreeding.

Furthermore, the way a species becomes extinct involves great suffering for many of its remaining members. Think of polar bears unable to mate or forage, trapped on ice floes as the polar ice melts. Think of endangered elephants and rhinos threatened by poachers, forced to watch members of their group get slaughtered for the sake of their tusks. Those who survive often lead a traumatized existence, at the same time as habitat loss also threatens them with starvation. Think of whales (many species now endangered) beached, gasping their last breath, because their bodies are stuffed full of the plastics with which the oceans are increasingly filled. More generally, habitat loss (a lot of it due to global warming) and habitat spoilage (for example, spoilage of the ocean by plastics) are the main mechanisms of species extinction in our world, and they typically inflict great suffering on individuals. If we care about the lives of individual creatures, we have powerful reasons to work against these modes of species destruction.

Finally, no creature is an island. Their good is in all cases some type of social good, exercised with and toward others.[27] Some creatures need a larger group for normal social life than others. Dolphins are more social than many birds. Still, even the less social (birds who may pair-bond with a mate for life and interact rarely with others), depend on the existence of a breeding community that is large enough so the population does not suffer, eventually, the health defects of inbreeding. Even for parrots, the good of each individual requires the health and diversity of a surrounding species community, and in some cases an inter-species community.

In short: it is the individual creature who is the end of our efforts and the central concern of a theory of justice. But species have crucial roles to play in the lives of individuals, giving us reason to care greatly about the current dangers that many species face.

A VIEW ABOUT THE BASIS OF RIGHTS

By making the fulfillment of Central Capabilities mandatory for political justice, the CA holds that animals have rights to support for the capabilities central to their various forms of life, up to some reasonable threshold, and in ways limited by the reasonable claims of others. (As chapter 7 will make clear, these limits include a self-defense principle.) The rights are claims inherent in the dignity of each individual animal. They demand fulfillment. Just as we make claims on one another for a chance to live, to speak, to enjoy good health, and so forth, so too does every animal. But a right is only real if it can in principle be legally enforced. And even though at this point in world history humans are the legislators and the enforcers, there is no reason why humans should enforce only human rights and not the rights of other sentient beings.

But a reader might find the CA interesting and even important in defining goals and aspirations, without yet being convinced that animals really have *rights* to the things on the Capabilities List, or that their absence is a sign of *injustice* and *rights violation*. So at this point we must say more.

Part of our task is to think well about duties. Rights are usually thought to be correlated with duties. So, if every animal has a bundle of rights, who has the associated duties? People who deny that animals have rights often do so because they can see no reasonable answer to this question. The problem is still thornier: rights are correlated not only with duties, but with law. Rights, as Korsgaard argues convincingly (drawing on Kant), and as I myself believe, are conceptually related to laws. Therefore, to say that a creature has a right to something is also to say that there should be laws protecting that entitlement. But we can imagine people who think that the very idea of laws protecting animal entitlements is impossibly utopian. Such people will resist the idea that animals have rights. What can we say to them? Who has the duties to vindicate these rights, eventually using law to do so?

Here Kant, as extended by Korsgaard, has the correct answer: the rights of animals are "imperfect rights"—meaning rights not against any definite person or animal, but, rather, against all human beings, against humanity imagined as capable of collective action.[28] (In chapter 10, I'll consider whether animals have any rights against other animals, such as the right not to be eaten, that ought to be enforced somehow, in a just society.) Imperfect rights are rights of individuals against wrongful treatment, where we are as yet uncertain how to organize effective action. In such cases, our most immediate duty as individuals will be to try to organize the group in such a way that all rights will be protected.

But why should we grant that animals have any rights at all? Most ethical views suggest something far weaker: that we should treat animals humanely out of beneficence or compassion. However, that is not strong enough: whenever individual sentient creatures are being wronged, injustice is being done. The CA fleshes out an attractive picture of animal dignity and striving as themselves demanding responsive protection from laws and institutions. Can we say more about the basis of these rights? If we can't, then the CA may seem to many readers an attractive ideal, but one without direct implications for what we ought to do.

Here again, Korsgaard's Kant gives us assistance. Kant believed that for human beings, rights are bulwarks against domination. We all find ourselves in the world, extremely vulnerable to domination by others. Without rights (understood as legally enforceable ethical claims), we would not be able to use resources to support our needs without being continually threatened by the domination of others. At the base of our rights is a very simple idea: every human being has a right to be where he or she is. Prior to owning or using anything, you have a right simply to be where you are. Therefore, there is injustice if things are divided up in such a way that some are unable to live. In this way, Kant grounds not only property rights, but also a right to democratic participation, to having a share of control over what happens in the world.

However, human beings are not the only sentient creatures who are thrown into the world and who need to avoid domination if they are to live decently. Kant himself thought that animals were simply property, and that his argument entitled human beings so to use them. But Korsgaard objects: other animals have a situation just like ours, thrown into the world, striving to live, vulnerable to domination. Right now all the other animals are dominated by humans. This seems to be injustice, by Kant's own argument: other animals too must have the right to be where they are, and, like us, a stake in what happens. They have ends of their own, and may not be subjected to our domination without injustice.[29]

This intuitive idea of a right to be where you are is deep, and it is no surprise that it is already recognized in some of our laws and institutions. In her recent book *Wildlife as Property Owners: A New Conception of Animal Rights*,[30] legal scholar Karen Bradshaw studies the many ways in which laws have already granted animals rights to a habitat and some types of property. Of course, like all our laws regarding animals, these are patchy and incomplete, but they show that people who live with animals in the "wild" are sensitive to the Kantian argument without formally making it. These animals are there, they have a right to be there, we have no right to throw them out.

This is an idea that can and must be given substance by law, as I'll elaborate in chapter 12. But this idea of interspecies law is not entirely one-way, giving humans all the duties and animals only rights. Animals too can be legally obligated, and their rights can have legal bounds so that the multispecies world will be able to live together. We are already familiar with this idea in thinking about companion animals, who, as chapter 9 will elaborate, are prohibited from harming both people and other animals in specified ways. Usually it's the "owner" who is envisaged as having duties—not to allow "her" dog to bite children, not to allow "her" cat to eat a neighbor's bird. But we can without difficulty reformulate these duties as duties of the animal in question—that must be exercised through collaboration, and teaching. Similarly, the legal duties of young children and people with severe cognitive disabilities are actually *theirs*, though they are exercised through the watchful agency of "collaborators."

THE NEW APPROACH IN ACTION

The CA maps a destination. It does not tell us how to get there. It is, I said, like a virtual constitution for the animals of the world. But there is no nation in which animals are citizens, though they should be seen as citizens with rights whose nonfulfillment is injustice. Because we are only at the beginning of a political journey toward justice for animals, any implementation of the ideas of the CA must be piecemeal, including working toward better international treaties and agreements, better federal statutes in each nation, and the improvement of many state and local laws, which for the foreseeable future will remain a bewildering and uncoordinated patchwork. Chapter 12 will explore the patchwork further.

At this point, however, it helps to have a foretaste of where we are heading in practical and legal terms. One such example may help carry our discussion further: a happy harbinger of what may be a new era in law, in the form of a remarkable 2016 opinion by the US Court of Appeals for the Ninth Circuit. In *Natural Resources Defense Council, Inc. v. Pritzker*,[31] the Ninth Circuit ruled that the US Navy violated the law in seeking to continue a sonar program that impacted the behavior of whales.[32] To some extent, the opinion is a technical exercise in statutory interpretation of the Marine Mammal Protection Act:[33] the court says that the fact that a program has "negligible impact" on marine mammals does not exempt it from a separate statutory requirement, namely that it establish means of "effecting the least practicable adverse impact on" marine mammal species.[34] What is significant, and fascinating, is that the argument relies heavily on a consideration of whale capabilities that the program disrupts:

> Effects from exposures below 180 dB can cause short-term disruption or abandonment of natural behavior patterns. These behavioral disruptions can cause affected marine mammals to stop communicating with each other, to flee or avoid an ensonified area, to cease foraging for food, to separate from their calves, and to interrupt mating. LFA sonar can also cause heightened stress responses from marine mammals. Such behavioral disruptions can force marine mammals to make trade-offs like delaying migration, delaying reproduction, reducing growth, or migrating with reduced energy reserves.[35]

The opinion does not give whales legal standing (entitlement to bring a claim in court, a notion I'll discuss at length in chapter 12); no such radical legal move is necessary to reach the clear result that the program is unacceptable. Because the whales did not have standing, they had to depend on the luck of having protection through the Marine Mammal Protection Act, a law made by human legislators, but with some concern for the interests of whales.

The whales also had to depend on ethically inflected wonder—on judges who read the law imaginatively, taking very seriously a set of obstructions to the whales' form of life that did not involve the infliction of pain. The opinion—written (for a unanimous three-judge panel) by Judge Ronald Gould, who sits in and has long lived in the state of Washington, where whale watching is a common pastime—concluded that obstructing a characteristic form of life-activity, even without pain, is an "adverse impact."[36] I imagine this judge as someone who has really looked at whales, with curiosity and wonder. But whether he or his clerks have really gone out whale watching or not, the opinion displays ethical and imaginative attunement of a type increasingly seen in coastal areas of the US, perhaps in the Seattle area above all. It sees whales as complex beings with an active form of life that includes emotional well-being, affiliation, and free movement: in short, a variety of species-specific forms of agency. The opinion goes well beyond Bentham, and it also steers clear of the "So Like Us" approach. Nor, like the Kantian, does it view whales as merely "passive citizens." It is a harbinger, it is to be hoped, of a new era in the law of animal welfare, and animal justice.

6

SENTIENCE AND STRIVING

A Working Boundary

That's how animals set out to move and act: the most immediate cause of their movement is desire, and this comes about either through perception or through imagination and thought.[1]

Aristotle, *On the Movement of Animals*

Now we have seen the CA in action, an approach based on the forms of life of sentient animals. As a theory of basic justice, it aims at supporting their strivings in central areas, focusing not just on pain but on the diverse goals each type of creature aims to attain (with much latitude for individual diversity and choice within a species).

But who are these sentient creatures? These are the ones whom my theory deems entitled to just treatment. The CA is a minimal theory of justice that can serve as an ideal "virtual constitution" to guide our diverse efforts in local, national, and international lawmaking. Understanding injustice as wrongful impeding of a sentient animal's characteristic life-activities, I have imagined minimal justice as protection of Central Animal Capabilities, up to a reasonable threshold.

But which creatures ought to be treated as ends? Given my understanding of justice and injustice, this boils down to the question: Which creatures are capable of significant striving? Of being not just damaged but wrongfully thwarted in their striving? The CA itself supplies answers to this question through its emphasis on significant striving. But we must now get specific about what the theory tells us.

The creatures discussed in the CA, the creatures whose significant striving the theory requires us to protect, must, it seems, be capable of perception and desire, and of moving in response to that combination. By perception I mean (however difficult it is to get at this in practical terms) the capacity to focus on objects in the world, in a way that's not just a causal collision, that has real directedness or what philosophers call intentionality. The world *looks like something* to these creatures. They have some sort of subjective experience. With desire, it is similar: the creatures we are looking for don't just mechanically jump away from harm or move toward food; they have a felt orientation toward what is seen as good and a felt aversion to what is seen as bad. That is what makes their striving significant. They are not just automata.

In other words, they possess that elusive property known as *sentience*. The world looks like something to them, and they strive for the good as they see it. Sometimes sentience is reduced to the ability to feel pain; but it is really a much broader notion, the notion of having a subjective point of view on the world. I think it's helpful to open the idea of sentience up this way, before we get to the difficult scientific debates about how to show that a given animal is sentient, which usually focus rather narrowly on pain. What I'm saying is that my core notion of injustice can apply only to creatures who are capable of significant striving, and that involves not just felt pain and pleasure, but also perceptual awareness and in most cases the ability to move toward or away from objects as the animal's view dictates. Often this will involve not just desires but also emotions, since emotions have evolved as ways living creatures take in news about how things are with their most important goals and projects.

By now, after a lot of fascinating work, scientists are in general agreement that most animals—including all mammals, all birds, and teleost (hard-boned) fish—are such creatures, difficult though these scientific

debates have been. Other cases (insects, crustaceans, cephalopods, cartilaginous fish) are more obscure. And then there is the case of plants,
which some scientists want to move into the justice camp, so to speak.
I'll present these debates, but the theory is the important thing: for we are
making new discoveries all the time, and if we have the theory as a template, we can easily regroup, classifying creatures differently.

My conclusion is in one sense neo-Aristotelian: animals are complex
creatures striving for their characteristic ends, with the aid of perception/
imagination/thought and of desires and emotions of many kinds. All of
these abilities are not in the least mysterious: they have evolutionary/
explanatory value.

Everything in this chapter is humble and disputable, as to the appli-
cation of the ethical intuition; new knowledge may change my tentative
conclusions.

THE EVIDENCE AND THE PITFALLS

One pitfall we must beware of is a kind of anthropocentric complacency:
human researchers think it is as clear as day that human beings have consciousness (however we define that elusive item), emotions, imagination,
subjectively felt perceptions, and cognitions of many types. (Scientists typically define cognition broadly, as any process through which a creature
acquires, processes, uses, or stores information, so there is a considerable
overlap between these categories: perception and imagination are forms
of cognition, emotions typically have cognitive or information-bearing
elements.) Briefly, during the heyday of behaviorism, some psychologists suggested that human beings had none of these things, but were just
stimulus-response mechanisms. However, this idea so clashed with life
experience that it never penetrated very far into the world of biological
research, and by now it has been abandoned.

Despite biology's general return to a more humanistic conception
of human beings, involving rich forms of intentionality (inner focusing
on outward objects), and what I have called *significant striving*, striving

imbued with personal meaning, the epistemic difficulties of such a conception need to be squarely confronted, as they typically are by philosophers discussing the "problem of other minds," but not so often by scientists doing research on animal intelligence. For the fact is that our evidence for the humanistic picture of human beings is complicated and uncertain. We have access to our own subjective experience, but even that is shaky. We know that we do not always know what we are doing, or what our emotions and intentions really are. As for other humans, what leads us to make the leap from self to other? The same things, really, that we will rely on (very cautiously) when we talk about other animals: biology, behavior, inference to the best explanation, and interpretive imagination. We know that other humans have a neuroanatomy like our own, and we reason that its deliverances are likely to be similar: if we have subjective awareness through the operations of our neural mechanism, so too, very likely, do others with similar neuroanatomy. That's the simplest account, and a highly plausible one. We see others behave in ways that suggest the types of actions that, when we undertake them, are accompanied by subjective awareness of many kinds—so we reason that the best explanation of that similarity of behavior would be to posit a similarity of experiential underpinnings. But what really justifies us in making these imaginative leaps from self to others? How do we really know that this putative friend, talking and laughing, is not a clever machine?

I don't want to say that we have no reason to ascribe mental life to other humans. I want to say instead, that we do; but not the sort of knockdown evidence that is typically demanded in the case of non-human animals. Failure to recognize the difficulty of our own case leads researchers to set the bar impossibly high in theirs. In both cases, the evidence and the difficulties are roughly similar.

The first source of evidence scientists use in tackling the issue of animal awareness is *neuroanatomy*. If it is sufficiently similar to our own, then explanatory parsimony suggests that its functions are very likely to be similar: it plays the same evolutionary role. If in us it produces perceptual experiences, feelings, and emotions, it is highly likely that it does so in other similarly equipped creatures—including other human beings. So far so reasonably good. Any hypothesis to the contrary is likely to be unnecessarily baroque, treating similar cases dissimilarly.

The converse, however, is not true. That is, if we see a neuroanatomy that is far removed from our own (no neocortex, perhaps not even a centralized brain), we cannot rightly infer that the functions of whatever system takes its place must be extremely different. For a long time, mistakes were made in this way: no neocortex, said scientists, then no cognitions, pains, or emotions. But we have learned by now that evolution is devious, and follows, often, convergent paths to a similar goal. Thus, as we'll see, humans and birds diverged so far back on the evolutionary tree that they have many large neuroanatomical dissimilarities. And yet: birds inhabit the same world of nature humans do, and face an array of challenges not too dissimilar to those we face. As it turns out, birds have adapted to face those challenges, but with strikingly different structures. Similarity of structure is pretty good evidence, then, of similar function (including its subjective properties); but difference of structure is not good evidence of difference of function, when we can study the way the creature functions independently and try to figure out how it does so.

At this point we need to bear in mind that subjective experience is not an idle frill: it plays many crucial explanatory roles. To take the simplest case, the feeling of pain is useful in keeping animals alive, and has no doubt evolved to serve a vital role in signaling the presence of harmful substances. So pain is linked usefully to animal behavior, and has evolved because of its survival value.

The second, and in many ways, most important piece of evidence is, consequently, *behavior*, under a variety of experimental and observational conditions. Behavior is crucial, but it is not easy to interpret. Some moving creatures may be harm-avoiding mechanisms without subjective awareness. We'll see that scientists have figured out ways to distinguish those from creatures who have genuine awareness. Here, pain plays a useful role, since it is a sharp subjective experience that typically has clear

behavioral consequences. But these experiments are themselves controversial and multiply interpreted.

Scientists and many philosophers alike at this point use *inference to the best explanation*, just as we ourselves do when we ascribe mental states to other humans in ordinary life.[2] Inference of this type is fraught with uncertainty (have we really defeated competing explanations?), and it is at best imprecise. Used in conjunction with other clues, however, as scientists typically use it, it gets us to a reasonably secure conclusion. Philosopher Michael Tye makes a lot of progress by using this strategy. On pain, for example, he writes:

> The hypothesis that there is one phenomenal quality in me that causes groaning, bodily tension, withdrawal behavior, etc., and a different phenomenal quality in you that has these effects is more complex, and it is ad hoc. A difference is postulated without any evidence, without any reason to suppose that there is a difference. . . . My final conclusion, then, is that it *is* rational for me to accept that you feel pain when I see you bloodied by your broken bike, for it provides the best available explanation of your behavior. What goes for pain goes for fear and the visual consciousness of red. Indeed, it goes for feelings and experiences generally.[3]

Sometimes these promising inferences are blocked by overemphasis on a difference or differences between humans and other animals. Particularly common is what I'll call the *false lure of language*. Scientists often tend to think that human awareness is linguistic in structure, and that a creature without language must have a totally different kind of awareness, if any at all. But of course, human perceptual and emotional experience is not always linguistic in form. We get used to reporting on our experience by using language, but that's a translation game. It isn't as though sentences go through our head as we have the experience, or at least not very often. We're used to reading novels that give detailed linguistic accounts of human experience, but that is an artful rendering of something that takes place in our own minds with great compression and little verbal elaboration. Novelists even portray in elaborate language the inner lives of children; but they acknowledge that they are attempting to render something that occurs very differently within the child. As Henry James wrote in his preface to *What Maisie Knew*, "Small children have many more perceptions than they have terms to translate them; their vision is at any moment much richer, their apprehension even constantly stronger, than their . . . vocabulary."[4] But it is not only children of whom this is true: probably only novelists command the vocabulary of novelists, and that no doubt not completely, when they are moving rapidly through their own lives. For this reason Proust boldly claimed that the only fully realized life is literature, meaning that the novelist's rich language goes beyond the gappiness, dullness, and impoverishment of daily experience. We should not believe Proust in his contention that the novelist's language is *superior* to most people's daily experiences. We should always remember that it is very *different*.

Human experience, in short, is far from novelistic, and it usually isn't even particularly verbal: it often uses pictorial and sonic representations. Even when it's to some degree verbal, it isn't crisp and precise the way a sentence describing it will aspire to be. And on the rare occasions when our experience is highly demarcated into sophisticated patterns, these won't all be linguistic; some will be pictorial and even musical. We all begin life not knowing how to use language, and not even knowing how to demarcate our own bodies from those of others. At this early stage we have deep and powerful perceptions and emotions, many of which persist and influence adult awareness.

When novelists attempt to write from the point of view of a non-human animal, they are accused of illegitimate anthropomorphism. Sometimes criticism of some sort is due, if the novelist has not bothered to investigate the life-world of that type of creature, but has lazily imagined the animal as rather like a human in a costume. Novelists do not always err in this way.[5] What the critic forgets however, is that a novel describing the world from the points of view of various human characters

is also guilty of the anthropomorphism, if we can call it that, of pretend-
ing our gappy, messy inner worlds are articulated into crisp and eloquent
sentences characteristic of the literary construct, a "human being."

Steering clear of the false lure of language is very difficult. Equally
difficult, in connected ways, is steering clear of the *false lure of metacognition.* Many people, including some scientists and philosophers, are enam-
ored of the idea that what sets humans apart is reflexive self-awareness,
awareness *of* one's own mental states. Sometimes consciousness is defined
in terms of such metacognitions, and anything lacking it is held to lack
consciousness. As Tye and others have convincingly argued (and really,
it's surprising that anyone ever held a different view), most of our experience goes on without reflexive awareness as we pursue our lives in the
world. We see, hear, feel. Things feel and look like something to us: and
yet most of the time we do not turn the laser beam of reflection on those
states, although certainly at times we do. The false lure in this case is two-
fold: we are lured into thinking that this particular ability to reflect on
one's states is a necessary condition of feeling pain and having many other
subjective experiences. This is false, as we know every day. And then, second, we err by believing that only humans have this trait. Experiments
have shown, however, that quite a few animals have it. We don't have to
look for an exalted light beam going on in their heads; we can infer this
ability from what they are able to do. One key is the practice of deception:
to deceive another animal about where some choice food is located, for
example, an animal needs the ability to think about appearances, how a
given set of indicators will appear to, be read by, the animal being de-
ceived. As we'll later see, animals as different as dogs and crows practice
deception, showing that they have metacognition. Metacognition, then,
is not the be-all and end-all that some have thought it, putting a creature
on a pedestal; nor is it the special exalted property of humans alone. It's
an ordinary ability that is useful to many creatures for whom hiding and
deceiving are useful, and useful, no doubt, in many other ways. To give
just one more example, we'll later encounter birds who probably have to
be able to think about how the female bird will view that elaborate bower

they are making, or that endlessly rehearsed song they are singing—just as we select a new outfit by thinking about what others (maybe particular others) will think of it.

Metacognition, although just a small part of conscious awareness, is useful to us in proving conscious awareness. If we encounter a creature who is capable of deceiving another creature in a way that shows awareness of how the world appears to that creature, then surely that creature does, a fortiori, have basic awareness: the world appears a certain way.[6] Sometimes this can be useful, where we are inclined strongly to doubt that there is something the world looks like and feels like to a given type of creature. Where birds are in question, the analysis of deception can open minds. But of course, metacognition, while sufficient for ordinary conscious awareness, is not necessary for it.[7]

WHAT IS SENTIENCE, AND HOW DO WE FIND IT?

How do we figure out which creatures have what is usually known as sentience? Well, first, we need to define what we're looking for.

First: we must always bear in mind that animals have evolved through natural selection. Their major attributes and abilities do something for them, or they would very likely not have been selected. So sentience is not just a nice admirable trait, it is a useful trait, and we need to bear that in mind at all times, lest we get sidetracked by a tendency to ooh and ah over subjectivity. Sentience does something for the creature, or it would not be there. Even without a theory of selection, Aristotle emphasized that animals were teleological (end-directed) systems aiming at survival and reproduction, and should be understood to have just those systems and attributes that promoted their integrated system of goals. Aristotle knew nothing of evolution, but we, who do know how it works, have all the more reason to believe that most structures in animals are there for some purpose. Of course, there is occasionally something useless. (Aristotle mentions the appendix.) But on the whole, everything is "for the sake of something," and all the abilities are integrated into an overall successful life-form. Now that we know about evolution we have all the more reason to follow Aristotle's approach, preferring explanations that show how things are indeed functional and apt.

Scientists divide "sentience" into three elements.

1. Nociception, which literally means "apprehending the harmful."
2. Subjective sensory awareness: the world looks/feels a certain way.
3. A sense of significance or salience.

Scientists tend to focus obsessively on pain, so that's why the first rubric is nociception, being aware of what is harmful, an ability necessary to survive, and prompting aversive behavior. With our more comprehensive focus on fitness and striving, however, we should really also include awareness of things that are good for the creature, prompting movement toward that thing. Aristotle imagines a thirsty animal saying to itself (in effect), "Drink for me"; and then, being a lucky animal, "Here's drink."[8] "Here's drink" would be nociception's opposite, perception of the good. Animals need the awareness of where food and drink are to be found just as much as they need the ability to avoid pain and danger. So let's call this one: *apprehending the good and the bad*.

But a creature could have that ability and still be like an automaton, reacting to stimuli with no felt awareness. Scientists typically use the term "nociception" to describe a reflex operation of the peripheral nervous system that by itself involves no subjective awareness of pain.[9] (Focusing on pain, they have no corresponding term for reflex awareness of food or other good things.) Some creatures, it will turn out, probably are more or less like automata. (I'll argue that not only plants but some animals are like this.) So, the second thing we are looking for, in addition, is subjective awareness: the world looks a certain way to the creature; it has a felt point of view. Again, let's not focus obsessively on pain, but think about seeing colors, feeling desire and pleasure, as well as pain and distress. Pain plays a large part in research because it is easier to test for than other subjective conditions; but we should think about the wide range of things a creature needs. This is our ordinary notion of *conscious awareness*.

To give an example of ordinary awareness at work in an intelligent creature, we have to translate their thoughts into our language, and we should not seek poetic frills, because the awareness of most intelligent animals is highly practical. Let me, then, return to Empress of Blandings, since Wodehouse captures with insight and humor the sorts of thoughts that this remarkable pig might have, after being kidnapped, driven all over Shropshire, and then returned to her own home sty:

> She looked about her, happy to be back in the old familiar surround-
> ings. It was pleasant to feel settled once more. She was a philosopher
> and could take things as they came, but she did like a quiet life. All that
> whizzing about in cars and being dumped in strange kitchens didn't do
> a pig of regular habits any good.
>
> There seemed to be edible substances in the trough beside her. She
> rose, and inspected it. Yes, substances, plainly edible. It was a little late,
> perhaps, but one could always do with a snack. . . . She lowered her noble
> head and got down to it.[10]

Wodehouse's description is not far from Aristotle's animal "practi-cal syllogism," which contains the premises "Drink for me," and "Here's drink"—and the conclusion is the action of drinking.[11] Both writers cap-ture the way in which perception and desire combine in an intelligent life that seeks diverse good things: food, quiet, stability. That's everyday sentience, and it's obvious that most vertebrates have it.

Subjective awareness is useful to creatures. Pain is a great incentiv-izer of aversive movement, just as desire and pleasure are of movement toward something. We know this from observing human beings who have lost the ability to feel pain in some part of their body (for example, by having all the nerves removed in an arm). This is a person at high risk of harm. She will have to watch that arm all the time in case it might come in contact with something sharp, or hot, or grating: pain will not be there to inform her to draw the limb quickly away. Similarly, when you've had Novocaine at the dentist, you will bite and damage your tongue if you try to eat too soon afterward. In short, subjective awareness is really useful, and we can understand why nature selected for it. It's not just a fancy ooh-ah thing, it is a part of animal survival equipment. It is logical that lots of creatures would have it.

But there is something more. I have spoken of *significant striving*. Creatures pursue some goals as vital to their lives, and neglect others that are more trivial. Sensory experience reports both the major and the trivial, but to make choices and act in the world creatures need a sense of significance, a stronger "oomph" to certain experiences, whether aversive or propulsive. This "oomph" is typically understood to be the evolutionary role of emotions, and we'll discuss that role later on. For now, let's just stick to a simpler case, pain. If a pain is small, the creature may or may not move to avoid it. If it is great, aversive movement is usually expected. But there's a catch: sometimes it is possible to feel even a very substantial pain without that pain seeming *bad*. This doesn't happen under normal life conditions, but we know that the way some opiates work is exactly this way: the sensation is there, but you don't mind it. A type of dissociation has set in. So we can see that, in theory at least, the sensation and its significance can come apart. Maybe a true-believer ascetic thinks hunger is fine, maybe even good, because it's a sign that he is moving toward his goal. And many people at many times have had such dissociative experiences about their sexual desires: the strong urge is there, but it is felt as a sign of sin or danger, and therefore prompts not a search for gratification but aversive efforts. It is likely that these types of dissociation of perceptual experience from life-meaning are uncommon in non-human animals when they are not injected with a dissociation-inducing drug. Their cultures do not warp them in the way that many human cultures warp us. (That's what Walt Whitman meant when he wrote, "I think I could turn and live with animals. . . . They do not lie awake in the dark and weep for their sins.") Still, we need to build into our picture the idea of significance, since without that, selection of movement and activity is likely to be random, ill-directed for attaining the creature's goals. Empress of Blandings did not simply see edible substances, she attributed great significance to those substances.

Because subjectivity and meaning usually go together, and indeed subjectivity would not be much use unless it communicated goals that had significance for the animal's activities, the real question is whether we are entitled to attribute subjective awareness to animals. Some scientists are skeptics. Marian Stamp Dawkins comments:

> Are animals conscious like us because they have many brain structures in common with us, or are they not like us because they lack some cru-cial pathway that prevents them from going that extra mile into con-scious experience? . . . The elusive source of our own consciousness and its infuriating refusal to be tied down to particular neural structures leaves us, at the moment, completely unable to distinguish between these quite opposite views of animal consciousness.[12]

Dawkins, notice, is thinking of consciousness as a mysterious, some-what hidden entity. She seems not to be thinking of what I've been talking about: ordinary daily subjective awareness of objects. Otherwise, as Tye argues repeatedly and effectively, it would be odd to treat it as mysteri-ous and unknown. Explanations of behavior that appeal to psychological structures and do not reduce them in every case to a particular neural mechanism are actually preferable to reductive explanations when we're dealing with behavior that is multiply realizable in different neural struc-tures, since these explanations are simpler and have greater predictive power.

It's the same thing with geometry. For example, to explain why a bronze sphere of radius r will fit through a wooden hoop of radius slightly greater than r, we don't need to invoke atom charts giving all the spe-cific trajectories of the atoms of bronze and wood respectively, even if we know them. That level of specificity is irrelevant, cluttering the mind with predictively otiose material. The laws of geometry give an explanation that holds good for this case and also for an indefinite number of further cases, with spheres made of gold, or marble, or any other solid material, and ditto with hoops. Nobody is claiming that spheres are not each made of some specific material; it's just that the specificity of the matter is not helpful when we're explaining what we're trying to explain.[13]

There are good reasons why scientists today almost universally attribute subjective experience (and a sense of significance or salience) to many animals: pain is a very good teacher of life-preserving behavior. It alerts animals to danger that may lead to impairment or even loss of life. And it trains the memory, motivating creatures to avoid an event that has caused pain in the past.[14] (Thus Empress of Blandings has now learned a preference for staying in her own sty, and an aversion to uncertain modes of transportation.) The same goes with good things, in the other direction.

EXPERIMENTAL CONFIRMATION: THE CASE OF FISH

But even if we are ready to believe that similar behavior requires a similar type of explanation, and that if awareness is crucial in our case there's a presumption in favor of its being crucial in the case of goal-seeking and goal-avoiding animals, we still have more work to do. Particularly in cases where neural structures are profoundly different, it's important to probe the relevant behavior experimentally, to see how far our working hypothesis makes sense. Again: we are looking for subjective awareness. Experimentally, we are almost always going to find this in areas that also have significance or meaning for the creature, because awareness of trivia does not alter behavior.

Most experimental scientists have concluded that fish feel pain.[15] The leaders of the pro camp are biologists Victoria Braithwaite at Pennsylvania State University and Lynne Sneddon at the University of Liverpool. But there are skeptics: in 2013, James Rose, Professor Emeritus at the University of Wyoming, published a paper with six colleagues, in the journal *Fish and Fisheries*, titled "Can Fish Really Feel Pain?," giving a negative answer to that question.[16] The approach of the "no" authors is question-begging, since it begins from the premise that only creatures with a neocortex can feel pain; since fish obviously lack a neocortex, they can't really feel pain, whatever experiments suggest. It's not good method to assert one's conclusion as a premise of one's argument, and I am not sure that this paper really merits refutation. One obvious problem is that there is by now an overwhelming consensus that birds have subjective experiences of many kinds, and yet birds do not have a neocortex. Still, it's useful to ask why Braithwaite and Sneddon concluded that fish do feel pain. After all, we've insisted that nociception is not sufficient for subjective awareness, and we'll later see that some creatures have nociception and avoidance behavior without subjective awareness.

As it turns out, their ingenious experiments, summarized in Braithwaite's book *Do Fish Feel Pain?*[17] are convincing. First, they carefully examine the fish neuroanatomy, finding nerves that contain both A-delta and C fibers, the two types that are associated with pain in humans and other mammals. A-delta fibers signal the sharp initial pain of an injury (say, touching the hot stove), whereas C fibers signal the subsequent sensation of the damage, which is likely to be a duller, more throbbing sensation. So fish may not have a neocortex, but they do have the right type of equipment. Next, Braithwaite and Sneddon subjected the skin of trouts to painful stimuli in the area where sensitive nerve tissue had been found.[18] There were four treatment groups: one group was injected with bee venom; one with vinegar; one with a neutral saline solution; and one group was handled but not injected, to rule out behavioral effects of merely being handled. The fish in the first two groups, but not the third and fourth, showed evidence of distress: elevated gill beats, rubbing their lips against the tank, rocking from side to side. Their next step relied on a simple fact: creatures given a pain-relieving drug such as morphine will not feel pain. (Fish are known to be responsive physically to morphine.) The administration of morphine removed the distress behavior.

All of this strongly suggested that the fish were *feeling* pain and not just engaging in reflex nociceptive behavior. The next step confirmed that conclusion. Fish typically are very wary of a new object suddenly introduced in their environment. The experimenters built a tower of red Lego blocks and put it in their tank. The fish who had not been injected avoided the tower. The fish who had been injected, however, failed to alter their behavior in the usual way. It seemed that they were unable to function properly: they wandered near the strange object, apparently distracted. This behavioral change suggests that they were really feeling something that was a sufficiently powerful signal to distract them and alter their awareness of other parts of their environment. And then the clincher: when they gave the fish in groups one and two morphine, they once again returned to their ordinary watchful behavior.[19] Braithwaite points out that this experiment is very different from one done with snails in which morphine blocks a nociceptive nerve signal that stimulates a reflex response: in the case of the fish, "novel object avoidance isn't a reflexive response because it involves awareness which is a cognitive process—the cognitive process is impaired because of the subjective feeling caused by the acetic acid."[20]

Other variants of these experiments, which I won't elaborate here, were tried out over a long period of time, further confirming the team's conclusions.

In short: we have *neuroanatomy, behavior* for which the best explanation is a subjective sensation of pain, and the *significance of pain for goals* (pursuit and avoidance).

EMOTIONS: A ROAD MAP OF SIGNIFICANCE

Animals typically have many subjective feeling-states. But we now know that they have another closely related piece of equipment: emotions. Not just *pain*, then, but also *fear*, and a bunch of others. Depending on the animal and its form of life and cognition, these may include *joy, grief* (if the creature has an idea of death and the loss of what is precious), *anger* (if the creature has causal reasoning), *compassion* (if the creature has a clear distinction between self and other and some capacity for *empathy*, by which I mean putting oneself imaginatively in the place of the other), maybe *envy* and *jealousy*. As the great biological expert on this topic, Frans de Waal, emphasizes in a recent book, these are names for general categories, but in the world we often find mixed emotions and subtle species distinctions.[21]

Emotions are often closely associated with feelings, but they are not reducible to feelings, because they involve not just a stabbing sensation (for example), but a cognition of important good or bad. Emotions are where we definitively move from subjectivity to *significance*, the third item on my list. From a time when behaviorists thought that no advanced psychology of animal (or human) behavior would allude to emotions, we have now come full circle to a world in which biologists see emotions as key to evolutionary fitness. Animals need to become aware of how things are in the world with respect to their most important goals and projects. Emotions fill that need: they are in effect cognitions of salience, of what the great psychologist Richard Lazarus called "core relational themes."[22] As Frans de Waal reports, neuroscientists, like so many humans (philosophers not least) used to disparage emotions, contrasting them strongly with "reason." No longer: "As a result of Damasio's insights and other studies since, modern neuroscience has ditched the whole idea of emotions and rationality as opposing forces, like oil and water, that don't mix. Emotions are an essential part of our intellect."[23]

What were Damasio's insights?[24] Antonio Damasio's primary concern, in *Descartes' Error*, is to convince his reader that the emotion/reason distinction is inaccurate and misleading: emotions are forms of intelligent awareness. They are "just as cognitive as other percepts,"[25] and they supply the organism with essential aspects of practical reason. They serve as "internal guides" concerning the relationship between subject and circumstances.[26] His secondary aim is to show that emotional functioning in humans is connected with particular centers in the brain.

The case from which Damasio starts is the sad history of Phineas Gage, a construction foreman who, in 1848, suffered a bizarre accident:

an explosion drove an iron bar through his brain. Gage was not killed; indeed, he made an amazing recovery. His knowledge and his perceptual capacities were unaltered. But his emotional life was altered completely. He seemed to be like a child, with no stable sense of what was important and what was not. He was fitful, intemperate, obscene. It was as if he didn't care about one thing more than another. He seemed bizarrely detached from the reality of his conduct. So he could not make good choices, and he could not sustain good relationships with the people around him.

Damasio discovered a modern Gage by accident, in a patient named Elliot, a formerly successful businessman who had a benign brain tumor. Elliot was weirdly cool, detached, and ironic, indifferent even to intrusive discussion of personal matters—as if it were not really about him. He had not previously been this way; he had been an affectionate husband and father. He retained lots of cognitive functions: he could perform calculations, had a fine memory for dates and names, and the ability to discuss abstract topics and general world affairs. After surgery to remove the tumor (which took part of the damaged frontal lobe with it), he was even less able to care about things or to rank priorities. He could stick obsessively to a task and perform it very well; but on a whim he might shift his attention and do something completely different. "One might say that Elliot had become irrational concerning the larger frame of behavior, which pertained to his main priority."[27] On intelligence tests, Elliot showed as unimpaired. Even the cognitive tasks (sorting, and so on) that are often used to test frontal lobe damage were a breeze to him. Standard IQ tests revealed a superior intellect. Two things were out of order: his emotions, and his capacities for setting priorities and making decisions. Emotionally, he lacked all sense that something was at stake for him in the events he could coolly narrate. "He was always controlled, always describing scenes as a dispassionate, uninvolved spectator. Nowhere was there a sense of his own suffering, even though he was the protagonist. . . . He seemed to approach life on the same neutral note."[28] Damasio's idea was that this failure—which clearly seemed connected with his brain damage (even Elliot himself could remember that he was different before) explained his decision-making failure. How can one set priorities well in life, if no one thing seems more important than any other? Even though Elliot could reason his way through a problem, he lacked the kind of engagement that would give him a sense of what to do.[29]

Damasio's research confirms the work of Lazarus and other cognitive psychologists: emotions provide the animal (in this case human) with a map of how the world relates to its own set of goals and projects. Without that sense, decision-making and action are derailed. Damasio suggests further that these operations have their seat in a specific region of the frontal lobe, the region that was known to have been affected in Elliot's operation, and which a colleague of Damasio's has reconstructed as the likely site of Phineas Gage's brain damage. Such conclusions are extremely interesting. They do not suggest in any way that emotions are non-intentional physiological processes: indeed, the whole thrust of Damasio's argument is strongly anti-reductionistic. All cognitive processes have their roots in brain function, and this does not mean that we should think of them as noncognitive feelings. The point Damasio makes is that the same is true of emotions: they help us sort out the relationship between ourselves and the world. But the fact that the healthy functioning of a particular area of the brain is necessary for these processes is relevant and very interesting, though we would need to inform ourselves about each species, especially in creatures like birds who have a very different neuroanatomy.

These are the conclusions de Waal is talking about. As he rightly says, these and related studies have reoriented scientists' attitudes to emotion and animal intelligence. Indeed, de Waal ends up concluding that although it is clear that most animals do have feelings of many sorts, we know much less about their feelings than we do about their emotions, since emotions, being securely tethered to the world and to action, and being parts of the animal's intelligent equipment for life, are as accessible as beliefs are, as part of the explanation of an animal's behavior, whereas feelings, though there, are often more elusive: what it actually feels like, subjectively, to be this or that type of animal is always going to remain somewhat mysterious, though the feeling of pain is very likely an exception. Emotions typically feel like something, but there is little constancy in these feelings, even within a species. Sometimes, too, emotions are internalized and not part of conscious awareness, as with a fear of death that guides our actions all the time but is rarely noticed, and certainly not always accompanied by trembling or shaking.

SENTIENCE AND STRIVING

Now we're in a position to sketch the life of the sort of creature our theory of justice has in mind: a life of *significant striving*. Two more ingredients are required: *desire*, and *movement from place to place*. (These were already insisted on by Aristotle.) Perception and subjective feelings, including those of pleasure and pain, plus the information about the good conveyed in emotions, inform the animal about where benefit and harm are to be found. This in turn triggers pro-desire or aversion, which typically, other things equal, triggers movement toward or away. Some aspects of sentience, particularly pain and pleasure, are usually conceptually linked to desires and action tendencies, and emotions are very tightly so linked. Desire and emotion are coextensive with perception whenever the animal moves from place to place in search of its goals. Fear does not guarantee movement away, since other emotional factors (for example, love of offspring) might intervene. And some emotions have only unclear and highly general action tendencies: love and compassion often lead to helping behavior, but the connection to action may be broken by distance, or lack of a clear way forward. That is why Aristotle's "practical syllogism" for animals always includes a step that he calls a "premise of the possible": such as "here's (something to) drink."[30] Something, in other words, that presents itself as a way forward in the present circumstance. To the extent that an animal is capable of planning, the step may be just the first step in a chain that leads to the good result in the end. For example, those corvids who hide their food in such a way as to deceive other corvids, using their own experience of having been robbed as a guide, hide the food as an intermediate step to enjoying it later, in a world of competition.

These abilities all go tightly together, but not exceptionlessly. I've said that there are creatures who have nociception without sentience. (We'll soon come back to this.) These creatures do move from place to place, but they don't have subjective perception, emotions, or desires (a form of subjectivity). Then there are other creatures who appear to move to and away from things without having the physical equipment for nociception (cartilaginous fish). And some creatures (the ones that Aristotle called "stationary animals," sponges, anemones, etc.) may possibly have some ability to avoid the harmful without either sentience or whole-body movement from place to place. These hard cases will concern us later. I am claiming that a necessary and sufficient condition for being a subject of a theory of justice is the possession of what I can call the "standard animal package": sentience, emotion, cognitive awareness of objects, movement toward the good and away from the bad. To such creatures the world is endowed with meaning: things are experienced subjectively as relevant to their well-being. They are responsive to the good as good and averse to the bad as bad. Here we come back to the great truth in Utilitarianism: there is a dividing line in nature created by sentience, the great uniter of the animals. We need, however, to couch this truth in a broader way: it isn't just the ability to feel pain (and pleasure), but also the ability to have subjective perceptual experiences of many types, emotional experiences, and the cognitive awareness of good and bad: the whole of what I've called the "standard package."

Suppose we found a creature who pursues a species-typical form of life, moving toward the good and away from the bad, but who had lost (or who never had) the ability to feel pain and pleasure (perhaps through some damage to its sympathetic nervous system). Does this creature fall under my theory of justice or not? Would we be committing injustice by doing to this creature what would normally be painful? (Tye describes an actual case of a girl born without the ability to feel pain.[31]) First, in my theory, pain is a threshold, but not the only thing that matters, and this maimed creature is very different from a creature whose whole form of life involves non-sentient robotic movement. Pain is not the only form of sentience (the world seeming a certain way to the creature), although it is an especially conspicuous form, and for this reason easy to focus on when doing experiments. Sentience is subjective awareness, and this comes in many varieties, including subjective visual, auditory, and other sensory awareness. The imagined creature is injured, and given that its form of life would typically include pain-sentience, it is likely to be very short-lived. Pain is useful, indeed crucial for the creatures who have it. This creature will have to be constantly on guard lest it be cut, burned, and so forth. But that means that to live for even a day, it must have some type of sentience in my enlarged sense, even if not the ability to feel pain: perceptual awareness above all. It must watch its limbs with subjectively registering perception, and be constantly aware of them. Even if some of its senses are damaged, then, in this case the sense of touch, it is sentient. Helen Keller could not see or hear, but she was keenly sensitive to touch, and used that sense to stay alive and to communicate. So this creature, sort of an inverse of Helen Keller, is a subject of justice, albeit an unfortunate and highly vulnerable one. The theory is about the whole form of life, not (as for Bentham) about pain as the only thing that matters. If we find striving and subjective awareness of some type, however handicapped, then the creature is sentient. Such atypical cases can be dealt with on a case-by-case basis, but we should typically go by expected normal species traits when setting forth our idea of the threshold of the theory of justice. The goal of the theory is to protect individuals, but epistemically the species is where we are best equipped to begin.

This brings us to another important observation. For a creature to have a flourishing life, it needs to have, insofar as possible, the abilities that enable it to be part of its own species community. It is there that it will have friendship and community, offspring and family, if at all—even though for some creatures, such as dogs, the relevant community also includes members of another species. This is why it's so crucial to teach human children with cognitive disabilities to use some type of language, often sign language, but not important to teach chimpanzees to use sign language. They can learn it, but it plays no role in its form of life with other chimpanzees. When, then, we encounter disability in another species, it is similarly important to try as hard as we can to bring the disabled creature in touch with the characteristic abilities of its species community, whether individually or by some type of extra assistance. For example, a German shepherd with hip dysplasia can have a good life with a special wheelchair for the rear limbs. There are countless similar cases, where the life can be relatively whole with supplementation. (In the case of dogs, whose community prominently includes humans, supplementation is important for membership in that larger community, not just the community of dogs.) So for my hypothetical creature who can't feel pain (apparently there are around a hundred humans in the world with this defect), it would be important to ask what form of life can be imagined to remedy the disability. If there is none, then the creature's deficiencies will have to be made up for by watchful surrogates. So: epistemically we build the theory of justice around the species norm, then we try to extend justice to every species member.

As we do this we should always bear in mind that a wide range of creatures learn their abilities through teaching within the species group culture, not just through inheritance (see chapter 4). A general tendency may be inherited, but its specific realization often depends on cultural learning, one reason why the presence of a representative species group is so essential for animal flourishing.

Significant striving, then, includes subjective perception of things that are helpful and harmful (the world looks like this to the animal), plus a variety of subjective attitudes, such as pain and pleasure, and, in addition, numerous other subjective states that motivate behavior: desires and emotions. The sentient animals we are describing have all of these abilities. Now we must ask what difference this makes for a theory of justice.

CREATURES AND THE WORKING BOUNDARY

Where, then, do we draw the line, where justice is concerned? Which creatures are included, and which does our current evidence seem to exclude? First of all, we must always keep our eyes and minds open, drawing the line humbly and tentatively, aware that our knowledge is highly incomplete. The theory about what a creature must be like to receive justice is far more secure than are specific conclusions about which creatures are in this group. Still, it is worth applying the general theory, to give a general sense of where it leads us. I leave mammals to one side, since it is obvious by now, given scientific consensus, that my theory of justice includes them all.

Fish

Fish, as we've seen, are definitely sentient creatures, and, beyond that, creatures of striving and flourishing, creatures to whom my theory applies. This has been demonstrated to the satisfaction of the vast majority of scientists, and to my own. There is a great deal more to say about fish, and readers will find it accessibly retold in biologist Jonathan Balcombe's book, *What a Fish Knows*. They are capable of surprising feats of intelligence, including transitive inference.[32] They have a variety of sophisticated modes of sensing the world, including keen sight, hearing, and smell—and these also register subjectively, as we know from experiments showing that fish are fooled by optical illusions.[33] They even have a sense we lack: an ability to sense objects through electrical waves. They are capable of many emotions, including fear and joy, probably some variety of love. They have a rich social life, including pair-bonding. In short, they have very complicated and fascinating lives, and seem to deserve our concern and restraint every bit as much as the mammals do. As Braithwaite puts it: "Given all this, I see no reason why we should not extend to fish the same welfare considerations that we currently extend to birds and mammals."[34] It is exhilarating to learn a great deal more about these remarkable members of our world.

So far I have been speaking, as do Braithwaite and Balcombe, of "bony" or "teleost" fish, which comprise about 96 percent of the species we know. A very different story should be told about cartilaginous or "elasmobranch" fish, which include sharks and stingrays.[35] These creatures are historically far removed from the teleosts: the two groups diverged way back in the Devonian and Cretaceous periods. So although people run the two groups together mentally and call both "fish," they are extremely different in all respects. Because there is no evidence that elasmobranch fish have an anatomy sufficient for nociception—they have "a general lack of nociceptive receptors"[36]—there is good reason to conclude that they are not sentient. One consequence is that they feed on species that are in fact noxious: they are found with dozens of stingray barbs in their mouths. They do wriggle and try to get away when movement is interfered with, but as we'll see, this is true of many creatures who give no evidence of sentience. And they continue undisturbed at their feeding even when severed in two, behavior we do not find in sentient creatures. As Tye concludes, "For elasmobranchs, so far as I am aware, there is *no* behavior, the best explanation of which is that they feel pain."[37]

Birds

Fish sentience continues to be debated, though a clear consensus is emerging. The sentience of birds is no longer in doubt. This was not always the case. Until very recently, the small size of bird brains and their lack of a neocortex led to a widespread view that birds were "lovely automata capable only of stereotyped activity."[38] Since the 1990s, particularly, our knowledge of birds has grown rapidly, as "[c]omplex cognitive concepts, such as planning for the future or theory-of-mind, were translated into carefully controlled tests. The results have been eye-opening, and hard to disavow by skeptics due to the rigor of the experiments."[39] Indeed, de Waal continues, it is our knowledge of the highly sophisticated and flexible intelligence of birds that has, more than any other field of animal studies, revolutionized science's overall picture of intelligence:

> We used to think in terms of a linear ladder of intelligence with human on top, but nowadays we realize it is more like a bush with lots of different branches, in which each species evolves the mental powers it needs to survive.[40]

For a long time, understanding was impeded by a blinkered view of anatomy: no neocortex, no or very little intelligence. As scientist William Thorpe already summarized in 1963, "There is no doubt that this pre-conceived notion, based on a misconceived view of brain mechanisms, hindered the development of experimental studies of bird learning."[41] By now, a close look at birds' proverbially weak brains shows that those brains are actually rich in neurons, and that through convergent evolution the bird brain organizes them differently, in clusters rather than layers; but the cells themselves are "basically the same, capable of rapid and re-petitive firing, and the way they function is equally sophisticated, flexible, and inventive."[42]

Equally revolutionary, toppling old stereotypes, has been the study of bird behavior. We now know that birds possess great adaptability to their environment, and a wide range of highly developed capacities. This knowledge has been the fruit of work by a large number of scientists, each group specializing, typically, in one species or group of species. Parrots and corvids have been shown to have exceptional conceptual intelligence and flexibility. Corvids use, and make, tools better than most any other non-human animal.[43] Parrots, as has been memorably shown by Irene Pepperberg in her initially mocked but by now heralded experiments with Alex, a gray parrot, turn out to have wide-ranging and sophisticated minds.[44] At every turn, Pepperberg's experiments were scoffed at by peo-ple who were determined that "only humans can do X." But by now the rigor of her work, combined with similar work by others on parrots and corvids, has silenced the skepticism.

Where language and expression are concerned, it isn't just parrots who have linguistic talents. It turns out that birdsong is not just lovely, it is also a highly intelligent system of communication. In many species, song is endlessly rehearsed—even when birds are alone they are practicing—and individual differences in fluency are appreciated by other (especially female) birds. Birds have an anatomy that would be the envy of many human singers: the syrinx, the bird analogue of our larynx, can sound two notes at one time. So birdsong involves complicated aesthetic capacities, but it also has combinatorial powers akin to language, in at least some species. The calls of the chickadee, for example, have been ranked "one of the most sophisticated and exacting systems of communication of any land animal," complete with a syntax that can generate an open-ended number of call types.[45]

Language is part of social interaction, and birds are among the most sophisticated social animals, forming long-lasting pair-bonds (80 percent of species are monogamous) and teaching a wide range of behaviors to their young, a striking instance of cultural learning. Feeding nestlings is taxing, requiring intense parental communication and attention. Equally impressive is the attention some species devote to aesthetic matters in constructing their dwellings: the bowerbird is an extraordinary artist. Magpies pass the mirror test, showing especially keen awareness of self and other, while corvids in general excel in reciprocity accompanied by gift giving.[46] In the process, birds clearly experience a wide range of emotions, including fear, but also love and grief. And they not only feel their own pain, they are keenly sensitive to the pain of others of their kind.[47]

Equally impressive are abilities that are difficult to compare at all to human abilities, especially the marvelous powers birds have to map their spatial location, partly by sight (birds have the most advanced visual system of any vertebrate, particularly sensitive to color distinctions), and partly by smell. Birds thus find their way to and from distant destinations, an ability in which they so surpass humans that the operations of the bird GPS system are still poorly understood.[48]

I've spent this much time on birds because the error of anatomical analogy is tenacious, and many people still think birds are stupid and couldn't possibly be sentient. But where striving is concerned, these fragile and relatively weak creatures are among the most successful strivers, with keen senses and a flexible form of life that has enabled them to flourish, each sort, in its own environment.

Reptiles

Reptiles are related to birds (birds descend from dinosaurs), although birds at some point became warm-blooded and reptiles remain cold-blooded. Like birds, they lack a neocortex. Their behavior shows far less flexibility and sophistication. Although both behavior and neuroanatomy have been less studied by scientists, both behavior and physiology suggest that they are probably sentient, undergoing not just pain but other sensory experiences (although their different sensory modalities seem unconnected from one another, as is not the case in birds). At least the hypothesis of sentience is probably to be preferred to the opposite, when explaining their behavior.[49]

Cephalopods

Now we turn to invertebrates, entering a realm of considerable uncertainty and debate. Among these, the cephalopods (squid, cuttlefish, octopuses) are the strongest candidates for sentience. Octopuses can learn to open a child-proof cap that is designed to thwart human children. Peter Godfrey-Smith's detailed study of this whole group of creatures presents a powerful argument that they have a sentient internal life, and mainstream scientists such as Braithwaite are, though hesitant, inclined to agree with that conclusion.[50] Godfrey-Smith (a philosopher of science) concludes that this group is "an island of mental complexity in the sea of invertebrate animals . . . an independent experiment in the evolution of large brains and complex behavior."[51] Having once had protective shells and then at some point having lost them, octopuses were enormously vulnerable, and developed very large and complex brains to survive. Godfrey-Smith points out that a typical octopus brain contains a number of neurons comparable to those in the brain of a dog or a young human child. But these neurons are dispersed throughout its entire body, making the octopus sentient all over and giving its limbs a remarkable degree of agency and independence. And they don't just rise to the challenges of their environment, they manipulate it: for example, by squirting water at laboratory light bulbs to make them go out. (They dislike light.) Studying fish made researchers understand that there can be sentience without a neocortex; studying the octopus has made them realize that there can be sentience in the invertebrate world, though among scientists the jury is still out.[52]

Crustaceans

With crustaceans (shrimp, crabs, lobsters) things are not clear-cut, although emerging knowledge has led to a reaction against the common practice of dropping lobsters alive into boiling water. Experiments with hermit crabs, in particular, have led scientists at least to debate whether they feel pain. Here's what happened in Belfast scientist Robert Elwood's experiments.[53] Hermit crab shells were rigged up to an electricity source that delivered small shocks to the crabs. Their reaction was to abandon the shells, even if no empty shell was currently available—unusual behavior, suggesting that the pain was unpleasant, since the crabs were making themselves highly vulnerable. (Hermit crabs use empty snail shells and often change shells.) The shocked crabs demonstrated altered behavior even when the shock was no longer present, showing, it would seem, a memory of the unpleasant experience lasting at least twenty seconds. Elwood concluded that the crabs feel pain and also remember it, something that other scientists and even Tye, who interprets behavior in a generous light, still doubt. Elwood has certainly shown that crabs and shrimp have more intelligence than we had previously thought. And we have been wrong about sentience before. Here, however, partly for anatomical reasons (crustaceans have many, many fewer neurons than cephalopods and even than honey bees), we still cannot reach a definite conclusion. We should probably err on the side of caution while we try to learn more.

Insects

Insect brains have considerable isomorphism in structure with mammal brains, and some insects (honey bees) have an impressively large number of neurons. The bee brain contains around one million neurons; given its small size, neural density is ten times greater than a mammal's cerebral cortex. Anatomically, then, sentience is not impossible.[54] On the other hand, insect behavior is in some key respects very unlike mammal behavior. Insects do not protect injured parts. They continue to feed even when severely injured: tsetse flies, for example, feed when dismembered, and locusts continue to feed while being eaten by mantises. Insects in general do not react to stimuli that would be very painful to mammals. So there are reasons to doubt that insects feel pain. Bees seem to be an exception to this rule, displaying avoidance learning.

More generally, the case of bees suggests that we need to learn more. It appears that experiments can induce in them a state approximating anxiety or fear. The bees were strapped into harnesses that made them immobile. They then learned to associate one odor with a pleasant taste (sugar) and another with an unpleasant taste (quinine). Once this association was established, the bees typically extended their mouths on smelling the smell indicative of good things, and retracted their mouths when they smelled the "ominous" odor. They were then divided into two groups. One group was violently shaken (the way a hive might be shaken by a badger). The other was not. The experimenters made use of the general truth that anxious subjects are pessimistic, expecting bad things, whereas non-anxious subjects are more optimistic. When presented with in-between odors, the shaken bees were much less likely to extend their mouths to try them than the unshaken bees. It seems that they interpreted the ambiguous stimulus more negatively. It does seem that they were in a state rather like a state of anxiety, inducing a pessimistic cognitive bias. But do they really feel this subjectively? The experimenters argue that this has been established as securely as it has for rats and other mammals. There is room for caution. For example, it is possible that the shaking simply caused a decrease in the shaken bees' abilities to discern odors generally.[55] The experiments, though highly suggestive, seem less conclusive than Braithwaite's and Sneddon's experiments with fish. But, given that bee anatomy at least permits sentience, and that bee behavior in general does not rule it out, we should probably continue to debate whether bees are sentient.

Aristotle's "Stationary Animals": Cnidarians (corals, jellyfish, sea anemones), and Porifera (sponges)

Ever since Aristotle, scientists have classified certain rather plantlike creatures as not plants, but animals. By "rather plantlike," I mean fixed, not moving from place to place. Aristotle referred to as "stationary animals" a group of creatures that we would now call Cnidarians (corals, jellyfish, sea anemones) and Porifera (sponges). Some (jellyfish) actually do move, but in general they don't exhibit the type of goal-directed movement toward an object of desire that my model urges us to look for. Cnidarians have no brains and no central nervous system, but they do have nets of neural tissue that seem to play a perceptual role. And they live, reproduce (sexually), and die as individual entities. Thus, scientists today agree with Aristotle that they have the sense of touch and are not merely tropistic entities like plants. Porifera are simpler entities, and branched off from the common ancestor of all Animalia before all the others. Sponges have no nervous systems at all, but they do have neurons and they do coordinate their activities, and they do reproduce, live, and die as individuals, thus making them animals rather than plants. However, none of these creatures seem at all likely to have sentience.

WHAT ABOUT PLANTS?

Where animals are concerned, I've laid out some general criteria for having interests grounded in justice, and I've tried to draw some conclusions about which types of animals meet these conditions. Line-drawing should always be tentative, and we should be more definite about the general criteria than about who meets them, given the incompleteness of our knowledge. But I have spoken throughout of animals, implicitly omitting plants from the theory of justice. Many people would disagree. I must now confront this issue.

Plants are clearly what we might call teleonomic systems. That is, they are organized forms of functioning that for the most part work to sustain life and also to reproduce. Those are basic functions of the living, and plants are indubitably alive. Minerals and other substances obey definite laws in their motions, but plants are self-nourishing and self-propagating and minerals are not. Plants have this in common with animals. And their behavior is lawlike: that is, we can predict that in a variety of situations, plants will do what it takes to remain alive and flourish, and to reproduce their species.

Throughout history there have been debates about whether plants are sentient. Aristotle denied this, distinguishing them even from those "stationary animals," sponges and anemones, which seemed to him to exercise rudimentary forms of perception, touch in particular, although they lacked the distance senses, hearing, sight, and smell, which are crucial to the life-functions of animals who move from place to place to get what they need. But this boundary between plants and stationary animals is difficult to defend: Doesn't a Venus flytrap sense its prey? Don't all plants sense heat and cold, light and darkness?

Some distinguished botanists have held that plants not only perceive, but have what I've called sentience. In his great work on animal ethics, the Greek Platonist Porphyry (see chapter 2) denied this: unlike animals, he said, plants are not owed justice because they do not experience pain and fear. But some eminent modern botanists drew the opposite conclusion. Darwin's grandfather, Erasmus Darwin, did experiments with plants, around 1800, that convinced him that they felt both pain and "irritability."[56] In the mid-nineteenth century, German biologist Gustav Fechner argued that plants have emotions, since it seemed that talking to them could improve their health and growth. And the great Indian botanist Jagadish Chandra Bose (1858–1937) contended that plants have something like a nervous system. Bose developed an instrument that he called a crescograph, to record the minute movements of plants.[57] He established that plants are minutely sensitive to many external stimuli, including heat, cold, light, and noise. By showing how flexible and intense these reactions were, he sought to convince people that plants have subjective feelings, including the feeling of pain. Bose was no crank; his achievements garnered him a knighthood, and he was greatly respected. But did he succeed in establishing sentience, or only a weaker conclusion? A further problem is that scientists have not been able to replicate his findings.[58]

Recently there is a group of scientists who call themselves "plant neurobiologists," who study information networks in plants, comparing them to animal nervous systems.[59] They have been strongly criticized by a group of leading botanists, who co-authored a letter in 2007 saying that their conclusions are "founded on superficial analogies and questionable extrapolations."[60] Their experiments show that plants transmit information about the intensity and even the color of light to other plants through electrical signals. But these cascading reactions do not constitute sufficient evidence of sentience or cognitive appraisal.

Despite these intriguing pieces of evidence that plants are far more sensitive to external conditions than we may have thought, there are several reasons why it seems implausible to ascribe sentience to them. Let's start with *neuroanatomy*. Plants do not have brains. They also don't have anything like a central nervous system, specialized networks of cells that perform the function of signaling. We should be cautious, remembering that we were wrong about birds and fish: a neocortex is not necessary for sentience. Still, those creatures do have a recognizable central nervous organization, even if different from that of mammals.

What about *behavior*? Given the lack of structural similarity between plants and animals, we should be very hesitant about *inference to the best explanation*, asking whether there are other ways of explaining the admittedly responsive reactions that are observed. And it appears that there are. Plants are rigid and tropistic. Their roots grow in the direction of gravity, exhibiting *geotropism*. They also exhibit *phototropism*, turning to the light.

They have seasonal rhythms. But these are fixed and inflexible, built into their species nature. Tropism is like animal behavior in one way: it is life-sustaining and self-nourishing behavior. But it lacks the sort of situational flexibility that makes us conclude that fish are sentient creatures. Nothing like the Braithwaite experiments, which pretty clearly show subjective feelings as key determinants of behavior, exists for plants. Without this it is difficult to think of them as *intending* anything, *striving* for a good life.

Nor do plants exhibit the sort of individual variation in reactions, the flexible agency, that is characteristic of fish and birds: you can be sure they will behave as their species behaves.

Plants, moreover, are not individual creatures at all. Animals are born one by one and die one by one. During life they are demarcated from one another. However much they respond to one another, one animal does not feel the pain of another, and the food that one eats does not nourish another (apart from the gestational period). The evident fact that they are, as Aristotle puts it, "one in number" is a large part of what underlies our strong intuition that what happens to *each* matters, that *each* should be treated as an end. When philosophers propose—and both Utilitarians and Buddhists have proposed—that pleasure and pain form a single system, and that our task is to maximize the former and minimize the latter, this runs afoul of our very basic ethical intuition that each life is the only life some creature will ever have, and that each life has its own significance. I have already invoked this intuition in arguing that for ethics, it is the individual creature that is the end, not the species. But plants are not individuals in this sense. It is impossible to say clearly when a plant is born or dies: cuttings, splicings, rooting of seedlings, the seasonal rebirth of flowers from bulbs, all these normal practices and events show us that a plant is basically a cluster entity, a *they*, rather than an *it*. Even when we are deeply attached to a particular tree, we cannot be sure what it is for the tree to survive, if seeds or a cutting should take root. For plants, it seems important that the species be preserved, but I have argued that this is not an imperative of *justice*, but a different type of ethical concern, perhaps more like the type of concern we have for an ecosystem.

We can still have deep concern for the preservation of a tree, but it seems to me that it is different from the type of concern we have for an animal who has only one life to live, and when it ends (often with agonizing suffering), that's that.

I conclude that plants do not have entitlements based upon justice. They can be harmed, but not done an injustice. Ethical concern of some sort still seems essential. The natural environment has ethical importance, both instrumental (it supports the capabilities of a sentient creature) and intrinsic; we have ethical duties to attend to it. (In general, I avoid the term "moral status" in this book, because I think moral status is not a single thing, and I am talking about a very particular thing, justice.) But these are not the type of duties we have to a creature who is born, tries to live well, suffers, and dies.

ETHICAL CONSEQUENCES

I have argued that creatures of surprisingly varied types have a place in the theory of justice, and that we should keep an open mind about others, since our knowledge is incomplete. This suggests that our duties are huge, stifling even. How can we face up to them? But let's remember that the justice-membership of a creature does not yet tell us *what* it is owed. There is no ladder of nature. Creatures strive for flourishing in manifold ways that don't line up to be graded on a single scale, and complexity of life does not determine justice-eligibility. Level and complexity of life, however, do determine precisely *what* is a harm to a justice-eligible creature. Human beings are not *better* or *higher* than dolphins; but there are things that are serious harms and wrongs to a human being that would not be wrongs to a dolphin: for example, the denial of an education conferring basic literacy. On the other hand, the ability to swim unfettered through large tracts of water is a key ability in the life-forms of fish and marine mammals, but to deprive humans of a chance to swim for endless miles is no injustice. And so forth.

When we consider justice and injustice, in short, we need to bear in mind the form of life of each creature. The goal is that each creature gets a decent chance to flourish in its own way. When we humans impede that flourishing—and we are omnipresent in these lives, since we control the earth, the seas, even the skies—we need to correct our overweening ways.

One thing we can say for sure—the great truth in Utilitarianism—is that pain is very bad for all sentient beings. So its wanton infliction (infliction that does not further the animal's own good) is always, in my theory, an injustice for sentient creatures. In my next chapter, I'll argue that whether a painless death is a harm to a creature depends on some specific factors about its form of life. If death is not even a harm, it is likely that it is not an injustice. In chapters 9 and 10, I will ponder, similarly, the issue of confinement, concluding that it is sometimes an injustice and sometimes not. And in chapter 8, I will consider cases where we currently commit injustice for weighty human reasons—but may be able to transcend those dilemmas through new scientific and medical possibilities. Once we digest these arguments, the demands of my theory may look like requirements that serious and sensitive human beings could live with, or at least strive to fulfill more and more adequately as time goes on.

7

THE HARM OF DEATH

What should we think about the genuinely painless death of an animal who has lived a decently rich life for a reasonable length of time? Is such a death a harm to the animal? And is it ethically permissible for us to cause it?

Bentham thought that killing an animal humanely (painlessly) is morally acceptable, if for some "useful" human purpose and not merely "wantonly"—either sadistically or for amusement. Recent Utilitarians such as R. M. Hare and Peter Singer basically concur, thus making room for at least some animal killing as ethically acceptable, although their arguments condemn most meat eating in today's world, grounded as it is in the pain-inflicting practices of the factory farming industry. Many theorists in many eras—from ancient Hindu, Buddhist, and Platonist thinkers to contemporary philosophers such as Christine Korsgaard and Tom Regan—have drawn a more radical line: it is always wrong to kill animals for human purposes. Killing for human use could be justified only if animals were rightly seen as the property of humans. They are not property, however; they are subjects of lives: so killing must stop. In this chapter, I will take a very uneasy position between these two groups (though closer to the second), showing where the Capabilities Approach leads us, when combined with a philosophical inquiry into the harm of death.

This issue is among the most urgent and difficult for any book on animal ethics. All too often, however, the issue is confronted with insufficient philosophical clarity. Death is not an easy topic. It is far from obvious why and under what circumstances death is bad for a creature, and if that is unclear it is also unclear when terminating a sentient life is harmful and even impermissible. My main objection to the second group is that they do not investigate this question sufficiently; I believe when we do, the answer is complicated. Let's step back and think hard about the harm of death—with some help from the history of philosophy. And let's not forget to distinguish two different things that might be bad: the process of dying, and the condition of being dead. Let's begin with humans, then extend our reflections to animals. Along the way, we'll see how the Capabilities Approach helps us zero in on the relevant questions.

Animals kill one another, and these killings also raise ethical issues for us, since in some cases we can intervene. However, I do not discuss those issues in this chapter; they await us in chapter 10, after we discuss the whole issue of "the wild" and our responsibilities for ethical stewardship in various domains. This chapter, then, focuses solely on what we humans do when we kill animals.

It is important to say at the start that with respect to current human practices, this chapter starts on the fringe. Most human killings of animals are not painless. Nor, even more important, do they follow a full, rich life. Animals raised for food in the factory farming industry have lives that are impaired and painful from the very start. In the introduction, I described the life of sows in gestation crates. In chapter 9, I'll describe the impaired lives of chickens and dairy cattle. I return to these issues in chapter 12, asking what law has done and must do about these practices. Here, then, I'm discussing the issue of mammals and fish humanely raised for food, which is a tiny minority of what takes place all over the world. I dwell on this fringe issue because it is genuinely complicated from the ethical viewpoint, whereas the horrors of the factory farming industry are not complicated, and should be condemned by all ethically sensitive people.

Another related issue I discuss elsewhere is the decision of a companion of a dog or cat to terminate that creature's life. In chapter 9, I claim that when such a choice is ethical it is because the human being knows the animal well, understands its form of life, and responds to indications from the animal that its current diminished existence is intolerably painful or shameful. When humans terminate the life of a companion animal for the sake of their own convenience, or because they don't feel like paying for medical treatment, this is always wrong, just as it would be wrong to terminate the life of a disabled child or elderly relative because it is too inconvenient or too expensive to provide care. Here, then, I discuss only cases where the animal life is reasonably healthy—which, for obvious reasons, is usually the case with animals whom we kill for food—although the animals killed in the factory farm industry are hardly truly thriving.

I begin with a problem about death that has long plagued philosophers thinking about human life. We need to see this problem as clearly as we can in the human case before we approach animal lives, where ethical debates are so much less developed.

"DEATH IS NOTHING TO US"

The fear of death causes a lot of pain in human lives—sometimes consciously, sometimes through a background sense of heaviness and discontent. So thought the radical fourth-century BCE Greek philosopher Epicurus (341–270 BCE), and he is at least partly right. Even if this fear does not produce all the evils that he, and his Roman disciple Lucretius (c. 99–c. 55 BCE), associated with it, including envy, war, sexual violence, herdlike submissiveness to religious authorities, even premature suicide, it is at any rate pretty troublesome. But Epicurus believed that there is no good reason for fearing death: death does not harm us. He put his view in this pithy way: "Death, that most terrifying of evils, is nothing to us. For when we are there, death is not; and when death is there, we are not."[1]

Epicurus does not deny that the process of dying is often painful. He left a deathbed letter describing his own excruciating pain from dysentery and urinary obstruction. He thought, however, that this pain could be counterbalanced by pleasures of friendship and memory that he continued to exercise even then: so he claimed to have a net balance of pleasure over pain on his deathbed. That, however, is not his big issue: he is talking about the badness of having ended one's life, of being dead.

Here's how we can reconstruct his argument:

1. An event can be good or bad for someone only if, at the time when the event is present, that person exists as a subject of at least possible experience.
2. The time after a person dies is a time at which that person does not exist as a subject of possible experience.
3. Hence the condition of being dead is not bad for that person.
4. It is irrational to fear a future event unless that event, when it comes, will be bad for one.
5. It is irrational to fear death.

Notice that the argument works with a notion of possible, not actual experience. Epicurus is not saying, "What you don't feel can't be bad for you," an obviously unconvincing claim, since many things that happen out of our immediate perceptual field can be bad for us: deaths of loved ones, asymptomatic cancers, a fire burning through one's house while one sleeps in blissful ignorance. He is saying that if there is no "you" in the world at all, then there is nothing for the idea of badness or deprivation to attach to, or the idea of benefit, either.

Epicurus and Lucretius do not simply assume that there is no afterlife; in fact they argue for this conclusion at length, using their atomic theory of the person. This, however, needn't concern us. Their intended audience feared death largely, they opined, because of a fear of posthumous punishment. So getting rid of the afterlife disposed of most reasons to fear death, or so they thought. Today people who believe in an afterlife typically think that this possibility makes things better, not worse; what they fear is precisely that there is nothing after death. Consequently, arguing that there is no afterlife tends only to magnify the fear of nothingness most of us have anyway. (This was true of lots of people in the Greek and Roman world too, as we see from critiques of the Epicureans by their contemporaries.) And even people who believe in a happy afterlife still fear death as the end of life. This fear of nothingness, of the end, should be our focus. And since we are ultimately aiming at political and legal principles that can be broadly shared in pluralistic societies, we must not build them on any contentious hypothesis about an afterlife. So let's follow Epicurus in assuming that all possible individual experience ends at death, or at least that the issue of posthumous survival is one we have no right to rely on in framing political principles.

Epicurus's argument is extremely powerful. There are few arguments from Greco-Roman antiquity that recent philosophers have taken so seriously, and eagerly debated. It seems very counterintuitive, since most of us do think that in most circumstances (where the person is still functioning and does not have overwhelming pain) death is bad and harms the person. But, says Epicurus, how can that be, when there is no person for harm to attach to? Maybe we dread the loss of life's pleasures, but when the curtain has finally fallen, there is no loss, because there is no you. Lucretius vividly depicts the irrationality of most people, who imagine a little them attending their own funeral and witnessing themselves deprived of all the good things:

> So he feels sorry for himself: he fails
> To make the real distinction that exists
> Between his castoff body, and the man
> Who stands beside it, grieving, and imputes
> Some of his sentimental feelings to it.

We're just contradicting ourselves: we imagine we are still there, and yet the whole point of our grief is the fact that we are not still there.

Some philosophers try to defeat this powerful argument by pointing to cases in which we ought to concede that things we don't know about, and perhaps even can never know about, are admittedly bad for us.[2] Thus, a person who has been betrayed and never learns of this fact has still been harmed, or so some people think. A person who has lost all higher mental functioning in an accident and isn't aware of this as a diminished condition has still been harmed (and might even recover damages). We may even dream up cases in which it is impossible for the person ever to learn of the bad thing, and even in such cases, we still often think that a harm has befallen the person.[3]

Yes, but. All of these examples involve a persisting subject who has at least a strong claim to be the original person. The diminished person might sue for damages only because there is a plaintiff in the world. (If the accident put the person in a permanent vegetative condition, then we should probably doubt that there is actually a person in the world, and maybe our sense that the person has been harmed really does partake in Lucretian doublethink.) However, take the person out entirely, and things are very different: To what subject should we attach terms such as "bad" and "harmed"? So far, then, Epicurus and Lucretius are undefeated.

THE INTERRUPTION ARGUMENT: AND TWO FALSE CONSOLERS

It is no surprise, however, that there is more to say. We can now introduce what I have called the "interruption argument," an argument first introduced, I believe, by classical scholar David Furley, extended by me, and independently elaborated by philosopher Jeff McMahan.[4] This argument says that death often affects the shape of a life by interrupting projects that unfold over time, rendering them, in whole or in part, empty and vain. We pursue many things as preparation for later things: for example, studying for the LSAT, even going to law school, not as choice-worthy activities in themselves but as necessary preparations for a career as a lawyer. If death cuts us short in the preparatory stage, it renders those activities pointless. Much that younger adults do is of this nature. Death is bad because it alters, retrospectively, the intended shape of activities we undertake in life, rendering many of our actions empty and pointless.

Furley focused on deaths that are conventionally deemed premature, but in "The Damage of Death" I extended this argument to any death that interrupts activities that unfold over time. And I noted that a large proportion of human activities are like this: projects involving work, family life, friendship, and much more. People typically do not have a master plan, but they do have a series of projects that unfold over time, projects that can be interrupted. We could try not to invest ourselves in temporally extended projects, so as to avoid the risk that some of them will be rendered fruitless by death. In fact, this is what Epicurus and Lucretius recommend. (They think contemplation of the order of the universe is complete in a moment, for example.) But in that case we would be forfeiting a lot of human value: the unfolding shape of love and friendship, the intergenerational dynamics of family life, and many more mundane pursuits, such as planting a garden, starting to read a long novel, etc. And there is also the sheer pleasure of going on living, seeing what happens to one's plans and projects next. When the movie projector breaks down in the middle of a movie, you feel you have missed out on something. Death, similarly, cuts short the pleasant flow of life's many projects. We don't have to have a grand master plan in order to have a diverse range of projects we pursue over time. Even when our activities are repetitions of activities we have performed many times before, they derive thickness and meaning from memory, our awareness of repetition, and our desire to repeat again. This is why rituals are often so emotionally rich: they acquire more meaning from the fact that we recall, for example, when we have attended a Passover seder in the past, and how the same people have grown and changed. We are, in short, temporal beings, both swimming in a river of time and, at the same time, standing apart from any single moment to observe the sequence. (Marcel Proust captures this aspect of human time beautifully.) By the same token, when we don't repeat ourselves, but take up a new pursuit, the worth of the new derives meaning from the awareness that it *is* new, and this too is an aspect of our relationship to time.

Many or even most human deaths damage the person's life retroactively, then, by interrupting temporally extended projects. We know some people who seem to live differently, taking each moment as it comes; but this is unusual, and perhaps most commonly found at the end of a long life, when a person decides that it is time to wrap things up and not to undertake activities that involve planning and temporal flow. When my grandmother died at 104, after a healthy life, it seemed less bad, at least, than most human deaths—precisely because she did to a degree seek to wrap things up—although her love of daily projects (interacting with her family, caring for her fine furniture) still gave her life a temporally interruptible structure. Epicurus, then, builds his argument on an impoverished picture of human life and value. If we accept a richer and more realistic view, many or even most deaths are bad for the person who dies, not in the illogical way imagined by Lucretius, but in a perfectly straightforward way: they change the life that was lived, and for the worse.

The capabilities view and the interruption argument are allies. The CA emphasizes the way life-activities unfold over time and refuses to think of pleasure and pain as static and momentary, as Utilitarians typically do. Nor does the interruption argument establish a hierarchy, as the "So Like Us" approach does: its claims about interruption and harm are descriptive, and it does not claim that interruptible lives are nobler or better than other lives; here again it dovetails with the claims of the CA. The argument does not establish a ranking, but it does single out a characteristic feature of animal lives that render them vulnerable to harm in a very specific way. When a life contains a temporal unfolding of which the subject is aware and which the subject values, death can harm it. However, not all creatures have lives like that—though many more than Bentham thought—and therefore the argument does not establish that death is a harm to all creatures. I'll return to this important fact.

Some philosophers have tried to defend Epicurus's conclusion, if not his argument, by pointing to ways in which death can actually be good for people, by rounding out a life and preventing boredom and loss of meaning.[5] Bernard Williams argued that all human projects are bound to become meaningless and boring if extended indefinitely. Even though death may appear an interruption, then, it is better than what Williams dubbed "the tedium of immortality." He takes as his example Janáček's opera *The Makropulos Case*, in which singer E.M. at last deliberately ends her life at 341, by refusing her regular infusion of the immortality drug.[6] Williams reads her as having wearied of all the pursuits life offers, and argues that this is true of human desire in general. I think this is overreaching, based on an atypical case. As I pointed out in "The Damage of Death," Elina Makropulos got tired of life because she was repeatedly objectified and exploited by the men in her life. Her suicide shows not a necessary truth of human desire, but the fact that relations between the sexes need to change, or at least E.M. needs to meet some new men!

Another consoler whom, in "The Damage of Death," I called "Younger Martha," made a different argument to the same conclusion. In *The Therapy of Desire*, published in 1994, I said that death was a necessary condition for most sorts of human value, giving a kind of limit against which striving, sacrifice, and other good human pursuits have their point.[7] Taking as my slogan Wallace Stevens's poem "Sunday Morning," in which the poet concludes, "Death is the mother of beauty," I tried to argue that a life without death would necessarily lack love, friendship, the virtues, and even athletic excellence, in their usual human forms. I now think this argument was mistaken: what is needed for these pursuits to have their usual human worth is some sense of striving and resistance, but not necessarily death. We can easily imagine death removed while thinking that people will go on being able to exhibit courage, resistance to suffering, the ability to be generous and to sacrifice, etc. Given that eternal pain might be thought to be worse than death, the possibility of sacrifice might even increase. And because people like repetition and don't insist on a grand narrative structure, there is no reason to suppose that an end point is a necessary condition of most human value.

Philosophers have made much of the fact that humans often see their lives as having a narrative structure. Jeff McMahan sees this aspect of human life as making us more valuable than other animals, who, in his view, have no sense of narrative structure. (He hasn't considered the elaborate practices of many species surrounding birth and death, and he just says "animals" without showing curiosity about different species.) I have utterly rejected this ladder-of-being approach; narrative structure is our way of doing things (for some people anyway), but other species have their own ways, and ours would not be appropriate for most of them. However, thinking about narrative structure does sometimes help us think about when a human or animal death is bad for the creature, and to that extent Younger Martha has a point: for humans who care a lot about narrative structure, a death that rounds off the story is preferable, for example, to interruption, or a long decline, or perhaps even to immortal repetition. As I said, many people like repetition and find meaning in many different ways, so I think Younger Martha was wrong to impose this norm on all lives. Older Martha thinks that there are many ways to imagine an immortal life that would not be boring in the least. It would have the same lead character, so to speak, engaging in many different episodes, trying new careers, and so forth. But the lack of a single narrative arc does not render it boring or not worthwhile. It would be less like a novel by Jane Austen and more like the "loose and baggy monsters" of Tolstoy and Dostoyevsky, or the joyful embrace of the rituals of daily life we find in James Joyce. Still, for those who share Henry James's disdain for the "loose and baggy," considerations of narrative unity may help explain why, for those people, some deaths, including earlier deaths, are preferable to others. I can't help feeling that anyone with such an aesthetic is bound to find real human life unsatisfying, but since that is not my purpose here, I will not develop this point further.

In short: lives unfold in time, and for a creature highly conscious of time and who lives, as humans typically do, in both the past and the future as well as the present, death can be a harm by interrupting the temporal flow—although, as we just said, not always and not for all people. The Capabilities Approach gives us a way of looking at characteristic activities that supports these judgments, by asking us at all times to consider the creature's whole form of life, including its temporal shape. A focus on maximizing moment-to-moment happiness, by contrast, omits temporally extended projects. So far, then, our theory fits well with judgments we are inclined to make. It can give both temporality and narrative structure the weight that they have in human and many animal lives, and it can also do justice to the fact that many human and animal life-activities are not so grandiose, but are delightful, and valuably human, anyway.

ANIMALS WE KILL: UTILITARIAN ARGUMENTS AND BEYOND

Now to animal deaths. First, once again, we should emphatically reject the contention of some philosophers that narrative structure, or susceptibility to significant interruption by death, makes human lives better than other animal lives. But differences in species' relation to time do make a difference in what can be a harm for a creature. The fact that humans derive relatively little information about the world from the sense of smell means that the loss of smell (though at times a symptom of disease) is not in itself the huge loss it would be to most other animals, who depend on it greatly. The loss of hearing would be fatal to a whale, for whom it is the primary source of information about the world, whereas many humans live well without hearing. Let's now start thinking about the role of death in non-human animal lives.

As I've said, the case of companion animals is special, and will concern us in chapter 9. Here the animal's communications with a sensitive human companion convey a set of advanced directives, so to speak, indicating when and whether death is a harm. On the whole, our laws do not permit a human to opt in advance for physician-assisted suicide once flourishing living is no longer possible, but I think they probably should. If an animal is in a state of chronic pain and/or cognitive disability, most companions, reading the animal's signals, choose death, and that death, I think, is not a harm. Such deaths are chosen for the sake of the animal. If done with sensitivity, and not with ulterior motives (say, to get rid of an expensive burden of care, or to inherit a fortune), they are acceptable and not a harm.

All this is very far from what happens when we eat animals. (I'll use the food case as my central example, but much animal experimentation has the same problem.) Here we are usually not making a proxy judgment on behalf of the animal, we are pleasing ourselves and using the animal as means to our own ends. I have asked the reader to reject without further argument the factory farming industry, which gives all the animals involved painful and cramped lives without the exercise of characteristic life-activities, such as free movement, social relations, fresh air, and choices of how to spend one's day. Let's consider the best cases of humane farming, where the animal has a reasonably good life: good food, fresh air, the companionship of other animals, etc.—and then is killed in a genuinely painless manner.

Some animals we kill for food are very young animals, who have had no chance to unfold their characteristic form of life in mature functioning. It seems to me that the Capabilities Approach, even when supplemented by the interruption argument, requires us to reject those practices. The CA involves a sense of morally inflected wonder at the variety of forms of life in nature, and those lives exert a moral claim that they may be permitted to develop and unfold themselves. The transition from childhood to maturity is salient in all animal communities, and is part of the awareness of young creatures. It is reasonable to suppose that young creatures learn to seek maturity as a central goal. When that is not reached, they do suffer a grievous type of interruption.

But there are other cases, in which the humanely farmed animal has lived an adult life for a reasonable period of time. Nature does not appoint any particular span for any of us, and dying before illness and decline set in does not seem obviously repugnant. In the human case, I argued that such deaths are harms only because of the interruption argument. So we need to investigate further.

Bentham thought that non-human animals, unlike humans, do not fear death in advance. He rather hastily concluded that for this reason death is not a harm for non-human animals, if painless and not preceded by painful practices. He simply asserted the point about fear, without evidence, and it isn't correct: animals of many types recognize threats when they are at hand, and fear impending death as a result. Many plan their movements in order to avoid threats they either have experienced or have learned about from other animals. So his argument is unconvincing, and we should do better.[8]

Modern Utilitarians do somewhat better. Both Peter Singer and Jeff McMahan insist on the superior worth of human lives, alleging that only humans give a narrative structure to their lives. I have already rejected that factual claim, and I have also rejected the idea of superiority they draw from it. Even were it true that human lives and only human lives exhibit "narrative structure," that does not make human lives better, just different. We should also reject, as we did in chapter 3, these Utilitarians' commitment to a "container" model, according to which what is important about a life is the amount of pleasure or satisfaction it contains.[9] This picture, entailing that one life might in principle be replaced by another that contained a similar amount of pleasure, does not do justice to the integrated living of lives: we, and other animals as well, are not bottles into which pleasures flow, we are agents pursuing goals, and each is valuable in its own right. John Stuart Mill understood this point and modified Utilitarianism to make room for the separateness and dignity of lives. So let us consider from now on a type of Utilitarianism that agrees with Mill on this point.

However, recent Utilitarians also employ a version of the interruption argument, and here we may cautiously follow them. What does this argument actually show for the question of whether, and when, death is a harm for a variety of non-human animals? Death is clearly a harm, as I've said, if it comes too early, interrupting development before adult functioning is reached, when a creature is aware of that development. It is also a harm to the extent that the animal pursues temporally extended projects, or even repeated projects with memory and awareness of repetition. Singer and McMahan seem to think this true of only a small number of species (apes, whales, and elephants). But we should not follow them: we should learn from research. Temporally extended projects are clearly present in the lives of all primates, elephants, birds, rodents, cattle, pigs, marine mammals, dogs, cats, and horses. So death can be a harm for these creatures, and it would be wrong to inflict that harm. Few today eat dogs, cats, horses, elephants, apes, and rodents, but many eat whales, birds, pigs, and cattle.

We also recall that chapter 6 concluded that there are some animals who appear not to be sentient at all, or minimally so. This is true of the animals whom Aristotle called "stationary," i.e., sponges, anemones; also most or all insects; and possibly crustaceans—though emphatically not cephalopods. We do no harm to non-sentient creatures when we kill them, and since they do not feel pain we need not worry too much about the manner, although it is always a good wager to kill painlessly, since we may learn more and decide we were wrong, as we seem to be doing in the case of lobsters.

Another group of animals, who were of interest to Bentham, were those whom he called "pests," i.e., animals who constantly attempt to harm us. Many of these (roaches, mosquitoes, flies) are insects anyway, but we should also put street rats (not lab rats) into this category. Here Bentham thought that killing was acceptable by a principle of self-defense, and I basically agree. However, most sensible self-defense statutes require the assailed to retreat first, before using deadly force. The analogue in this case would be for humans to use nonlethal means of self-defense, such as contraception, rather than killing, wherever they can. We already have such methods for insects, and for rats their use has recently been shown to be even more effective than lethal methods in reducing populations.[10]

We now get to the heart of the matter. The primary food animals are cattle, pigs, birds, and fish. (Lambs have already been struck off the list, with veal calves, by the adulthood principle.) Before we use the interruption argument, we ought to study the cognitive life of each animal. Pigs are extraordinarily intelligent, and clearly have a sense of temporal projects. Birds are marvelous and highly elaborate planners, so it seems to me utterly implausible that chickens would fail to possess this common avian capacity. Cattle too seem clearly above the "interruption" line. So even humane killing of these creatures inflicts a serious harm, and is wrong for that reason.

But it is plausible that there are some creatures, some types of fish perhaps, for which the interruption argument does not kick in. They live in a perpetual present with no prolonged projects to be interrupted, and they do not remember the routines they repeatedly execute. Research is not terribly clear on this point: if a type of fish lives in a perpetual present, then it seems wrong to impute temporal emotions, such as fear, to that fish, as some scientists do (see chapter 6). But it seems likely that fear has been prematurely ascribed on the basis of aversive behavior. All right, suppose we become convinced that there are such moment-to-moment creatures. Utilitarian philosopher R. M. Hare imagines a fish painlessly killed by a stun mallet expertly wielded by his local fishmonger.[11] This fish has been swimming around freely, having a good (adult) life until just before that moment. Fish authority Victoria Braithwaite describes "more humane" fisheries where such practices are used on a large scale. The morality of fish-eating is a complicated matter that I think is best left to the judgment of each individual, but Braithwaite records that she herself eats (humanely killed) fish.[12] For his part, Balcombe views the morality of fish-eating as a serious matter, and he abstains from consuming fish.[13] Hare judges that eating a fish killed in that way is morally acceptable. In a reply to Hare's article, Peter Singer agrees, although he says that he himself does not eat humanely killed fish because a public figure needs a much simpler policy.

If my argument is correct, death is not a harm for these creatures. Although intuitively we think of death as the ultimate thwarting of all striving, in this case it does not thwart the animal's projects, because there are no temporally extended projects to be thwarted. Epicurus is correct about these creatures, although he was wrong about humans and most animals. Fish are subjects of justice in that they can be wronged by the infliction of pain, by starvation, by painful deaths. But, if my argument is correct, they are not harmed by a painless death in the midst of a thriving life. Do we even need to wait until the fish reaches adulthood? Do they have any consciousness of maturity as a goal? It seems that they don't, if they really live in the moment. Still, one can imagine that a very young fish has a fleeting awareness of being small while other fish are big, so the case is unclear. Therefore it is always good to err on the side of caution and avoid killing baby fish.

For quite a few years, I have eaten fish around four times a week, though our increasing knowledge of their cognitive lives makes me have many qualms and doubts. The high protein needs of aging women, especially those like me with a high level of physical exercise, combined with my difficulty digesting lentils and beans, make it hard for me to transition to a totally vegan diet. By current calculations, a seventy-four-year-old woman weighing 115 pounds and with a high rate of physical activity needs between seventy and one hundred grams of protein per day. During the process of writing this book, I made a serious attempt to transition to a mostly vegetarian diet, eating fish only once or at most twice a week. That is not clearly morally better, since the dairy industry (I was eating a lot of yogurt) is less humane than a humane fish factory. I kept trying to transition toward lentils, but with bad digestive reactions. And I discovered by sheer chance that the dietary change had made me weaker. I had been attributing my athletic decline to "just aging." But by sheer chance, in May 2021, the leftovers of a meal served after my daughter's memorial service, including a large amount of halibut, an excellent protein source, were left with me. After eating halibut every day for a week, I discovered a sudden improvement in muscular function, and I am now back to the higher fish consumption.[14]

What should I think about this ethically? The interruption argument gives me something to say to myself, but I am not at ease. The argument could be wrong. Or it could be right, but be wrong about fish. It does not help that the alternative of a dairy-heavy vegetarian diet seems morally worse, given the suffering of animals in the dairy industry.

IN FAVOR OF MORAL DIFFICULTY

It currently seems likely that painless death is not a harm to fish in the way that it is for animals with different types of cognitive lives and projects.

Fish are usually killed as adults, and if they are happily swimming around and truly painlessly killed, one could maintain that death is not a harm to fish at all, although we must be open to new learning.

I am therefore inclined to say that people like me are not using fish only as means to our own ends, because they are not inflicting harm. It is not always wrong to use a person or creature as a means: I used my research assistants as means to improving my manuscript; I use doctors as means to keep my health good. The problem comes when we use a person as a *mere* means, meaning that we do not respect the person's dignity and harmfully exploit the person in various ways. I would be exploiting my research assistants, for example, if I bullied or harassed them, or failed to pay the promised wage. But if there is respect and no harm, I think we should conclude that the person is not being used as a *mere* means. In chapter 9, I will argue that shearing sheep for their wool is use, but not *mere* use: the sheep are not harmed and are usually even benefited. So the question is whether killing fish in order to eat them is that sort of non-harmful use, or a pernicious, harmful form of *mere* use.

In the sheep-shearing case, we can imagine a type of hypothetical consent, as in the case of the sensitively euthanized dog or cat. (*This wool is heavy and annoying; I consent to being relieved of it.*) But it is difficult to imagine the fish giving that type of tacit consent to being killed.

There are four moral problems I feel here. First, we are judge and jury in our own case, and the possibility of special pleading is always looming, as it has been throughout this chapter. Why did I focus as I do on the interruption argument? Why do I interpret the evidence about fish as I do? I try to be in good faith, but for good reasons we should be skeptical when there is such a blatant conflict of interest.

Second, the habit of instrumental use of sentient beings is a type of habit that can spread to cases where the interruption argument does not even putatively let us off the hook. If fish, why not humanely farmed meat from all sources? We dull our moral alertness at our peril.

Third, and a related issue: If fish for food, why not fishing for sport? One useful purpose is very like another, and if we argue that there is no harm, we may migrate out to approval of not just fishing but, who knows, hunting as well. Of course, I have stipulated that the death must be painless. That is never the case with line fishing and net fishing, but a revised form of these practices could be imagined. Hunting, if it is done by highly skilled shooters, can be painless, although most actual hunters are not highly skilled.

Fourth, there is the sheer brute fact of the instrumental use of another sentient being. Even if it doesn't actually harm the being, it is still a kind of domination over that other life. It claims an authority that seems unjustified. This is the truth in veganism. Who told us we could do this? I reject the vegan argument in the sheep-shearing case, but the case of eating fish remains unusually difficult. Don't our species-specific capacities for moral deliberation mean that we must be more cautious in this case, where so much is unknown? If the type of life and species-specific capacities affect what can be a harm to a sentient creature, so too do they affect what can be wrongdoing in a sentient creature. With our specific life-form comes responsibility.

ALTERNATIVES?

What can we do, what should we do, as we struggle with these complexities? First of all, we can grapple with them, which is progress. But agonizing does not make current conduct right. And we now face a familiar question in political thought: Should we be gradualists or revolutionaries? In other words, should we encourage ourselves and others to make many changes that will improve the lives of animals while not arriving at ethical blamelessness (as my argument has construed that goal)? Some people think of this sort of gradual improvement as an objectionable liberal "revisionism": nothing less than the full revolutionary change that we can imagine before us seems enough. In every movement for justice this debate has arisen. And it has different answers in different cases. It will surprise few readers of my work that I am at heart a liberal revisionist, but with a revolutionary streak.

Some evils, such as slavery, seem so abominable that only a complete, total, and sudden abolition seems morally acceptable. In this category I would place the factory food industry, the use of animals for fur, and the hunting of animals for sport. If we can't bring about abolition right away, we had better at least refuse to participate, right now, and totally.

Other evils appear different: once the conscience of humanity is aroused, we can work over time to change our culture and eventually to re-move the evil. Sexism seems to me such a case: it is so manifold, so deeply woven into the fabric of every society's daily life, that abolition at a stroke is not feasible, and refusing to participate in diseased institutions is likely to prove both personally difficult and counterproductive—although in the early days of feminism some separatist feminists tried this course. In this category I would place non-harmful killings of animals (by the interrup-tion argument) that are still instances of instrumental use and domination from which we ought to shrink. I do believe, then, that humane farming, at least for fish, is a big step forward, though not the final destination. Rather in the manner that many people try to reduce their carbon footprint, though unable, still, to go over to zero carbon, we can decrease gradually the extent to which our lives rely on these unsavory practices.

We must now put a further issue on the table: cost. At least at present, humanely sourced fish is pretty expensive, as also are free-range eggs. So by advocating a transition to that sort of diet, we are ignoring issues of class and economic capacity, the fact that this morally superior choice, and therefore the gradual transition I recommend, is available only with sacrifice to poorer families. (The same may also be true of a high-quality vegan diet, though it is difficult to do the necessary calculations.) If, as we often say in philosophy, ought entails can—that is, it can't be obligatory unless it is possible—it's not clear that we can recommend the diet I've described (even with qualms) as a moral norm for all. And yet the cost will not come down until it is chosen by many. That issue will confront us again in the next chapter, when we consider how this and other apparently tragic dilemmas might be resolved.

To think further and better about this moral transition, let's turn, then, to the issue of tragic dilemmas.

8

TRAGIC CONFLICTS AND HOW
TO MOVE BEYOND THEM

The interests of human beings and other animals often conflict. Some conflicts are over land and resources: elephants and villagers, for example, competing to use the same space, the same trees. Many medical experiments that save both human and animal lives inflict harm on animals. In numerous cases, vulnerable populations claim that their very existence as a people requires continuing cruel practices that cause animals great pain. These conflicts are messy and hard to think about. Some, at least, seem very grave. If we want to defend the CA, we need to discuss this issue, since it may seem that valuing plural capabilities just lands us in a mess. In this chapter, I argue that reflecting about the idea of tragic dilemmas will help us move forward.

Two common approaches to these tragic dilemmas are, I believe, pernicious. The first is what we might call the *weeping-and-wailing approach*: people wring their hands and say how terrible things in our current world are, without even showing curiosity about what might make things better. The second, closely related, approach is what we might call *self-hating defeatism*: it is because of human overreaching that we got to the bad place where we currently are, and there is nothing to do about it except to give up a lot of our ambitions and to live a reduced and chastened lifestyle. (Many Greek tragedies end with this message.) Both are common today. Often, the term "the Anthropocene" is used both descriptively, to describe our era of human world domination, and normatively, to name an evil and express a strongly negative reaction to that evil.

What is wrong in both is the absence of forward movement. We can't undo the past that brought about the bad situation, but we may be able to figure out ways to move beyond it. And although human ambition has caused many problems in our world, it can also be a source of improvement.

WHAT ARE TRAGIC DILEMMAS?

Tragic dilemmas are so called because of their prominence in ancient Greek tragedy. A typical case is Aeschylus's King Agamemnon, who is told by the gods that he must either kill his own daughter, Iphigenia, as a sacrifice to the gods, or suffer the destruction of his entire army (including the king and his daughter). Stricken to the core, he cries out: "Which of these is without evils?" It's important that no bad action of Agamemnon's led to his predicament.[1]

Agamemnon's case is not just difficult to decide. Indeed, as I described it, it may not be difficult at all, since the second alternative involves causing the death of all. Still, both alternatives require him to do something morally horrible. Either kill his own daughter, for whom he has paternal responsibility, or kill the whole army, for which he has a commander's responsibility. (Let's assume he has no third alternative, such as retreat.) And since we like to think that doing what we ought to do is always in our power—"ought implies can"—the existence of such dilemmas is an affront to our sense of competence and control. It's bad enough when the universe inflicts loss. It is worse when it inflicts a moral taint on well-meaning people.

Life is full of tragic dilemmas, large and small. They are caused by the fact that people, with good reason, cherish plural values, and events out of their control make it impossible to fulfill the moral demands of all. Sometimes they are forced by the exigencies of war. In civil war, family members often find themselves on opposite sides of the battle lines, encountering tragic dilemmas between their duty to their cause and their duty to their kin. Not surprisingly, the tragic aspects of civil war have been central to tragic literature in many cultures.

Tragic dilemmas are not just a matter of weighing up the costs and benefits. We should always try to do this, in order to try to figure out what to do. But in such cases, in addition, we should notice that there is a special *type* of cost, involving the fact that whatever one does, one will violate an important norm to which one has committed oneself.[2]

What should follow from this? It seems that a proper reaction would involve both an acknowledgment of serious guilt at the action one is taking and, then, a resolve to atone in whatever way one can in the future, reaffirming one's general commitment to the value that has lost out in the crisis situation.[3] Beyond this, good planning may be able to prevent such tragedies from afflicting good people in the future.

Here we arrive at the philosopher G. W. F. Hegel's approach to tragedy, which I follow. Tragic clashes between two spheres of value, he argued, stimulate the imagination to think ahead and change the world: for it would be better if one could find a way to prevent the tragic choice from arising in the first place. The bad choice is before us, now; but the next time let's try to figure out how to prevent it.

This isn't always possible, but as Hegel understood, tragedy stimulates the moral imagination to envisage a world that would be free of the dilemma that causes so much horror to the protagonists, producing what he called a "canceling" or "sublation" (*Aufhebung*) of the dilemma. Talking about the dilemma in Sophocles's *Antigone*, where the state has ordered Antigone to violate her sacred religious duty, Hegel said that the modern liberal state has figured out ways to protect both civic order and people's right to honor their religious obligations.

It's not as easy as he suggested, but it's good aim to work with. George

Washington wrote to the Quakers in 1789 that they would not be required to perform military service: "I assure you very explicitly, that in my opinion the conscientious scruples of all men should be treated with great delicacy and tenderness: and it is my wish and desire, that the laws may always be as extensively accommodated to them, as a due regard for the protection and essential interests of the nation may justify and permit." Many tragic dilemmas, though not all, are "sublated" by that idea, in exactly the way Hegel recommended.

Once we grasp Hegel's idea, many daily tragedies look simply outrageous. Concerned parents often feel torn in a painful way between the obligations of the workplace and the obligations of childcare. The workplaces we know were originally designed for men who didn't do much childcare. These workplaces usually lacked the flexibility that parents needed. Today, people often try to imagine scheduling that relieves parents of these painful conflicts. (Often, but not often enough.) For example, they try not to require people to be in the office during times when schools and childcare centers are closed. So: don't endure guilty choice-making in silence, change the world.

Hegelian change is not always possible, but who knows what we can do until we exercise political imagination? The governments of the Indian states of Kerala and Tamil Nadu noticed that many poor parents were keeping their children out of school because only the child's labor enabled the whole family to survive. But keeping children out of school doomed such families to a subsistence living standard, rather than solving their problem. The state governments did two Hegelian things: First, school hours were set up in several different packages, so that parents could choose the hours that were compatible with some continued work for their child. Second, and more important, the government subsidized a nutritious midday meal for all children who were in school. The caloric and protein content were appointed by law, and it more than made up for the child's lost earnings. Subsequently, the Indian Supreme Court ordered all the schools in all states to offer the midday meal, and they continue to mandate its protein level and caloric content.

What the government did here is right in line with the Capabilities Approach. First, they identified plural ends that a just society must achieve: health and education. Then, second, they saw that the current situation created a tragic conflict between two important capabilities. They analyzed them, convincing people that both were genuinely important values that must be respected. Third—rather than just ignoring or de-prioritizing one of the two capabilities—they imagined a solution that would allow both capabilities to be fulfilled up to a reasonable threshold level. All three of these steps must be gone through in applying the CA to a situation that looks like a tragic dilemma.

Can Hegelian imagination help us with the dilemmas that infect our dealings with other animals? I believe it can, if we face squarely the moral gravity of these predicaments. Let's look at four areas of moral unease: medical experimentation, meat eating, questions raised by the hunting practices of threatened traditional cultures, and, finally, larger and more general conflicts over space and resources. In each case, let's ask Hegel's question: What changes in society and law would "sublate" or cancel the dilemma—if indeed it is truly tragic?

MEDICAL RESEARCH USING ANIMALS

Medical experimentation at present has a tragic shape. On the one hand is the imperative of saving both human and animal lives, to which research using animals has contributed greatly in the past. On the other hand, experiments have inflicted horrible torment on animals and have caused countless premature deaths. The treatment of research animals has also been highly insensitive to their complex forms of life. Isolation in solo cages is the norm, despite the fact that research has shown that even rats and mice are complexly social creatures.

Very few defenders of animal rights seek the abrupt termination of all research using animals. There is too much to be gained, including for the animals themselves. Thus, Peter Singer has adopted a nuanced position, holding that in some cases animal experimentation is justified.[4] What needs to be asked, however, is not simply whether experiments are on balance justified, but whether and when they are tragic, violating a moral norm. If they are tragic, this will put us on notice that we must move as quickly as possible to "sublate" the tragedy by changes in our practices.

Let's break this down into three issues. One is the harm caused to many animals by incapacitation and premature death, even if painless and preceded by a flourishing life. Second is the harm inflicted on animals by subjecting them to pain during research, whether or not ending in death. Third is the deprivation inflicted on animals with or without death, due to their experimental conditions. All three, right now, appear to pose tragic dilemmas: experimenters must violate a moral norm in order not to give up an important good. Without great changes in the way scientists do experiments, the second problem can be solved in a way that removes tragedy. Pain mitigation is now the norm in research guidelines. The first and third issues are more recalcitrant, awaiting new modes of research.

Let's address the third problem. Consider the conditions in which research animals typically live. All they have is a bare, lonely cage, as if they were just things without complex forms of life. People who are outraged by the impoverished environments given many animals in zoos often fail to be aware that the typical life of a research animal is far more impoverished.

The Capabilities Approach recommends mapping out, as best we can, the whole form of life of each type of creature and aiming for decent lives, attending not just to pleasure and pain, but also to movement, stimulation, and friendship. Thus it sets a much more demanding goal than most current research guidelines, which focus on mitigation of pain. But its demands should be reasonably easy to meet if people really think about them. All this presupposes that we're talking about research that does not in its intrinsic nature inflict disease and pain. There is much we can learn from animals while treating them well. Some animals should not be held in confinement at all: I'll discuss this in chapter 10. But for those for whom confinement might be ethically acceptable, the "confinement" should be a world full of possibilities for exploration, bonding, good nutrition, and free movement. This goal is of course very far from being realized, but the CA at least focuses our eyes on an enriched, and possible, image of the goal.

Where research inflicting incapacitation and death is concerned, regulation and law have made some progress. The "3Rs," the mantra of the Nuffield Council in Britain (2005)—*reduction, refinement,* and *replacement*—have become the watchwords of all regulatory bodies: reduce the harms, refine techniques so as to produce fewer harms, and, where possible, replace research involving animals with other types of research.[5] The guidelines developed by the council are relatively weak, on account of often-mentioned disagreements among its members. Still, not everything that used to be routine is permitted today. The council articulates as a distant goal for researchers a world without animal research; and, in the meantime, insists on a case-by-case justification for the research that is still done.[6] And the council usefully notes that a culture of regulation, though highly desirable, all things considered, can insulate people from moral reflection. The report, though not a legally enforceable document, is still a harbinger of progress. Legislation implementing these ideas is the next step for each country.

The entire debate over limitation and regulation, however, is deeply flawed by *scala naturae* thinking: thus, even in the writings of leading ethicists, what is permitted often depends on how "high" on the ladder a creature is judged to be, and rats, mice, and fish are treated as utterly unequal to large vertebrates. Especially suspect is the singling out of great apes for special protection.[7] Even the setup of the debate is problematic. Thus the Nuffield Council recognizes three positions:

1. There is something special about humans, and all humans possess some morally vital property that all animals lack (the *clear-line view*).

2. There is a hierarchy of moral importance with humans at the apex, followed by primates and then other mammalian species . . . with invertebrates and single-celled creatures arranged towards the bottom (the *moral sliding scale view*).

3. There is no categorical distinction between human and non-human animals, and that they are moral equals (the *moral equality view*).

Only options 1 and 2 are explicitly grounded in the *scala naturae*. But what is missing from the entire list, including the third option, is the idea that each type of creature has a distinctive form of life and that this form of life dictates what can and cannot be a harm for it. We can and should recognize salient differences among the species (with sentience used as a minimum threshold, as chapter 6 recommends), when we ask what harms a proposed form of research will do. But that emphatically does not mean lining up all the creatures in a hierarchy.

There is, further, a growing awareness that not all human purposes are important. Bentham already insisted on this point (see chapters 3 and 7), but we need to rediscover it. Thus, the testing of cosmetics on rabbits has come under heavy scrutiny, and people currently have non-tragic ethical options in the beauty area. The use of animal subjects in toxicology research, although it has increased in response to public anxiety about chemical risks, has also come under increasing criticism, with some leading bioethicists calling for its total elimination.

A different challenge to current thinking, and even to the Nuffield Council's gradual reform efforts, comes from mounting evidence that animal models are not very reliable. Scientific arguments in this area have become highly politicized, and it is difficult for the layperson to know whom to trust. The Nuffield Council is studiously agnostic about unreliability claims, probably because of disagreements among its members. More recently, Aysha Akhtar brings a growing body of scientific literature to bear on this question, arguing that we know for sure by now that a lot of animal-based research is unreliable and in that way imposes large costs on humans, through misguided treatments and the abandonment of others that might have proven superior. She concludes that, even if we focus just on humans, the costs of animal research outweigh the benefits.[8] In the same special issue, focusing on toxicity testing, Andrew Rowan concludes that the predictive value of animal testing is on average only 50 to

60 percent, but that in rodent studies it falls below 50 percent, less accurate than a coin toss.[9]

If this new line of argument is correct, research using animals does not pose a tragic dilemma, because nothing is gained by it. But it seems unlikely that such a sweeping conclusion is correct. For the areas in which animal studies are not useful, we should just drop them. And we should applaud the council's demand for a case-by-case justification based on solid evidence. But in other areas, great medical benefits, for both humans and other animals, are gained through immoral means.[10] To drop the potentially useful research with no substitute would itself harm both humans and other animals. At least there, then, we are currently stuck with a tragic dilemma, if we believe, as I do, that there is a moral imperative to save lives.

However, this is one case where we can clearly see Hegelian light at the end of the tunnel. Computer simulation and other technologies are developing rapidly, promising, rather than just *mitigation* of harm, a complete *replacement* of the use of animals, at least in cases where we would not permit similar research strategies using humans. Even the cautious Nuffield Council recommends the "third R," replacement, wherever possible. Ethicists go further, recommending massive investments in computer models. Given unreliability issues, these replacements promise benefits in quality as well as avoidance of ethical costs.

During the transition period, which should be as brief as possible, research animals must have decent housing conditions, and attention must be paid to their species-typical physical, psychological, and emotional needs. Strict limits on the infliction of pain must be enforced, and palliation of pain must be mandatory.

All this, and more, is put into codified form in the important recent work of Tom L. Beauchamp and David DeGrazia in their 2020 book, *Principles of Animal Research Ethics*,[11] which will, and should, shortly supplant the 3Rs approach as the normative set of guidelines in this area. It makes several distinct advances. First, Beauchamp and DeGrazia insist that all vertebrates and cephalopods are sentient, have a point of view on the world, and thus deserve serious moral consideration. They avoid all *scala naturae* ranking, although they hedge their bets by not criticizing it, either. Second, they formulate a set of principles that give guidance that is both more definite than that of the 3Rs and more wide-ranging, embracing, in effect, a Capabilities Approach to the protection of a species form of life.

Beauchamp and DeGrazia recommend three basic principles:

1. **The Principle of No Unnecessary Harm.** Animal subjects must not be harmed unless a particular harm is necessary for and morally justified by scientific purposes.
2. **The Principle of Basic Needs.** Animal subjects' basic needs must be met in the conduct of studies unless failure to meet specific basic needs is necessary for and morally justified by scientific purposes.
3. **The Principle of Upper Limits to Harm.** Animal subjects must not be caused to suffer for a lengthy period of time. In rare, extraordinary cases, exceptions may be made if the research is necessary for and morally justified by critically important social and scientific purposes.

They have a great deal more to say about each principle. They are certainly tougher than the 3Rs approach, though there are some obvious gaps, such as their agnosticism about whether the harm of premature death can be justified—but at least they do acknowledge the tragic nature of the choice: it is a harm. And they acknowledge that a Hegelian approach is superior to all harm-causing approaches by insisting that if there is any harm-free alternative, that must be preferred to any that harms animals.

Especially significant is their account of basic needs, which dovetails to a great extent with what the CA recommends. Their catalog includes the following:

Nutritious food and clean water
Safe shelter
Adequate stimulation, exercise, and opportunities for species-typical
   functioning

Sufficient rest to maintain physical and (where applicable) mental
  health

Veterinary care

For social species, access to compatible conspecifics or social group
  members

Freedom from significant experimental harms such as pain, distress,
  and suffering

Freedom from disease, injury, and disability

Freedom of movement with adequate space[12]

They then add: It is controversial whether the following is a basic need:

Freedom from premature death.

I would insist that it is a basic need (subject to the qualifications expressed in chapter 7); and I would strike out "where applicable," since all sentient creatures have a mental life. That is what sentience is. But overall, the list is a good one. Writing as a commentator, Frans de Waal points out that there is never any reason to keep an ape apart from a group of other apes, even for a short time. If the experimenter needs to isolate an individual for a period, this can be done by summoning the ape from its colony through a door or portal.[13] He notes that allowing primates to maintain their species-typical lives would produce better science, as well as being more humane. We can extend his point to all sentient animals.

We have not yet reached the Hegelian goal, a world free of tragedy— as measured, according to my approach, by the thresholds established under the Capabilities Lists for the world's creatures. Setting those thresholds is, as always, a disputed matter, about which there may continue to be reasonable disagreement. And even in the world where thresholds are met, there will be permissible research to be done, with a need for careful regulation. So Beauchamp and DeGrazia have made a valuable contribution to our progress toward minimal justice.

MEAT EATING AGAIN

Let's now return briefly to meat eating. Are there really tragic dilemmas here, and how common are they? Vegans will say that most if not
all people can quickly transition healthily to a plant-based diet, doing
themselves not harm but good in the process. I have cast at least some
doubt on this, citing the protein needs of aging people (and we might add
children) and mentioning that not everyone's digestive system can handle
massive amounts of beans, lentils, etc. So in that case there could be a
tragic dilemma for such an individual, since we have duties to ourselves
to maintain our health. Cost is also an issue for non-elite families. These
dilemmas are mitigated to some extent by chapter 7's alternative of humane farming (especially the painless death of a fish, who has no or few
temporally extended plans and projects). But difficulty is not completely
removed.

Another potential problem is the harm that could be done to animal
habitats by the massive change in crop growing that would be required if
everyone really transitioned to a vegan diet. This issue is unclear at present, but should be seriously studied.

But here too there is a Hegelian solution in the offing: artificial meat.
Virtually unknown when I began planning this book, it is now a massive
growth industry, with many different types of "meat" made from plant
ingredients. The reason these meat substitutes are popular is only partly
ethical; people also want the health benefits of lowered saturated fat content and, often, sodium content. This science is still in its infancy, since
substitute meat foods are said by some to lack variety of flavor and tex-
ture. And there is no artificial fish, so far as I am aware, for those of us
who love fish. Still, this is the future. We can see it and work for it. When
even baseball stadiums offer veggie dogs and veggie burgers,[14] the future
of *Aufhebung* is at hand. Laboratory grown meat, which is "real" meat
from animal stem cells, but produced without animal killing, is already
available, and on the market, at least in Singapore. Again, investment in
these developments seems amply warranted, and by now there are enough

animal-friendly chefs that we can expect these imaginative people will carry on from current beginnings.

CULTURAL PRESERVATION?

Cruel practices have recently acquired cultural/political chic, in the form of an appeal to the cultural rights of long-subordinated indigenous peoples. Consider three examples.[15]

In 2009, the Kwa-Zulu Natal department of Agriculture publicly defended Zulu bull-killing at an annual festival as a "cultural ceremony" protected by Section 31 of the South African Constitution, which "enshrines the right of every human being to practice his/her religion, culture, and language."[16] The bulls are slaughtered in a slow, torturous practice that involves "gouging out its eyes, pulling out its tongue and tail, tying its testicles in a knot and shoving sand and mud down its throat."[17] The Zulu defend the practice as a key rite of passage, necessary to sustain their traditions.

The Chippewa people hunt white-tailed deer as a necessary part of their material survival and cultural integrity. They claim that venison not only provides essential nourishment, but also fosters bonds of community, and, by ritual sharing with less physically able members of the people, fosters a sense of the equal dignity of all community members. The hunt itself is structured by prayers and rules that are central to the Chippewa belief system.[18]

The International Convention for the Regulation of Whaling (ICRW) contains a "cultural exemption": the regulations limiting harpooning do not apply "to aborigines dwelling on the coasts of the territories" of the contracting parties, provided that they used traditional fishing vessels, did not carry guns, and intended to whale for local consumption only. This last provision is routinely disregarded, and much of the whale meat is sold for commercial use in restaurants and markets, particularly in Greenland (see also chapter 12). Still, Denmark so energetically defended the cultural exception that they publicly said that they did not care whether the indigenous people sold the whale meat to tourists, and that the whalers could even use baseball bats to kill whales if they wanted to.[19]

If people are really interested in defending the powerless from the abuse of power, there is no group of intelligent and sentient beings more dominated and less respected in today's world than are non-human animals, who also have cultures. So this way of making the case for culture seems seriously off: far from empowering the powerless, it further disempowers the entirely powerless.

But there is much more to say. Appeals to culture have two virtually insuperable problems of logic and definition. The first of these we may call the "who's in, who's out" problem. Who are "the Inuit people"? All people of Inuit origin who live anywhere in the world? Only a particular geographically bounded group (those in Greenland, for example)? Since by no means all Inuit people practice whaling, this question must be answered if one is to support the claim that "Inuit culture" requires whaling. Moreover, one must offer a definition of the notion of "culture" itself, since there are many competing definitions.[20]

Combined with this issue is the "whose voices count" problem. Most appeals to the values of a culture attend to the voices of the powerful leaders of that group, usually male. They ignore women, critical voices, alienated voices, and so forth.[21] In this case, the young male hunters are being heard, and all sorts of other people with Inuit credentials are not being heard: women, those who moved away out of dissatisfaction with tradition, those who criticize tradition, and so forth. Cultures are neither monolithic nor static: they are scenes of debate and contestation, and they are in motion.[22] To grant supremacy to a narrow subgroup who defend archaic practices, rejecting other dissonant voices, is to make a decision. But what could the normative basis for that decision possibly be?[23]

All these problems afflict the appeal to culture, when used to defend aboriginal whaling. Matthew Scully's book *Dominion* shows that the Makah were inspired by Japanese pro-whaling forces to embrace a tradition they had not pursued for many years. Those whose voices were heard were those who followed this Japanese influence.[24] Scully admits that the Inuit hunters of Alaska have a more serious claim to be "real-life" aboriginal whalers. And yet his study shows that "most Eskimos who hunt whales today are not primitives struggling to subsist in the harsh fringes of civilization. They are young men for whom whaling is a passion and, as we are told, an act of cultural self-affirmation. They whale, not because they must, but because they want to."[25] Scully concludes that the practice is not all that different from trophy hunting, especially since the lifestyles of Alaskan natives are today largely reliant on the petroleum industry. Their alleged respect for "custom" is also selective, since the methods used to remove the whales from the waters are usually far from traditional.[26]

In short, appeals to culture parade as if they had normative force, but they never tell us where that force is coming from. All sorts of bad practices are highly traditional: for example, domestic violence, racism, child sexual abuse, and, of course, the torture of animals. The fact that these practices have been around for a long time is not a point in their favor.[27] If tradition has a normative force, its defenders have to try harder to say what that force is.

The argument cannot simply be that cultures collapse if they reject some prominent value that they once held. Even though it is likely that the values involved in Nazism were deeply woven into German cultural traditions, German culture of a recognizable sort has survived the utter rejection of Nazism. All cultures have begun to reject gender discrimination, with struggle but without utter cultural collapse. Christian cultures were once profoundly hostile to Jews, Muslims, and Hindus; now they are far less so, and they have reinvented their culture in order to show respect for the religious commitments of non-Christians. And although Lord Devlin predicted in 1958 that British culture would not survive without legal prohibitions of same-sex acts, history has shown him wrong.[28]

And what of the culture of whales themselves? Although proponents of aboriginal cultural rights often speak of these groups' respect for nature, it is impossible to see whaling as a sign of respect for the life and culture of the whale. As Anthony D'Amato and Sudhir Chopra rightly

comment, "[N]o one asked the bowhead whether the gangs of men clubbing and harpooning them were demonstrating respect."[29]

In an excellent recent article, philosophers Breena Holland and Amy
Linch have pointed out that it diminishes native peoples to view them
as mere slaves of the past.[30] Culture is itself a "tool kit" (here they appeal
to the work of sociologist Ann Swidler) out of which people continue to
construct their own stories. There are many groups who practiced cruelty
toward animals in the past, but some have adapted, as a result of ethical
argument. They argue that it is more respectful of a traditional society
to expect them to deliberate and move forward. Indeed, as philosopher
Jonathan Lear has shown in *Radical Hope*, his moving study of the Crow,
a group can find utterly unforeseen ways of moving forward even when
seemingly faced with utter cultural devastation.[31] So I conclude there is no
truly tragic dilemma here, because it is possible to reconceive one of the
ends so that it can still be respected while respecting the lives of animals.

Linch and Holland seem content with humane killing. I would go
further, returning to Hegel's question and to the CA: What would it be
to imagine a world in which the tragic dilemma between causing the destruction of a culture or people and causing pain and harm to animals
would no longer exist? Here Hegel's original source of inspiration, Greek
theater, leads us to the answer: a group can retain the value of a practice
that holds the group together by theatricalizing it and removing lethal
means altogether. Greek tragic drama was very likely a cultural modification, in which theater took the place of human sacrifice. No longer
would a young person be slaughtered on the altar; instead, the sacrifice
of Iphigenia takes place as theater, reminding the group of its history and
also celebrating its progress beyond such understandings of cultural tradition.[32] Similarly, sports can be seen as a theatrical substitute for lethal
combat (although in the case of football, one might wonder whether the
lethal possibilities have been entirely removed).

Solutions need to come from the groups themselves, but, given
the growing popularity of cultural tourism, it is not hard to imagine
the groups themselves understanding the potential of ritual theater for

cultural survival. The long-standing success of the Cherokee historical drama *Unto These Hills*, which has been one of North Carolina's major cultural attractions since 1950, is evidence of what the future could hold for the Zulu, the Chippewa, and the Inuit.[33]

I conclude that we should not tolerate animal killing as a form of cultural expression, any more than we now tolerate violence against women as a cultural expression of masculinity. All groups are capable of change, and change must be demanded of all, out of respect for their own ethical capacities, and out of respect, first and foremost, for the animals. All human beings are under a collective obligation to work for better laws and institutions.

CONFLICTS OVER SPACE AND RESOURCES

So far, our tragedies yield to imagination and work. Far more tenacious are the pervasive tragic dilemmas caused by human-animal conflicts over space and resources. In Africa, despite widespread efforts to protect and preserve elephants, their presence often inflicts great hardship on villagers, who need the trees that elephants are debarking for their own food. This sort of conflict is common, involving many animal species. The very resurgence and success of a species is often prelude to conflict, such as conflicts over space between humans and mountain lions in our Western states. These conflicts are very basic: on the one side, the capability of animals to live their entire form of life, involving numerous capabilities on the list; on the other, the needs of impoverished humans for capabilities to lead healthy lives.

The first step in thinking well about such cases is to analyze the conflict clearly. Do both sides really involve pushing people below the threshold of a genuinely major capability? Not all interests are of equal weight. Humans, for example, can adapt to a smaller space more easily than can most large animals, as the success of cities has taught us; so we should not think that when humans are asked to do that in order to support the flourishing of an animal group, this is necessarily tragic. Nor do human financial interests by themselves generate tragedy. Thus, efforts by ranchers in Wyoming to cull herds of wild horses—and to impede breeding corridors that would strengthen the health of species members—involve economic interests that are not essential for health and survival. Better results for all parties can be obtained by better scientific understanding of the role of wild horses in the larger ecosystem.[34]

Often, however, the interests are weightier: health and survival on both sides. Then much depends on the numbers. With coyotes in cities, because their numbers are relatively small and their threat to humans and domesticated animals containable, patterns of live-and-let-live are already evolving.[35] With the more dangerous mountain lions, although one intrepid hiker recently had to strangle the animal in self-defense,[36] and other such cases will undoubtedly occur, it is possible to capture lions in a humane way and ship them away to a wildlife rehabilitation facility, with the possibility of later release back into the wild—as has happened with the siblings of the dead lion.[37]

Elephants in themselves do not threaten humans. But they need a lot of space and they consume a lot of tree bark and plants. Humans also take up a lot of space and have many urgent uses for trees and plants. That type of competition can be alleviated by the creation of wildlife refuges with clear rules—often handsomely supported by ecotourism. But as long as animals freely enter areas of human habitation, there will be truly tragic scenarios.

These scenarios are exacerbated by rural poverty, which makes the competition for resources with large animals more desperate, and may even lead humans to side with poachers, in search of financial gain. A Hegelian solution will therefore have to be complex: it will have to promote clearly demarcated and secure wildlife refuges, but also help communities make the most of community lands.[38] Interventions that strengthen the rule of law in Africa are also crucial for ending poaching, as are interventions on the demand side.

We must now discuss population control. Human population growth is part of the problem, and sensible controls must be part of the solution.

Draconian imposition of fixed numbers has some large ethical drawbacks, as Amartya Sen argued in his influential paper "Fertility and Coercion."[39] Fortunately, the apparent dilemma between freedom and population control is only apparent, because evidence shows that the most effective way of limiting population is educating women, an intervention that promotes freedom rather than limiting it. But women and men will choose to limit their families only when public sanitation and available health care give them reason to believe that two children can survive to adulthood.

Should animal contraception also be discussed? Many large animals, including elephants, rhinos, giraffes, tigers, and lions are so endangered that limiting population would be irrational, and what we need to do is to preserve and increase numbers. But there are other cases of conflict in which animal contraception might be cautiously investigated, so long as research is carefully done and harm is not caused to the animal. For wild animals, we don't know enough about the potential harms at present. The contraceptives proposed for wild horses seem to have harmful side effects. But that does not mean more research should not be done. As with human contraceptives, research should continue until a safe option is found.

By focusing on specific cases of human-animal conflict, I have avoided, it will be said, the largest conflict of all. In a world where humans are starving and dying from lack of medical care, can we possibly justify spending any substantial amount of time and money at all in caring for other animals? This, roughly, was the shocked response of some young development thinkers in our Human Development and Capability Association when I presented some of this work. I do indeed hold that we should not give any absolute priority to human interests, as these objectors appear to wish me to do. I hold that all creatures count equally. But I also insist that the dilemma is falsely posed: most of the current threats to human life from poverty and disease come from the absence of effective governmental institutions, not from "natural" limits to the earth's capacities. We can and should envisage, and work for, a multispecies world in which all have opportunities for flourishing. And we should, I think, go even further, insisting that an ethical attunement to the lives of animals and a sense of wonder at their complexity and dignity is part of our humanity, without which human life itself is impoverished.

In general: whenever we think we have to inflict hardship on animals in order to preserve a healthy human community, we ought to step back, asking how we got into that bad situation, and what we might do to produce a future world in which that grim choice does not arise. Weeping and wailing is self-indulgent when we have work to do. The dilemmas are genuinely difficult, and there is no guarantee that there will not be at least some irreparable loss. But let's see what can be done. Hegelian optimism will not satisfy people who get pleasure out of thinking how inexorably bad everything is, and who love to believe that the Anthropocene is an apocalypse because of our sinful overreaching. I just don't believe that. I think we can deliberate well, and create a feasible multispecies world. The only question is: Will we?

9

ANIMALS WHO LIVE WITH US

Animal companions live in a majority of human homes in the United States: 67 percent by one recent account.[1] People cherish their companion dogs and cats and often have very strong emotional bonds with them (as they also do with horses and some other animals who live close to the home). Norms of mutuality and concern are on the rise. According to recent surveys, between 89 and 99 percent of people who live with a dog or cat believe the animal is a member of the family.[2]

In antiquity, genuine reciprocity and respect was not uncommon between humans and animals who lived alongside them. When Odysseus returns to Ithaca after an absence of twenty years, he finds his beloved hunting dog, Argos, lying neglected on a heap of manure, his coat infested with ticks.[3] Despite advanced age and neglect, however, Argos is the only sentient creature in Ithaca (including Odysseus's wife, Penelope, and his friend Eumaeus, the swineherd), who recognizes Odysseus beneath his disguise as a beggar. The mutual respect and concern between the two is evident: Argos attempts to get up and go to Odysseus, but is too ill to do so, and simply wags his tail. Odysseus (unable to recognize him in public because of his disguise) refers to him as a "noble dog," and tears come to his eyes. Argos, apparently fulfilled by having seen his beloved human again, lies down and dies.[4]

The same story that shows us the depth of loyalty and concern that may exist between humans and companion animals also shows, however, the dark side of human relationships with their animal companions: for neglect and abuse, particularly when a dog is too old to be instrumentally useful, has also been the common lot of dogs and cats, and Argos has been shamefully abused by the suitors. Indeed, Odysseus knows that some dogs are treated badly throughout their lives: he contrasts Argos's noble appearance (despite the squalor of his current predicament) with the situation of other dogs that "beg around tables and are kept merely for show."[5]

In the ancient Greek world, dogs typically worked alongside humans, got plenty of exercise, and were commonly respected for their activity. The mutually respectful symbiosis of Odysseus and Argos has persisted, wherever humans and dogs are partners in shared goals. At Rousham House, a country estate in Steeple Aston, outside Oxford, a visitor may see the grave of Ringwood, an "otterhound of extraordinary sagacity," whose epitaph was composed by no less a poet than Alexander Pope, a visitor to the estate and a famous lover of dogs. (He wrote a good deal in praise of his own favorite companion, a Great Dane named "Bounce.") Today, however, when dogs do less work and often live in more cramped conditions, there has been a devolution in the relationship, as the word "pet" indicates, and many dogs are treated as toys and ornaments. When people note recent improvements in respect and concern, it is against the background of a previous decline.

Still, all too often dogs and cats are regarded as property, owned by a human and consequently living at the sufferance of the human—not ends in themselves, but appendages: useful sometimes for protection, sometimes for emotional support, sometimes as cute toys to play with, sometimes as valuable trophies showing the human's status.

Today many contest that view, believing that dogs and cats are not property but companions, members of the household, just as precious as other members. They demand greater access for their companion animals—in parks, hotels, airplanes. This shift is lurching and inconstant, and it coexists with a great deal of abusive and neglectful behavior. Very often the same people who want to bring their dogs and cats with them on airplanes are at the same time neglecting them by under-exercising them and giving them inconsistent or deficient support in learning social limits. They no longer see these animals as property, but they also don't fully respect and attend to them. And often these same people buy dogs from puppy mills that have raised them abusively and neglectfully, infecting them with numerous diseases. Even when a human household somehow acquires a healthy animal, its human members often choose the animal because they like the way it looks, or they have seen it in a movie—knowing nothing about the specific needs of that type of animal for exercise and companionship. So the initially healthy animal often becomes anxious and antisocial, like a neglected child. In short, many of the same people who believe they love a companion animal are often the ones who abuse them.[6]

Our improving relationship with companion animals remains defective, a work in progress at best, a type of relationship that would in many cases be regarded as morally heinous and legally actionable were the creature in question a human child.

This chapter will ask what the Capabilities Approach has to say about our moral/political obligations to animals who live with us and about how we can best promote their capabilities—in partnership with them. I'll focus on dogs and cats, but later extend the analysis to horses and other companionate or working animals. In the process, I will explore and to a considerable extent agree with the idea that companion animals should be thought of as fellow citizens, an idea developed in an important recent book, *Zoopolis*, co-authored by philosophers Sue Donaldson and Will Kymlicka.[7] In chapter 5, I already announced that the CA treats animals as active citizens. In this chapter we will begin to see what that means in practice.

SYMBIOTIC FLOURISHING

The Capabilities Approach asks us to respect the characteristic form of life of an animal kind. Although each individual sentient animal is to be treated as an end, a good way of starting to formulate political guidelines for the treatment of species members is to consider the species form of life—including the range of individual variations that are typically found within it. And, although we can certainly grant that elephants and even whales may under certain circumstances develop important relationships with members of other species, including humans, there is such a thing as the unimpeded flourishing of an elephant or whale leading an elephant or whale way of life. I do not believe that this observation means "the wild" is a place conducive to wild animal flourishing, as I argue in the next chapter. Nor do I believe that the right way for us to behave toward wild animals, in a world where we dominate everywhere, is to leave them alone—as if that were even conceivable. Still, it is at least possible to imagine an elephant form of life without humans in it, and it is possible to imagine that life going well.

With companion animals, things are otherwise. Over millennia, these animals have been bred by humans to be useful for human purposes. They have developed psychological traits, such as docility and responsiveness, and even physical traits, such as "neoteny" (the retention of juvenile features such as a large head and large round eyes in the adult animal), that make them seem appealing and nonthreatening to humans. Above all, they have developed vulnerability and dependency.

This means two further things: First, we cannot describe their species form of life without putting a relationship with humans at its very heart. And this symbiotic relationship is asymmetrical. It is possible to encounter humans who do not have deep relationships with other animals—in fact, we encounter such humans all the time. My Capabilities List mentions the *opportunity* to have rewarding relations with other animals as a valuable human capability, but not everyone will want to use it.

For companion animals, by contrast, there is no real possibility of their flourishing except in an asymmetrically dependent relationship with humans. Feral dogs and cats do poorly and die soon. And if a strain should evolve that could live apart, as has happened with wild horses, that is a substantially different species, and that evolution took long eons of evolutionary time. If domesticated dogs and cats (and not some new strain of canine or feline) are to flourish, it is in a form of asymmetrical dependency with us.

Sometimes domesticated animals are compared to slaves. The comparison mistakes the depth and, in one way, the iniquity, of what we have done. Slaves were oppressed, but they were perfectly capable of freedom and self-direction, and when they got it, they grabbed it with alacrity. The damage done by slavery was profound, but it was reversible. No child of a slave is biologically marked for slavery (although the social damages of slavery are ongoing and not yet undone). But if we were to sign an Emancipation Proclamation for all dogs, cats, and non-feral horses, that would not spell happiness for those creatures or their descendants. Quite the opposite: it would spell misery and death. Humans have created creatures like Aristotle's hypothetical "natural slaves," whose very biological nature destines them for an asymmetrically symbiotic relationship.

ABOLITIONISM?

We can debate the morality by which, in remote prehistory, humans (no doubt by much trial and error, over millennia) bred domestic dogs from wild canines and domestic cats from wild felines. One might even see something good in it, arguing that the domestic species are more protected than their wild forebears from the hazards of nature. However, it is perfectly clear that the aim of those remote humans was not to protect, it was to use. For a variety of human purposes, including hunting, herding, and companionship, wild canines were not reliable, just as they would be unreliable today. And while I have said that some of the relationships that emerged in herding and hunting were reciprocal and affectionate, the ur-humans who ultimately bred an Argos were not aiming at respect or love; they wanted the work to get done reliably, and by a non-threatening creature. Domestication would be analogous, then, not to slavery but to the deliberate creation by breeding of a race of "natural slaves" who could live and flourish only in a relationship of asymmetrical dependency.

What should we think of that unsavory past? We should certainly insist that vulnerability and dependency, even when asymmetrical, are not per se bad. Phases of the human life cycle—childhood, old age, and temporary disability—all involve asymmetrical vulnerability and dependency, and there is nothing low or undignified about that. Many humans who live with us are asymmetrically dependent throughout their lives: people with severe genetic disabilities, particularly cognitive disabilities. We love these people, or should, and do not think that there is anything morally wrong about cherishing them as they are and helping them to flourish in their own way. Indeed, today at least, we think that there is something terribly wrong with not doing that.[8]

The case of companion animals, however, is not the same. People with disabilities are not deliberately bred to be asymmetrically dependent. They are accidents of the genetic lottery, and though today the tendency is to bring such pregnancies to term and help the resulting child flourish, rather than to abort the fetus, such children are not created deliberately. Even advocates for people with Down syndrome or other genetically rooted disabilities would think it unethical to deliberately arrange to give birth to a child with Down syndrome, given the medical problems and social difficulties such a person will live with—even if it were to give a child with Down syndrome already in one's household a companion.

And imagine the moral horror of deliberately breeding an entire subtype of humans with cognitive disabilities, genetically distinct from other humans, in order to have undemanding and docile household help. Probably this ugly idea would have occurred to some humans if not for the fact that most human adults with cognitive disabilities are not physically robust, but have other physical problems that would make the hideous experiment a failure; or else, as with humans on the autism spectrum, they might be physically robust but not docile and obedient.

We can see that moral humans, seeing the evil fruits of that experiment, would call for an end to the deliberate breeding of that type of human. In my thought experiment, that would be easy, because so far the subservient type was not a separate species, but had been specially bred in every individual case, by the implantation of eggs containing the relevant gene, etc.

Some animal advocates, who call themselves "abolitionists," are in favor of exactly that course, where domestic dogs and cats are concerned. Gary Francione, the leader of this movement, writes that the only way to undo the terrible wrong we humans have done to these once-wild creatures is systematically to forbid reproduction, until they eventually die out.[9]

One can see the allure of this argument. But it has a number of problems. First, like other arguments concerning reparations for past evils, it is vague about who bears accountability and guilt. The best way of thinking about reparations is as a symbolic statement of apology—but even that is maddeningly unspecific: Who is apologizing on behalf of whom and with what warrant? And it is at best a kind of useless hand-wringing, when what is needed are bold forward-looking steps to improve the lives of animals who are alive today. Why should people today, who may intensely love dogs and cats, or who may respect them even if they do not love them, atone for their very creation by humans so remote in time that we cannot even imagine them?

Second, Francione's proposal inflicts by force a massive trauma on the very beings whom the abolitionist claims to respect. One cannot wish a species away with a magic wand. Extinction, as I said in chapter 5, always occurs by way of harming existing species members: in the Francione case, by a mass involuntary worldwide sterilization movement that would involve some centralized ministry rounding up all the existing dogs and cats, taking them from their homes, and neutering them—rather in the way that in India, under the Emergency, Sanjay Gandhi arranged for members of the lower castes to be rounded up and forcibly sterilized in order to deal with a burgeoning population. Even those of us who reject the idea that animals are property might come to cherish property rights as a bulwark against the invading army of activists, indifferent to the wishes of the animals themselves and those who live closely with them. Nor would the mass forced sterilization be painless for the dogs and cats. Sterilization can be acceptable and even in many cases advisable, as I'll argue later. But Francione sterilization would fracture ongoing relationships. The sterilization I approve is either done by companion humans with a view to preventing litters who could not find good homes, or, when practiced on strays, is done to prevent mass starvation and misery for subsequent strays.

A more plausible abolitionist argument, one not based on the idea of undoing past wrongs, might be that the symbiotic relationship between humans and companion animals is an ongoing injustice. But this argument cannot succeed without first addressing the issue of flourishing: Can dogs and cats, in their symbiotic relationships with humans, lead flourishing lives or not?

The only possible justification for deliberately causing the extinction of a species is that its individual members cannot have lives worth living. But dogs and cats can have flourishing and healthy lives, if humans treat them as they should—a big "if," to be spelled out later, but doable. If bred for symbiosis, they were also bred for robust health—apart from cases that I shall discuss shortly. Nor, like children with severe disabilities, are they stigmatized in their own species community. They have lots of friendships available to them—with other members of their own species, with animals of different species, and with the humans who live with them. They are asymmetrically dependent, but it is typically not a painful dependency, marred by isolation and illness.

It might be true that if we could go back into human prehistory we should not domesticate animals. This will remain unclear, because we do not know enough about the prehistory of domestication. But guilt over the remote past does not suggest a useful policy for the present. Dogs and cats are here. They can live flourishing and joyful lives, albeit symbiotic lives of asymmetrical dependency. But why should we think that so bad?

Dependency can be dignified. Rather than, with Francione, ruing the past and trying to undo it, we should face the present—the existence of these symbiotic species—and co-create a future. Let's now spell out the terms of that future.

But first there is a place in the lives of dogs and cats where abolition of a kind is called for, I believe. As Bernard Rollin, a philosophical expert in veterinary ethics, has shown, the most popular breeds of dogs are often the most afflicted with genetic diseases. Bred to an exacting breed standard, they suffer the fate of all inbred populations: they are unhealthy. The Labrador retriever, the number one breed (in popularity) today, is at risk for over sixty genetic diseases. The same is true of other popular breeds, such as the German shepherd, the English and French bulldog, the pug, and many others. Inbreeding is dictated by American Kennel Club (AKC) standards, but it is bad veterinary medicine. And it is bad for individual animals bred in this way.

As Rollin says: people would be horrified if humans bred their children like that, selecting for traits that pleased them aesthetically but, at the same time, saddling the child with a risky and very likely painful existence. I enjoy the National Dog Show, and am in awe of the canine beauty onstage there. But the time for the abolition of aesthetic inbreeding has come. It is inhumane. It is breeding for human vanity and, often, for breeder profit, not for mutually respectful symbiosis.

There are some good reasons for breeding dogs. One is work: certain breeds can perform tasks (herding sheep, being Seeing Eye dogs) that others cannot. Since I will defend work when the conditions are humane, we have a reason to tolerate a type of breeding, but not with the exacting aesthetic standards of the AKC, if an existing breed has genetic defects. Some hybridization is compatible with retaining the useful qualities of a breed. Second, people differ in their ability to provide homes for dogs of different sizes and athletic requirements. Although the current regime in my city, where only rescue or shelter dogs may be legally acquired by pet stores, is a good response to the horrors of puppy mills (see chapter 12), this humane practice is compatible with the continued legality of legitimate breeders, who, as I reconceive them, would breed animals to fit with different lifestyles and accommodations, but without the extreme inbreeding of AKC standards. In short: the goal of good dog lives requires the abolition of most breeding that currently exists, but it justifies some continued breeding to fit dogs for different situations and contexts. A companion can then select a companion dog knowing approximately what size it will be, how much exercise it will need, whether it will be a suitable companion for children, and so forth.

It is too intrusive to outlaw AKC breeding with a single stroke. But combining a pro-adoption policy with a strong ethical campaign against too-inbred "pure" breeds should work in pretty short order. People already prefer healthy hybrids to English bulldogs, who can barely breathe.

This sort of abolition does no harm to animals, just the reverse. And it is easily within our power, unlike a return to a prehistory when dogs and cats did not exist.

FROM PROPERTY TO CITIZENSHIP

Throughout the history of human relationships with companion animals, they have been regarded as property. They have been bought and sold, and they have been regarded as totally under the control of the "owner." Women and slaves, too, used to be regarded as property. Slaves were always bought and sold; women in many societies were literally bought and sold as well, though other societies substituted the more polite fiction of courtship followed by "coverture," the full loss of a woman's legal rights upon marriage. For slaves, the property status meant no genuine legal protection, even against murder. Women did slightly better: thus, wife murder was usually a crime—although wife rape and wife beating were seen as a normal exercise of owner privilege.

Similarly, dogs and cats used to be regarded, and to some extent still are, as things, to be bought and sold. Law protected them against some abuses, but not against many others. Today, although the term "companion animal" has become more current, the term "owner" persists, and dogs and cats are still legally bought and sold in most places, although adoption from a shelter is gaining ground.

The property status meant treatment as simply an object of the owner's interests. Pieces of property are not ends; they are means to someone else's ends. The big truth in the Kantian view is that a being cannot gain respect as an end unless it ceases to be regarded as property.[10]

For slaves and women, the remedy was emancipation: full adult autonomy. For the reasons I have explored, this remedy is not fully appropriate to dogs and cats, who need human partnership and asymmetrical care. But there are two other analogies we now need to consider: children, and adults with severe disabilities. Children, too, used to count as property: they could be used for hard labor by their parents, and no laws prevented parents from physically or sexually abusing them. People with disabilities similarly lacked protection; whether they were treated kindly or cruelly was a matter of luck. Now, by contrast, children and people with disabilities are regarded as citizens with rights of their own, as ends in themselves—although they need partnership with temporary or permanent human "collaborators" in order to exercise their rights, and although the collaborator as legal guardian has certain decisional powers over choices for them.[11] What would it be, then, to treat dogs and cats the way we now (ought to) treat children and adults with cognitive disabilities?

It means, first of all, that they ought to be treated as ends, not means, and that both policy and law should take cognizance of their interests, protecting them against both abuse and neglect. While human companionship is a legal status (usually through adoption) that gives the human companion certain rights, it also gives the human many duties, and the status is revocable, if the duties are not fulfilled. Just as children can be removed from an abusive or neglectful home and put up for adoption, so too dogs and cats. As a faculty member, I was recently required to complete an online training about how to recognize child abuse and neglect, and I was struck by the fact that the scenarios described as "concerning" and/or "reportable" are the common lot of a large proportion of dogs and cats: for example, being left alone without company for hours at a time, being given too little or deficient food and water, not being given enough access to fresh air and exercise. But in their case, law intervenes only at the extremes of cruelty.

The analogy also suggests that companion animals are equal citizens, whose interests should be taken into account when public decisions are made. Their voices should be heard. The case of children is peculiar, because they are typically denied the vote on grounds that they are immature and will be enfranchised later. So let's consider adults with severe cognitive disabilities. These people have full legal rights, including the right to vote, even though they will need to rely on a "collaborator" to exercise many of these rights. If their rights are infringed, the "collaborator" can go to court on their behalf.

By contrast, companion animals at present lack all legal standing in the US, meaning that they cannot go to court as the plaintiff of an action, represented by an advocate. Their voices are consequently all too rarely heard when policies are made. I will challenge this legal situation in chapter 12. What would it mean to consider companion animals as fellow citizens? Sue Donaldson and Will Kymlicka have made this excellent proposal, but we need to say more about what it means. There are many theories of citizenship, its rights and its duties. Donaldson and Kymlicka make valuable suggestions, especially their proposal, drawn from disability rights, that citizens may exercise political agency while still being dependent on collaborators who try to understand their preferences. But I want to dwell, first, on the meaning of citizenship, as the CA articulates it.

According to the CA, then, citizenship for companion animals means, above all, that these animals are ends whose species-specific capabilities ought to be fostered by public policy, up to a suitable threshold, as spelled out in a basic law of some sort.

And citizenship also means that companion animals should be given decisional input into policies that affect their lives—one thing the capability of "practical reason" means in a political context. That is a type of political agency, whether it is exercised by traditional forms of democratic action or not. What forms might the fulfillment of this capability take, where animals are concerned?

When my friend Cass Sunstein was up for confirmation as head of the Office of Information and Regulatory Affairs in the Obama administration, his writings were read by his political opponents, among them his fine article "Standing for Animals," which documents the absurdities to which the lack of legal standing for animals has led, and argues for reform.[12] Conservative internet celebrity Glenn Beck wrote frequently alleging that Sunstein was "the most dangerous man in America,"[13] because "he thinks that your dog ought to be able to sue you."[14] Such were the internet conspiracy theories of a simpler era. This one had the advantage of truth.

Yes, indeed. For me, as for Sunstein (as I'll elaborate in chapter 12), a dog should be able to sue (for example, bringing an action to demand enforcements of under-enforced laws against cruelty), and to exercise, through a human representative, any of the fundamental legal rights of a citizen. Of course, this will be done by a human "collaborator," in just the way that humans with severe disabilities are represented in court by a collaborator. So this proposal is no more absurd than the idea that an aging parent, suffering from a mental disability, should still be able to sue a nursing home over deficient care—represented, once again, by a human "collaborator." (And let's not forget that you and I, too, need to hire a lawyer to sue for protection of our legal rights.) But what about the vote? I am sure Beck would regard the idea of animals voting as even more nightmarish than animals suing. Imagine a polling place where a group of dogs and cats have gathered to register their preferences, in the company of their frequently neglectful owners—so the ill-exercised animals will be yapping and biting, creating chaos. This is the Beck nightmare.

But the idea of each individual animal going to the polls and casting a vote for candidates for election is utterly the wrong way to conceive of representation for dogs and cats. My basic idea, similar to that of Donaldson and Kymlicka, is that the preferences and demands they do express in their daily lives will be translated into policy through suitable use of companionship, collaboration, and representation. One idea would be to have in each city and state an Office of Domestic Animal Welfare, whose human members would be charged with systematically examining the welfare of dogs and cats and promoting that welfare (those capabilities) through a variety of policies—in more or less the way that a department of child welfare operates in a well-functioning city or state. This would entail a lot of learning, including observation of how dogs and cats of many different types live, conversations with their human companions, and simply attending to the signals the animals themselves send about their welfare. Just as true attention to the capabilities of people with disabilities revealed that they are greatly impeded by lack of disability access to buildings and public transportation, and buildings and buses were consequently redesigned to promote greater capability, so too due attention to the preferences of companion animals can produce policies protecting their capabilities—with a prod from federal law where needed, as proved crucial in the disability case. Towns and cities would then be required to make suitable spaces available to companion animals, enhancing their ability to move freely and exercise, just as they are currently required to provide wheelchair access on buses and ramps in buildings.

As we'll see in the next section, the citizenship idea would impose on human companions further specific duties to promote the capabilities of the animals who live with them. And, since citizenship is reciprocal, it would impose duties on the animals as well: not to bite people or other animals, not to urinate and defecate in inappropriate places, not to be a nuisance in airports. If animals are cited for violations, their human companion must bear the cost, but it seems right to cite the animal, since holding accountable is a sign of respect. The breeding process that resulted in domestication means that these duties can usually be reliably fulfilled, given appropriate education—whereas we cannot expect a tiger or even a chimpanzee to observe similar duties. That is why these animals should not be kept as companion animals.

Obviously these duties must be exercised by the human companion and the animal acting in concert. Well-cared-for animals learn not to be a nuisance when they are shown sufficient respect for their learning abilities and their human companions care enough to spend time with them. And when cities and towns make spaces for exercise available to animals they are more likely to behave well in more confined spaces.

Humans must also compromise: not expecting dogs not to bark at all, for example. And they should be educated to understand dog body language, reading signs that a dog is not liking a certain type of behavior, learning not to hug a dog suddenly, or to put a hand directly in a dog's face. If an interaction goes poorly, it is not always the dog who is to blame!

GENERAL AND SPECIAL OBLIGATIONS

All humans have a collective obligation to secure and protect animal capabilities. This is just as true of wild as of companion animals, as my next chapter will argue. But the case of companion animals is somewhat more straightforward, because they have a fixed residence within an existing city, and a state, whose institutions should ultimately be responsible for making and enforcing laws that protect their welfare. All people in a given area, then, are responsible for supporting policies and laws that adequately protect domestic animal capabilities, whether they live with an animal companion or not.

However, there are also some special obligations that belong to people who choose to bring a companion animal into their home. As Keith Burgess-Jackson argues in an excellent article, this decision is analogous to the decision to have a child: it involves (or should) taking responsibility for the welfare of a vulnerable being who comes to live with you.[13] Parents who have a child become responsible for its nutrition and health care, for preventing cruelty and abuse, for making sure the child has opportunities for learning and stimulation, for exercise and play, and above all for sheltering love. The same is true of the decision to adopt a companion dog or cat. This decision, however, is often made with appalling casualness, and the large population of dogs and cats in shelters—and on the street—shows that people often regard an animal as a whim and feel it is perfectly all right to abandon the animal if they move away, or simply don't feel like caring for it any longer. (This has happened outrageously often as society reopens after COVID.) Parents who treat a human child this way would be charged with crimes. And even when people think they love their companion animal, there is still a great deal of ignorance about what that special responsibility entails. Many animals are ill-nourished. Many if not most dogs are under-exercised. And many human companions think that a companion animal is at their disposal—meaning fun to play with when they feel like it, but fine to leave alone when they are too busy or don't feel like it. (That's what many people think having a "pet" means: having a live toy.) Cats often do all right when neglected, but dogs need interaction and affection, and often do not get enough. People also do far too little research on the particular type of dog or cat they adopt, and choose a type that looks nice or is popular, without asking whether their lifestyle fits with what the animal needs. Some kinds of dogs should never be kept in a small urban apartment, and they become restless and even aggressive when cooped up for much of the day. Others are more adaptable. But all dogs need exercise, sensory stimulation, and a great deal of love and affection.

Finally, since we are talking about a multispecies society, dogs need education to be good citizens, just as children do, and this too is a special responsibility of the human companion. Hygiene comes easily to dogs, but they do need to be housebroken. They also need to learn not to bite or leap up on strangers. Cats should learn not to chase the local birds—or should be prevented from doing so if they can't learn. Pro-social behavior can and should be taught gently, through positive reinforcement, as with children. A child who has not been toilet-trained or taught to wash or not to bite has suffered from criminal neglect, and so too with dogs, I believe. Custody of an animal is a privilege that should be revoked in cases of severe or repeated neglect. The two sets of responsibilities complement and reinforce one another. Special ethical responsibilities don't really protect animals unless there is institutional and legal enforcement. That's where the collective responsibilities kick in.

The primary difference between companion and wild animals, as we'll see later, is that in the case of the latter, special responsibilities belong to people with an institutional role (for example, officials in a wildlife reserve) that officially gives them such a responsibility as part of their employment. People should not adopt a wild animal into their home.

PROMOTING SYMBIOTIC CAPABILITIES

Let's now consider the large rubrics of the Capabilities List, asking what version of each we ought to protect for animals who live in human households—remembering that all the capabilities of these animals are in some sense symbiotic.

Life and Health

Right now most jurisdictions give companion animals some protections. They are required to be inoculated against rabies and some other diseases. Increasingly, humans are required to adopt and not to purchase from a puppy mill, thus curbing many other diseases. Severe neglect may lead to citations for animal cruelty. But the protections are thin and incomplete. Sometimes shelters impose additional requirements on people who adopt from them. Still, there is no enforcement of regular veterinary care, regular exercise, or high-quality nutrition. We have only to consider the difference between children and companion animals to see how much more could, and I think should, be done. Children are now watched by a large range of public officials.

As I mentioned, all faculty and administrators in my university, for example, are mandatory reporters for child abuse and neglect, simply because our university has some programs involving young people under the age of eighteen. There are detailed definitions of mandatory reportable neglect. Thus, should I observe a child, well-dressed and apparently well-fed, left off at the locked school door before it is opened in the morning,

I am required to report the parents for neglect, since the doorway of a school is considered an unsafe place.

Not so for companion animals. Lack of grooming, apparent lack of adequate nutrition, and lack of regular exercise are simply not noticed, and if they are, there is nobody to whom these should or would be reported. Only in a very extreme case, where neighbors notice systematic neglect, would reporting ever happen. My view is that companion animals and children should be treated alike: an office overseeing animal welfare should take these complaints, and neighbors should receive training in their duties as mandatory reporters. Unfortunately, this is not enough, either for children or for animals: nobody can tell how good or bad the nutrition in the home is, for example. Children at least get a nutritious school lunch, but dogs and cats may get very inferior food all the time. Here public information and persuasion are our best allies. But because genuinely nutritious food for dogs is expensive, a public program should help nonaffluent families.

As for veterinary care: it is a sad fact that millions of children in the US lack health insurance, so it comes as no surprise that more millions of companion animals lack insurance too. When insurance is absent, care is often inadequate. Affluent families purchase health care for their children, or are insured through employment. And affluent families often purchase private medical insurance for their companion animals, which is relatively inexpensive and pretty good. So the problem is how to make sure companion animals in nonaffluent families—and in neglectful affluent families—are covered for the care they need. I favor a requirement, when adopting an animal from a shelter, that the human enroll the animal in an insurance program, in just the way that a person who takes on the ownership of a car is required to have auto insurance. Because animal insurance is currently not terribly costly, such a requirement would not greatly diminish the number of adoptions. This would make animals temporarily better off than children in the US, since it is abhorrent to Americans to curtail anyone's freedom to bear children by conditioning this choice on medical insurance, and there is no comprehensive health insurance subsidized for them once they arrive in the world. But that problem, an egregious injustice, urgently needs to be solved too. And for both there must be a public arrangement that makes the insurance afford-able for nonaffluent families.

People sometimes say that it is immoral to give a companion animal expensive medical care, when so many poor humans are suffering. This is a very confused objection. It is like saying that people should not take care of their own children's medical needs just because not all children have health insurance. The objector has confused special and general re-sponsibilities. Having adopted a companion animal (having decided to have a child), human adults have special responsibilities to support that animal with adequate medical care. But we also all have a general re-sponsibility to make it possible for nonaffluent people to afford to meet their special responsibilities, and indeed to enforce them when people are neglectful.

People often treat different members of their household differently, without justification—securing extensive and aggressive cancer treatment for an elderly relative and yet, when a dog has cancer, opting to euthanize the dog. This asymmetry, which seems to me totally immoral, is a vestige of the "pet" mentality: these creatures are optional toys, whom we may dispose of when things get tough. Responsible companions do not behave this way. There is indeed a place for euthanasia in the lives of dogs and cats; I believe there is a similar place for physician-assisted suicide in the lives of humans, but readers may doubt the latter while agreeing with me about the former. The place is: when the animal sends signals that life is just not worth living anymore, whether on account of intolerable pain or a sense of shame and degradation. A wonderful German shepherd I knew, Bear, who lived with a friend of mine, had hip dysplasia, the lot of so many like him, as a result of inbreeding. With a wheelchair supporting his hind legs, Bear was able to enjoy life, walking all around, and depending on his human companion only to carry him upstairs. But when he became in-continent, he was so ashamed and so miserable that his signals suggested his life was no longer worth living, and these signals were followed.

Bodily Integrity

Law already forbids some obvious forms of cruelty to animal bodies: beating, sexual assault, training the animal for use in fights with other animals. But there are some forms that are still popular. Let's consider just two: declawing (cats) and tail docking (dogs). These examples will show what the CA can supply that a Utilitarian approach cannot. The CA forbids all bodily alterations, even painless ones, that remove a central element in that creature's characteristic form of life, just on account of convenience or aesthetic considerations.

People want to declaw cats because they care about furniture, curtains, etc. They doubt the efficacy of training, and don't want to invest time in it. Declawing, like any other medical procedure, can be done without pain, as when one extracts a tooth. So the objection to it cannot be on Utilitarian grounds. Here the CA proves its superiority once again. The problem with declawing is that it stops cats from exercising a prominent part of their form of life, which does involve use of the claws to climb and to gain traction. If a declawed cat goes outdoors, it will be unable to climb trees and unable to defend itself. Declawing an outdoor cat is real cruelty. But even for an indoor cat, declawing makes the cat's paws virtually useless for traction, for climbing, for scratching. That of course is the entire point, to turn a cat into a convenient non-cat. The reply to the person who asks about declawing should be: if you do not want to live with a cat, don't adopt a cat. Shelters who offer cat adoption often, rightly, ask would-be adopters to sign a document promising not to declaw, and imposing stringent financial penalties on them should they be found to have violated the agreement.[16] Companions, meanwhile, should provide a home environment with ample occasions for clawing and scratching: if scratching posts are attractive enough, furniture is likely to survive.

Tail docking in certain breeds of dogs is less discussed, but equally significant. Again, the issue is one that pits aesthetics and convenience against an animal's form of life. Tails used to be docked out of mistaken health concerns: it was thought that undocked boxers and other related dog breeds were more prone to rabies. Today, as F. Barbara Orlans writes, people cite a variety of reasons: "Not wishing to break with tradition, improving appearance, preventing dogs from injuring themselves while involved in shooting and hunting, better hygiene, and providing for more harmonious cohabitation with humans in confined living conditions."[17] Fifty breeds are customarily docked.

Since tail docking is usually performed on newborn puppies without anesthesia, pain is an issue, but perhaps not an insuperable one, since an anesthetic could be given. The primary proponents of docking are breeders who sell dogs for show and feel that for economic reasons they must defer to a traditional aesthetic. The primary opponents are veterinarians (whose professional associations in the UK and Europe forbid docking), and the Council of Europe, whose Multilateral Convention for the Protection of Pet Animals forbids docking along with atrocities such as ear cropping, teeth removal, and the especially ghastly procedure of vocal cord removal (called "devocalization").

Two plausible reasons given in favor of docking are prevention of tail injuries and hygiene. Data on the first are inconclusive at best, and it is tempting to say that you can prevent all injuries to a dog by amputating the parts of its body that might be injured, but that is not a compelling reason for amputation. The hygiene objection can be met by better care and grooming, and it appears specious in any case because many long-haired breeds are not docked. Docking is first an aesthetic preference and second a choice for convenience over care. Such reasons should not be permitted to interfere with an animal's structural and functional integrity.

The tail is an organ of balance, a large sentient organ composed of vertebrae and muscles. It is used not only for movement but also for communication (of friendliness, playfulness, defensiveness, aggression, etc.). It also carries a scent gland used to mark territory. There should, then, be no doubt that even if the pain of the initial surgery were removed, an objection based on the animal's capabilities would decisively forbid the practice.

Mobility and Public Space

The Capabilities List speaks of freedom of movement as a key human capability. For humans, it is clearly *enough* mobility that is required. Nobody would argue that every person should be able to walk or drive everywhere. There could be no property rights or protections for personal privacy without laws against trespass, unwarranted search and seizure, and so forth. My rights of movement are also restricted by traffic laws, by laws governing the ownership and use of motor vehicles, and much more—and above all by the rights of others. I am not only not permitted to commit assault and battery, I am also not permitted to stalk someone or to harass them, which also typically means not entering their personal space unbidden, even if it is not their own property.

All of this is true of companion animals as well: their mobility rights are rightly limited in similar ways. Typically, however, they are limited in many further ways. Many cats are not permitted to go outdoors at all. Dogs are restricted by leash laws and by a dearth of dog parks where they can run unleashed. Even people very conscientious about their special obligations often have a hard time getting enough exercise for their dogs, given the standard design of public space.

Let's talk about cats first. Donaldson and Kymlicka argue that it is ethically wrong to keep a cat entirely indoors, and they might seem to be on strong capability grounds when they do so. Cats do love to climb, to run in the grass, etc. However, in urban and even many suburban environments it is clear that the hazards of the outdoors take years off the average life of a cat. There are good data on this that have convinced most concerned US cat lovers. (Donaldson and Kymlicka live in Canada.) Motor vehicles, animal viruses, predatory animals such as larger dogs or even coyotes, these are the unavoidable risks of the outdoors, and cats cannot be trained to avoid them. Cats, unlike dogs, and more like humans, adapt well to a more indoor life, and to somewhat less exercise. Therefore, many great lovers of cats argue that it is unethical *not* to keep a cat indoors, unless you are in a safe rural environment with no predators. I'm with the second group. Humans can live good indoor lives, and in cities we all do. Cats are similarly adaptable.

Dogs are different. Need for exercise depends on the breed, but all need quite a lot, and rarely get enough. A fenced-in yard is ideal, but not available to all. And even the dog with a yard wants a change of scene. Unfortunately, in cities people can't always even find good places to run with a dog on a leash, far less to let a dog play, explore, socialize with other dogs in a free and unleashed environment. Just as the design of public space has undergone a revolution in order to make space accessible to people with disabilities, so too space needs to be redesigned for accessibility to dogs. But care must also be taken: for unfortunately, many dogs are ill-trained and may bite children, adults, and other dogs. That is the reason for leash laws. There are also people who are allergic to dogs and therefore don't want to be nuzzled even by a very nice dog.

Unlike Donaldson and Kymlicka, then, I am not hostile to leash laws; they have their place. But I wholeheartedly agree that we need to create many more spaces, especially in urban environments, where dogs (and humans) can romp and play. (There need to be many playgrounds for human children too.) Dog parks need to be easier to access, and larger, and with more engaging opportunities for climbing and jumping. Just as disability access required retrofitting existing space, so too here: existing parks need to be differently configured, and this should be part of urban planning, not a niche concern pressed only by a vocal minority.

Sexuality and Reproduction

Unlike humans, dogs and cats cannot direct their own sex lives by advanced planning and consent. They cannot choose to use contraception, even when burdened by many births. Humans must either limit access to their companion animals by keeping them indoors during their fertile period or at least consider spaying or neutering them if they think limiting birth is in the interests of the animal, and/or the potential new animals that would be born.

The CA suggests that in a well-behaved world, each animal, male or female, would have at least one or two chances at sex and reproduction: that seems a reasonable threshold, if a low one, given the importance of the capability and the life-experiences it yields. There are several reasons to spay or neuter following this initial experience of sexuality/pregnancy/ birth: preventing exhaustion to the female animal from repeated pregnancies; the difficulty of keeping non-neutered male cats as companions (aggression, spraying); and, above all, the harms to the many litters of puppies and kittens who would not find suitable homes and would likely either be abandoned or swell the already overburdened population of shelters. If we think of the parent animal's own hypothetical consent, we can easily imagine, given the strong attachment of female animals to their offspring, that they would not want offspring to live a miserable life, and would therefore consent to the operation.

Unfortunately, ours is far from a perfect world. There are so many feral cats living miserable lives (and reproducing all the while), and so many unwanted puppies, that the ideal solution is, for now, too permissive. A good policy probably dictates the spaying or neutering of all strays (many countries already practice this as a matter of public policy), and at least urging human companions to neuter their companion animals in advance of reproduction—unless they commit to keeping the offspring or finding truly suitable homes for them. That can be, and often is, a condition of adoption. Pro-animal NGOs such as Friends of Animals operate active spay/neuter programs as an important contribution to animal welfare. The fewer animals end up in shelters, the more likely that those who are there will find suitable homes.[18]

In some countries there are additional reasons for spaying/neutering, in the damage done by feral cats to native birds and mammals. Australia has embarked on a ghastly program of cat extermination.[19] A sounder policy, used in many places, is to sterilize feral cats, and that policy can be expected, if pursued intelligently, to lead to good results. I do believe that a self-defense principle permits us to kill animals (for example, rats) who threaten the life and safety of humans and other animals, but killing (which must be humane, as the Australian program is not) should be a last resort, after contraception has been tried.

Education and Training

I've already said that a multispecies society requires all to accept responsibilities for the well-being of others, and this means that a responsible human companion will educate her companion animal in good social behavior: not biting, not soiling the rug, and so forth. But education is not just control: it is a development of the animal's social maturity, and dogs, like children, are full of eagerness to learn, and derive pleasure from mastering a social habit, so this is not a dreary activity unless humans make it so.

Work

The Human Capabilities List does not even include work as a separate category: only as a place where discrimination may not be present, and where affiliation may be fostered. This omission reflects not the unimportance but the ubiquity of work. People may not love the work they do, and some people, whether through affluence or through retirement, may not work at all, but such people are rare. For companion animals, by contrast, work is not ubiquitous. Cats rarely work. Dogs work if they belong to breeds that can be trained for specialized functions: herding, hunting, rescuing, guiding, and a variety of olfactory detective occupations (sniffing for explosives, for drugs, even for COVID). Donaldson and Kymlicka are extremely critical of putting animals to work, and they come to the conclusion that animals should work only when they wish to, and only as much as they wish to.

Working dogs are often trained using negative reinforcement; they are often given hours that give them little opportunity for play and affection. It is also true that some of the things dogs have been bred to do, like foxhunting, are themselves inhumane. But reforming work practices does not mean abolishing them. And for dogs as for humans, a job well done can be a huge source of satisfaction. Think again of Argos: he was listless, lying on the dung heap, because he was too old to work, and had a sense of lost status and uselessness. That's what I would feel if I were forced to retire. And I think many dogs of the relevant breeds lead richer and more fulfilling lives if employed than sitting around idle in someone's house. Very much the same is true of horses, of the type bred for hunter-jumper activity: they have the joy of a good athlete at executing their jumps well, and putting them out to pasture before age dictates this is to remove a great source of meaning. In short: if on-balance work adds meaning and richness to the animal's life, then, as with all of us, the animal must accept the regular hours that a decent workplace requires (meaning hours that give ample time for play and companionship). That does mean that sometimes they work when they don't feel like it, but that is true of all of us.

All working animals, including humans, are in one sense used as means to the ends of the workplace. But what decent societies strive to achieve is the treatment of a worker as above all an end, even in the context of serving various useful functions.

Stimulation and Play

Corresponding to the capability of Senses, Imagination and Thought and the capability of Play is the need for all companion animals to have environments that stimulate their senses and their curiosity and that invite them to enjoy play, both with other animals and with humans. A large proportion of companion dogs, especially, are bored. If the human takes them out for just one or two brief walks, and leaves them alone in the house the rest of the time—common behavior of busy working humans—they grow listless, often put on weight and acquire diseases such as diabetes, and, in general just don't enjoy life. Adopting a dog means taking responsibility for giving the dog a cognitively varied and interesting life: appropriate exercise in a variety of environments, varied and tasty food, and opportunities to play with other animals, as well as playtime with a non-bored and affectionately engaged human. Animal behavior expert Barbara Smuts, whom I'll discuss in chapter 11, makes a further important point: the dog needs to be able to call the shots, at least some of the time. Thus, when out walking with her companion dog, Safi, she allows Safi to decide on the route about half of the time, following an interesting smell or trail. Most humans don't do this: they have their fixed running or walking route, and the dog has to come along. Curiosity is extinguished, and, once again, the dog has a boring life. Many humans drag their children along with them in a similar fashion, but this is bad parenting, and good parenting involves taking the child, often, where the child wants to go.

Affiliation and Practical Reason

These are the key capabilities on the human list, in that they organize all the others and suffuse them, coloring everything else. For dogs and cats, *practical reason* is closely associated with being treated as an end. To have a life of practical reason, for symbiotic animals, is not to go off on their own: that cannot be a good life for a dog or cat. It means, instead, within the larger relationship with a human, having one's interests respected; having sufficient options, in short, across all the central dog or cat capabilities; being able to live a good life that is the creature's own, not one that is dictated solely by the interests of humans. And because this good life will never be a solitary life, but always one intertwined with humans (and often with other animals), it is crucial that the relationship with humans be a mutually affectionate and mutually respectful relationship. If affection and respect are there, and if humans really learn to think of the companion animal as an independent being with its own ends, not just a toy or instrument, all the rest will follow.

COMPANION ANIMALS NOT INSIDE THE HOUSE: HORSES, CATTLE, SHEEP, CHICKENS

I have focused extensively on cats and dogs, but they offer a good paradigm for related cases. I think horses (of non-wild species) are a very similar case, although they do not live inside the house. They are highly interactive, get pleasure and meaning from a good relationship with humans, and can take joy in their own excellence and the partnership it involves. Nor would they have good lives if turned loose to make their way through the world on their own. This isn't to say that the world of horseback riding is not full of cruelty and corruption, but it should be possible, given what I've said so far, to recognize it and work against it.

There is one thing to add, however, related to my argument about the abolition of specialized dog breeding linked to disease: the entire industry of thoroughbred horse racing needs to be abolished. Horses are bred to have such stick-thin legs that they often break from the slightest cause, dooming the animal to a premature death. They have abnormally small hearts, and a multitude of other health problems. This is all about money, not about the animal, and I think that the breeding of such animals must be made illegal, and sooner rather than later. Steeplechase racing has similar health issues. A steeplechase horse must have greater strength and stamina than a thoroughbred raced on the track; but apparently the health problems are similar or even greater.[20] Hunter-jumpers are different and can lead fine healthy symbiotic lives with their human companions, as can dressage horses.

As for cattle, oxen are working animals who, if treated well, flourish in their work. What about dairy cattle? As Donaldson and Kymlicka discuss, the dairy industry at present is a moral horror.[21] Bred to produce abundant milk, dairy cows have weak bones through depletion of calcium. In addition, cows are separated from their calves at birth (to maximize the share of their milk that goes to humans), and kept continuously pregnant, which results in many health problems. I agree with Donaldson and Kymlicka that it is possible to imagine a reformed dairy industry. But it would not be commercially profitable, since calves would use a lot of the mother's milk, and the mother would not be continuously pregnant. They imagine that cow's milk might then become a luxury good, "resulting in a limited but stable cow community."[22]

Things are much better with sheep. Actual sheep are often not treated very well, but, unlike some vegans and like Donaldson and Kymlicka, I have no principled objection to the human use of animal products, so long as the animal is able to carry on its characteristic animal life. Use need not be exploitative, and domestic sheep need to be shorn, since they do not shed their wool automatically. It is good for them, relieving them of a burden. Indeed, not to shear them would be an abuse. So we can easily imagine ethical conditions under which humans shear sheep and use their wool. In addition, humans may ethically gather sheep droppings and use them for fertilizer. As Donaldson and Kymlicka say, "These uses seem to be utterly benign—the sheep are just doing what sheep do, and humans are benefiting from this uncoerced activity."[23] Indeed, they add, viewing the sheep as citizens we note that this is a major opportunity for them to contribute to the common good.[24]

What about chickens (the ones who are raised for their eggs, not for slaughter)? Again, the current commercial system of egg production is unacceptable, involving abusive confinement, the killing of male chicks, and the killing of hens once their egg production drops off. But here we can easily imagine an ethical reform that would be sustainable, and it is already in place on some farms. Free-range domesticated hens produce a large number of eggs. They can be allowed to incubate some, and raise young, and there will still be many left. There seems nothing wrong with the human use of these surplus eggs, so long as the chickens have plenty of room to live good chicken lives, roaming around, forming relationships, having plenty of time to explore and play.[25]

Vegans, like abolitionists, deny the possibility of mutually beneficial symbiosis. We need to look carefully at each case, but I believe symbiosis, in the case of animals both inside and outside the house, is possible.

Other barnyard animals are raised for slaughter, and I leave that topic for my chapter on law. Are there other animals who are quasi-companions? Most of the animals kept in homes under this description—hamsters, gerbils, parakeets, goldfish, turtles, canaries—are not really symbiotic animals at all: they are captive wild animals, even if they are in a private home, not a zoo. My next chapter will take up that topic.

To summarize: numerous animal species, usually through deliberate breeding in prehistory, are thoroughly symbiotic with humans. They live in our homes or alongside them. There need be nothing wrong with that, so long as they are treated not as "pets" or property, but as active dependent citizens, with their own lives to live. They would not be able to live well if simply turned loose. Changing our old ways, based on the property paradigm, will not be easy, but it is a revolution already in progress with dogs, cats, and horses, and there are even isolated examples of reformed human behavior with chickens, sheep, and dairy cattle. Abolitionism is no good for these animals, who will flourish only in partnership with humans. Nor is the vegan idea of nonuse a sound guide to ethical behavior. The CA is a far better guide, using the animal's own characteristic way of life as a benchmark.

10

THE "WILD" AND HUMAN
RESPONSIBILITY

Be thou me, impetuous one!
Drive my dead thoughts over the universe
Like wither'd leaves to quicken a new birth!
Percy Bysshe Shelley, "Ode to the West Wind"

Killing, the most criminal act recognized by human laws, Nature does
once to every being that lives; and in a large proportion of cases, after
protracted tortures such as only the greatest monsters whom we read
of ever purposely inflicted on their living fellow-creatures.
J. S. Mill, "Nature"

Should we try to leave non-domesticated animals alone in "the wild," their
evolutionary habitat, but also a place full of cruelty, scarcity, and casual
death, or should we actively intervene to protect wild animals? If the latter, in what ways? And what is "the wild"? Does it even exist? Whose interests does this concept serve?

In this chapter, I grapple with difficult questions raised by the idea of
"wildlife" and "the wild," questions such as: Do we have a responsibility
to protect "wild" animals from scarcity and disease? How can and should
we do this, without violating these animals' form of life? Given that zoos

historically have been cruel to wild animals and have served human interests rather than the interests of the animals they imprison, can we legitimately keep at least some wild animals in zoos of some type, and, if so, which animals and zoos of what type? Can we envisage such a thing as a cooperative multispecies society, where "wild" animals are concerned? And what about predation of vulnerable animals by other animals? Could it possibly be our responsibility to limit that?

My answers to these questions will be, in some cases, controversial; in some cases one may accept the general outlines of the Capabilities Approach and differ about these applications. Indeed, in terms of the community of animal lovers, this is likely to be the most controversial chapter of the book.[1] But my conclusions, albeit provocative, are also tentative, since we are searching for new ways to think and act in a world dominated, everywhere, by human power and activity.

Beginning with a skeptical examination of the Romantic credentials of a common Western idea of "the wild" and of "Nature," I argue that this idea is made by humans for human purposes and does not serve or even very much consider the interests of other animals. Moreover, today at any rate, there is no such thing as "the wild," no space, that is, that is not controlled by humans: the pretense that "the wild" exists is a way of avoiding responsibility.

Next, having already considered the situation of animals with whom humans live on a daily basis and who have evolved to be symbiotic with humans, and having defended there a version of the idea of a "multispecies society," and of animals as our fellow citizens, I proceed to ask: How far can and should this idea be extended to "wild animals"? What are our responsibilities as de facto guardians to protect "wild" animal lives?

"THE WILD" AS ROMANTIC DREAM

The fascination of an idea of "wild" Nature lies deep in the thinking of the modern environmental movement. The idea is entrancing, but also, I believe, deeply confusing. Before we can make progress, we have to understand its cultural origins and the work it was meant to do for those who employed it.

Here, in a nutshell, is the Romantic idea of Nature: Human society is stale, predictable, effete. It lacks powerful sources of energy and renewal. People are alienated from one another and from themselves. The Industrial Revolution has made cities foul places where the human spirit is frequently crushed (as in Blake's "dark Satanic mills"). By contrast, out there somewhere—on the mountains, in the oceans, even in the wild West wind—there beckons something truer, deeper, something uncorrupt and sublime, a type of vital energy that can restore us, because it is the analogue of our own deepest depths. Other animals are a large part of this "wild": of Nature's mysterious and vital energy. (Think of Blake's "Tyger, tyger, burning bright.") The typical Romantic scenario is that of a solitary walk in wild Nature: Chateaubriand visiting Niagara Falls (although he never actually went there); Rousseau's *Reveries of a Solitary Walker*; Goethe's Werther flinging himself into the embrace of the winds; Shelley feeling, even, that he himself *is* the wind; Wordsworth's lonely wandering ending in a more tranquil epiphany of golden daffodils; Henry David Thoreau taking to the woods around Walden Pond. "Wild" Nature summons us to deep emotions of wonder and awe, and through those emotions we are renewed.

Is this constellation of emotions helpful in thinking about how we ought to approach other animals? I believe it is not. The Romantic idea of "the wild" is born of human anxieties, particularly about urban and industrial life. Nature, in this conception, is supposed to do something for us; the idea has little to do with what we are supposed to do for Nature and other animals. The narcissism of the concept is usually explicit, as in Shelley's constant "I," or in Wordsworth's final lines: "For oft, when on my couch I lie, / In vacant or in pensive mood, / They flash upon that inward eye / Which is the bliss of solitude; / And then my heart with pleasure fills, / And dances with the daffodils." Blake's "Tyger," similarly, is clearly an emblem of something in the human psyche, and the poem tells us nothing about how Blake would like us to treat real tigers.

Many nineteenth-century Romantics even had the idea that peasants and other poor people were part of Nature or closer to Nature, and ought to stay there in rural poverty rather than venture into the city and try to get educated. Tolstoy's Levin finds peace when he drops his urban sophistication and joins the natural work life of the peasants. (And what would real peasants have thought of that pretension?) Thomas Hardy skewered the fiction in *Jude the Obscure*, showing its dire consequences for real poor people with intelligence and ambition; but the fiction endured. E. M. Forster still believes it when he represents Leonard Bast, in *Howards End*, as better off in the country: his mistake was to move to London and try to educate himself. Instead of peasants, think other animals, and you will see where I am going. Oh those animals, so far below us, how alive, how robust they are! If only for a brief five-day safari we could share (from a safe distance) their world of violence and scarcity. Of course, we would never dream of living that life, but we feel a frisson by brief contact, and we feel more alive. (Many people on eco-safari think and talk in exactly this way.)

Nor is the Romantic fiction the peculiar property of newly industrial Europe and North America. Other societies have other variants on the idea of "natural" purity, energy, and virtue. We see it in ancient Roman obsessions with farming and agriculture as renewing sources; in Gandhi's idea that the virtue of India's people will be restored by rural poverty, spinning one's own cloth, and so forth. People in many places seem to need to believe that their urban sophistication is bad and that they will become happier and better if they blend somehow with "wild" Nature. Usually the "blending" is pretty bogus, as with Chateaubriand's description of a place he didn't bother to visit, as, also, with the immense sophistication with which the Romantic poets lay claim to rural simplicity. Fine, it's still good poetry. My point is that this is an idea by and about human beings, not about Nature or animals or what they require of us. And the wonder involved in the Romantic sublime is similarly egocentric. It is not the sort of wonder I've been talking about since chapter 1, the wonder that really turns us outward.

Some good has come of the Romantic idea of Nature. Because people wanted a certain type of experience, they preserved places that seemed to offer it. The Sierra Club and much in American conservationism had this origin, as did preservationist movements elsewhere. Often, today, people find physical and spiritual refreshment in "wild" places, and countries that have preserved them offer people a genuine good that has vanished in other places. But the good is all too often accidental: it is about us, not them. And there is much bad: glorification of game hunting, whaling, and fishing, and today's ghastly theater of what might be called sado-tourism, in which people lay out a lot of money to see animals tear other animals limb from limb, rather like captive slaves and lions in those long-ago gladiatorial games.

THE "WILD" IS NOT GOOD, AND IT DOESN'T EXIST ANYWAY

If by Nature and "the wild" we mean the way things go when humans do not intervene, that way is not so good for non-human animals.[2] For millennia, Nature has meant hunger, excruciating pain, often the extinction of entire groups. When we compare "the wild" to the factory farming industry, or to the less ethically sensitive forms of zoo captivity, it looks somewhat more benign; but used as a source of normative thinking in itself, the idea of Nature does not offer useful guidance. As John Stuart Mill correctly says, Nature is cruel and thoughtless.

Even the time-honored idea of the "balance of nature" has by now been decisively refuted by modern ecological thinking. When humans do not intervene, Nature does not attain a stable or balanced condition, nor does it attain the condition that is best for other creatures or for the environment.[3] Indeed, to the extent that natural ecosystems do sustain themselves stably, it is only on account of various forms of human intervention. The "balance of nature" idea looks different from the Romantic idea, but it is really a form of it: our (urban) lives are marred by competitive anxiety and envy, but Nature is peaceful and balanced. This idea has its roots in human need and fantasy and is not supported by evidence.

There are certainly some good reasons not to intervene in the lives of "wild" animals. Two such reasons are (1) that we are ignorant and will make many mistakes, and (2) that intervention is often objectionably paternalistic, when what we ought to do is respect animals' choice of a way of life. These are prima facie reasons only, however. Ignorance can be replaced by knowledge, as our ignorance of what is good for the children and the companion animals who live with us has, for the most part, been replaced by knowledge. Where we remain ignorant, society believes that ignorance in such matters is not excusable: thus, a parent who refuses vaccinations for her children (or indeed for companion animals) is (in most circumstances) blameworthy for the ignorance that underlies that choice. As for autonomy: we typically do not accuse governments of acting with objectionable paternalism when they adopt comprehensive Social Security or health insurance measures—or, indeed, when they adopt laws defining murder, rape, and theft as crimes and enforcing those laws. Where the basic wherewithal of life is concerned, we feel that people have a right to be protected (although anti-paternalists rightly insist that where adults are concerned, health choices remain personal to at least some extent). If we shrug our shoulders when animals are starving, aren't we saying that animals don't matter? And if we defend our hands-off policy by pleading ignorance of their good, how plausible is that plea when we're talking about matters of basic survival?

But this discussion, interesting though it is, presupposes that there is such a thing in the world as "wild" Nature: spaces that are not under human control and supervision. It presupposes that it is possible for humans to leave animals alone. That presupposition is false. However large the tracts of land may be, all land in our world is thoroughly under human control. Thus "wild animals" in Africa live on animal refuges maintained by the governments of various nations, who control admission to them, defend them from poachers (only sometimes successfully), and support the lives of animals in them through a range of strategies (including spraying for tsetse flies and many other matters). There would be no rhinos or elephants left in the world if humans did not intervene. In the US, "wild horses" and other "wild" creatures live under the jurisdiction of our nation and its states. To the extent that they have limited rights of non-intervention, free movement, and even a type of property rights, that is because human law has seen fit to give them these rights.[4] Humans are in control everywhere. Humans decide what habitats to protect for animals, and leave the animals only what they decide not to use.

The air and the oceans might appear to be more genuinely "wild," but what can happen in them is controlled in many ways by both national and international law, and shaped pervasively by human activity. As Hal's story in the introduction and the discussion of the US Navy's sonar program in chapter 5 show us, the lives of whales and other marine species are constantly interfered with by human use of the oceans— by sonic disturbance, commercial whaling, plastic pollution, and much more. Chapter 12 will discuss what law has done so far to protect marine life, and how little, really, law has been able to do to rein in human greed. As for the air, as Jean-Pierre's story in the introduction reminds us, humans are polluting the air in ways that interfere greatly with the lives of birds. Human architecture and urban lighting cause countless bird deaths every year: light draws birds to it, disrupts their circadian rhythms, and alters migration patterns.[5] Human activity also alters, and often destroys, bird habitats.

A book like this might grant that the current status quo is that humans dominate everywhere, but could still recommend that humans simply back off and leave all the "wild" animals in all of these spaces to do the best they can for themselves. Even that proposal would require active human intervention to stop human practices that interfere with animal lives: poaching, hunting, whaling. And it would be, it seems, a gross abnegation of responsibility: we have caused all these problems, and we turn our backs on them, saying, "Well, you are wild animals, so live with it as best you can." It is not clear what would be accomplished by this pretense of a hands-off policy. It would not really be hands-off, it would simply be a decision not to try to remedy the problems that our ubiquitous activity has caused for animals. Quite apart from the issue of species protection, which, as in chapter 5, I leave to some extent to one side, it seems like a very callous policy.

Nor is it clear that we can ethically be standoffish, even in instances where we have not caused the problem. If we are there looking on, in control of and monitoring animal habitats, it seems like callous steward-ship indeed if we permit mass starvation, disease, and other thoroughly "natural" types of pain and torment. We would be watching these calamities, but refusing to stop them. We'll get to predation later, and that issue is truly difficult. But what about starvation and preventable disease, things that existing wild animal refuges routinely try to prevent—and things that very likely have human co-causes?

An example is instructive: in Kyrgyzstan, a national park called Ala-Archa has created spaces that wild animals control. Thus the park is divided into three zones: one where humans may hike and picnic, one where animals live without human interference, and one where the same animals breed and nurture young, again without interference—so to speak. The rationale is that rare species such as the snow leopard need protection if they are to sustain themselves and reproduce, and that all species function best in a multispecies world if the reproductive activities are segregated to some extent from other life-activities. Thus, on a recent visit I saw only squirrels and magpies. All of this of course is totally artificial and requires constant intervention. Each habitat is set up and maintained so that animals can enjoy flourishing species-specific lives. Although I could not get near the two other zones, I know that internally there is much management there as well, fostering successful feeding and reproduction. This arrangement is much better for animals than the one that would exist if all creatures collided together. We could even hypothesize that it's the one that the animals would choose if they spoke, since it's the one that best promotes health and flourishing. But in saying that, we are saying that animals, like humans, don't choose to be abandoned without protectors: their hypothetical choice is for a world with decent stewardship promoting their flourishing. A non-"wild" world.

Here's another example, introduced just in case you still insist that the skies are the last frontier of true animal freedom. New Zealand, unlike Australia, has no non-domesticated midsize mammals. But it does have a variety of rodents, mainly introduced by white settlers: rabbits, squirrels, mice, rats. And of course, it has domesticated animals, dogs and cats, many of which wander at large. But the islands contain an amazing variety of birds—not predatory birds, which might have an edge in the competition with the rodents, but many species of small songbirds and several types of parrots. As you can easily imagine, the little birds and to some extent the parrots are at risk from the rodents and the cats. And if the "course of nature" had prevailed, many avian species would by now be extinct, and, more germane to my argument, many small birds would have been torn apart and died in agony. Outside Wellington, I visited a bird sanctuary that is in effect a large avian semi-zoo. Humans may enter and hike, though they have to pass inspection lest they feed the birds or carry in with them any rodent, dog, or cat. But rodents, dogs, and cats are kept out by a large and very high netting. It is three-sided, meaning that birds may leave if they choose to do so, seeking food outside. But it is carefully calculated to be a barrier too high for any of the usual rodent suspects to cross: indeed a demonstration at the entrance shows how high rabbits can jump, how high cats jump, and what sort of thwarting of the climbing capabilities of each has been put in place. Birds are free—precisely because the space is curated.

These two cases show that freedom and autonomy for animals are not incompatible with intelligent human stewardship. Indeed, they typically require stewardship, because Nature is not a glorious site of freedom.

If humans try to renounce stewardship, in a world where they are ubiquitously on the scene, shaping every habitat in which every animal lives, this is not an ethically defensible choice or one that promotes good animal lives. The only options before us, in the world as it is, are types and degrees of stewardship. We need to face this fact head-on, or else we will not have a good debate about how to exercise the power that we indubitably have.

PRINCIPLES OF ETHICAL STEWARDSHIP: WILD ANIMALS AND THEIR HABITATS

First, then, here are some general principles to guide us as we steer our course in a world that we dominate, for better or for worse. (And right now it is mainly for the worse.)

Principle 1. Every wild animal habitat is a human-dominated space.

Animals need good habitats in order to have flourishing lives. But humans control all the habitats, on land, sea, and in the air. Often, this "control" is diffuse and chaotic, and there is power without authority. This situation permits countless injuries to "wild" animals, from poaching to asphyxiation from pollution. Accepting Principle 1 as a starting point is the beginning of accountability and true deliberation about how animal capabilities can be protected.

Principle 2. Human causal responsibility for bad habitats is often concealed and can rarely, if ever, be ruled out.

It is tempting to think that humans are responsible for obvious harms such as poaching, hunting, and whaling, and maybe even for harms that, while less obvious, are clearly human in origin (the plastics in the oceans, sonic disruption from sonar, shipping, and oil rigs),[6] but not for other harms that seem to come from "Nature," such as drought, famine, and loss of a typical space to search for food (such as ice floes, on which polar bears must navigate the oceans to find sustenance). But a little reflection will show that this line cannot be clearly drawn, if drawn at all. Human activity is central in climate change, which is a key to habitat damage for many species, causing droughts, famines, floods, and fires. Human activity pollutes the air. Human population spreads out into formerly animal spaces, reducing their space and their food. Mill was certainly right to say that "Nature" never was a fostering environment for animal lives. Today, however, the largest "natural" problems facing animals are of human origin. We should proceed as if nothing is "just Nature," and all the big bad things are mainly us. In short, we should never let ourselves off the hook.

Principle 3. Stewardship is not companionship, and wild animals are not companion animals.

What remains of a notion of "the wild," in my approach, is a warning not to treat wild animals as if they were companion animals. They have not evolved to be symbiotic with humans, and their form of life is only incidentally intertwined with ours. There may sometimes be friendships between humans and wild animals (see chapter 11), but that possibility requires great humility and deference to the wild animal's form of life.

There will be delicate lines to be drawn: when to give medical care to an injured animal, how far to back off. The following section will investigate some of these. The touchstone should always be a picture of the ideal flourishing of that type of creature, and we should interfere with that picture, typically, only at the margins of the frame, sustaining habitats, removing dangers, and at times addressing disease, but not treating the wild creatures, whether fledgling birds or orphaned elephants, as if they were our household pets. This emphatically does not mean leaving animals alone, as if we bore no responsibility for their predicament. It means finding solutions that are respectful of what the animal needs in order to live as itself.

STEWARDSHIP AND THE CAPABILITIES

Now, as in chapter 9, let's consider the large rubrics on the Capabilities List, giving examples of ways in which humans can—and often, ethically, must—protect animal capabilities. There are so many species to consider that I can give only a sketch of what the CA would recommend.

Life, Health, Bodily Integrity

First, and most urgent, humans must *end human practices that directly violate wild animal life, health, and bodily integrity*. Poaching is an obvious case, and more effective global cooperation is urgently needed to stop this criminal trade, both policing it at its source and banning the sale of all ivory worldwide. Commercial whaling, and other forms of hunting wild animals for profit or amusement, should also be banned and effectively policed. Animal parts (trophies of the hunt) should be prohibited from being exported from the nation where a killing has occurred and imported into the hunter's nation. Some nations and states have begun to do this. It is also important to stop the importation of young wild animals into zoos in a rich country, as with the Swaziland eighteen, which I discuss in the next section, and as with orcas taken from their pods to amuse visitors in marine theme parks. These practices don't kill the animal, but they violate its health and bodily integrity by ripping it from its group context and putting it into a context that cannot support either physical or mental health.

Second, humans must *stop practices that heedlessly cause animal death and suffering*, even though humans did not intend to harm animals: they just did not think well enough to foresee the harm. The use of single-use plastic items and their disposal, ultimately, in the ocean is such a practice, and we must not only stop it, but also clean up what is already there as best we can, since plastic lives more or less forever. Another such practice is bright lighting on urban buildings, which lures thousands of migrating birds to their doom. Around a billion bird deaths are caused in this manner annually, in the US alone.[7] It is possible to dim lighting at high-migration times without harming human activity, or to use bird-proof glass. Cities such as my own, which are key parts of migration patterns, bear a heavy responsibility for these deaths (see the conclusion). In this same category I would place the use of sonar in the sea, and the use of air guns by oil riggers trying to chart the ocean floor, which cause sonic disturbances very damaging to marine mammals (see chapter 12).

These first two steps can and must be taken right now. Far more difficult is the third: humans must *protect wild animal habitats from damages due to climate change and other environmental factors that likely have a human origin*. I said that one principle is that you don't let yourself off the hook easily, and it is ethically responsible to assume that droughts, famines, floods, shrinkage of glacier ice, and so many other environmental conditions threatening the lives of wild animals are ultimately of human origin. At any rate, we should be proactive, presuming our own responsibility. But it is so difficult to know exactly what to do. Stopping climate change requires a global will that is not yet established, and even if it is, it won't reverse changes that have already taken place. So what about animals who are suffering right now? For famine and drought, we must take steps already known to be effective for human populations, which will benefit both humans and animals. The hardest cases are those where climate change threatens to make a form of life unlivable in the future. We cannot replace the ice that polar bears used to walk on to find their food. So we must focus on preventing further loss.

The fourth follows naturally: we must *limit our own use of scarce habitat resources* in order to leave room for animals. I discussed these conflicts in chapter 8, and they clearly entail limiting human population growth and protecting many spaces so that they remain clear of human habitation.

Fifth, I would argue that we must *use our knowledge—wisely and deliberately—to protect wild animal lives*. Large wild animal reserves protect animals by spraying for tsetse flies and other deadly threats. This is where human activity crosses a boundary between remediation of human harms and proactive protection. But it seems unthinkable not to cross that line, since humans are managing these wildlife reserves, presumably for the sake of the animals in them, not just for human tourists and the money they bring in. What about *veterinary care*? Here we run a grave risk of upsetting the animal's form of life, if intervention is too frequent and too disruptive. However, given our ubiquitous presence near wild animal lives, medical intervention is increasingly seen as a moral imperative that can be fulfilled with respect and understanding. In areas of human habitation, local authorities advise inhabitants what to do—and what not to do—if they find an apparently abandoned small bird, or rabbit, or deer.[8] Many animal lives are saved in this way without making the wild animal into a household pet: they are given emergency care and returned to their family. In a decent zoo, animals routinely have veterinary surgery for life-threatening problems. Just one recent example was the daring hip replacement performed on a tiger at Brookfield Zoo in Chicago.[9] Should this sort of capability-preserving intervention also be attempted in wildlife reserves, which are in effect large non-enclosed zoos? This is an evolving field of specialization in veterinary medicine, and such experts will be trained to be thoroughly familiar with animal habitats and forms of life. As time goes on, they will make many difficult judgment calls in this area.[10] It does seem intolerable that a tiger gets to be able to walk again because it happens to be in a zoo in Chicago, whereas a tiger in a large animal reserve in Asia would not get the same care—just because the reserve is larger than the zoo! (And what other relevant difference is there, other than that the reserve is a better habitat?)

There are many difficult questions human experts will need to explore as time goes on, and as the interpenetration between human and animal lives becomes ever greater. The Capabilities Approach offers good guidance where Utilitarian approaches do not: the aim should always be that the animal should be protected in its ability to live a full species-characteristic form of life (or to depart from that species norm if it chooses to do so). Conflicts will remain between the good of one species and that of others, predation being the main such case. But typically the measures that protect animal habitats in general are good for all the animals in those habitats.

Senses, Imagination, Thought; Emotions; Practical Reason; Affiliation; Other Species; Play; Control Over Environment

The rest of the capabilities on the list take care of themselves once life, health, and bodily integrity are protected. (As before, I leave predation for special later treatment.) If an animal's habitat is free from grievous intrusions and dangers, if it offers enough space for healthy movement, group activity, and enough quality nutrition, then animal lives will not be deadened by monotony (as in bad zoos), stifled by fear, or lacking in opportunities for self-direction, including affiliation and play, both with a species group, and in good relationships with other species.

ARE ZOOS ETHICALLY PERMISSIBLE?

One useful thing the idea of the "wild" has done for us is to cast doubt on the ethical permissibility of zoos and marine theme parks. But I'll argue that, as usual, the idea of the "wild" gives us crude and inaccurate guidance.

"Zoo" in this discussion is a relative term. It means a space in which animals live that is (a) much smaller and (b) considerably more confined than the large animal reserves that are, for the most part, what's left of the idea of the "wild" on land. Of course, there are wild animals outside of these protected zones, but they are increasingly living in a non-wild way, in regular contact with human beings and human habitations. We should remember that large animal reserves are also somewhat confined: keepers track all the movements of virtually all the animals, and are able to relocate them if need be (for environmental or health reasons). Zoos also feed and care for the animals in them, albeit often badly—and keepers on animal reserves do so only at the margins, addressing extreme cases of famine and drought. But there is a continuum. The Arnhem ape colony, a research facility (see chapter 11), is not very confined—the whole island is inhabited by the apes. So it is counted here as a zoo, but it is several steps in the direction of a large reserve, and it does not admit tourists. The size of a "zoo" is dictated, usually, by its tourist clientele: as the area gets larger, more complex arrangements need to be made so that people can see the animals—in San Diego, mainly from a tram above the animals. So that zoo moves in the direction of a large animal reserve; such reserves also have a tourist clientele (economically crucial for the nations that maintain such reserves), and they too arrange to move people around, typically by jeep, so that they can see the animals.

The typical zoo of fifty years ago was very often a place of animal torture, little better than a circus. Animals were kept in cramped drab enclosures without any of the flora of their typical habitat. One would often, for example, see a single elephant standing on concrete (bad for their feet) in a bare enclosure with no trees or grass. Zoo animals were fed inappropriate food, and, worse still, the public was often encouraged to feed them and often to touch them. They usually had little or no social life with members of their own species. Sometimes they were herded around using physical cruelty rather than positive reinforcement. Often (particularly in marine theme parks) they were forced to perform tricks that humans like but that are not part of the creature's normal repertory. The similarity between zoos and circuses goes deep, since zoos were conceived of as entertainment for a human public, not as providing any benefit for the animals. (Again, we should not romanticize large animal reserves, which, similarly, are maintained as a tourist industry.)

Today there is progress, but it is very uneven, in part because zoos are unevenly regulated. (Nonprofit zoos face heavier regulation than for-profits, for example.) Some countries regulate a lot, some very little or not at all. Thus, India has given constitutional rights to circus animals (see chapter12), but in most countries animals don't have any legal standing. And in both for-profit and nonprofit zoos (which have to get money from donors), there is always a danger of exploitation and abuse, particularly of animals such as elephants that draw in the public. The presence of money does not all by itself mean that zoos must be bad. Universities, arts organizations, and many other entities have to raise money from donors, legislatures, or from the public. If they pursue their mission with integrity, that is good rather than bad. So our question is, can zoos ever be said to pursue an animal-friendly mission with integrity?

Circuses are rapidly dropping their exploitation of large mammals such as lions and elephants, and going over either to a completely human acrobatic show or to one that involves only humans and symbiotic companion animals such as horses. Why wouldn't that be the right future for zoos too, even if that meant, as it would, that zoos would cease to exist, except as research facilities off-limits to tourists? What, in other words, can be said on behalf of zoos, from the point of view of people who seek the flourishing of animals?

The difference of degree between zoos and large reserves is very important from the capabilities perspective: the large spaces in Kenya and Botswana mean that animals don't have to be restrained, and they can, albeit with careful stewarding of the habitat, more or less go about their normal lives, and cultivate their normal social relationships. That's a good goal: if we are dealing with a smaller space, that is what we ought to look for.

One point often made in defense of zoos is that zoos educate the public, especially children. If children grow up seeing no "wild" animals, they will not care for them or support policies to enhance their welfare. Eco-tourism offers wonderful opportunities, but only, in most cases, for the affluent. This point is important, but the educational goal cannot be well served by zoos that offer the animal a miserable, usually solitary, life. If children are to learn, they need really to learn, seeing the typical life-form of the animal in a habitat that is also reasonably typical. Here Utilitarian approaches give bad guidance, suggesting that the absence of pain is the main thing. The CA demands much more: social life and free movement in a group-typical space.

Our world makes so many new resources available for learning—documentaries of all sorts—that do not require distortion of the animals' daily life, beyond the extent to which the omnipresence and control of human beings has already distorted it. Wonderful films of many types are available to stimulate wonder in younger and older viewers. The excellent documentaries *Blackfish* and *Sonic Sea* expose the damage done to marine mammals by ripping them from their habitat or polluting it with damaging noise and trash. *The Ivory Game* instructs its viewers soberly about how elephants are murdered by the international criminal conspiracy of ivory poaching and ivory sales. Some popular films of this sort seem to me inferior: for example, the Oscar-winning *My Octopus Teacher*, which has many beautiful and wonder-inspiring moments, but focuses too much on what a romanticized relationship with a (female) octopus offers the human being who is the film's protagonist. Still, in the process, viewers can't help learning and wondering. In short: we don't need zoos to educate us, given the extent and quality of these new resources. As time goes on, new resources will be developed: virtual reality experiences, interactive video engagements.

Zoos, however, also house valuable scientific research that enhances our knowledge of animal abilities and promotes animal health. Some of this research is very difficult to do in an open space. (Obviously this varies greatly with the species.) Research done in confinement has greatly enhanced our knowledge of primate intelligence and primate emotions. It has shown how versatile and intelligent many birds are. It has demonstrated that Asian female elephants can recognize themselves in a mirror. (Although a lot of fine elephant research has been done "in the wild," this particular test would have been difficult to administer, as herds graze over hundreds of miles.) Research on animal cognition benefits animals by enhancing our understanding of their real form of life and by winning them new respect that conduces to better treatment. It isn't possible to apply the Capabilities Approach well without learning a lot more about animal abilities and forms of life. Furthermore, some devastating animal diseases have been cured or controlled through zoo research—for example, the herpes infections that often doom small elephants. Most zoos do not do significant research, but some do.

Here we have some truly valuable goals whose pursuits in some cases may require a degree of spatial control. They do not, however, require an unhealthy, emotionally estranging, or sensorily deficient confinement. Indeed, Frans de Waal makes the point that research done on animals not living in their normal social and physical conditions is likely to get misleading results.[11] He points out that there is no reason why primate research need ever isolate one animal from its social community.

Finally, zoos may protect animals from a variety of threats. Where a species is threatened with extinction, controlled reproduction in a zoo environment may be a lifeline, temporarily at least. And where poaching cannot be successfully controlled in larger spaces, zoos may protect the vulnerable.

These points make a case for the continued existence of zoos, meaning relatively small, confined spaces carefully monitored and controlled by humans, somewhat more than would be the case in a large animal reserve in Africa. But for which animals do these arguments work?

The essential normative question, I've argued, is how we can support the capabilities of animals to lead a type of life characteristic of their species. From the point of view of that question, relevant issues will be amount and type of space, flora and other aspects of what we might call a "facilitating environment"—borrowing a term from psychoanalyst Donald Winnicott's account of how human beings develop well in childhood only if they have support of many types from other humans and from their surroundings. This will include the availability of social interactions, the availability of sensory stimulation, the provision of a suitable and characteristic diet, the absence of crippling emotional stress, the ability to play and develop. Notice that these capabilities are often highly compromised in "the wild," which, as we've said, is all too often a place of devastating hunger, disease, fear, and torture. It would be grotesque to argue that because "the wild" contains famine, drought, and poachers, the good confined space must introduce these things. It would be equally grotesque, I think, to argue that because small animals are food for larger animals in "the wild," a good confined space must arrange for that sort of predation. But I'll treat that point more fully in my next section. What we should be seeking are spaces that really are "facilitating environments" for the exercise of animal capabilities. Often, larger reserves are such environments, but unstably, given the danger of poaching. In cases where an animal can conduct the full range of its characteristic activities, including social activities, in a "zoo," that could be advantageous for the animal.

Luckily, however, we do not need to argue against Romantics and in favor of managed environments. To repeat: a large nature reserve in

Africa is different from the San Diego Zoo in degree, not in kind. Both are highly managed spaces, both indeed are also spectator-friendly spaces. (The Kyrgyzstan enclosures I described are unusual, but sagely chosen, non-spectatorial spaces, but these too are highly managed.) If we think that confinement is in and of itself morally unacceptable, then we have to reject the whole modern world, for all the spaces in which animals live are confined and managed spaces, though sometimes the confinement escapes our notice because the spaces are so large.

Using this insight as a guide, I reach the general conclusion that a smaller confined space is justified if and only if the animals within it have access to their characteristic form of life, spatially, sensorily, nutritionally, socially, emotionally. If zoos are managed intelligently, this goal can be achieved for many animals, including monkeys, perhaps great apes, and some types of birds. In the marine area, most fish can be included in a marine theme park if tanks are large enough. And virtually all small mammals, as well as most reptiles and amphibians, can do fine in a confined space of the right sort.

Now we've narrowed the field, and we arrive at the most difficult cases. Elephants, given their need for movement over large stretches of terrain and their immense need for food (typically including bark stripped from trees)—and given their social nature, with young being raised by at least four females, while mature males go off on their own and meet up with the group only at breeding time—are virtually impossible to keep ethically, even in the best zoos, such as San Diego, though this zoo does understand the need for space and therefore restricts spectatorship to distant aerial viewings. Wild herds can roam over fifty miles in a single day. So elephants need much more space than even a large zoo can afford, and they do not have a good health or breeding record in confinement: there is an alarmingly high occurrence of stillbirth, and of reproductive complications.[12] Moreover, most zoos are very far from being like San Diego. Since the early 1990s, more than twenty US zoos have shut down their elephant exhibits on ethical grounds, or have announced a plan to do so. In 2011, the Association of Zoos and Aquariums announced tough guidelines concerning acreage and other conditions; but even these are not sufficient. The director of the Detroit Zoo, which closed its elephant exhibit in 2004, said this:

> For us, as hard as we tried, we realized that realistically nothing we could do was going to give them an opportunity to thrive. [He alludes to deficiencies in both the physical and the social environment.] So there were just so many things that we realized were major compromises for the elephants, and that no matter how much we love elephants and want to be near elephants and see elephants, we said this is just fundamentally wrong for us to do this.[13]

Unfortunately, however, many zoos are not this ethically sensitive. They know that elephants are a great draw for the public. Whether zoos are for-profit, needing revenue directly, or nonprofit, needing donors, elephants are big business. This fact, combined with zoos' elephant breeding problems, has led to nefarious schemes to bring elephants from Africa to US zoos, fraudulent projects in which elephants are taken from a larger environment to small inadequate zoos with false tales about famine and drought.

Consider the story of the Swaziland 18, whose story has been told at length in "The Swazi 17" by Charles Siebert, in the *New York Times Magazine*.[14] These were elephants who were rounded up and shipped off to zoos in the US under the (demonstrably false) pretext that a drought was threatening rhino and elephant populations, and that the only way to preserve the rhinos was either to kill the elephants or to relocate them to the US. Only seventeen elephants were actually shipped: it is believed that the eighteenth elephant died from a gastrointestinal disease before the trip. The organization Friends of Animals got a temporary injunction from a federal judge, who scheduled an emergency hearing that very night. By that time, however, the elephants, spirited onto the planes under cover of night, were already on board and sedated, so the judge let the plane go. The fact that the elephants were boarded without notifying the judge and the advocates was not technically illegal, since a stay had not been filed with the injunction, but it was underhanded. The elephants were dispersed to different zoos, including Dallas and Wichita. Elephants are big money for zoos, whether directly (in the case of for-profit zoos) or in terms of donor and public support (in the case of nonprofits). Friends of Animals is now working on action getting such transfers classified as "for commercial purposes," which are illegal under international treaty law.

We should be very clear that most zoos are commercial enterprises of one sort or another (for-profit or donor-supported). Large animal reserves also have their commercial side, but at least part of their role is to protect animals for their own sake.

For all the other large mammals—rhinos, giraffes, bears, polar bears, cheetahs, hyenas, lions, tigers, and others—we should ask, about each, what a "facilitating environment" is, and whether such an environment can be offered by a relatively small, enclosed space. In favor of permissibility for the smaller space will be any special hazards and dangers the animal faces in its larger world (polar bears from the melting of glaciers, rhinos from aggressive poaching), and the good that might be done for the animals themselves by research that cannot be done in the wild. Always we should demand a result that is good for the animals themselves, or, as Winnicott would put it, "good-enough," even though there may also be collateral benefits for human visitors. We should emphatically reject solutions that treat animals like pets of human visitors, as with the story of Knut the polar bear, which I describe in chapter 11. But the blanket preference for totally uncurated spaces is both unrealistic (there aren't any) and bad for some animals (they would not wish to be poached, starved, etc.). However, we must be on the lookout for fraud, as in the false pretense of drought in the case of the Swazi 18. I believe that most of the larger land mammals on my list cannot thrive in zoos, although it is possible that bears and apes can, if conditions are socially and physically good enough (as with the Arnhem colony). Crucial for all species who develop through cultural learning is the presence of a typical and large enough social group. It isn't enough to say, "Now we have five chimpanzees," or whatever: they have formed a cultural group of the right sort, with all the characteristic types and roles.

Turning to the seas and the skies: very large marine mammals, such as orcas and whales, cannot be ethically kept in a marine theme park. The 2013 documentary film *Blackfish* showed how badly orcas live in captivity, especially when, as typically, they are taken from their pods at a very young age, and thus unable to learn the appropriate behaviors of orca life from elder orcas.[15] The case of Tilikum showed the destructive rage to which this cruel deprivation gave rise. The film caused a surge of protest in the viewing public, leading eventually to a correct decision by Sea-World that it would no longer breed orcas or stage shows.[16] More recently, California has passed the Orca Welfare and Safety Act (2016), aimed at phasing out all captivity for orcas and ensuring the humane treatment of those that remain in captivity. The law makes it illegal to breed orcas in captivity, and also to use captive orcas in a public entertainment. In 2020, SeaWorld started using its remaining orcas in educational shows, exhibiting natural behavior with live science-based narration—though how they can exhibit "natural" behavior, given the absence of a large typical group, is unclear.[17] Orcas are highly cultural, learning most behavior from their group in very specific ways: for example, they are one of the few non-human species to have menopause, and females who stop giving birth at forty and live into their eighties play a key role in instructing the young and imparting norms.[18] Without this structure, young orcas are as much adrift as the Wild Boy of Aveyron, who lacked access to human cultural learning.

Dolphins are a different case, and a very difficult one, since they are so social and so interactive that they can to some extent thrive in captivity. They have even been known to take tricks learned in captivity back into "the wild" and teach them to their young.[19] On the one hand, it seems objectionably demeaning to see these marvelously intelligent mammals used for amusement. On the other, joy in skilled athletic performance is a prominent feature of many animal lives, and what is clearly part of the flourishing of sheepdogs, retrievers, and hunter-jumper horses should not be deemed inauthentic or off-limits simply because the creature is "wild" and learned the behavior from humans. Indeed, we should probably reject the idea that all human-animal cooperation and reciprocity is inappropriate for a "wild" creature. What, then, is the right line to draw?

Thomas White explores this issue with characteristic balance and sensitivity.[20] He focuses on features of dolphin lives he has already explored earlier in his book: their extreme sociality, and their need to roam in a very large space with a large group of other dolphins. Even sensitive zoos that treat dolphins well, he argues, don't provide them with enough space or a large enough group. They do protect them from many dangers. But this, says White, is a double-edged sword, since dolphins so protected lose their ability to survive in the wild. So in the end he concludes that captivity is ethically unacceptable.

These are excellent arguments, and I am inclined to support them. Dolphins certainly need large spaces and a representative social group, although they are also highly adaptable, and thrive in a variety of settings. An intermediate solution could be a much larger and partly open pen, where dolphins might go and come, and mingle with humans only as much as they wish. Dolphin Reef in Eilat, Israel, may be such a place, though it remains controversial.[21]

Above all, dolphins ought to be treated with respect, as powerful and wonderful creatures of high intelligence who have their own ideas about what they would like to do. That also means respecting their interactivity, ingenuity, and sense of humor, traits that they sometimes exercise toward humans and other species, as well as other dolphins.

Birds come in many varieties. Some don't typically cover large stretches of terrain: parrots, magpies, and crows. Others do, and seem unduly confined when put in an aviary. Some are highly social; some are loners. Birders love to go look for each species in its characteristic place, and that ought to be a preferred way to see birds, though a curated yet free space like the New Zealand enclosure with its protective sides and open roof, is also appropriate. As we understand different species of birds better than we currently do, we will be able to come up with species-specific recommendations.

All these questions are hard, and good zoos wrestle with them daily. The revolution in thinking that good zoos now exemplify has to be required of all zoos through better regulation, and we must all keep asking the hard questions, guided by the idea of respect for forms of life.

To summarize: the CA gives us good guidance as we think about the ethics of zoos. The touchstone should be the animal's form of life: Can zoos provide a reasonable opportunity for that? When they can, I think zoos are permissible, though caution must always be exercised, given the role of human domination (and, often, human greed) in all zoos. When they can't, we must exercise stewardship in a different way, protecting animals in large wildlife preserves and sanctuaries.

PREDATION AND SUFFERING

The "wild," we've said, is a place of both scarcity and violence. Today many people who care about animals think that we ought to inhibit human violence against animals (poaching, hunting, whaling) but do nothing to interfere with "Nature"'s violence (hunger, drought, predation). Can this common attitude be defended?

The approach this book has developed focuses on the life-chances of individual creatures: they ought to have the chance to live flourishing lives. Suffering and the chance to exercise various forms of agency are the twin things that matter. From the perspective of creatures who are victims of "Nature"'s violence, the fact that it's all "Nature" is no consolation. As Mill says, they often suffer even more horribly: starving is among the most painful forms of death, as is being torn limb from limb by a pack of wild dogs. A bullet to the brain would definitely be better than that, even if the former deaths are "natural" and the latter human-inflicted.

Nor do we actually think in the hands-off way I've characterized, when we are aware of our own control and stewardship. In defending human action to protect animals against floods, famine, and drought, I am not making a radical proposal, I am reporting common thinking and practices. Just as nations that have animal reservations inhibit poaching, so they inhibit the influence of "natural" disasters—*most of which have human causes in the background anyway.* When we can do this, then, it seems that we must.

Predation, however, seems different. Stewards of large animal reservations not only do not inhibit predation, they often strongly encourage it. They behave, then, very differently from companions of domesticated animals, who typically do not encourage their companion dogs and cats to feast on little birds or to hunt foxes, even though that behavior is part of the typical repertory for some breeds of dogs and cats. Companions, that is, typically treat their companion animals rather like children: they channel natural aggression in the direction of some form of substitute activity, preventing frustration of instincts, but also preventing harm to others. Just as a child is steered in the direction of competitive sports rather than human carnage, so a cat is steered to a scratching post rather than to a bird. Isn't the animal's capability to lead its characteristic form of life being frustrated? Yes and no. A capability may be described in multiple ways. We could say that what is typical of cats is the capability to kill small birds. We could also say that what is typical, and crucial, is the capability to exercise predatory capacities and avoid the pain of frustration. What is inherited is a general tendency that may be expressed in more than one way. In a multispecies world, where we all have to inhibit some behaviors in order to live peacefully together, it makes sense to focus on the latter, more general, description of the capability, unless we have overwhelming evidence that this approach doesn't work, that cats without bird-killing are depressed and miserable. This is not what evidence shows us. A cat needs some outlet for its predatory nature—just as a human does. But there is no reason why this outlet must be one that inflicts horrible suffering on a victim.

Why don't we think this way when we're dealing with predation in "the wild"? There is a good reason for the asymmetry. We are very ignorant, and if we tried to interfere with predation on a large scale we would very likely cause disaster on a large scale. We basically have no idea of how species numbers would change, what shortages would be created, and we are totally unprepared for dealing with the likely consequences of such interventions. The only way we could protect weaker creatures from predation is by turning larger animal reservations into zoos of the bad old sort, with each creature or group in its own enclosure. This would be the wrong direction to go. Short of going down that road, however, there is no feasible idea of substitute behaviors comparable to the role of such a concept in the lives of companion dogs and cats. In a typical zoo setting, people may try to arrange a substitute: for example, giving a tiger a weighted ball to exercise its predatory capacities, while feeding it meat that has been humanely killed.[22] Here is what the San Diego Zoo says about the diet of their leopards: "At the San Diego Zoo, our leopards are generally fed a commercial ground meat diet made for zoo carnivores, and are offered an occasional large bone, thawed rabbit, or sheep carcass. To keep their hunting skills sharp, wildlife care specialists occasionally offer the cats a meatball 'hunt,' where part of their food is rolled into balls and hidden throughout their habitat."[23] This displaces the torture from the hunt to a factory farm visitors do not see. That is not an improvement. However: synthetic lab-grown meat or even plant-based meat would be far superior. Even a humanely killed animal would be superior, since predation deaths are usually very painful. Without separate enclosures, however, such substitutions would not be possible.

Philosopher Jeff McMahan, in a newspaper op-ed, has speculatively suggested engineering predation out of existence.[24] That idea would solve the separate enclosures problem, but it simply doesn't show respect for most of these animals, who should not be blamed for their tendencies. (They have not evolved to be educable like dogs and cats, and though many of them exhibit social learning, it comes from a predator species community.) And elimination would surely create a chaos of population overgrowth that we are unprepared to deal with.

Those, then, are the good reasons for moving very cautiously against predation, if at all. On the other hand, the suffering of vulnerable creatures and their premature deaths matter greatly and seem to demand some type of intelligent action. It simply is not part of the form of life of these creatures to be eaten by predators. Their form of life is their own, and they seek to live it undisturbed, just as we do, even though at times we too are also prey for aggressors. These species would not have survived if they were not pretty good at escape. To say that it is the destiny of antelopes to be torn apart by predators is like saying that it is the destiny of women to be raped. Both are terribly wrong, and demean the suffering of victims. It is an unfortunate fact that in "the wild," animals' desires for peaceful life meet so frequently with frustration and pain. The situation looks like one of the tragic dilemmas we discussed in chapter 8, only the world does not easily offer a Hegelian solution.

There are also some very bad reasons for not moving against predation. Part of the Romantic idea of "the wild" is a yearning for violence. Blake's Tyger and Shelley's West Wind are emblems of what some humans feel they have lost by becoming hypercivilized. A longing for (putatively) lost aggression lies behind a lot of people's fascination with large predatory animals and indeed with the spectacle of predation itself. People who manage animal reservations know that predation is a sure tourist draw. On my visit to a fine reservation in Botswana, I found that one of the most eagerly sought-after sights was that of a rare species of wild dog leaping in a pack upon an antelope and tearing that animal limb from limb even before it was dead. From the start of the hunt through its excruciating death scene and the obligatory division of the spoils to the final scene in which the vultures cleaned the carcass, rich tourists in my jeep watched with avidity, leaving their tent colony at 4:00 a.m. to do so; and it was a rare one or two who reacted with horror and aversion. People have unsavory sadistic tendencies, and they fashion entertainments to gratify them. Just as the Romans satisfied bloodlust in part through violence involving animals (including elephants, to which Cicero and Pliny strongly objected, although they didn't object to the torture of humans), so too today my highly respectable Botswana tourist establishment was making money from vicarious sadism. Moreover, the animal reservation is geared as a whole to this exercise: the wild dogs are highly endangered, and much effort is made to preserve them. I am agnostic about the desirability of preserving that species, but I think here the key concern prompting preservation is a bad one: money from sado-tourism.

There are some modest interventions with predation that we should contemplate, while holding off on the larger issue. The first is not to make money from sado-tourism. Just as foxhunting, another human sport torturing animals to satisfy human sadism, has been rendered illegal, I would argue for restricting predation to spaces with no humans, as has wisely been done in Kyrgyzstan. There would be a lot less carnage if it were not semi-staged for a human audience. In a large reservation it may not be possible to keep humans entirely away from predators, but there's no need to make a point of taking tourists to see predation, much of which occurs at dusk and at night anyway.

Second, where there are instances of animal-animal cruelty under human stewardship, we may cautiously find at least some ways to intervene in favor of the weaker: for example, protecting the weaker or rejected member of a litter or a nest from destruction, as is often done. The New Zealand bird reservation is a marvelous instance of this. They keep out the rabbits, rats, mice, and cats, who have plenty of food anyway, since those are very resilient species. Of course, this displaces the predation done by these creatures onto other small creatures outside the reservation, so my approval is questionable. But New Zealand's birds are extremely vulnerable, because they did not evolve to escape this type of predator— the predatory species are mostly not indigenous to New Zealand. And people can and do provide some substitute food for the other animals that does not involve predation. Cats may be fed humanely killed meat or fish, which is at least somewhat better, or plant-based or lab-grown meat, better yet. So I think on balance the nation's decision to protect the birds is defensible.

How much further can we go in this direction? We need to press this question all the time. A pair of rare piping plovers, who have nested at Montrose Beach in Chicago, found to their dismay that a skunk had eaten their two eggs, which were close to hatching. They then laid another egg, and the Park District installed a new stronger enclosure around the nest to protect it. Will anyone dare object to that on grounds of "unnatural-ness"? In late July 2021, four chicks were hatched, and two have been suc-cessfully raised to young adulthood. Once hatched, the chicks were no longer confined to the enclosure, and two seem to have succumbed to predation, in the vulnerable period before learning to fly. Should there have been even more protection of the young chicks? Probably not, since they would then not have learned how to be plover adults.

Third, there are some instances of predation that are permissible in any case in my theory. Predation of insects does not inflict a harm of which the CA is cognizant. And predation of rats and some other nui-sance animals can be covered under a self-defense principle. This opens up food sources for many creatures.

In short, we need serious ongoing discussion of the predation prob-lem and what to do about it, and we need to keep searching for Hegelian solutions, such as substitute animal behaviors. (The rabbits and cats in Kyrgyzstan are engaging in substitute behavior when they find food with-out killing birds.) We need above all to convince people that predation is a problem. Too many people grow up excited and enthralled by predation, and this has had a bad effect on our entire culture. It's important to keep pointing out that antelopes were not made to be food, they were made to live antelope lives. The fact that so often they do not get to live those lives is a problem, and since we are in charge everywhere we need to figure out how much we can and should do about it.

"LIMINAL ANIMALS"

Some animals who used to live far from humans have now moved into areas of human habitation. They have become familiar members of urban ecosystems. Rats, mice, squirrels, raccoons, and wild birds such as pi-geons and Canada geese have lived alongside humans for a very long time. More recent denizens include coyotes, monkeys, deer, cougars, and even baboons and bears. The special problem these animals present is that they often compete with humans and can become aggressive toward companion animals and even children. This is a new area of research in animal ethics that is very exciting, and we need to know a good deal more about these animals in order to avoid a defensive exterminationist approach. I believe a self-defense principle is reasonable for pests, as I said in chapter 7. But often we make the mistake of thinking a creature is a pest simply because it frightens us. Coyotes, for example, are very shy, and usually do not approach humans. Cities have increasingly learned this, and are more likely to be cautious and gentle in their approach. Sometimes, too, the fault is our own: if humans feed coyotes, they become accustomed to hanging around human habitations, and this can lead them to become predators. These cases are fascinating, but raise no special theoretical issue that other issues of potential conflict that we have discussed do not already raise. They are already being discussed, in the current literature, with appeal to the Capabilities Approach.[25] So I treat them very briefly here, but think it is important to recognize that this is a category in some respects new, and always growing.

POPULATIONS AND HOW TO CONTROL THEM

One thing that often happens in "wild" spaces is population imbalance. Take elks in parts of North America. When they grow too numerous, they don't have enough food, and they suffer. People then suggest two things: introducing hunting, and introducing wolves as "natural" predators. Of course, the introduction of wolves is not "natural" at all: it's just hunting by other means, and is far more painful to the elks, at least if the hunters actually know how to shoot.

How should we think about such cases? First, we'd better recognize quickly that it is a matter of choice and stewardship, not "Nature." Second, we should ask why the problem exists. Wild horses in Wyoming are short of food because ranchers seek to monopolize all the grazing land for their cattle, for commercial reasons. So some baseline must be negotiated, in terms of a sensible distribution of the relevant animal and human property rights. Greed should not call the tune. This requires much pro-test activity and litigation. But even with a reasonable baseline, population problems will occur, as with the elks. I suggested in chapter 8 that human population control is imperative, as well as curbing human greed. But I also more tentatively suggested that just as we routinely use contraception for companion animals, so we should, carefully and gradually, consider this Hegelian solution to population imbalances for animals in "the wild," so long as the species is numerous. We still know too little, and research is in its infancy. With human contraception, the search for methods free from unpleasant side effects is ongoing. We can expect the search for ani-mal contraception to take many decades, especially since methods have to be designed for each species, and the approach to research must be more cautious than in the case of humans, where informed consent is possible. Still, that alternative seems preferable to the others that are on the table for that particular case (starving, being hunted by humans, and being torn up by wolves). At the very least, we should not be scared off from going down that path by charges of "playing God."

Given the position of humans in this world of today, we have all the power. We can't hide from that fact, and trying to hide is itself a choice with consequences. We have only the choice to exercise our stewardship cruelly and dumbly, or with intelligent concern for animal flourishing.

We can now see that the CA offers good guidance for our evolving treatment of both companion and wild animals. In the latter case, its ad-vantages over Utilitarian approaches are even clearer, because it gives us clear reasons to reject zoos, even when they inflict no pain. Keeping the animal's full form of life in mind leads to sounder policies, which respect animal sociability and animal striving.

11

THE CAPABILITIES
OF FRIENDSHIP[1]

One afternoon, when I looked into the cave, I found her, for the first time, not hidden away in utter darkness but crouching only a foot or two from where I knelt. "Well hello there," I said quietly, trying oh so hard not to frighten her. I scarcely dared to breathe. I wanted to reach out and touch her, but I couldn't risk it. She turned her head away, and I thought she would creep to the back of the cave, but no, she held her ground. In a moment, she began to wag her tail ever so slowly. It thumped against the side of the cave. With that gentle motion, all my defenses were instantly swept away. "Well then," I said to myself as she suddenly looked blurred to me, "I'm yours forever!"[2]

George Pitcher, *The Dogs Who Came to Stay*

Resting in the shade of a tree, Alex, Daphne and I lazily contemplate the landscape, dotted here and there with herds of zebra and impala. A breeze rises, fluffing up the hair on Daphne's head. I fiddle with a brightly colored stone and Alex leans over to peer at my find. Then he rests his head against the tree and dozes. I look past him at Daphne and our gazes meet. She makes a friendly face and moves a little bit closer. Daphne, too, begins to nap, and soon I'm drifting off as well, lulled to sleep by the sound of her gentle breathing and the birds flitting about

in the tree above. My body relaxes completely, secure in the presence
of my companions.[3]

> Primatologist Barbara Smuts, describing an afternoon
> nap with Alex and Daphne, who are baboons

Can there possibly be friendship between human beings and other animals? The Capabilities List mentions *affiliation* as central, and insists that
protecting the ability to have relationships of reciprocal concern requires
protecting institutions that nourish and sustain this capability. Where humans are concerned, we have lots of ways of protecting people's capabilities
for valuable forms of love and friendship. Laws protect families in various
ways, and forbid violence or abuse within them. Laws against workplace
sexual harassment are key to constructing workplaces in which there can
be genuine friendship, not simply domination. Workplace health and safety
laws also play a role, and perhaps especially laws limiting work hours, thus
allowing people time for family and friends. Good schools foster children's
developing capabilities for reciprocity and affiliation, while equipping
them with skills and interests that make friendships textured and rewarding. Laws protecting the freedoms of speech, religion, and association, and
personal privacy, construct spaces within which friendships may form. In
many other ways, the goal of affiliation can shape laws and institutions.

But what about other animals? I have already said a great deal about
affiliations among the animals themselves and the social structures that
sustain them. But what about friendships between humans and other animals? Is this a worthwhile ideal? Is it possible? Is it possible with regard
to wild animals or only companion animals? And what can we do to promote it if it is both worthwhile and possible? This book could be limited to preventing terrible abuses. But the Capabilities Approach is about
flourishing lives. And just as a human community that was well-fed and
educated and equipped with the political liberties would be hollow and
incomplete if it made no room for friendship and love, the same is true of
the large multispecies community that we ought to foster.

In this chapter, I'll argue for the possibility and the value of such friendships. But I will also argue that we cannot attain them without rethinking the relationships most people have with companion animals and even more radically rethinking our relationship to wild animals, ending some of the most common forms of domination and exploitation in which we now engage—including not only horrors such as trophy hunting, poaching, and whaling, but also quieter forms of domination in which wild animals are treated as objects for human amusement, rather than as subjects with their own lives to live.

This chapter, then, will be both an in-depth study of (part of) one capability, and at the same time the expression of a spirit in which I believe we ought to pursue all the capabilities. It will lead us back to the emotions of engagement that I discussed in chapter 1: wonder, compassion, and outrage. But we may now add: friendship and love.

WHAT IS FRIENDSHIP?

It is dangerous to model a general trait on the human experience of that trait. Even when we approach human beings in other places, we often go wrong by projecting our own customs onto others. But when we approach another species, the problem of projection always looms large. Study of the creature's form of life is an essential prerequisite for any meaningful reflection.

For example, when we think of animal perception we must think of forms of sight, hearing, and smell that are very different from our own, and also of senses we simply lack, such as perception through magnetic fields, or echolocation. The same is true for friendship: what we prefer is not necessarily what another species will prefer. We've seen that species of many types live with a reasonably large group of fellow species members. Friendship for an elephant will be friendship in the context of the female-led group; even though each elephant is a distinct individual, friends do not isolate themselves from the larger herd, except when mature males depart for their own comparatively solitary life. For dolphins, similarly, an extensive group is the essential reference point for all affiliations, and if friendship with a dolphin will be possible, it will be against this background.

Nonetheless, we can learn from ideals of human friendship, if we are careful to define friendship in a humble and open-ended way, not building in from the start a reference to human practices, but ready to learn.

A sine qua non for friendship, emphasized in discussions of the topic ever since Aristotle and Cicero, is that friends treat one another as *ends*, not simply as means to either gain or amusement. This is the feature of the Kantian approach to humans that Korsgaard and I incorporate in our approach to animals; obviously it is woefully lacking in most human dealings with animals.

Moreover, friendship is dynamic: friends are active, seeking to *benefit one another for the other's own sake*, not one's own. Not all benefit to others treats the other as an end. For example, for millennia men have treated their wives as trophies, taking care of them, but primarily in order to glorify the male's own status. Such instrumentalization is ubiquitous in human relationships with animals, even when they are well cared for. People may fuss over their "pets," and give them luxury food and grooming, without seeing them as more than toys for humans to play with.

Treating another person as an end always involves *respect for that person's form of life*. This is rarely commented on in discussions of human friendship, since it is taken for granted that humans share a basic form of life. However, it is important, because humans have different values and plans of life, and befriending someone on condition that this person will drop all her own plans and accept your values and choices is far from a true friendship. (Failure to think about this has marred many if not most relationships between men and women throughout millennia of human history.)

Respect for differing forms of life and activity is crucial if there are to be friendships between humans and other animals. It is lacking in most human-animal relationships. Even in the case of companion animals, there is a crucial distinction between arranging things for the human's convenience and genuinely respecting the animal's own form of life.

This sort of respect has been particularly lacking in human relations with "wild" animals. Even humans who have benign intentions may be deficient in real respect. Humans so often go into nature on autopilot, rather like the stereotype of the bad American tourist in a foreign country. This bad tourist has little real curiosity about the inhabitants and their culture; she doesn't study or learn, she doesn't even try to speak the language. She speaks only English, and she eats only American food because it is more familiar. But she oohs and aahs over the striking monuments these strange people have created. This is still typical American tourist behavior, alas, and it is also typical safari behavior toward "wild" animals. People love to see strange creatures and to marvel at "nature red in tooth and claw"—but with all too little genuine curiosity about the animal's form of life, and without any attempt at empathy with the animal's point of view. No friendship can take root on such arid soil.

And of course, this touristic behavior, defective though it is, is already much better than what we all too often see. At least the safari tourist goes to see what is there in its own setting—a far cry from many common behaviors of humans to animals. More often, "wild" animals are watched as they perform human-choreographed routines in zoos and theme parks that are little more than prison cells, and are prevented from living their species way of life in virtually all respects. Respect for species forms of life requires a lot of humility and a lot of learning.

Respect can be attained, though with difficulty, through intellectual learning, from the outside as it were, understanding similarities and differences. For friendship to begin to be possible, however, more is required: *empathy*, or at least a serious attempt at empathy; trying to see the world from that animal's perspective, to understand how an animal of that sort characteristically communicates and chooses, and to become attuned to the animal's way of seeing. We never attain fully accurate perspectival vision even with other humans, however close they are, and we should not expect that we would ever fully attain a view of the world from the point of view of a non-human animal. But it is crucial to try, and at times we can partially succeed.

All of these prerequisites for friendship might be there without friendship itself: so far, we have just a respectful relationship. But friendship involves more: shared activities and pleasures, delight in one another's company. Usually, then, friendship requires extended co-presence in the same place.

Friendship also requires trust, and trust takes time. So co-presence must be extended, not fleeting. It's interesting that among humans, love has a better chance of flourishing at a distance and in a brief time interval than does friendship, with its trust, commitment to the other's good, and pattern of shared activities. At present, this requirement seems to rule out friendship between humans and whales, because extended co-presence is possible only in the morally unacceptable confines of a theme park. Birds of most species are a challenge as well, although there are species of birds who can be friends with a suitably attuned human.

Respect for an animal's species form of life does not and, if it is friendship we are pursuing, should not, negate *attention to particularity*. Among humans this goes without saying: someone who treats people as interchangeable with one another is an unlikely candidate for friendship. So much is also true of friendships between humans and animals.

When a human friend respects another animal's form of life, she must understand how key capabilities are differently realized in the human species and the animal's species. For example: when we think about friendship we think, inter alia, about play. All animals engage in play, but what counts as play needs careful study: thus the play-biting of young wolves would not be acceptable in a human childcare center! Any possibility of friendship must begin by investigating these differences, against a highly general background of similarity. And there are differences, clearly, in the further specification of the key capability of affiliation. The structure of a human family varies across culture and time; but all known human families are very different from elephant families, in which young are reared by a cooperative group of females, while males after puberty leave the group to wander solo, except at mating time.

Human friendship depends a good deal on language and other forms of communication (music, art, gesture). Animals of most types are also flexible and highly skilled communicators, with many ways of signaling their experiences, preferences, fears, and desires to one another. The challenge is to construct a meeting place between human and animal communication systems. Sometimes the difficulty is simply one of understanding, and can be overcome by learning. Sometimes there are serious physical obstacles: we are unable to hear many of the sounds made by whales and elephants, for example, though recording equipment attuned to low-decibel sounds can capture the communication, and potentially translate it into something humans can hear.

A word about friendship and love. Sometimes people use the term "friendship" to mean a relationship that is emotionally weaker than love. I follow the Greeks and Romans, whose notions of *philia* and *amicitia* do not have that restriction. Some of the relationships I'll discuss are very emotionally intense. My primary reasons to speak of friendship and not love are to indicate, first, that it is *philia* and not *eros*: sexual desire and intimacy are not integral to the relationship (in cross-species cases they are absent); and, second, that friendship, like *philia*, involves reciprocity in good wishes, emotions, and good actions, whereas love, whether erotic or not, can be one-sided and can even exist when you never meet the object of your love. Many people love animals very deeply without knowing any particular animal intimately enough to form a friendship. Anyone who loves whales, as my daughter did, has to be content with love from afar, unreciprocated. I myself have no friendships with animals, though lots of love for them. I just am unable to shoulder the responsibility of caring for a dog, given my travel obligations, and I cannot go live with elephants, although I long to form a friendship with a group of elephants. So friendship is in that sense more exigent than love, though it may certainly include mutual love.

PARADIGMS OF HUMAN-ANIMAL FRIENDSHIP: COMPANION ANIMALS

Companion animals, when not treated as "pets," but allowed their own dignity and agency, can often become friends of the humans with whom they live. Many readers will have participated in such friendships, and many more will know of them from reports of many kinds. Still, it is useful to examine a paradigmatic case of such a friendship, so let's look further at the friendship between philosopher George Pitcher (1925–2018) and the two dogs, Lupa and Remus, with whom he and his partner, composer and music professor Ed Cone (1917–2004), lived in their house in Princeton, New Jersey, from 1977 to 1988 (Lupa's death) and 1991 (the death of Remus).[4] We met the two dogs in the introduction. Their story is narrated with extraordinary detail and empathy (including self-empathy) by Pitcher, who, not surprisingly, is one of the philosophers who reopened the topic of emotions in recent philosophy when it had been thought to be a topic not worth studying. And the story has the additional advantage of being one for which I can vouch from personal experience. As a friend of the two men, I often visited Princeton and stayed in their house on the golf course, and had many walks with George and the dogs. Remus was very social with me, though Lupa, as the book describes, always retained her fear of strangers, and usually sat under the grand piano when I was around.

Lupa had been a wild dog for quite a while, and her puppies were probably fathered by another member of the group of wild dogs. Prior to that, it seems that she had experienced abuse. Certain gestures, particularly a raised hand, inspired fear in her (see the introduction); and there was something about someone using the downstairs telephone (not other phones) that set her to cowering. George found her, with her newborn litter, shivering in the dark crawl space under a toolshed on their property. Initially her fear of strangers made her shrink back from all contact, and it took days before she would eat food left at the mouth of her "cave," weeks before she could be tempted to venture a little bit outside the "cave" to get the food. All the while, George spoke to her gently and reassuringly, trying to imagine what she had endured to inspire such fear, and "sensing . . . a huge vulnerability in her."[5] As the book makes clear, Pitcher is at the same time discovering, or rediscovering, his own vulnerability, having walled off many emotions after a difficult childhood. The episode described in the first epigraph marks the first time Lupa responds positively to his overtures, and from that moment on he is totally committed. Although Ed initially opposed having a dog, he too was won over, first to keep Lupa and one of her puppies outside, and later to welcome them into their home, meanwhile finding good homes for the other puppies. When they gave names to the two dogs (naming them after the she-wolf who suckled the two founders of Rome, and one of her two human "children"), this act "was an acknowledgment that they were, for us anyway, something like persons, and persons, moreover, who were now our responsibility. We were committing ourselves in a serious way, as one does in taking vows."[6] (Pitcher emphasizes that Ed was known for blunt truth-telling and utter seriousness, a trait that I experienced with gratitude and some discomfort when he offered critical comments on some of my writing about music.)

Pitcher acknowledges that the dogs were surrogate children for them. (As two gay men in that closeted time, they had no chance to marry or adopt.[7]) But he also stresses that the dogs also took other emotional roles: Lupa became a mother figure, and Remus was an intrepid companion. It would have been possible for the surrogate-child idea to lead to inappropriate treatment of the dogs, treatment not respectful of their canine lives; many people act this way, dressing up dogs in baby clothes, etc. I saw no hint of that bad behavior. Instead, there was constant attunement to their dog-specific desires and modes of expression—and to their particularity, their differences from one another and from other dogs. What the absence of human children did mean was that they were not distracted by other responsibilities, but could devote their full attention to Lupa and Remus.

From the beginning, Pitcher is an Aristotelian friend, treating Lupa and Remus as ends and benefiting them for their own sake, not his own.

He is always attuned to what each of them wants, with a high degree of sensitivity to each one's particular modes of expression: Remus's habit of "significant sitting" near an object he wanted, Lupa's different mode of expressing desire by "placing her paw gently on our knee and looking expectantly into our eyes, perhaps also whining softly."[8] Remus is capable of strong protest: when a friend's female dog for whom the men are dog-sitting dares to sleep in George's room, Remus endures this trespass patiently. But when the same dog arrives for a second visit, Remus surprises Pitcher by coming up to Pitcher's chair and peeing all over the rug. Although at first Pitcher was annoyed, he understood that "Remus had what he considered to be a legitimate gripe, and of course every right to express it. . . . I had to admit that this expression of his grievance was eloquent, bold, and original."[9] Pitcher also understands, and chronicles, Remus's mastery of deception and playacting to get things he wants.

And the dogs reciprocate. They offer both men their unqualified devotion—and show Pitcher what it is to express love. (At the time he found Lupa, Pitcher writes that he was seeing a psychiatrist in New York three times a week for his difficulty expressing love, and after a while the psychiatrist tells him that the dogs have done him more good than she has.) Just as the men are attuned to the dogs' communications, "so they in turn understood many of our words, actions, and even states of mind."[10] Seeing Pitcher in tears watching a TV documentary about a child with a congenital heart defect dying during a life-saving operation, "both dogs rushed to me, almost knocking me over backward, and, with plaintive whimpers, fervently licked my eyes, my cheeks, in an effort—which was totally successful—to comfort me."[11] Probably the dogs understood more than the narrative lets on. Pitcher glances lightly over his childhood in the book, but I know it made him feel unworthy of love and cut off from comfort; no doubt he identified with the lonely and sick little boy, and that was a reason for his strong response. The dogs' offer of unconditional love and comfort was exactly the best response to his lifelong sense of unworthiness.

So there are empathy and attunement on both sides, rich mutual communication, and a great deal of delight in shared activities. As for freedom: most companions of dogs never give the dog an option to go live in the wild, and for most it would be a cruel and risky option. But since Lupa had lived successfully as a wild dog, Pitcher believed he ought to give her a fair chance to go back to the wild life. One day as they are out on the golf course, Lupa, following the scent of a rabbit, dashes into the woods. George and Ed pointedly do not go after her, but wait to see what she will choose. As they approached home, with pessimism, there she was, worn-out from the chase, following slowly. "Her lips were drawn back from her slightly open jaws so that she seemed to be smiling. I saw for the first time that she was beautiful. She looked up at me as if to say, 'Boy, that was great fun!' but what I understood was that she was ours, now and forever."[12]

For many dog owners that "ours" is asymmetrical: the dog is a prize possession, and they emphatically do not see themselves as belonging to the dog. For George and Ed, it is just as true that they belonged to the dogs as that the dogs belonged to them. Lupa had a particular love of her collar, which she clearly saw as a "symbol of the bond that united her to us. . . . She wore it, so it seemed, with pride and a certain quiet joy."[13] She became anxious and listless when they had to take it off to groom her. "To restore her confidence, we had only to put the collar back on."[14] The men recognize an asymmetry: the dogs are utterly dependent on them in a way that they are not utterly dependent on the dogs. But they understand this asymmetry as a reason for immense responsibility, not for pride.

A sad asymmetry of human-dog friendship is an inevitable difference of life spans. Ed lived to be eighty-seven, and George to ninety-three. These well-cared-for dogs (and they had first-rate medical care) lived to be seventeen, in the case of Remus, and to something around that, in the case of Lupa, whose birth date they never knew—very long lives for these relatively large dogs. Inevitably, then, the story ends with canine aging and, eventually, two deaths—and with Pitcher learning something further about himself: how to mourn.

Many readers will have their own stories to tell, but this one, so skillfully narrated, gives us a paradigm of what friendship (and mutual love) can be, across the species barrier.

PARADIGMS OF ANIMAL-HUMAN FRIENDSHIP: WILD ANIMALS

Because wild animals do not share a dwelling with human beings, as do companion animals, the first obstacle to friendship is locational: Where are the two parties to meet, and on whose ground? Putting aside for the moment the difficult question whether there may ever be friendships between human beings and animals in captivity, we are then dealing with cases where the wild animal pursues its own species form of life in a space that is in a larger sense human-dominated, but that gives them plenty of room to move around and carry on as themselves, with their own species groups. How, then, could a friendship ever begin? Friendship requires living-with, and even if human beings sometimes form friendships online, cross-species relationships require bodily presence. So the human being must go to the place where the wild animals in question live, stay there for an extended period, succeed in being welcomed there, and ultimately be, so to speak, invited into relationship, despite being seen as strange and initially threatening. For some species, such as whales, this shared space cannot be found. Even though it is now possible to do a lot of up-close research under water that was previously impossible, the constraints on the human who ventures into that environment preclude shared activity and pleasure. Maybe this will change. Peter Godfrey-Smith's narratives of his dives in search of the reclusive octopus show great zest and pleasure; perhaps someday intrepid whale scientists will be able to live with whales, somehow, for extended periods. For many other species, however, determination, research expertise, grant money, and a deep love of the animal species can already propel researchers into a form of life in which a world may be genuinely co-created.

A paradigmatic example is ethologist Barbara Smuts's account of her relationships with the baboons in East Africa with whom she lived for many years.[15] Smuts was led to her work, she records, by profound curiosity. She believes that this curiosity about other animals is our evolutionary heritage from our human ancestors, but is usually overridden by modern life. "Each of us has inherited the capacity to feel our way into the being of another, but our fast-paced urban lifestyle rarely encourages us to do so."[16] Smuts went to the habitat of the baboons and lived there without human company. She emphasizes that for long periods of time she did not see or talk to another human being, which proved very helpful in learning to "feel [her] way" into the baboon life.[17] (The tourism analogy is useful here again: learning to speak French fluently is much easier with total immersion, and no opportunities to revert to English.)

Her first challenge was to convince the baboons that she was not a threat. Having prepared well for this challenge, she approached them gradually, with great sensitivity to their reactions, "tuning in" to the subtle signals of fear that they send one another when she moved too rapidly or too near. At first, mothers called their infants to them and gave them stern looks of warning. As time went on, however, and they saw Smuts responding to their signals, their behavior shifted: if they felt she was too close, they would give "dirty looks" *to her*—changing, as she notes, from treating her as an object to treating her as a subject with whom they could communicate. In the process of gaining their trust, Smuts "changed almost everything about me, including the way I walked and sat, the way I held my body, and the way I used my eyes and voice. I was learning a whole new way of being in the world—the way of the baboon."[18] She was obviously not a baboon, with her human body and way of moving; but she entered their world through attentive responsiveness to their signals, until they accepted her as a social being whom they could treat as a member of their group. Respect for personal space, immensely important in the baboon world, was essential to the ultimate familiarity and trust that the group and Smuts co-created. She learned, for example, not to ignore them when they approached, as scientists are often taught to do, but rather to communicate respect in baboon fashion, making brief eye contact and grunting. Eventually the troop and she could relax in one another's company, as in the example of Alex and Daphne quoted as this chapter's epigraph. By the end of the time, Smuts noticed that her whole sense of her own identity had shifted, had become more bodily, less intellectual.

Smuts's friendship is with the whole troop, not with one or two individuals. She got to know them all as particular individuals, even as "highly idiosyncratic individuals, as distinct from one another as we humans are."[19] She emphasizes that she might have formed more intimate individual relationships, and was sometimes encouraged by one or another baboon to do so—but the objectives of her research made her not wish to alter the behavior of the baboons to that extent. Thus, the apparent one-sidedness of the friendship—she was learning their ways and they were simply including her in an ongoing way of life—was chosen by her and might have been different, leading to greater particular intimacy. Sometimes that intimacy briefly did emerge. She mentions one incident in which she had a bad cold and fell asleep while the troop moved away—and woke to find one baboon named Plato by her side. She asked him where the others had gone, and he strode off confidently, with her at his side. "I felt as if we were friends, out together for an afternoon stroll."[20] However, this relationship is predicated on her being a good group member. And in another case, where the baboons offer her help, it is the entire group that assists her: in a rainstorm they all move to make room for her to sit down in a shelter they have chosen.

In becoming a friend, she plays by their rules, not they by hers, but they change, simply in the act of including her. She had come to their world, not they to hers, and like a good guest in a foreign country, she observed the customs that were in place. On this basis they treated her as a subject and group member, and protected her when she needed protection. Smuts concludes: "Developing relationships with birds or other animals when we enter their space is surprisingly easy, if we approach the experience with sensitivity and humility."[21]

Another similar narrative of group intimacy and eventual inclusion is Joyce Poole's memoir of her life with elephants in Kenya's Amboseli National Park in *Coming of Age with Elephants*.[22] Poole is less self-conscious than Smuts about the relationship-forming aspects of her research, but it emerges clearly that she was able to gain the trust not only of the matriarchal group of adult females who lead the herd, but also of male elephants, the primary objects of her research, who are typically solitary and resist relationship. She co-created a world with the elephants, and they learned to respond even to her highly human utterances, as when—a moment I captured in the introduction—she would sing "Amazing Grace" to Virginia, a matriarch, and her female group. "It was a ritual we had. . . . Virginia would stand silently, slowly opening and closing her amber eyes and moving the tip of her trunk. I sang for five or ten minutes, or for as long as they would listen."[23] (Here we see contributions from both sides, with the elephants learning a new pleasure in human song.)

Unlike Smuts, Poole was not far away from humans. She lived with a group of researchers, and interacted with many Kenyans of many different types. What the book makes clear is that creating and sustaining affectionate relationships was very hard in Poole's human world. She encountered pervasive sexism and one traumatizing incident of sexual assault. A loving intimate relationship with a Kenyan man painfully fell apart because interracial relationships were not tolerated by her white researcher community. She ended up being profoundly lonely on the human side, happy and engaged on the elephant side—reminding us that if humans sometimes form friendships, they also spoil them with unfortunate frequency, and through some vices unknown in the elephant world. Poole had strong incentives to think herself into the elephant mind-world, in the obtuseness and harshness of humanity as she came to see it.

Eventually, realizing that she was not going to have a child in the usual way, through a loving relationship, Poole went away, had a child (probably through artificial insemination, though she is reticent on this point), and clearly thought of herself as like an elephant: "I went through labor and the birth of my baby as an elephant would, surrounded and assisted by my female companions. . . . And when at last my child came into the world, she arrived like a baby elephant, amid great commotion and ceremony."[24] To Poole, mutual support and community are elephant traits, which she prefers to the usual traits of human society as she knows it: divisiveness, sexism, and selfishness. After an absence of two years, she returned to the Amboseli elephants. They surrounded her car, "and, with their trunks outstretched, deafened us with a cacophony of rumbles, trumpets, and screams until our bodies vibrated with the sound. They pressed against one another, urinating and defecating, their faces streaming with the fresh black stain of temporal gland secretions."[25] As Poole knows, this is a ceremony elephants typically reserve for family and group members who have been separated for a long time. It is also associated with the birth of a new baby elephant. Poole realized that they had recognized her, and were celebrating not only her return but also the child she brought back with her, "my tiny daughter, held out to them in my arms."[26]

Had the elephant matriarchs seen Poole as unfortunate because she was childless? Certainly they are likely to have responded intuitively to the deep depression and loneliness she describes as her state of mind for several years. Smuts shows us that Safi, her companion dog, intuitively perceived a depressed mood in Smuts before Smuts herself was fully conscious of her affliction. Elephants are at least as emotionally intelligent as dogs, and are famous for the subtlety of their empathetic perception. So it is not fanciful that they perceived in Poole a change from depression to joy. At the very least, they were welcoming her as a group member and celebrating a new life. But who knows: in the depth of their wise and understanding hearts they may have been cheering the transition from lonely woman to fulfilled elephant mother. It's no accident that she titles her memoir *Coming of Age with Elephants*. Humans did not understand her or help her "come of age"; they impeded in so many ways her desire to flourish as a woman.

These are cases of friendship, but they are predicated on going into the animals' world for long periods of time, which is rarely possible for most of us. Smuts insists, however, that such relationships are all around us if we seek them out. She gives a brief example of a mouse, though the relationship is a short one. Cynthia Townley describes befriending wild birds.[27] None of these cases offer, however, as described, the long-time trusting co-creation of a shared world that is evident in the experiences of Smuts and Poole. Smuts brings this out by juxtaposing the baboon narrative with a moving account of her long-term relationship with a companion dog, Safi. Because dogs can share a dwelling with humans, they can become friends in a deep and meaningful way with humans who inhabit the usual human world and do not travel to research stations in Africa. (Safi knows Smuts, she concludes, better than any human she has ever known, and is keenly aware of the nuances of her moods, as Smuts is of Safi's.) For most of us, such a shared life with wild animals is not really possible, if we respect their group way of life and their need for a large and relatively human-free habitat. The writings of these researchers give us, however, an imaginative paradigm of what such a friendship can be like. We can all cultivate the type of curiosity, empathy, and responsiveness to animal forms of life that these researchers learned in their work. And if friendship still eludes us, we can have unrequited love.

CAN THERE BE FRIENDSHIP WITH ANIMALS IN CAPTIVITY?

We now need to face a difficult question: Can there ever be friendships between humans and wild animals who are living in captivity? We've said that in a sense "the wild" is all human domination and in a larger sense captivity; but now we need to think about what is usually meant by "captivity": not huge game parks, but zoos, where humans and other animals encounter one another at close quarters. Here there is always room for skepticism about the context of domination—whether the potential human friend is a zoo employee, thus party to the domination, or just a visitor, who seems less fully implicated. Let's see to what extent this worry can be met.

Friendship is predicated, we said, on respect for species ways of life. So it is not compatible with practices that do violence to those ways of life. Particularly obvious is the common practice of taking a young elephant, or orca, away from its group and exploiting it in a zoo or theme park for the amusement of humans, as I discussed in chapter 10. Sometimes the public is hoodwinked into paying money to see a charade of friendship, with captive animals whose form of life has been destroyed. *Blackfish*, for example, showed the way in which SeaWorld theatricalized apparently affectionate relationships between trainers and captive orcas, as part of getting spectators to pay to see the stunts the orcas were painfully taught to perform. At times the trainers themselves appear to have been duped: some of those interviewed on camera obviously loved the animals with whom they worked and either were genuinely ignorant of the violence done to their way of life or were manipulated into turning a blind eye.

An omnipresent danger for both spectators and trainers is narcissism and lack of genuine curiosity: we so easily imagine the animal as like us, or project onto the animal human-like sentiments that are unlikely to be the animal's own reactions. Thus, humans can lull themselves into believing that they are participants or spectators in a friendship, rather than enablers of cruel capability violation. Genuine empathy must be based on knowledge, and zoos and theme parks have a strong interest in keeping both spectators and trainers ignorant of the animal's full form of life, so that they can indulge fantasies of friendship without recognizing how impoverished and deprived the zoo environment is.

A related pitfall is that of urging the animal to perform activities that are not characteristic because this amuses human visitors, or fits with their fantasies of friendship. Again, this may be done either through cynical exploitation or through good-faith obtuseness. I've already discussed ape sign language. Other tricks chimpanzees are taught to perform are worse still. Until very recently it was common, in movies and TV, to see chimps dressed in human clothes riding tricycles, or swaddled in diapers like babies.[28] These performances used to amuse humans by feeding a fantasy that the chimp is similar to a human child. This is not friendship, but a parody of it, by humans who lack genuine humility and curiosity.

Dolphins are a complicated case, as I discussed in chapter 10. They are very curious about humans, and happily interactive with them. In their unconfined lives, they often seek out humans and form cooperative activities with them. Hal Whitehead and Luke Rendell describe the way in which a group of coastal dolphins worked in tandem with coastal fishermen, helping them lure shellfish into their nets.[29] These cooperations are at least precursors to friendship. Whitehead and Rendell also show that dolphins who have learned tricks in a theme park and are then released into an unconfined sea habitat sometimes take those tricks with them, and teach them to their young. We might question, then, the inappropriateness of teaching tricks: if done using only positive reinforcement, it may be a joyful part of a cooperative interaction, and stimulating to these highly intelligent mammals—at least sometimes. In a semi-enclosed but not confined space, such as Shark Bay in Australia, there might possibly be beginnings of friendship of the Smuts-Poole variety.

What of animals who seem to do well with a smaller habitat? Can they form friendships in captivity? A sad and controversial history was that of Knut (2006–11), the orphan polar bear in the Berlin zoo who became a fan favorite and certainly had putative friendships with several of the zookeepers.[30] This case is difficult because Knut was rejected by his mother, and would have died had he not been in a zoo with friendly zookeepers, particularly Thomas Dörflein, who clearly loved the little bear, slept by his side, and fed him baby formula. Elephant matriarchs do rear young communally, so a baby whose mother is dead would not be abandoned. This appears not to be true of polar bears, and in the usual habitat of bears, this cub would probably not have had a chance at living its species form of life. Some animal activists did say that the zoo should have had the courage to let the young bear die.[31] But the public, who had already fallen in love with Knut, protested outside the zoo. I believe that the initial actions of the zookeepers were defensible, even laudable. And it remains unclear whether they had any option of giving Knut a normal life with other polar bears, even with the other polar bears in the zoo. So it is consequently unclear whether their treatment of Knut showed any lack of respect for Knut's species form of life; it might have been the best possible in the circumstances.

What the case certainly shows, however, is the public's lack of knowledge and curiosity about the characteristic form of life of polar bears. They wanted Knut to behave like a fluffy toy, and did not like his characteristic polar bear behavior. There was an uproar when Knut killed fish, and people talked of a violation of Germany's laws against animal cruelty. The zoo made little attempt to educate the public about what polar bears really are and do—and for obvious reasons, since they needed Knut to be cute and "harmless," and polar bears are no such thing. Knut was a financial bonanza for the zoo, which trademarked his name, sold all sorts of Knut products, and even exhibited his remains. Zoos always need money, and their motivations should in consequence always be carefully scrutinized.

There are better candidates for "captivity" friendships. Some research environments do offer confined animals something like a species form of life, and, at the same time, interaction with humans. Apes are the logical candidates for such potential friendships, because their species demands can often be met within a research facility. Zoos often don't care about the social lives of apes, or care only in an anthropocentric way, preferring to see them behave "like us." But today there are zoos with a more respectful research-oriented attitude. A scientist working in such a facility may form Smuts-type friendships. One example seems to be the relationship of biologist Jan van Hooff with the chimpanzee "Mama," the heroine of Frans de Waal's *Mama's Last Hug*.[32] The professor and the chimpanzee knew one another for forty years. (Van Hoof was de Waal's thesis adviser, so de Waal, too, knew Mama for a long time, and had a friendship with her.) The main point of the research was to study social structure and interactions among chimpanzees, so she lived her entire life with a sizable kinship group, characteristic of non-captive chimpanzee groups, whose matriarchal leader she eventually became. Van Hooff had observed failed attempts to house groups of apes when he worked in his youth for a NASA facility that prepared chimps to be sent into space. The deficiencies of the NASA installation in housing, feeding, and social opportunities inspired him to create the Arnhem colony, a two-acre island with about twenty-five chimpanzees that permitted both larger groupings and more intimate family retreats, as preferred by chimpanzees in "the wild." "So even though Mama was captive, she enjoyed a long life in her own social universe, rich with birth, death, sex, power dramas, friendships, family ties, and all other aspects of primate society."[33] It was the first large chimpanzee colony, although it has become a model for many around the world.

"One month before Mama turned fifty-nine and two months before Jan van Hooff's eightieth birthday, these two elderly hominids had an emotional reunion."[34] De Waal describes Mama's deathbed embrace of the professor in a way that makes their deep bond clear. Mama welcomed him with a huge grin, and patted his neck, a gesture of reassurance common among apes (and humans too). Reaching for Jan's head, she gently stroked his hair and embraced him with her long arms, trying to pull him closer. She kept patting his head and neck rhythmically, the way chimpanzees comfort an infant. There seems little doubt that Mama, weak and emaciated, was aware of her own diminishing condition, and aware, too, of Jan's fear and grief. The quality of this farewell gives us a small glimpse of the years of friendship that preceded it. And de Waal records his own friendship with Mama in the context of her role in the whole group of chimpanzees.

These relationships are friendships. And if they have limits—the animals are still captives—we need to remember that the "wild" is also, for chimpanzees, a captive zone where humans (poachers especially) frequently exercise a far more baneful tyranny. I see no reason why an environment this respectful (and de Waal proceeds to describe the group and its interrelationships and activities at length) cannot yield friendship, though perhaps this would have been impossible if the colony had been open to the public.

A very different relationship with a research animal is psychologist Irene Pepperberg's famous friendship with Alex (1976–2007), an African gray parrot with whom she interacted for thirty years. This relationship, which seems mutually affectionate and profoundly respectful, is described at length in Pepperberg's book *Alex & Me*, whose title, appropriately, puts Alex first.[35] Pepperberg's interaction with Alex, like van

Hooff's with Mama, was in the context of research. The research might initially seem objectionably anthropocentric, since it tests the ability of parrots to master human language and to reason in ways mediated by language. However, it was propelled throughout by respect for a creature for whom most scientists had no respect. Its objective was to convince the scientific community of the high intelligence of parrots, since it had been thought that a bird could not possibly perform complex feats of reasoning. And in the form of life of parrots (unlike that of chimpanzees) mimicry of whatever communicative sounds are around plays a central role. So language seems not like an alien imposition but rather a medium used to elicit characteristic displays of parrot rationality. Alex did not freely choose to enter the lab—Pepperberg bought him at a pet store—but once in the lab, he exercised control to an almost comical degree. He viewed himself as free to perform the tasks or to refuse them, and he found many ways of indicating boredom and even scorn, so the relationship was full of what it's hard not to call humorous banter. Parrots are generally agreed by scientists to be among the wittiest of the species.[36] And there appears no doubt of the mutual affection of the pair, although Alex did not have arms to hug Pepperberg as Mama hugged van Hooff. His death came very suddenly, at night, so Pepperberg had no opportunity to bid him farewell, but his loss devastated her, as she recounts. His last words to her—words he said every night as she left to go home—were "You be good. I love you. See you tomorrow." Sure, he's repeating what he heard Pepperberg say. But this exchange of farewells clearly became, over the years, genuinely mutual.

One serious concern about Alex and Irene Pepperberg as candidates for friendship is that Alex had no relationships with other parrots, other than the casual, and sometimes rather scornful, interactions he had with other parrots in the lab. But African gray parrots, unlike chimps, elephants, and dolphins, are not highly social and do not live in groups. Little is known about their behavior in the wild, but it is clear that because they are potential prey for many species, they have evolved to be lonely and secretive. They practice mimicry as a key survival skill: in the jungle they avoid detection by learning to imitate other animal and bird sounds. Alex, then, was not exiled from a rich communal life. He did lack a mate: parrots, like many birds, are monogamous and raise their young jointly. So his world did not have Mama's life "rich with birth" and "sex." But parrots are not chimps, and a group is definitely not necessary for their flourishing; whether a mate is, or whether some parrots are just loners, is unknown. Certainly he did not seem depressed or lonely, and it is possible that for parrots, as for humans, flourishing comes in different forms, single as well as coupled.

Friendships across species are possible in captivity, then, if there is respect for the animal's form of life, and for its Central Capabilities within that form of life, as essential bases for interaction and affection. Such friendships are not always available to people without specialized training and opportunities, but, as Smuts says, there are cases all around us that we should investigate further with curiosity and humility: parrots certainly; perhaps corvids and other birds; perhaps rodents of many different types.

FRIENDSHIP AS AN IDEAL: EXPANDING HUMAN CAPABILITIES

Some humans will be lucky enough to have friendships with "wild" animals. Many more will have friendships with dogs, cats, or horses. Many will have unrequited love for animals who remain distant. But all humans can learn from these paradigms of cross-species friendship. They expand our consciousness, teaching us new habits of humility and curiosity as we approach other creatures, including other humans.

Are these friendships as important for the "wild" animals as they are for us, and for companion animals? The importance is different. We control all animals' lives and at present are harming those lives: so friendship is an imperative for us as a correction of our exploitative ways. For companion animals, cross-species friendship is a great good, essential for flourishing. But "wild" animals themselves don't need those face-to-face friendships in order to flourish, though they do need humans to exercise their power with a nonexploitative and friendly cast of mind—"as if" friends, so to speak. But many good things add to all our lives without being absolutely necessary for flourishing, and I believe that in the cases I have discussed here, friendships with humans were a good in the "wild" animal lives.

If we think human-animal friendship is possible and a good goal, this will instruct our political and legal efforts and expand our capabilities. The ideal of friendship commits us all to ending some of the most exploitative forms of activity in which humans engage toward wild animals: not just hunting, factory farming, trophy hunting, poaching, and whaling, not just the torture of animals in experimental research, but also the many quieter forms of domination in which wild animals are treated as objects for human touristic amusement, rather than subjects with their own form of life to live. Both parties will gain. The Capabilities Approach, suitably opened up through knowledge of other species and their forms of life, offers us good guidance as we pursue this difficult goal.

12

THE ROLE OF LAW

ESSENTIAL BUT SO DIFFICULT

If animals have rights, this means that legal mechanisms to enforce them must either exist or be created. Rights and law, I argued in chapter 5, are conceptually independent. And rights mean that, where those structures do not yet exist, all humans, having the monopoly of lawmaking in this world, have a collective duty to create them as best we can. But there are huge difficulties in our way.

The idea of a virtual constitution is just a metaphor, in the absence of institutions that can enforce those rights. Our first difficulty is that in our world there is no such thing as an enforceable rights document. International law about human beings and international human rights documents are extremely weak and fragile. They can be legally enforced, basically, only through nations that support the contents of such a document. In the abstract, this is not such a bad thing, I believe, because the nation has moral importance: it is the largest unit we know that is fully accountable to people and a conduit for their voices and their autonomy (literally, their self-legislation). Human rights documents can have expressive and persuasive power, helping democratic electorates in each nation to take steps toward enforcement.

The situation of animal rights, however, is far more uncertain than that of human rights, for two very different reasons. First, there is nothing like a global consensus on these issues, and no agreement, even, that the welfare of animals ought to be a subject of global concern. That was once true about women, and yet, over time, the status of women under international human rights law (especially CEDAW, the Convention on the Elimination of All Forms of Discrimination Against Women) has made at least some progress. In that issue as with others where some progress has been made—racism, the rights of humans with disabilities and of LGBTQ people—status quo bias has made progress slow. Status quo bias is much stickier in the case of animals. I'll later discuss the lack of progress in an effort to end whaling globally through international treaty law. In all of these issues, greed and the desire to avoid the costs of change make progress even more uncertain.

But there is a further issue, preventing us from solving the problem through an expressive international rights treaty with nation-based implementation: Where are the animals and whose inhabitants are they? If animals are to be thought of as citizens, whose citizens are they? Companion animals are highly localized, a reason why my proposed solution to some of those issues, with its parallel to child welfare, can work; but most wild animals are not localized. They wander across borders. The skies and seas, above all, know no clear borders, though both have areas of nation-based jurisdiction. For many creatures who have been my concern in this book, even an expressive-persuasive document would have to be international to be fully inclusive. This problem has not stopped nations from addressing the needs of some birds and of marine mammals in their coastal waters, as we shall see. But it does mean that for concerned citizens to stop abusive practices by all the nations who pursue them is a tall order, requiring reliance on just those international institutions that are likely to be weak and easily bullied.

Even within nations, there is a huge gap between laws on the books and what is actually enforced, because animals do not have standing (a legal right to go to court as the plaintiff of an action), and human beings who care about animals usually cannot get standing to sue on their behalf, demanding enforcement of existing laws. On the books in the US we have some very promising laws at many levels that embody a Capabilities Approach. And yet, enforcement is sporadic at best. Our legislative process is plagued by gridlock, partisan division, and lobbying on behalf of financial interests, the meat industry being among the most powerful. In our current world, where there are no meaningful limits to the role of money in politics, it is difficult to make any progress against such entrenched interests.

A further problem is that at every level there is a messy plurality of frequently overlapping jurisdictions: federal, state, city or town, and county—often dealing with animals who move across jurisdiction lines. As an example of this problem, I'll later discuss the effort to stop "puppy mills," commercial for-profit breeders who raise puppies in shocking conditions and then sell them to pet stores, where they look cute and are usually bought without awareness of their origins or the medical issues they face as a result of their bad treatment.

A REALISTIC IDEAL

Law is both ideal and strategic. It is easy to be confused about what our best course should be. Should we map out an ideal situation, or should we begin with the defective materials we have and try to make things somewhat better? Some philosophers think that "ideal theory" and theory rooted in the real world, aiming at comparative progress, are two very different things, and that ideal theory is not very practical.[1] To me, however, it seems clear that the two are actually complementary. If we start from where we are and want to reach a destination, it is straightforward to plot a route from here to there if we once get clear about the destination. If we start and just want, somehow, to go to a "better" place, our course is not clear. Ideal theory directs our practical efforts. The ideal must be attainable and realistic; but I have tried to portray the ideals embodied in my Capabilities Approach in such a way as to show that they satisfy that demand.

The anti–ideal theory person may object that my proposals will be far too costly for modern societies to afford them. However, as chapter 8 has shown, cost is endogenous to the development of alternatives. Going over to a mostly meat-free diet is becoming easier all the time, with the development of meat substitutes and synthetic meat. The changes in urban space recommended in chapter 9 (more dog parks, for example) are far less costly than the changes required by the Americans with Disabilities Act. That act was driven by a moral imperative, and its costs were largely borne by the facilities, most of them private, that had to be reconfigured to conform to the law. Moreover, in both the dog park and the disability cases, the cost is primarily a one-time transition cost of restructuring. Beginning de novo, it is not more costly to design buildings with disability access than buildings without. Similarly, urban planning taking the needs of companion animals into account is expensive only when past planning has not done so.

The costliest part of my proposal is the prevention of habitat loss and the cleaning up of existing habitats. Like all bold environmental proposals, this will not be cost-free. But many of these costs are dictated in any case by human welfare. Jean-Pierre's air is the same air human beings breathe, and was made cleaner by the same Clean Air Act. Taking action to stop the melting of glaciers that inflicts harm on polar bears is part and parcel of a program addressing the human future in a time of global warming. Stopping the use of plastics that pollute the seas has transition costs, but quickly new solutions are replacing the old. Or rather, old solutions: many workplaces and even resorts are transitioning to models that replace single-use plastic with the recyclable cans of yesteryear, or even requiring people to bring their own refillable water bottles. As for the habitats of elephants and other large mammals, the cost of protecting large tracts of land for elephants to graze on can be made feasible by international cooperation, by addressing human overpopulation, and by the revenue from ecotourism that always follows well-preserved habitat spaces.

CURRENT RESOURCES

Let's see what law currently offers: both a lot (on paper) and a little (in practice). Initially I'll stick to the US, though international law and comparisons between nations will be important later.

Animals in the US (as in most other countries) already have legal rights, as defined under a wide range of state and federal laws.[2] Even though the public believes that the issue of "animal rights" is highly controversial, the fact is that legislation has given animals a considerable array of rights in recent years, amounting to a virtual "bill of rights"—though with many gaps and omissions. (Usually, animals raised for food and animals used in experimentation are exempted.)

State laws provide animals with a wide range of protections against cruelty, expansively construed. Laws standardly go well beyond protections against what we might call active cruelty (beatings, killings, and so forth), and impose on people in charge of animals (usually, owners) a wide range of affirmative duties: they must offer adequate food and shelter, they must not overwork animals. In New York—to take a representative example—anyone who has confined an animal must provide good air, water, shelter, and food.[3] Anyone who transports an animal in a cruel or inhumane manner faces criminal penalties. Animals transported by rail must be allowed out every five hours for rest, feeding, and water. Other laws forbid overworking or causing unnecessary suffering. California's laws against animal "torture" are even broader, defining "torture" to include negligent imposition of unnecessary suffering. As I've mentioned, these laws exempt animals raised for food and those used for medical or scientific purposes.

These laws have two further defects. First, they do nothing for animals not under the direct control of some human: they track the relationship of ownership and control. Second, they must be enforced by the state, but the state enforces them rarely, only in the most egregious cases. They remain, for the most part, just words on paper.

At the federal level, the US by now has passed a wide range of protective laws. Most of these statutes go back well before "animal rights" became a popular cause, and can hardly be regarded as cases of "political correctness." It may astonish many readers to learn that in 1966, in the middle of the Johnson administration, Congress passed a very comprehensive law, the Animal Welfare Act (AWA), which is broader than most state laws, in that, at its inception, it included animals used in scientific experimentation. Indeed, public outrage at the treatment of animals in research facilities was its main impetus.[4] This law, in its original form, protected all warm-blooded animals used in research or exhibitions, or as pets. It includes a wide range of civil and criminal penalties against mistreatment, and the Secretary of Agriculture is required to issue a detailed account of what "humane treatment" is for each species, governing "handling, housing, feeding, watering, sanitation, ventilation, shelter from extremes of weather and temperatures, adequate veterinary care."[5] Specific sections require minimum amounts of exercise for dogs and an environment suited to protect the "psychological well-being" of primates.[6] These primates must have the opportunity to form social groups and to have access to "environmental enrichment" that will allow them to express "noninjurious species-typical activities."[7] There is a flat ban on practices in which any animals are made to fight. In its species-specificity and in protections for free movement and psychological health, it goes beyond the Utilitarian approach toward what a Capabilities Approach would recommend.

As written, the law has salient omissions. One is the total omission of cold-blooded animals, an omission apparently motivated by one legislator's desire to insulate Maryland's National Hard Crab Derby from regulation. Another is the omission of killing itself. The act never says that experimenters cannot bring about the death of experimental animals—only that it must be kind to them as it does so. Third, by focusing on three categories—experimentation, exhibitions, and pets—the act exempts the factory food industry from regulation. Still worse, in 2002 the act was amended to exclude birds, and all rats and mice bred for use in research, thus defeating much of the original act's purpose. In 2002, the USDA agreed to protect birds not used in research and to draw up a standard of care for them, but they delayed and delayed, and the issue of unreasonable delay is currently being litigated.[8]

The Endangered Species Act (ESA) is aimed, obviously, at the preservation of species, not at the welfare of individual animals, but its mechanisms, including habitat protection and protection from disturbance, are good for individuals as well, and a species only goes extinct when its individual members suffer in a variety of ways.[9] So although I focus on individual welfare, and it is unfortunate that to obtain habitat protection one must show that the species is endangered, at least its remedies are good for many individual animals. Habitat is defined in a way congenial to the Capabilities Approach: it has to accommodate the behaviors characteristic of the species; and it requires that this determination be made using the best scientific evidence available, again congenial to the CA, which urges policy makers to consult current research about animal behavior and cognition.

Three statutes of note protect specific types of creatures. The Wild Free-Roaming Horses and Burros Act (WFHBA) addresses the situation of wild horses and burros, considered to be "living symbols of the historic and pioneer spirit of the West."[10] Despite this highly anthropocentric beginning, the act goes on to state that these species "contribute to the diversity of life forms within the nation and enrich the lives of the American people," a statement that apparently ascribes some intrinsic value to these creatures.[11] This law was in fact the project of a very concerned animal advocate, Velma Bronn Johnston, known to many as "Wild Horse Annie," and its original aim was to safeguard these animals.

More recently, however, the Bureau of Land Management (BLM), the federal agency in charge of implementing the WFHBA, is pushing a false narrative of exploding wild horse populations that allegedly threaten

America's public lands. Although baseless in most cases, BLM's cries reso-
nate with some elected officials, the public, and in some cases even with
wild horse advocates. The result has been the removal of tens of thousands of wild horses from public lands, in what seems to be a complete
abdication of BLM's responsibility under the act. Even the idea that horses
are too numerous derives not from sound science but from lobbying by
ranchers who graze their cattle on these lands. As the National Academy
of Sciences reported in 2013, BLM's management of wild horses lacks
scientifically rigorous methods to estimate the population sizes of horses
and burros, to model the effects of management actions on the animals,
or to assess the availability and use of forage on rangelands. BLM, who
commissioned this report, has never sought to correct these problems.

A law contemporary with the ESA and the WFHBA is the Marine
Mammal Protection Act (MMPA), which I have already discussed in
chapter 5 in connection with the navy's sonar program.[12] This law prohib-
its any "take" of marine mammals in US waters and by US citizens in international waters. It also bans the import/export and sale of any marine
mammal or marine mammal parts or products within the United States.
"Take" is defined as "to harass, hunt, capture, collect, or kill, or attempt
to harass, hunt, capture, collect or kill, any marine mammal."[13] The act
further defines harassment as "any act of pursuit, torment or annoyance
which has the potential to either: a. injure a marine mammal in the wild,
or b. disturb a marine mammal by causing disruption of behavioral patterns, which includes, but is not limited to, migration, breathing, nursing,
breeding, feeding, or sheltering."[14] It is a very well-written statute, with a
focus squarely on the animal's form of life as a whole, not just on killing
and the infliction of pain.

Thus, the decision in *NRDC v. Pritzker* was dictated by the statutory
language, not only by wise judging. It is the closest we get at the federal level
to the legal implementation of the Capabilities Approach. Enforcement is
to be shared between the US Fish and Wildlife Service (Department of
the Interior) and the National Oceanic and Atmospheric Administration
(Department of Commerce), each being given responsibility for specific

species. (Whales are under the Commerce Department, the reason why Penny Pritzker, then Secretary of Commerce, was the defendant in that landmark case.) Litigation has proven necessary to get the enforcement that the act requires, but in that case the NRDC was judged to have standing to sue (see below).

This law looks comparatively good, and it has in fact protected whales from "harassment," even against some very powerful interests. But one must bear in mind the fact that the US has never had a major commercial whaling industry, and therefore environmental groups do not need to contend against powerful commercial interests.

A third major statute protecting a specific group of animals, from a much earlier date, is the Migratory Bird Treaty Act (MBTA).[15] As its name indicates, this law arose out of a bilateral treaty between the US and Canada. It now embodies other bilateral agreements made with Mexico, Japan, and the former USSR. This law makes it illegal to "pursue, hunt, take capture, kill, attempt to take, capture, or kill, possess, offer for sale, sell, offer to barter, barter, offer to purchase, purchase, deliver for shipment, ship, export, import, cause to be shipped, exported, or imported, deliver for transportation, transport or cause to be transported, carry or cause to be carried, or receive for shipment, transportation, carriage, or export"[16] any bird or part of a bird. Penalties are stiff: fines up to $15,000, and imprisonment up to two years. The Secretary of the Interior is to make regulations determining which birds fall under the act's scope.

A first point that is obvious, and related to gaps in other laws, is that it is limited to "migratory birds," and thus exempts chickens, ducks, and most other game birds, all of which are standardly hunted, raised, and killed for food. Moreover, the act explicitly limits its scope to "bird species that are native to the United States or its territories."[17] This almost meaningless statement—since we have little information about the bird population of North America in prehistory, and in any case there was no United States then—leaves lots of room for the Department of the Interior to include or exclude.

There are other weaknesses. The act is centrally an anti-hunting and anti-poaching act. It says nothing clear about protection of the lives and capabilities of birds beyond that. One might have thought that habitat destruction and environmental degradation are sure ways of killing many birds (as Jean-Pierre's case reminds us). And indeed courts have sometimes interpreted the act to prohibit activities that cause environmental harm. In 1980, the DC Circuit held that the prohibition of killing birds "by any means and manner" suggests that killing by destroying habitats is banned by the act.[18] In 1999, a federal district court came to the same conclusion in a case involving an electric company that had failed to install inexpensive equipment on its power lines to prevent the death of birds by electrocution. The act, the court said, is not limited to hunting and poaching. Further, the fact that the company had no ill intent toward the birds was not relevant: the MBTA is a strict liability statute.[19] Other courts, however, have disagreed. In 1997, the Eighth Circuit, in a case dealing with deaths of birds due to timber harvesting and resulting habitat destruction, said that to read the Act as prohibiting habitat destruction "would stretch this 1918 statute far beyond the bounds of reason."[20] In a related case, the Ninth Circuit came to a similar conclusion.[21]

As for the authority the act grants to the Secretary of the Interior, this feature has made the Act expand and contract with each administration, sometimes dramatically. Prior to the Trump administration, the Department of the Interior had held that killing birds incidentally through toxic waste spills is illegal under the act.[22] The Trump administration changed course, limiting the Act to hunting and poaching.[23]

Each of these laws has serious gaps and flaws, but with all their deficiencies, the federal and state laws we currently have offer a surprising amount of protection to at least some animals.

TWO KEY LEGAL ISSUES: STANDING FOR ANIMALS. FIDUCIARY DUTIES

There is, however, a huge problem with all of existing laws: they are relatively rarely enforced, and there is no mechanism through which concerned citizens can intervene to demand their enforcement. Here we arrive at one of the most critical legal issues for anyone who cares about animal protection: the issue of standing.

"Standing" means entitlement to go to court as the plaintiff of an action. Typically, standing is given only to someone who has suffered a particular injury. A concerned third party usually does not have standing. This is a wise requirement on the whole, preventing a lot of meddlesome litigation. Consider two salient examples in recent years where standing was denied. In *Hollingsworth v. Perry*, the litigation surrounding same-sex marriage in California, the US Supreme Court ruled that the private citizens who had originally sought to ban same-sex marriage through Proposition 8 lacked standing to appeal when the ban was found unconstitutional by the appellate court and the state of California refused to defend the law.[24] These private citizens, the Court ruled, had not suffered the type of direct particular injury that conveys standing. In 2000, in *Elk Grove Unified School District v. Newdow*, Michael Newdow, arguing on behalf of his minor child, challenged the use of the words "under God" in the school's ritual Pledge of Allegiance as a violation of the Establishment Clause.[25] Although he had a very strong case, the Supreme Court—reluctant, very likely, to decide this highly controversial case—ruled that Newdow, being a noncustodial parent after a divorce, did not have standing to argue the case. In other words, even his parental concern and his strong arguments did not entitle him to go to court. It's a high bar to meet.

Still, since animals cannot go to court, and since the efforts of their most concerned allies typically fail for lack of standing, as did the conservationists in *Lujan v. Defenders of Wildlife*, and other similar human allies of animals in cases to be discussed shortly, we need to create an avenue into the courts for animals, whose interests otherwise will go unprotected.[26]

The only real solution to this problem is to grant standing to animals to enter court as plaintiffs in their own right, through a duly appointed fiduciary. The person who is injured need not be the one who appears in court. Minor children can be represented by their parents, and people with cognitive disabilities by a duly appointed guardian, or "collaborator," to use the term preferred in the disability movement. If Newdow had been a custodial parent, he would have had standing to argue, through the alleged injury to his daughter.

The problem, however, is that animals have never been given standing under US law. A court in India did give circus animals standing, holding that they are persons within the meaning of the Indian constitution's Article 21, which forbids deprivation of life or liberty without due process. The court wrote:

> Though not homosapiens, they are also beings entitled to dignified existence and humane treatment sans cruelty and torture. . . . Therefore, it is not only our fundamental duty to show compassion to our animal friends, but also to recognise and protect their rights. . . . If humans are entitled to fundamental rights, why not animals? [27]

Colombia, too, gives animals legal standing, as I discuss in my conclusion. Similarly, the US Congress could give animals standing under Article III if it so chose: there is no constitutional barrier to such a move, argues Cass Sunstein, an expert in this area, and I know of no scholar who disagrees.[28] So far, however, the US has taken a different route, denying animals direct standing and granting standing to humans to appear on behalf of animals in only a narrow range of cases.

One possible route to human litigation on behalf of animals might have been "informational standing," the right to obtain essential information. It seems highly plausible that concerned humans have a right to obtain information about animal treatment. But neither the AWA nor the MMPA expressly gives humans informational standing, and in the absence of an explicit provision, concerned humans have to fall back on the Administrative Procedure Act, which was interpreted to deny this sort of standing to human organizations seeking information on animal welfare, in *Animal Legal Defense Fund, Inc. v. Espy.*[29] Indeed, so far the record of attempts to invalidate so-called "ag-gag" laws that expressly prevent people from acquiring information about animal treatment in the factory farm industry, on free speech grounds, is quite mixed, as we'll later see.

The other plausible channel by which humans might acquire standing is that of concerned observers of mistreatment.[30] And this is what humans have tried to do again and again. Under existing law, however, they can acquire standing only if they meet two conditions: their injury must be "aesthetic" and not ethical or compassionate; and it must be very direct. If plaintiffs have only a principled interest in animal welfare, it is clear that they do not have standing, as *Lujan* clearly established.[31] If they have definite plans to study a species that is threatened, and they can show that the conduct they challenge reduces the supply of such creatures available for study, they can also very likely get standing.[32] But if the species is not endangered and they are simply concerned observers, they must show an "aesthetic" concern, and it must be very direct and immediate. Marc Jurnove, an employee and volunteer for animal welfare organizations, brought a suit against the Long Island Game Farm Wildlife Park and Children's Zoo for its inhumane treatment of animals.[33] (Note that this treatment was very likely illegal under New York State law, but nobody was enforcing the law.) What Jurnove had to say in order to have a chance of winning was that he was a regular visitor to the zoo, and had suffered injury to his "aesthetic interest in observing animals living under humane conditions."[34] His ethical concern as a worker for animal welfare did him no good at all. He was granted standing only because the injury was highly particular, his visits were frequent, and the injury was aesthetic. Even then, the panel was divided, because the bad treatment, they said, was caused by the zoo, not the government (the defendant).

Things have gone wildly astray. The basis for concern should be the harm to the animal, not Jurnove's aesthetic interest or even his ethical interest. Human interests are capricious and, really, irrelevant. What matters is the injury to the animal. Imagine if the criminal law were based on the aesthetic, or even ethical, reactions of bystanders, rather than the harms done to the actual victim. Law would then become wildly unpredictable, hostage to majority preferences. Nor is the frequency of Jurnove's visits of any real significance apart from some evidentiary significance: he has witnessed the bad conduct frequently. The human observer is a witness to a crime. He or she is not the victim. Animals are not protected by law so that we can feel aesthetic rapture or moral satisfaction. Laws on the books protect them as themselves. If those laws are not enforced, it is obvious that animals are the victims of governmental bad behavior and should be given standing to sue for law enforcement, through concerned human fiduciaries such as, perhaps, Jurnove.

Just such a change to current law was advocated already in 1972 by Justice Douglas in his dissent in *Sierra Club v. Morton*.[35] Standing, he wrote, should be expanded to include protection for those "inarticulate members of the ecological group" who cannot advocate for their own interests.[36] (And of course, as he does not say, we already give standing just in this way to minor children and humans with severe cognitive disabilities.) He noted that the primary impediment to this extension comes from federal agencies who are "notoriously under the control of powerful interests who manipulate them."[37] And he envisages a new day when "[t]here will be assurances that all of the forms of life which [the environment] represents will stand before the court—the pileated woodpecker as well as the coyote and bear, the lemmings as well as the trout in the streams."[38] If with "all forms of life" he means to extend standing beyond sentient animals, I respectfully disagree. But his examples are all from the animal realm.

Given that yesterday's dissents are sometimes tomorrow's majorities, this opinion may augur progress. Similarly, in *Cetacean Community v. Bush*,[39] an unsuccessful attempt to challenge the navy's sonar program prior to the successful *NRDC v. Pritzker*, the Ninth Circuit, though not granting standing to the plaintiff organizations, noted that "nothing in the text of Article III explicitly limits the ability to bring a claim in federal court to humans."[40] And they cited an earlier Ninth Circuit case in which the court stated that the Hawaiian palila bird "has legal status and wings its way into federal court as a plaintiff in its own right."[41] They insisted that this statement was "dicta," i.e., not part of an enforceable holding;

but such dicta can pave the way for later holdings. And in fact, in *NRDC v. Pritzker*, the Ninth Circuit engaged in a lengthy discussion of standing. While not granting standing to the whales themselves, they interpreted the interests and injuries of the NRDC broadly and generously, as *Cetacean Community* had not.

Standing for animals would be easy and straightforward if Congress were to act. There is no constitutional barrier to giving animals standing under Article III. If Congress does not act, it is not impossible that the courts will gradually go there.

If animals should have standing, who represents them? Throughout this book, I have argued—agreeing with Christine Korsgaard—that all humans have a collective obligation to secure animal rights. However, the current approach, according to which volunteer organizations or individuals try hard to get into court on animals' behalf, is disorganized and chance-governed, and needs to be replaced by a more orderly system. In the case of companion animals I have suggested local governmental bodies akin to those that now protect children from abuse and neglect. In many other cases, a statute has delegated enforcement to specific governmental bodies, such as the Department of Agriculture or the Department of the Interior. But this approach has been insufficient to stop a great deal of bad behavior—the reason why nonprofit organizations have tried so hard and in so many ways to get standing to sue for enforcement.

What would be better? We can borrow an idea from a familiar area of law: *fiduciary law*.⁴² A fiduciary is someone who has a legal obligation to advance a beneficiary's interests. (Standard examples are guardians, trustees, and conservators.) Typically the need for legal regulation arises from the fact that the fiduciary is in a powerful position vis-à-vis the beneficiary and the beneficiary is poorly placed to monitor the fiduciary's activities.⁴³ The fiduciary's job is not simply to do no damage to the beneficiary's interests, but to advance them actively, in accordance with that person's wishes and preferences. But there is always a danger that the fiduciary will instead promote his or her own interests.

For this reason, law imposes on fiduciaries two duties: the *duty of care* and the *duty of loyalty*. The duty of care involves "making decisions that would best advance the beneficiary's care, education, health, finances, and welfare, all the while doing so with an eye towards advancing the beneficiary's autonomy. This means that the fiduciary must try, as much as possible, to include the beneficiary in the decision-making process and familiarize herself with the beneficiary's values and interests."[44] The duty of loyalty involves being on guard against self-dealing, and states have adopted various monitoring requirements to ensure that fiduciaries are fulfilling this duty.

This is exactly what is needed, for each type of animal. And this approach fits particularly well with the Capabilities Approach: fiduciary law is not just concerned with avoiding pain or even harm to the beneficiary, but rather with actively advancing the beneficiary's interests in a broad way. In the case of companion animals, the human companion is the first-stage fiduciary, but I have proposed that government ought to monitor this arrangement zealously, with an eye to neglect. In other cases, government should designate a suitable animal welfare agency as the fiduciary for a specific type or types of animals. The fiduciary is supposed to be active in the animals' interests: thus, if the USDA is idle and harm is afoot, the designated agency could pursue the issue. In the case of wild animals, the fiduciary should not sit idly by if they are suffering from various harms (habitat spoilage, poaching, disease), but should actively intervene in the animals' interests.

Without reform of standing law, this arrangement has no teeth. But once animals have standing, a fiduciary arrangement can give the fiduciary standing to go to court on the animal or animals' behalf.

Law has been resourceful, where human interests are concerned. These good ideas have been operating for a long time to protect vulnerable human beings. There is no reason why, suitably altered, they cannot be transferred to animals.

Let's now look at three issues that exemplify and make vivid the gaps in law's current coverage. The first, the issue of puppy mills, shows the difficulty of enforcing the Animal Welfare Act in the absence of zeal on the part of the USDA, and, on the other hand, the resourcefulness of local jurisdictions in attempting to solve the problem. The second, the regulation of factory farming, shows what can be done in the complete absence of federal regulation, and yet the fierce resistance that all such efforts encounter. It also shows that other nations have made more progress with a more comprehensive approach. The third, the various harms done to whales and other marine mammals, shows the promise and yet the current weakness of international regulation.

PUPPY MILLS

Puppy mills are commercial for-profit breeders who breed for quantity and then sell young puppies to pet stores, where consumers often believe they are purchasing dogs from high-quality breeders. The Humane Society of the United States has closely monitored these breeders for many years, and publishes an annual report on a "horrible hundred" in order to document the nature and magnitude of the problem.[45] Many dogs are given low-quality nutrition, and often too little water. Many are given no or insufficient veterinary care, and often have diseases, parasites, and other problems. Puppy mill dogs typically have little room to move around and are often kept in cages, in unsanitary conditions that spread disease. They have too little shelter from heat and cold.

Many of these conditions violate the AWA. For three years, from 2017 to 2020, the USDA stopped reporting on its enforcement of the AWA, and enforcement actions against particular breeders declined by 90 percent. Inspectors reported that they were actively dissuaded from doing their jobs.[46] In February 2020, at the direction of Congress, the USDA was required to restore online data about enforcement actions. In 2019, the Humane Society won a lawsuit requiring the USDA to release comprehensive data to the public when requested. Its 2020 report contains comprehensive information on breeders in every state.

The puppy mill problem is nationwide at the point of purchase: pet shops in every state carry, or until very recently used to carry, dogs from these problematic breeders. But it is not nationwide at the point of origin. Missouri is its capital, with thirty problematic breeders. Next are Ohio with nine, Kansas and Wisconsin with eight, and Georgia with seven. (These numbers are unreliable because some states discourage local investigation.) In Missouri, which has topped the "horrible hundred" list for eight years, humane organizations have waged a legal struggle for years to regulate the bad breeders, but with repeated failures at the state level. A Puppy Mill Cruelty Prevention Act passed as a referendum in 2010, supported by the Humane Society, the ASPCA, and other groups, and bitterly opposed by agribusiness and breeder groups, the NRA, and, oddly, the Missouri Veterinary Medical Association. Under old regulations, a dog could be kept in a cage only six inches longer than her body and permanently confined there, exposed to the elements with no requirement for veterinary care. The new law mandated adequate food, sanitary and somewhat larger cages, veterinary care, and protection from extreme temperatures. Within two months of its passage, five bills to repeal or modify the law had been introduced. Governor Jay Nixon signed a much watered-down bill in 2011. The revised bill removed the requirement for outdoor exercise and allowed cage sizes to be set by the State Department of Agriculture.[47]

Still, the state does have an enforcement system, which some states do not, and occasionally closes down the worst offenders.[48]

Since point-of-origin regulation is undependable, a large number of states, cities, and counties are regulating at point of sale. The preferred strategy is to require pet shops to sell only rescue dogs from licensed shelters. Let's look at my own city's attempt to use this strategy. In 2014, the City of Chicago passed an ordinance requiring that all pet stores obtain their pets from an animal control center, a government-run kennel or training facility, or "a private, charitable, nonprofit humane society or animal rescue organization."[49] A further purpose of the law was to increase the shelter live-release rate—which did in fact increase, from 62 percent in 2016 to 92 percent in 2019. Pet stores began campaigning against the law immediately, since it cut off a profitable business. Some critics claimed that the law violated the US and Illinois constitutions, but the Seventh Circuit dismissed the claims as legally baseless.[50]

Meanwhile, it emerged that the law had been poorly drafted, allowing pet shop owners to evade its requirements. Puppy mill breeders only had to establish a "shell" nonprofit corporation and funnel the dogs to Chicago pet stores through that. An exposé by the *Chicago Tribune* showed that two puppy mill breeders, J.A.K.'s Puppies and Lonewolf Kennels (the former in Iowa, the latter in Missouri), had opened nonprofit corporations, fronts for the puppy mill, named Hobo K-9 Rescue and Dog Mother Rescue Society. Over a thousand dogs were sold in Chicago from these organizations. Interestingly, the two source states reacted in opposite ways to the exposé, Missouri doing nothing, and Iowa ultimately penalizing the mill, and other puppy mills in the state, to the tune of $600,000.[51]

Meanwhile, in Chicago, Alderman Brian Hopkins introduced an amendment to the law that requires pet shops to get pets from rescue groups with no ties to any for-profit breeder or entity. Further, it required pet shops to charge only a modest adoption fee, removing the incentive to sell expensive allegedly purebred dogs. After much debate, this amendment finally passed on April 12, 2021.[52] An odd feature of the process, showing the continued power of the puppy mill–pet store nexus, was the fact that Alderman Raymond Lopez, who had previously supported the ordinance, opposed the amendment—and was found to have accepted a campaign contribution from a pet shop owner. But Lopez did make a good point when he opposed the amendment's exclusion of "backyard breeding," a concession to the American Kennel Club. Hopkins argued that people who love their breeds will not raise them in cruel conditions; Lopez countered that a lot of the dogs who end up in shelters are overbred purebred dogs from just such breeders. He makes a point I made in chapter 9: dogs are abused not only by the obvious harms of the puppy mills, but also by being inbred and therefore subject to many diseases. Eager amateur "backyard breeders" are especially likely to ignore genetic screening.[53]

This lengthy drama shows how difficult it is to make progress on this issue at point of sale, when states do not properly regulate origins. Point-of-sale regulation is not just difficult, it is inherently narrow in jurisdiction. A Chicago resident who wants a puppy mill dog (perhaps in ignorance of the bad conditions, just seeking a cute puppy, rather than a mature shelter dog) has only to drive to the suburbs, where regulation is spotty at best, often a patchwork of inconsistent city and county rules.

The whole issue could be solved by zealous federal enforcement of the AWA; or by a new federal statute directed at this specific issue. States can do relatively little so long as there is at least one eager source state, and a lot of profit-oriented pet shops. Meanwhile, countless young dogs have no chance to develop and exercise their capabilities.

FACTORY FARMING (AND AG-GAG LAWS)

Chapters 1, 7, and 9 have mentioned some of the abuses of the factory farming industry. Farm animals lack protection under federal laws such as the AWA, the ESA, and the MBTA. They are also exempted from protection under the state anti-cruelty laws of thirty-seven states. And things are still worse: so successful has the effort of the factory farm industry been to insulate itself from criticism that many states have passed so-called "ag-gag" laws that criminalize whistleblower activity intended to bring these abuses to public attention.[54] (Undercover photography and video recording have been very effective in revealing abuses and motivating public outrage.)

The typical statute criminalizes undercover recording in an agricultural facility; some extend more broadly to recording in other types of businesses. At present, six states have "ag-gag" laws on the books: Alabama, Arkansas, Iowa, Missouri, Montana, and North Dakota (though lawsuits have been filed in Iowa and Arkansas, and two prior Iowa statutes have been ruled unconstitutional by courts). In five other states—North Carolina, Kansas, Utah, Wyoming, and Idaho, the laws have been struck down on the ground that they violate First Amendment rights. In eighteen states, ag-gag legislation has been introduced but defeated: Maine, New Hampshire, Vermont, New York, New Jersey, Pennsylvania, Florida,

Tennessee, Kentucky, Indiana, Illinois, Minnesota, Nebraska, Colorado, New Mexico, Arizona, California, and Washington. In the rest, the battle has so far not materialized.

This struggle shows the enormous importance of nonprofit legal organizations who fight the legal battles around the US. Meanwhile, information has emerged, and is easily available on the websites of these organizations, and in books such as Timothy Pachirat's impressive exposé, *Every Twelve Seconds: Industrial Slaughter and the Politics of Sight*,[55] which takes the reader into the concealed life of the slaughterhouse, seeing its daily activities from the viewpoint of a worker. (Pachirat was doing undercover research as an employee at a cattle-slaughter facility that he does not name.) Anyone who wants to find out what abuses the industry is so eager to conceal can access the information, thanks to the work of such courageous whistleblowers.

Federal law contributes little to the fight against abuse. Not only are all farm animals exempted from the AWA, but even the Humane Methods of Slaughter Act and the Twenty-Eight Hour Law, which regulates how animals must be treated in transport, exempts poultry, even though 95 percent of the animals raised for food in the US are poultry.

How are the states doing? We find much the same problem that the puppy mill issue presented: the states where most of the abuses occur do nothing, and the states that have passed good laws are by and large those where few abuses were occurring anyway (although the raising of chickens is not as geographically centralized as the raising of pigs and cattle). Abuses that have been made illegal by some states include the use of gestation crates (ten states), the use of veal confinement crates (nine states), and the use of hen confinement cages (eight states). California and Massachusetts are especially active regulators. But the states that regulate are not the large producers, so their point-of-origin regulations are not particularly significant.

For this reason, as in the case of the puppy mill problem, states have also adopted point-of-sale strategies: banning the sale of foie gras, made by force-feeding ducks and geese (California and New York City), banning the sale of veal and pork from animals raised in confinement crates (California and Massachusetts), and banning the sale of eggs from hens confined in a manner illegal under these states' laws (seven states). Meanwhile, other states have moved in the other direction. Iowa, the nation's largest egg-producing state and one of its largest pork producers, has adopted specific exemptions to anti-cruelty laws for practices involving farm animals. Some abuse is prosecuted, but it must be very extreme: for example, a case in which pig-farm workers beat pigs with metal rods and jammed pins into their faces. Iowa has also passed a law requiring any grocery store that participates in a federal program that subsidizes cage-free eggs to sell, as well, eggs from hens kept in confinement crates.

Point-of-sale strategies are not likely to advance rapidly, given that— unlike the regulation of pet stores—they put a financial burden on consumers. And point-of-origin strategies are doomed for the present, in the largest meat-producing states.

Europe, meanwhile, has been able to make a lot more progress, apparently because the EU is not in the grip of the factory farming industry to the extent that US federal lawmakers are. The European Convention for the Protection of Animals Kept for Farming Purposes, enacted in 1976, contains a wide array of protections for farm animals and sets up a system of monitoring.[56] The convention is further supplemented by species-specific regulations, including pens for pigs spacious enough for them to stand up, lie down, and socialize with other pigs. Pigs must also have enough hay, straw, and other materials to permit them to engage in their natural "investigation and manipulation activities."[57] Both food chickens and egg-laying hens also have reasonably robust protections. A directive for calves recognizes their social nature, requiring group housing for calves above eight weeks old. In short: Europe is moving in the direction of respecting animal capabilities.

Even though the EU law is pretty protective, some nations, for example, Austria and Sweden, have gone even further in protecting pigs and chickens.[58]

Concerned US readers may be despondent at this point. From the point of view of this book, these highly intelligent and complex animals should not be raised for food in the first place. If even these incremental reforms toward humane treatment are so unsuccessful, how can we expect the goals of this book to be realized? Admittedly, the United States is a difficult nation in which to hope, given the huge power of the meat industry over our political life. Still, the progress that has been made through law and lawyering, especially against ag-gag laws, is impressive. And as more information is out there, public sentiments really are changing. The new popularity of plant-based imitation meat, and the prospect of synthetic meat, may prove the game changers worldwide.

THE FUTURE FOR WHALES: THE WEAKNESS OF INTERNATIONAL LAW[59]

For centuries, whales have been seen in seemingly contradictory ways: as awe-inspiring and beautiful animals, but also as animals from whom human beings can make a great profit. Great literature contains both views. D. H. Lawrence, so critical in many respects of industrial capitalism, took the first approach in his poem "Whales Weep Not!" (1909):

They say the sea is cold, but the sea contains
the hottest blood of all, and the wildest, the most urgent.

All the whales in the wider deeps, hot are they, as they urge
on and on, and dive beneath the icebergs.
The right whales, the sperm-whales, the hammer-heads, the killers
there they blow, there they blow, hot wild white breath out of
the sea!

Consider, by contrast, this extract from Obed Macy's *The History of Nantucket* (1835):

In the year 1690 some persons were on a high hill observing the whales spouting and sporting with each other, when one observed: there— pointing to the sea—is a green pasture where our children's grand-children will go for bread.

Herman Melville, who cites the Macy passage among the many extracts with which he begins *Moby-Dick*, is drawn in both directions, accepting the industry of whaling with no criticism, while at the same time emphasizing the awe-inspiring properties of its prey. As we shall soon see, contemporary international law is also pulled in both directions, one faction trying to end lethal cruelty to whales, the other faction seeking only to preserve whale "stocks" for future exploitation.

Whaling, the sole focus of international efforts to date, is only one small part of the harm done to whales in international waters. Sound is a whale's most important form of communication with other whales, and disruption of their sonic environment disrupts their form of life in many ways, as *NRDC v. Pritzker* rightly concluded. But there are many disruptions other than those caused by the US Navy. Other nations also use sonar. The global shipping industry makes a great deal of noise all over the world. And the oil and gas industry causes sonic disruption not only by the noise of oil rigs that drill for undersea oil, but also by the cartographic operations searching for oil. In order to chart the contours of the ocean floor, these companies use high-powered air guns that explode air downward through the deep, and this happens at regular intervals, and more or less all over the globe. An excellent exploration of these disruptions is in the justly lauded 2016 documentary film *Sonic Sea*, directed by Daniel Hinerfeld and Michelle Dougherty.[60] These sonic bursts can even in some cases cause brain injury and death to whales. So the fact that international law has not seen fit even to discuss regulating sonic disruption shows how timid it is and how little it aims to accomplish.

What is wrong with whaling? In the terms of this book, the answer is evident: it ends prematurely the lives of these complex sentient animals, using them as objects from which humans can extract meat, oil, and other useful products. But that is what is wrong with the killing of most animals for food, as chapter 7 has argued. It may certainly be added that the industry of whaling is cruel: harpooning inflicts a long, slow death, sometimes made more painful by clubbing. New technology has changed things somewhat: now many whales are caught using a shell harpoon with an explosive head detonating inside the whale, which shortens the time of dying. Still, it is a bad death. And yet, most animals killed for food also have a bad death, at the end of a bad life, and the whale was at least free before, and thus does much better than most cows, pigs, and chickens. Before we embark on a critique of current practices, then, it is important to say that whaling does not involve any evil that these other common practices do not. It is thus hypocritical for nations such as the US, which does little whaling, to gripe about the whaling done by other nations while overlooking the heinous practices in which they are implicated every day. Unfortunately this (justified) charge of hypocrisy often retards attempts to protect whales under international law.

Another issue to be clear about is the nature of the evil against which legal protection is sought. Here there are two factions. For one faction (basically the same faction that wants to use whales as means to human ends), the only evil to be prevented is the extinction of one or more species of whales, thus the end of (one part of) a lucrative industry. This faction typically speaks of "whale stocks," as if the individual whale were insignificant. For others, and for me, the evil is the needless and cruel deaths of individual whales. The species matters because continued reproduction and diversity of the species are usually essential for individual health and flourishing, including social interaction.

Whales within US jurisdiction do reasonably well. The MMPA protects individual whales not only from killing but also from "harassment," and the *Pritzker* case shows how protective courts can be, even against powerful military interests. Orcas have not always been protected from "harassment," as the infamous conduct shown in *Blackfish* demonstrates, but things have now changed, at least in California, thanks to the Orca

Welfare and Safety Act. Orcas flourish, meanwhile, in the wild in US coastal waters, especially off of the San Juan Islands in Washington.

That is not to say that the US does not hunt whales. Beluga whale hunting, monitored by the Alaska Beluga Whale Committee, kills about three hundred whales a year. Two indigenous groups hunt endangered species against the protests of animal rights groups: the bowhead whale is hunted for "subsistence" by nine indigenous Alaskan communities, and the Makah in Washington State have resumed hunting the gray whale. Both hunts are defended using appeals to cultural rights of the type I discussed in chapter 8.

Now, however, we come to what goes on in international waters. All hunting of whales, including hunts conducted by US actors, are regulated by a treaty signed in 1946, the International Convention for the Regulation of Whaling (ICRW). This convention sets up a monitoring group, the International Whaling Commission (IWC).[61]

The ICRW was aimed not at ending the killing of whales but at sustainable use. It was motivated by evidence of depletion of "whale stocks." In its preamble, Dean Acheson, then US secretary of state, described whales as "wards of the entire world" and a "common resource." The word "resource" suggests that whales are seen as objects for human use. And indeed, when the convention was drafted, there was no thought of banning commercial whaling entirely: the goal was a quota system for each member nation. Two forms of whaling were explicitly permitted outside the announced quotas: aboriginal whaling, and whaling "for scientific purposes." Both then and now, a nation that does not agree to a particular provision may remain a member of the IWC while opting out of that provision. And any change requires assent by three-fourths of the nations.

With these provisions in place, the stage was already set for stagnation—despite the fact that US Secretary of the Interior C. Girard Davidson heralded the treaty as pointing to "a more peaceful and happy future for mankind." (The future happiness of whales was not mentioned!) And yet without the opt-out, many nations seriously engaged in whaling, including Russia, Japan, and Norway, would not have joined the IWC in the first place.

At first, commercial whaling was permitted, with a quota system and careful monitoring procedures. In 1982, however, a complete moratorium on commercial whaling was instituted. Intended to be temporary until stocks recovered, the moratorium endures, since there has been no agreement about circumstances that would justify resumption. This disagreement has only intensified: some members of the IWC have increasingly shifted to an animal rights viewpoint, with a general ethical objection to whaling, while other members are eager to resume the commercial practice. Enforcement has always been weak, since the treaty gives each nation the task of disciplining its own members. And Norway and Iceland have simply opted out of the moratorium and conduct legal commercial whaling operations.

Other nations, meanwhile, exploit the exceptions granted under the treaty. Let us consider each of these in turn. The purpose of the scientific exception was to understand whale biology. Just as medical students gain knowledge by dissection, so too it was thought that knowledge of the whale required whale cadavers. But whereas human beings are not murdered for the purposes of medical science, there being a sufficient supply of cadavers by natural death, it was reasoned that whale cadavers were typically lost in the deep, and that the occasional beached whale might not be representative of the species. So killing for research, some nations argued, is required.

Even were such claims of scientific purpose always made in good faith, our world has changed. New technology has made it possible to study whales up close in the deep itself without killing them, as Hal Whitehead and Luke Rendell routinely do, using deep-sea descent equipment and especially deep-sea photography. The new equipment doesn't explore the insides, but just as a good doctor can combine what we already know about human anatomy with a clinical examination of a patient to get an accurate result, so too can the scientist studying whales. The whole idea that we must kill in order to know has never been accepted for any other animal species; by now it is possible to make progress with other methods.

Appeals to scientific purpose, especially those mounted by Japan, have failed to convince. In March 2014, the International Court of Justice (ICJ) ruled that Japan's program of scientific whaling in the Antarctic, known as JARPA II, was not justifiable under international law, because it did not have merit as a scientific program. The case was brought by Australia, with New Zealand intervening.[62] The court pointed to the lack of scientific findings and peer-reviewed studies from the program. Many environmental organizations saw the entire practice as commercial whaling in disguise, and it is difficult not to agree.

Japan, however, did not give up: they announced that they would "redesign" the program, and their right to do so has been defended by the Institute of Cetacean Research (ICR), a Japanese NGO that claims to be an independent research organization, although it sells the "by-products" of whale dissection commercially as food. (Significantly, in the Sea Shepherd case, to be described shortly, the ICR is described by the Ninth Circuit, not contentiously but straightforwardly, as "Japanese researchers who perform lethal whaling in the Southern Ocean.")

The court's decision was cautious. It did not address claims that whales have a right to life, and it defined the purpose of the ICRW as that of balancing conservation with sustainable exploitation. Nor did it object to the whole idea of giving special permits for scientific research; it only said that Japan's program did not qualify. After 2014, Japan reduced the number of whales caught in the Southern Ocean, but continued the practice. In 2015, Japan submitted a new plan for "scientific" whaling, and prevented a repeat lawsuit by modifying its optional declaration on the jurisdiction of the ICJ, removing from that court's jurisdiction all disputes relating to living marine animals.

The issue is now moot, because Japan, frustrated by the increasing opposition it faced in the increasingly conservationist IWC, left the commission in December 2018, and resumed commercial whaling in 2019, although not in the Antarctic. In 2020, the ICR states that its research now uses only nonlethal methods.[63] Apparently, then, it is conceding that its genuine scientific work does not require whale death. Once commercial whaling is out in the open, the veil is no longer needed.

What can and should be done? Little is to be hoped for at present from the IWC, a weak and increasingly conflict-ridden body that powerful nations feel free to ignore. Resistance by extreme environmental action groups has also failed. Especially notorious has been the activity of the Sea Shepherd Conservation Society, a group who believe that whales have an inherent right to life. In order to fight for the cause of whales, it has repeatedly interfered with Japanese whaling activities in the Antarctic. Sea Shepherd does this in a very aggressive manner, which many environmental groups deplore—rightly, in my view. For example, it throws bottles filled with butyric acid onto whaling vessels and attempts to obstruct the whalers' vision. The group and its founder, Paul Watson, argue that this is the only effective way to disrupt the whaling, because mere protest has not been effective, nor has international law. But the tactic has backfired legally. The ICR sued Sea Shepherd under the Alien Tort Statute (a law originally designed to make it possible to sue sea pirates in US courts), asking for an injunction against the group, claiming its actions constitute piracy. A federal district court ruled in favor of Sea Shepherd, saying the ICR had not shown that the group's actions constitute piracy, though it expressed disapproval of Sea Shepherd's tactics. On appeal, the Ninth Circuit reversed,[64] with the lead opinion written by Judge Alex Kozinski, shortly before his sudden retirement and public disgrace.[65] Sea Shepherd's leader, Paul Watson, stopped the aggressive activities in 2017, citing new anti-terrorism laws passed by Japan.

In short, "scientific" whaling has not been halted by either legal or extra-legal means, and at this point the pretense of science is no longer needed, since nations have returned to open commercial whaling. The IWC is revealed as hopelessly impotent—a problem familiar from the history of international human rights law.

What about the other exception made in the convention, aboriginal subsistence whaling (known as ASW)? In chapter 8, I questioned the claims made by the Makah and the Inuit that whaling is necessary for cultural survival. I can now add that not all indigenous peoples agree with these arguments. The Maori have represented to the IWC their great respect for whales and their desire to distance themselves from lethal practices.[66]

As to the claim that whale meat is necessary to meet nutritional needs, this too does not stand up to scrutiny. The IWC refers to "trade in items that are by-products of subsistence catches."[67] Obviously enough, trade in whale products means that there is a surplus going beyond immediate nutritional needs. And this surplus standardly includes meat: whale meat ends up in tourist restaurants in Greenland. To the objection that if whale meat is sold in restaurants it cannot be essential for the survival of the Inuit people, Greenland responded: "With respect to restaurants it [Greenland] noted that it did not control who could eat particular products within Greenland and saw no problem with tourists eating whale meat in restaurants. . . . The nutritional value of local foods is better and more environmentally sound than flying in imported foods from the west along with the associated health problems this can bring."[68] But a preference for local foods on health grounds (quite apart from the fact that there are serious health issues connected to the consumption of whale meat) is completely different from a need for food for survival. Where acute hunger is a problem, that problem should be addressed by sound public policy across the board. This, in fact, Denmark has done: Greenland's Inuit people (almost 90 percent of Greenland's inhabitants), are in fact quite wealthy, thanks in large part to ample subsidies from Denmark.

The IWC shows its weakness by deferring to such empty nonarguments. Despite the grimness of the current situation, however, I believe that there is a better future for marine mammals ahead. So many international and national groups are taking up their cause. So much state-level and nation-level progress has been made. So many fine films, such as *Blackfish* and *Sonic Sea*, have alerted people to the plight of whales and dolphins. So many excellent books are being written about the beauty of whales and their current plight.[69] So many whale watchers have brought their own sense of wonder into courtrooms and legislatures. So many skilled lawyers and law students, inspired by the tasks that need to be accomplished, are entering this field of practice. Wonder, compassion, and outrage are rising all around us. Much more remains to be done. International law is weak. For the present we must approach these issues through domestic laws (as is also true of human rights), and through an international protest movement. But I have confidence that humanity is getting its act together.

LAW IS ALL OF US

As this chapter has shown, the world's legal systems are in a primitive condition, where the lives of animals are concerned. Entitlements, I've said, entail laws to make them real: if not actual laws, the possibility of such laws in the future. A lot of progress has been made at the local and state, and even at the national, level in various nations—though always unevenly in the US, failing to protect the animals raised in the meat industry. For all animals, furthermore, the problem of standing impedes real progress, since laws in the US have not yet treated animals as full subjects of justice, capable of standing in a court of law (with a suitable surrogate) in their own right. Standing could be given them by a vote of Congress, and yet we all know how far in the future that vote is likely to be. Meanwhile, in the international realm, the cause of animals appears very uncertain, since even those bodies that exist are wracked with conflict and impotent to rein in defectors.

What can be done? In all these cases, the remedy really requires the evolving consciousness of humanity to generate solutions. That this can happen, we can see by contemplating the progress of women. Women all over the world were once treated, under law, as objects or property for men's use and control. A married woman had no independent legal agency: she could not sue, or manage her own finances. Above all, women had no say in the future of law, because they could not vote. In 1893, New Zealand became the first nation to grant suffrage to women.[70] In 2015, Saudi Arabia became the last. As the result of a courageous effort by many women and men, women have gradually improved laws on sexual assault and sexual harassment, won entry to universities, parliaments, and the world of employment. The story is terribly unfinished, but after millennia of stagnation there has been a burst of energy all over the world.

The same thing can happen, and, I believe, is happening, with the rights of animals. Indeed, it has begun to happen. The future that Jeremy Bentham confidently predicted has taken too long to arrive. But it is on its way, attainable if we will make it so. The obstacles are the same as in the case of women: greed, and pride. By pride, I mean the belief of the dominant group that it is above it all, and that the subordinated group isn't fully real.[71] Dante depicts the proud as bent over like hoops, so that they can only see themselves and can't look out at the world, or the faces of others. For millennia, in just that way, much of humanity has been looking only at humanity, and never turning outward to look, really look, at the other sentient beings with whom we share this small and fragile planet. By now things have changed, though partially and unevenly. There is more looking, more wonder, and, in that connection, more compassion and outrage at what we have done and are doing.

The future is us. Will we really see? Will we extend a hand of friendship to our fellow creatures? And will we do the difficult work of changing the ways we live, and changing our laws and institutions? I don't know. It is in all our hands. The work takes many types of people: scientists who work with dedication and commitment to describe the abilities of animals and their complex forms of life; activists who selflessly give their lives for the sake of species whose languages most people don't try to understand (even calling them "dumb beasts"); legislators and judges who make good, and often unpopular, decisions; lawyers who bring cases against abusers, one case at a time; teachers and parents who raise children who look at the world with undiminished wonder. Even the market has its place in the effort: if synthetic meat did not potentially make money, people would not work so hard to create and market it.

I think the philosopher too has a place in this work. That's why I have written this book.

CONCLUSION

"Animals are in trouble all over the world. Our world is dominated by humans everywhere: on land, in the seas, and in the air. No non-human animal escapes human domination. Much of the time, that domination inflicts wrongful injury on animals: whether through the barbarous cruelties of the factory meat industry, through poaching and game hunting, through habitat destruction, through pollution of the air and the seas, or through neglect of the companion animals that people purport to love."

That's where I began this book, and that is where we are today. This book has not by itself changed the terrible situation of animals, for which we all bear a collective responsibility. But I hope that the intervening chapters have helped to awaken or strengthen the three emotions I discussed in my first chapter: wonder at the complexity and diversity of animal lives, compassion for what all too often befalls those lives in our human-dominated world, and a productive future-directed outrage ("Transition-Anger," to use my terminology) aimed at rectifying the situation.

However, this book is not just about arousing those emotions and urging productive action. It is also a book of philosophical theory, aimed

311

at describing a view that can direct these efforts and at showing that it is better than other theories now in use. The struggle to improve the lot of animals and to rectify abuses needs many things: courageous activism; committed and resourceful legal work; organizations dedicated to animal lives and their committed participants; donations to those organizations; creative and rigorous scientific research; efforts to communicate the beauty, the amazing capacities, and the current plights of animals to a mass audience through journalism, film, and visual art. All readers of this book can find their own roles in the effort, depending on their situations and capacities. Even within philosophy, many different projects make valuable contributions: insights into the nature of mind, into perception and sentience, into the structure of emotions, these and other projects make distinctive contributions to understanding animal lives.

But the struggle also needs an overarching philosophical-political theory. Theories direct the efforts that people make, marking some things as salient and neglecting others, urging law to direct its efforts in this way rather than that. And all too often defective theories direct things badly, ignoring issues of great importance and focusing entirely on a narrow or distorted range of concerns. Theory gives lawyers and politicians a lens through which to see the world, and often encourages them to ignore important things that people see quite well in their daily lives. Once that has happened, the need for theory becomes much greater than before, because now we need not just one more theory, but a counter-theory, one that by cogent arguments will show the defects in bad theories and then propose a replacement—often thereby rescuing people's daily perceptions from neglect and impotence.

The theories that have guided humanity so far in addressing animal lives have each been promising in some ways, but crude or distorting in others. All of my three defective theories can ultimately revise their claims so as to accept political principles based on the Capabilities Approach, or so I think. Korsgaard's Kantian view can emphasize her deep insight that animals are ends in themselves and deemphasize claims about human moral specialness that are a distraction to a principled political consensus.

Utilitarians can work with the subtle insights of Mill's theory, rather than Bentham's more reductive view. Even the anthropocentric "So Like Us" approach can become part of the "overlapping consensus" if it downplays similarity to humans as a source of legal and political principles and embraces wonder and respect for difference. There is reason to think that such a theory could go in that direction, given that the view is originally inspired by Christian views of all nature as God's creation, and of the human being as a responsible steward rather than an arrogant dominator. And recently, the most sensitive philosophical exponent of a "So Like Us" approach, Thomas White, when asked to write an essay on ethics for a group of expert dolphin scientists, recommended to them as the best guiding theory—not his former anthropocentric theory, but, instead, the Capabilities Approach![1]

The Capabilities Approach can respond better than these other theories to the facts we now know about animal lives: about the amazing diversity of animal abilities and activities, about their capacities for valuing, for forming social networks, about their capacities for cultural learning, about friendship and love. If Jeremy Bentham came face-to-face with Hal the whale, or Lupa the dog, or Empress of Blandings (Bentham was very fond of a free-ranging pig, who used to accompany him on walks),[2] he, being a person of wide-ranging sensitivity and intelligence, would very likely see all these aspects of both creatures' lives. But there is no room in his official theory for much of what a concerned friend of animals can see. The CA is built around the idea that we must look and see what each animal life contains and values, and must protect, non-reductively, the most important elements in that whole diverse set of strivings. I've shown how the CA directs our practical thought well when we ask whether zoos are acceptable, when we frame laws and policies about both companion and wild animals, when we confront the weaknesses of international law in protecting marine mammals from harassment, when we try to articulate what is horrible about the factory farm industry, and when we try to specify the harm of puppy mills. These are but examples, and there are countless other issues where a species-specific approach, oriented to forms of life, can help us imagine a more just world.

Politicians and academics often speak of "global justice" as a goal we ought to pursue. But all too often their efforts and projects are not truly global. By that term they typically mean justice for human beings, no matter where they live. That of course is already a noble goal toward which we ought to aspire. But in the process we must not forget that a justice that is truly global is a justice that takes up the burden of protecting the rights of all sentient creatures, no matter where *they* live, on land, in the sea, or in the air. And it must really be *justice*—concerned, as I have said, with removing barriers to sentient creatures who strive to attain their ends.

Ours is a time of a great awakening: to our kinship with a world of remarkable intelligent creatures, and to real accountability for our treatment of them. The Capabilities Approach is the best theoretical ally of all concerned humans working toward that awakening and that accountability. We have a collective responsibility to vindicate the rights of animals, and finally, we are beginning to face up to that responsibility. But we need an adequate theory to direct us. I think we now have one, though no doubt it has many flaws and will be improved by future work.

The task seems daunting. There are so many bad things going on, so much suffering, so much frustration of animal striving toward free movement, health, and social life. And the frustration and suffering make so much money for many people. Animals are so terribly weak in this world, and the allies of animals often seem to be terribly weak as well—against the power of the meat industry, the guile of poachers, the unending stream of plastic trash, the noise pollution from the undersea "air bombs" of the oil industry. However, I believe that our time is a time of great hope for the future of animals.

Let's think for a moment about hope.[3] Having hope does not depend on the probabilities. If your relative is ill, you can hope even if the prospects look pretty bad; and you can have fear, hope's opposite, even if the prospects look good. The two emotions are different angles of vision, different ways of seeing an uncertain future that we do not control. And the two emotions are different in the efforts they inspire. Fear immobilizes people and often turns them weak-willed. Hope buoys people up and gives them wings. It's like seeing a glass as half full rather than half empty; but the angle of vision makes a huge practical difference. For this reason Immanuel Kant said that we all have a duty to cultivate hope in ourselves, to sustain us in our practical efforts. I think Kant is right. We must all be people of hope, if we think that our efforts are important and, indeed, are our collective responsibility.

We can cultivate hope simply by bootstrapping it out of our wonder and our love. But we also have specific reasons to have hope at this particular time. So many people know so much more about animals these days, see them (up close or on film), care about them accurately, rather than only through narcissistic fantasy. This revolution in awareness has already led to concrete political developments.

- Take the recent reinstatement of a raft of protections for birds under the Migratory Bird Treaty Act of 1918 that were removed during the previous administration.[4] Once again, the accidental killing of birds in the course of industrial activity is a violation of the Act.
- Take the sweeping Animal Welfare (Sentience) Bill recently introduced in Britain's House of Lords, which uses recent scientific work on animal sentience and emotion, and would require the government to consider how all its policies—not just those dealing directly with animals—affect the welfare of sentient animals.[5] This bill will eventually be implemented by a set of more specific laws, and it appears to have widespread support.
- Take the remarkable decision of the US District Court for the Southern District of Ohio, on October 20, 2021, that hippos are legal persons, under a US law that permits "interested persons" to request permission to take depositions for use in a foreign legal proceeding— the first time any US court has recognized animals as legal persons. The hippos, brought to Colombia by Pablo Escobar, have become very numerous, leading the government to plan to kill a lot of them. Because Colombian law allows legal standing for animals, the hippos are the plaintiffs in a Colombian lawsuit to stop the killing, and US

experts seek to be deposed in the case. So, by a very odd route, without changing our country's more restrictive ideas of standing, a US court has created a momentous conclusion.[6] (It is not a precedent, because it is based on Colombian law's decision to grant the hippos legal standing, but it is highly suggestive; and the more inclusive idea of standing in Colombian law is also a reason for optimism.)[7]

- Take the passage of the Bird Safe Buildings Act by the Illinois state legislature in July 2021. This law, signed by Governor Pritzker, will require the use of bird-friendly construction techniques for all new construction or renovation of Illinois state-owned buildings. At least 90 percent of the exposed façade material on new state buildings will need to be made of glass that helps stop bird collisions. It will also require that, when possible, outside building lighting is appropriately shielded to protect wildlife.[8] Private construction, for example in our own university, is also beginning to follow the Act's guidelines.

These and so many other concrete political developments show that change is possible, and they also show that change depends on all of us: such changes are political and fragile, depending on the involvement of concerned citizens in the political process, which is one way that all of us can, and should, exercise our collective responsibility.

But for this same reason, given the instability of our political process, they may seem terribly fragile and not precisely reasons for hope. Hope, I've said, does not need reasons. However, if we are looking for courage in our hoping, it does help to fix our minds on instances of progress rather than regress—although terrible news, such as the recent oil spill off the coast of California, which has already killed countless marine creatures,[9] can also inspire outrage and political action. For a pretty solid example of a good change, very unlikely to be reversed, think, then, about the remarkable, almost incredible, consumer success of plant-based meat products—soon to be followed by the further option of lab-grown meat that is "actual meat" without killing any animals, marketed by the US company Eat Just, and now approved for sale in Singapore, and shortly, no doubt, elsewhere.[10] Change is held back by the money people make by exploiting animals. But now money can be made by enterprises that do great good. These developments show that friends of animals can increasingly triumph without painful sacrifice and struggle, as people seek a healthier diet and as more and more people, given the choice, make a choice for justice.

Every reader can come up with similar examples of things that can be done and are being done, many of them mentioned in this book. Thinking of these things makes hope easier, and renews our spirits as we strive. For, after all, we are all animals in our own specific way, striving for goals we value, and often being thwarted. Not always, however, and not when we can band together sufficiently in pursuit of shared goals.

I hope that the readers of this book will be moved, in their own many different ways, to make a choice for justice and become lovers of animal life: with wonder, with compassion, with outrage—and with hope.

Acknowledgments

This book has developed over a number of years, so I have many people to thank. First and most, I am so deeply grateful to my late daughter, Rachel Nussbaum Wichert (1972–2019), a lawyer who worked as a Government Affairs Attorney for Friends of Animals, at their Wildlife Division in Denver, focusing particularly on marine mammals. I discuss her contributions in the introduction, and one can see them everywhere here. Through Rachel I got to know the staff at Friends of Animals and learned so much from them and from their inspiring legal work. So I owe them much as well—especially Michael Harris, Director of the Wildlife Division, and Priscilla Feral, the Director of the overall organization. Rachel's husband Gerd continues her love of orcas and other whales, and I am grateful to him for his warm support for this project.

During the time I have been preparing this book, I've been lucky to have superbly gifted and attentive research assistants, who all contributed greatly to this book, even more than is usual for a book of mine, since this one required so much research and learning. In chronological order: Matthew Guillod, Jared Mayer, Tony Leyh, Claudia Hogg-Blake, and Cameron Steckbeck. In the last stages of the work, I presented the draft in a seminar with twelve marvelous students, some from law and some from philosophy, and their comments were so valuable that I must mention them all by name: Franchesca Alamo, Michael Buchanan, Spencer Caro,

Ben Conroy, Kristen De Man, Benjamin Elmore, Micah Gibson, Jack Johanning, Psi Simon, Cameron Steckbeck, Nico Thompson-Lleras, Andres Vodanovic.

As always, the tough criticisms of my colleagues at the University of Chicago Law School at Work-In-Progress Workshops and in written comments on chapters have contributed immensely to the book, and I am especially grateful to: Lee Fennell, Brian Leiter, Saul Levmore, and Richard McAdams. I presented early drafts at workshops at the NYU Law School and Yale Law School, and a related lecture at the Harvard Political Science Graduate Student conference, and learned a lot each time. Particular thanks are due to Sam Scheffler, Jeremy Waldron, Thomas Nagel, Priya Menon, and Doug Kysar.

My editor Stuart Roberts at Simon & Schuster has been amazing, sending me the most helpful comments throughout.

Bibliography

Ackerman, Jennifer. 2016. *The Genius of Birds*. New York: Penguin Books.
———. 2020. *The Bird Way: A New Look at How Birds Talk, Work, Play, Parent, and Think*. New York: Penguin Press.
Aguirre, Jessica Camille. 2019. "Australia Is Deadly Serious About Killing Millions of Cats." *New York Times*, April 25.
Akhtar, Aysha. 2015. "The Flaws and Human Harms of Animal Experimentation." *Cambridge Quarterly of Healthcare Ethics* 24, no. 4: 407–19.
Alter, Robert. 2004. *The Five Books of Moses: A Translation with Commentary*. New York: W. W. Norton.
American Anti-Vivisection Society v. United States Department of Agriculture, 946 F.3d 615 (D.C. Cir. 2020).
Amos, Jonathan. 2015. "Knut Polar Bear Death Riddle Solved." BBC News, August 27.
Angier, Natalie. 2021. "What Has Four Legs, a Trunk and a Behavioral Database?" *New York Times*, June 4.
Animal Legal Defense Fund. 2021. "Animals Recognized as Legal Persons for the First Time in U.S. Court." October 20. https://aldf.org/article/animals-recognized-as-legal-persons-for-the-first-time-in-u-s-court/.
Animal Legal Defense Fund v. Espy, 23 F.3d 496 (D.C. Cir. 1994).
Animal Legal Defense Fund v. Glickman, 154 F.3d 426 (D.C. Cir. 1998).
Animal Welfare Act (AWA), 7 U.S.C. § 2131 et seq (1966).
Associated Press. 2020. "Iowa AG: Groups Involved in Puppy-Laundering Ring to Disband." March 25. https://apnews.com/article/8f5dada41cb7a4afc25403d4c93365f5.
Balcombe, Jonathan. 2016. *What a Fish Knows: The Inner Lives of Our Underwater Cousins*. New York: Scientific American/Farrar, Straus and Giroux.
Batson, C. Daniel. 2011. *Altruism in Humans*. New York: Oxford University Press.
Beam, Christopher. 2009. "Get This Rat a Lawyer!" *Slate*, September 14.
Beauchamp, Tom L., and David DeGrazia. 2020. *Principles of Animal Research Ethics*. New York: Oxford University Press.

Bekoff, Marc. 2008. *The Emotional Lives of Animals: A Leading Scientist Explores Animal Joy, Sorrow, and Empathy—and Why They Matter.* San Francisco: New World Library.

Bendik-Keymer, Jeremy. 2017. "The Reasonableness of Wonder." *Journal of Human Development and Capabilities* 18, no. 3: 337–55.

———. 2021a. "Beneficial Relations Between Species and the Moral Responsibility of Wondering." *Environmental Politics* 30. https://doi.org/10.1080/09644016.2020.1868818.

———. 2021b. "The Other Species Capability and the Power of Wonder." *Journal of Human Development and Capabilities* 22, no. 1: 154–79. https://doi.org/10.1080/19452829.2020.1869191.

Benhabib, Seyla. 1995. "Cultural Complexity, Moral Independence, and the Global Dialogical Community." In *Women, Culture and Development*, edited by Martha C. Nussbaum and Jonathan Glover. Oxford, UK: Oxford University Press.

Bentham, Jeremy. (1780) 1948. *An Introduction to the Principles of Morals and Legislation.* Reprint, New York: Hafner.

———. 2013. *Not Paul, but Jesus.* Project Gutenberg. https://www.gutenberg.org/ebooks/42984.

Berger, Karen. 2020. "Snorkeling and Diving with Dolphins in Eilat, Israel." *BucketTripper.* February 25. https://www.buckettripper.com/snorkeling-and-diving-with-dolphins-in-eilat-israel/.

Bever, Lindsey. 2019. "A Trail Runner Survived a Life-or-Death 'Wrestling Match' with a Mountain Lion. Here's His Story." *Washington Post*, February 15.

BirdLife International. 2017. "10 Amazing Birds That Have Gone Extinct." January 24. https://www.birdlife.org/news/2017/01/24/10-amazing-birds-have-gone-extinct/.

Botkin, Daniel B. 1996. "Adjusting Law to Nature's Discordant Harmonies." *Duke Environmental Law & Policy Forum* 7: 25–38.

Bradshaw, Karen. 2020. *Wildlife as Property Owners: A New Conception of Animal Rights.* Chicago: University of Chicago Press.

Braithwaite, Victoria. 2010. *Do Fish Feel Pain?* New York: Oxford University Press.

Brink, David O. 2013. *Mill's Progressive Principles.* Oxford, UK: Clarendon Press.

Brulliard, Karin. 2018. "A Judge Just Raised Deep Questions About Chimpanzees' Legal Rights." *Washington Post*, May 9.

Brulliard, Karin, and William Wan. 2019. "Caged Raccoons Drooled in 100-Degree Heat. But Federal Enforcement Has Faded." *Washington Post*, August 22.

Burgess-Jackson, Keith. 1998. "Doing Right by Our Animal Companions." *The Journal of Ethics* 2: 159–85.

Burkert, Walter. 1966. "Greek Tragedy and Sacrificial Ritual." *Greek, Roman and Byzantine Studies* 7: 87–121.

Campos Boralevi, Lea. 1984. *Bentham and the Oppressed.* Berlin: Walter de Gruyter.

Carrington, Damian. 2020. "No-Kill, Lab-Grown Meat to Go on Sale for First Time." *Guardian*, December 1.

Cetacean Community v. Bush, 386 F.3d. 1169 (9th Cir. 2004).

Chicago Zoological Society. 2021. "Media Statement: Update on Amur Tiger's Second Surgery at Brookfield Zoo." February 1. https://www.czs.org/Chicago-Zoo logical-Society/About/Press-room/2021-Press-Releases/Update-on-Amur-Tiger's -Second-Surgery-at-Brookfield.

Colb, Sherry F. 2013. *Mind If I Order the Cheeseburger?: And Other Questions People Ask Vegans*. New York: Lantern Books.

Cole, David. 2014. "Our Nudge in Chief." *The Atlantic*, May.

Comay del Junco, Elena. 2020. "Aristotle's Cosmological Ethics." PhD diss. Chicago: University of Chicago.

Community of Hippopotamuses Living in the Magdalena River v. Ministerio de Ambiente y Desarrollo Sostenible, 1:21MC00023 (S.D. Ohio 2021).

Connor, Michael. 2021. "Progress, Change and Opportunity: Managing Wild Horses on the Public Lands." The Hill, March 12.

Cowperthwaite, Gabriela, dir. 2013. *Blackfish*. CNN Films.

Crawley, William. 2006. "Peter Singer Defends Animal Experimentation." BBC, November 26.

Damasio, Antonio. 1994. *Descartes' Error: Emotion, Reason and the Human Brain*. New York: G. P. Putnam's Sons.

D'Amato, Anthony, and Sudhir K. Chopra. 1991. "Whales: Their Emerging Right to Life." *The American Journal of International Law* 85, no. 1: 21–62.

Dawkins, Marian Stamp. 2012. *Why Animals Matter: Animal Consciousness, Animal Welfare, and Human Well-Being*. New York: Oxford University Press.

de Lazari-Radek, Katarzyna and Peter Singer. 2014. *The Point of View of the Universe: Sidgwick and Contemporary Ethics*. New York: Oxford University Press.

Delon, Nicolas. 2021. "Animal Capabilities and Freedom in the City." *Journal of Human Development and Capabilities* 22, no. 1: 131–53. https://doi.org/10.1080 /19452829.2020.1869190.

Devlin, Patrick. 1959. *The Enforcement of Morals*. Oxford, UK: Oxford University Press.

de Waal, Frans. 1989. *Peacemaking Among Primates*. Cambridge, MA: Harvard University Press.

———. 1996. *Good Natured: The Origins of Right and Wrong in Humans and Other Animals*. Cambridge, MA: Harvard University Press.

———. 2006. *Primates and Philosophers: How Morality Evolved*. Princeton, NJ: Princeton University Press.

———. 2019. *Mama's Last Hug: Animal Emotions and What They Tell Us About Ourselves*. New York: W. W. Norton.

Dickens, Charles. (1854) 2021. *Hard Times*. Project Gutenberg. https://www.guten berg.org/ebooks/786.

Donaldson, Sue, and Will Kymlicka. 2011. *Zoopolis: A Political Theory of Animal Rights*. Oxford, UK: Oxford University Press.

Dorsey, Kurkpatrick. 2014. *Whales and Nations: Environmental Diplomacy on the High Seas*. Seattle: University of Washington Press.

Dworkin, Gerald. 1988. *The Theory and Practice of Autonomy*. Cambridge, UK: Cambridge University Press.

Elk Grove Unified School District v. Newdow, 542 U.S.1 (2004).

Elster, Jon. 1983. *Sour Grapes: Studies in the Subversion of Rationality*. Cambridge, UK: Cambridge University Press.

Emery, Nathan. 2016. *Bird Brain: An Exploration of Avian Intelligence*. Princeton, NJ: Princeton University Press.

Endangered Species Act (ESA), 16 U.S.C. § 1531 et seq (1973).

European Parliament and Council, Regulation No. 2008/20/EC, L47/5 (2018).

Favre, David. 2000. "Equitable Self-Ownership for Animals." *Duke Law Journal* 50: 473–502.

———. 2010. "Living Property: A New Status for Animals Within the Legal System." *Marquette Law Review* 93: 1021–70.

Feingold, Lindsey. 2019. "Big Cities, Bright Lights and up to 1 Billion Bird Collisions." NPR, April 7.

Fischer, John Martin. 1993. *The Metaphysics of Death*. Palo Alto, CA: Stanford University Press.

———. 2019. *Death, Immortality, and Meaning in Life*. New York: Oxford University Press.

Fitzmaurice, Malgosia. 2015. *Whaling and International Law*. Cambridge, UK: Cambridge University Press.

———. 2017. "International Convention for the Regulation of Whaling." United Nations Audiovisual Library of International Law. https://legal.un.org/avl/pdf/ha/icrw/icrw_e.pdf.

Francione, Gary L. 2008. *Animals as Persons: Essays on the Abolition of Animal Exploitation*. New York: Columbia University Press.

Francione, Gary L., and Anna Charlton. 2015. *Animal Rights: The Abolitionist Approach*. New York: Exempla Press.

Friedman, Lisa. 2021. "Trump Administration, in Parting Gift to Industry, Reverses Bird Protections," *New York Times*, January 5.

Friedman, Lisa, and Catrin Einhorn. 2021. "Biden Administration Restores Bird Protections, Repealing Trump Rule." *New York Times*, September 29.

Fujise, Dr. Yoshihiro. 2020. "Foreword." In *Technical Reports of the Institute of Cetacean Research (TERPEP-ICR)*, no. 4, December. Tokyo: Institute of Cetacean Research (ICR).

Furley, David. 1986. "Nothing to Us?" In *The Norms of Nature*, edited by Malcom Schofield and Gisela Striker. Cambridge, UK: Cambridge University Press.

Giggs, Rebecca. 2020. *Fathoms: The World in the Whale*. New York: Simon & Schuster.

Gillespie, Alexander. 2005. *Whaling Diplomacy: Defining Issues in International Environmental Law*. Northampton, MA: Edward Elgar.

Godfrey-Smith, Peter. 2016. *Other Minds: The Octopus, the Sea, and the Deep Origins of Consciousness*. New York: Farrar, Straus and Giroux.

Gordon, Yvonne. 2020. "A Fun-Loving Dolphin Disappears into the Deep, and Ireland Fears the Worst." *Washington Post*, October 23.

Gowdy, Barbara. 1999. *The White Bone*. New York: HarperCollins.

Hare, Richard M. 1999. "Why I Am Only a Demi-Vegetarian." In *Singer and His Critics*, edited by Dale Jamieson. Hoboken, NJ: Wiley-Blackwell.

Harris, Michael Ray. 2021. "What Happy Deserves: Elephants Have Rights Too, at Least They Should." New York *Daily News*, August 30.

Harvey, Fiona. 2021. "Animals to Be Formally Recognised as Sentient Beings in UK Law." *Guardian*, May 12.

Hasan, Zoya, Aziz Z. Huq, Martha C. Nussbaum, and Vidhu Verma, eds. 2018. *The Empire of Disgust: Prejudice, Discrimination, and Policy in India and the U.S.* New York: Oxford University Press.

Hegedus, Chris, and D. A. Pennebaker, dirs. 2016. *Unlocking the Cage*. Pennebaker Hegedus Films and HBO Documentary Films.

Hinerfeld, Daniel, and Michelle Dougherty, dirs. 2016. *Sonic Sea*. Imaginary Forces.

Holland, Breena, and Amy Linch. 2017. "Cultural Killing and Human-Animal Capability Conflict." *Journal of Human Development and Capabilities* 18, no. 3 (June): 322–36.

Hollingsworth v. Perry, 570 U.S. 693 (2013).

Holman, Gregory J. 2020. "Missouri Tops 'Horrible Hundred' Puppy Mill Report Again, but Has More Enforcement Than Some States." *Springfield News-Leader*, May 11.

Horwitz, Joshua. 2015. *War of the Whales: A True Story*. Reprint edition. New York: Simon & Schuster.

Humane Society of the United States v. Babbitt, 46 F.3d 93 (D.C. Cir. 1995).

Institute of Cetacean Research v. Sea Shepherd Conservation Society, 725 F.3d 940 (9th Cir. 2013).

James, Henry. (1897) 2021. *What Maisie Knew*. Project Gutenberg. https://www.gutenberg.org/ebooks/7118.

Japan Whaling Association v. American Cetacean Society, 478 U.S. 221 (1986).

Kahan, Dan M., and Tracey L. Meares. 2014. "When Rights Are Wrong." *Boston Review*, August 5.

Kant, Immanuel. (1788) 1955. *Critique of Practical Reason*. Translated by Mary Gregor. 2nd ed. Cambridge, UK: Cambridge University Press.

———. (1798) 1974. *Anthropology from a Pragmatic Point of View*. Translated by Mary Gregor. The Hague: Martinus Nijhoff.

———. (1785) 2012. *Groundwork of the Metaphysics of Morals*. Translated by Mary Gregor and Jens Timmermann. 2nd ed. Cambridge, UK: Cambridge University Press.

Karpinski, Stanislaw, et al. 1999. "Systemic Signaling and Acclimation in Response to Excess Excitation Energy in Arabidopsis." *Science* 284, no. 5414 (April 23): 654–57.

Katz, Jon. 2004. *The New Work of Dogs: Tending to Life, Love, and Family*. New York: Random House.

Kitcher, Philip. 2015. "Experimental Animals." *Philosophy & Public Affairs* 43, no. 4 (Fall): 287–311.

Kittay, Eva. 1999. *Love's Labor: Essays on Women, Equality, and Dependency*. New York: Routledge.

Korsgaard, Christine. 1981. "The Standpoint of Practical Reason," PhD diss. Cambridge, MA: Harvard University.

———. 1996a. *Creating the Kingdom of Ends*. New York: Cambridge University Press.

———. 1996b. *The Sources of Normativity*. Cambridge, UK: Cambridge University Press.

———. 2004. "Fellow Creatures: Kantian Ethics and Our Duties to Animals." In *Tanner Lectures on Human Values*, vols. 25/26, edited by Grethe B Peterson. Salt Lake City: University of Utah Press.

———. 2006. "Morality and the Distinctiveness of Human Action." In de Waal, *Primates and Philosophers: How Morality Evolved*, edited by Stephen Macedo and Josiah Ober. Princeton, NJ: Princeton University Press.

———. 2013. "Kantian Ethics, Animals, and the Law." *Oxford Journal of Legal Studies* 33, no. 4 (Winter): 629–48.

———. 2018a. "The Claims of Animals and the Needs of Strangers: Two Cases of Imperfect Right." *Journal of Practical Ethics* 6, no. 1 (July): 19–51.

———. 2018b. *Fellow Creatures: Our Obligations to the Other Animals*. New York: Oxford University Press.

Kraut, Richard H. 2010. "What Is Intrinsic Goodness?" *Classical Philology* 105, no. 4 (October 1): 450–62.

Lazarus, Richard. 1991. *Emotion and Adaptation*. New York: Oxford University Press.

Lear, Jonathan. 2008. *Radical Hope: Ethics in the Face of Cultural Devastation*. Cambridge, MA: Harvard University Press.

Lee, Ascha. 2021. "UChicago Animal Rights Philosopher Fights for Bronx Zoo Elephant's Freedom." WBBM, August 30.

Lee, Jadran. 2003. "Bentham on Animals," PhD diss. Chicago: University of Chicago.

Leonard, Pat. 2020. "Study: Air Pollution Laws Aimed at Human Health Also Help Birds." *Cornell Chronicle*, November 24.

Levenson, Eric. 2021. "What We Know So Far About the California Oil Spill." CNN, October 5.

Linch, Amy. 2021. "Friendship in Captivity? Plato's Lysis as a Guide to Interspecies Justice." *Journal of Human Development and Capabilities* 22, no. 1: 108–30. https://doi.org/10.1080/19452829.2020.1865289.

"List of Migratory Birds." 50 C.F.R. 10.13 (2000). https://www.govinfo.gov/app/details/CFR-2000-title50-vol1/CFR-2000-title50-vol1-sec10-13.

Lujan v. Defenders of Wildlife, 504 U.S. 555 (1992).

Lupo, Lisa. 2019. "Rodent Fertility Control: What It Is and Why It's Important." Pest Control Technology, April 12.

Maestripieri, Dario, and Jill M. Mateo, eds. 2009. *Maternal Effects in Mammals*. Chicago: University of Chicago Press.

Marine Mammal Protection Act (MMPA), 16 U.S.C. § 1361 et seq (1972).

Maritain, Jacques. 1951. *Man and the State*. Chicago: University of Chicago Press.

Mayer, Jared B. 2020. "Memorandum to Martha C. Nussbaum." November 17.

McMahan, Jeff. 2002. *The Ethics of Killing: Problems at the Margins of Life*. New York: Oxford University Press.

———. 2010. "The Meat Eaters." *New York Times*. September 19.

Migratory Bird Treaty Act (MBTA), 16 U.S.C. § 703 et seq (1918).

Mill, John Stuart. 1963. *The Collected Works of John Stuart Mill*, edited by J. M. Robson. Toronto: University of Toronto Press.

Moss, Cynthia. 1988. *Elephant Memories: Thirteen Years in the Life of an Elephant Family*. Chicago: University of Chicago Press.

Municipal Code of Chicago, § 4-384-015 (2014).

Nagel, Thomas. 1979. *Mortal Questions*. Cambridge, UK: Cambridge University Press.

Nair v. Union of India, Kerala High Court, no. 155/1999, June 2000.

Narayan, Uma. 1997. *Dislocating Cultures: Identities, Traditions, and Third-World Feminism*. New York: Routledge.

National Research Council. 2013. *Workforce Needs in Veterinary Medicine*. Washington, DC: National Academies Press.

Natural Resources Defense Council, Inc. v. Pritzker, 828 F.3d 1125 (9th Cir. 2016).

Newton County Wildlife Association v. United States Forest Service, 113 F.3d 110 (8th Cir. 1997).

NineMSN. 2017. "Berlin Zoo's Baby Polar Bear Must Die: Activists" March 21. https://web.archive.org/web/20070701010523/http://news.ninemsn.com.au/article.aspx?id=255770.

North Slope Borough v. Andrus, 486 F.Supp. 332 (D.C. Cir. 1980).

Nozick, Robert. 1974. *Anarchy, State, and Utopia*. New York: Basic Books.

Nuffield Council on Bioethics. 2005. *The Ethics of Research Involving Animals*. https://

www.nuffieldbioethics.org/assets/pdfs/The-ethics-of-research-involving-ani
mals-full-report.pdf.

Nussbaum, Martha C. 1978. *Aristotle's De Motu Animalium*. Princeton, NJ: Princeton
University Press.

———. 1986. *The Fragility of Goodness: Luck and Ethics in Greek Tragedy and Philosophy*. Cambridge, UK: Cambridge University Press.

———. 1994. *The Therapy of Desire: Theory and Practice in Hellenistic Ethics*. Princeton, NJ: Princeton University Press.

———. 1996. *Poetic Justice: The Literary Imagination and Public Life*. Boston: Beacon Press.

———. 2000a. "The Costs of Tragedy: Some Moral Limits of Cost-Benefit Analysis."
In *Cost-Benefit Analysis: Legal, Economic and Philosophical Perspectives*, edited by
Matthew D. Adler and Eric A. Posner. Chicago: University of Chicago Press.

———. 2000b. *Women and Human Development: The Capabilities Approach*. New
York: Cambridge University Press.

———. 2001. *Upheavals of Thought: The Intelligence of Emotions*. New York: Cambridge University Press.

———. 2004. *Hiding from Humanity: Disgust, Shame, and the Law*. Princeton, NJ:
Princeton University Press.

———. (2004) 2005. "Mill Between Bentham and Aristotle." *Daedalus*, 60–68. Re-
printed in *Economics and Happiness*, edited by Lulgino Bruni and Pier Luigi Porta.
Oxford, UK: Oxford University Press, 170–83.

———. 2006. *Frontiers of Justice: Disability, Nationality, Species Membership*. Cambridge, MA: Harvard University Press.

———. 2008. "Human Dignity and Political Entitlements." In *Human Dignity and
Bioethics: Essays Commissioned by the President's Council on Bioethics*. Washington, DC: President's Council on Bioethics, 351–80.

———. 2010a. *From Disgust to Humanity: Sexual Orientation and Constitutional Law*.
New York: Oxford University Press.

———. 2010b. "Mill's Feminism: Liberal, Radical, and Queer." In *John Stuart Mill:
Thought and Influence*, edited by Georgios Varouxakis and Paul Kelly. London:
Routledge.

———. 2010c. "Response to Kraut." *Classical Philology* 105, no. 4, 463–70.

———. 2011. "Perfectionist Liberalism and Political Liberalism." *Philosophy and Public Affairs* 39, no. 1 (Winter): 3–45.

———. 2012. *Creating Capabilities: The Human Development Approach*. Cambridge,
MA: Harvard University Press.

———. 2013. "The Damage of Death: Incomplete Arguments and False Consola-
tions." In *The Metaphysics and Ethics of Death*, edited by James S. Taylor. New
York: Oxford University Press.

———. 2016a. *Anger and Forgiveness: Resentment, Generosity, Justice*. New York: Oxford University Press.

————. 2016b. "Aspiration and the Capabilities List." *Journal of Human Development and Capabilities* 17: 1–8.

————. 2018a. *The Monarchy of Fear: A Philosopher Looks at Our Political Crisis*. New York: Simon & Schuster.

————. 2018b. "Why Freedom of Speech Is an Important Right and Why Animals Should Have It." *Denver Law Review* 95, no. 4 (January): 843–55.

————. 2019. "Preface: Amartya Sen and the HDCA." *Journal of Human Development and Capabilities* 20, no. 2 (April): 124–26.

————. 2021. *Citadels of Pride: Sexual Abuse, Accountability, and Reconciliation*. New York: W. W. Norton.

Nussbaum, Martha C., and Hilary Putnam. 1992. "Changing Aristotle's Mind." In *Essays on Aristotle's De Anima*, edited by Martha C. Nussbaum and Amélie Oksenberg Rorty. Oxford, UK: Clarendon Press.

Nussbaum (Wichert), Rachel, and Martha C. Nussbaum. 2017a. "Legal Protection for Whales: Capabilities, Entitlements, and Culture." In *Animals, Race, and Multiculturalism*, edited by Luis Cordeiro Rodrigues and Les Mitchell. Cham, Switzerland: Palgrave Macmillan.

————. 2017b. "Scientific Whaling? The Scientific Research Exception and the Future of the International Whaling Commission." *Journal of Human Development and Capabilities* 18, no. 3 (October): 356–69.

————. 2019. "The Legal Status of Whales and Dolphins: From Bentham to the Capabilities Approach." In *Agency and Democracy in Development Ethics*, 259–88, edited by Lori Keleher and Stacy J. Kosko. Cambridge, UK: Cambridge University Press.

————. 2021. "Can There Be Friendship Between Human Beings and Wild Animals?" *Journal of Human Development and Capabilities* 22, no. 1 (January): 87–107.

Nuwer, Rachel. 2019. "This Songbird Is Nearly Extinct in the Wild. An International Treaty Could Help Save It—But Won't." *New York Times*, March 15.

Orlans, Barbara F., Tom L. Beauchamp, Rebecca Dresser, David B. Morton, and John P. Gluck. 1998. *The Human Use of Animals: Case Studies in Ethical Choice*. New York: Oxford University Press.

Osborne, Emily. 2021. "New Law Will Protect Illinois Birds from Deadly Building Collisions." Audubon Great Lakes, July 29.

Pachirat, Timothy. 2011. *Every Twelve Seconds: Industrial Slaughter and the Politics of Sight*. New Haven: Yale University Press.

Palila v. Hawaii Department of Land and Natural Resources, 639 F.2d 495 (9th Cir. 1981).

Part Pet Shop v. City of Chicago, 872 F.3d 495 (7th Cir. 2017).

Pepperberg, Irene. 1999. *The Alex Studies: Cognitive and Communicative Abilities of Grey Parrots*. Cambridge, MA: Harvard University Press.

————. 2008. *Alex & Me*. New York: HarperCollins.

Piscopo, Susan. 2004. "Injuries Associated with Steeplechase Racing." *The Horse*, August 1. https://thehorse.com/16147/injuries-associated-with-steeplechase-racing/.

Pitcher, George. 1995. *The Dogs Who Came to Stay*. New York: Dutton.

Platt, John R. 2021. "I Know Why the Caged Songbird Goes Extinct." *The Revelator*, March 3.

Poole, Joyce. 1997. *Coming of Age with Elephants: A Memoir*. New York: Hyperion.

Poole, Joyce, et al. 2021. "The Elephant Ethogram." Elephant Voices, May. https://www.elephantvoices.org/elephant-ethogram.html.

Rawls, John. 1986. *Political Liberalism*. Expanded ed. New York: Columbia University Press.

"Regulations Governing Take of Migratory Birds," 50 C.F.R. 10 (2021). https://www.govinfo.gov/app/details/FR-2021-01-07/2021-00054.

Renkl, Margaret. 2021. "Think Twice Before Helping That Baby Bird You Found." *New York Times*, June 7.

Rollin, Bernard. 1995. *Farm Animal Welfare: Social, Bioethical, and Research Issues*. Ames: Iowa State University Press.

———. 2018. " 'We Always Hurt the Things We Love'—Unnoticed Abuse of Companion Animals." *Animals* 8 (September 18): 157.

Rose, James D., et al. 2013. "Can Fish Really Feel Pain?" *Fish and Fisheries* 15, no. 1 (January): 97–133.

Rott, Nathan. 2021. "Biden Moves to Make It Illegal (Again) to Accidentally Kill Migratory Birds." NPR, March 9.

Rowan, Andrew. 2015. "Ending the Use of Animals in Toxicity Studies and Risk Evaluation." *Cambridge Quarterly of Healthcare Ethics* 24, no. 4 (October): 448–58.

Russell, W. M. S., and R. L. Burch. 2012. "Guidelines for Ethical Conduct in the Care and Use of Nonhuman Animals in Research." American Psychological Association Committee on Animal Research and Ethics, February 24.

Safina, Carl. 2015. *Beyond Words: What Animals Think and Feel*. New York: Picador.

———. 2020. *Becoming Wild: How Animal Cultures Raise Families, Create Beauty, and Achieve Peace*. New York: Henry Holt.

Samuels, Gabriel. 2016. "Chimpanzees Have Rights, Says Argentine Judge as She Orders Cecilia be Released from Zoo." *The Independent*, November 7.

Schneewind, Jerome B. 1998. *The Invention of Autonomy: A History of Modern Moral Philosophy*. New York: Cambridge University Press.

Schultz, Bart. 2004. *Henry Sidgwick: Eye of the Universe: An Intellectual Biography*. New York: Cambridge University Press.

Scott, Elizabeth S., and Ben Chen. 2019. "Fiduciary Principles in Family Law." In *Oxford Handbook of Fiduciary Law*, edited by Evan J. Criddle, Paul B. Miller, and Robert H. Sitkoff. New York: Oxford University Press.

Scruton, Roger. 1999. *On Hunting: A Short Polemic*. London: Vintage UK.

Scully, Matthew. 2002. *Dominion: The Power of Man, the Suffering of Animals, and the Call to Mercy*. New York: St. Martin's Press.

Seattle Audubon Society v. Evans, 952 F.2d 297 (9th Cir. 1991).

Sen, Amartya. 1983. *Poverty and Famines: An Essay on Entitlement and Deprivation*, Reprint ed. New York: Oxford University Press.

———. 1996. "Fertility and Coercion." *The University of Chicago Law Review* 63, no. 3: 1035–61.

———. 2009. *The Idea of Justice*. Cambridge, MA: Harvard University Press.

Shah, Sonia. 2019. "Indian High Court Recognizes Animals as Legal Entities." *Nonhuman Rights Blog*, July 10. https://www.nonhumanrights.org/blog/punjab-haryana-animal-rights/.

Shapiro, Paul. 2007. "Pork Industry Should Phase Out Gestation Crates." *Globe Gazette*, January 10.

Siebert, Charles. 2019a. "The Swazi 17." *New York Times Magazine*, July 14.

———. 2019b. "They Called It a 'Rescue.' But Are Elephants Really Better Off?" *New York Times*, July 9.

Sierra Club v. Morton, 405 U.S. 727 (1972).

Sidgwick, Henry. (1907) 1981. *The Methods of Ethics*. Reprint of 7th ed. London: Macmillan; Indianapolis: Hackett.

Singer, Peter. 1975. *Animal Liberation: A New Ethics for Our Treatment of Animals*. New York: HarperCollins.

———. 2011. *Practical Ethics*. Cambridge, UK: Cambridge University Press.

Smuts, Barbara. 2001. "Encounters with Animal Minds." *Journal of Consciousness Studies* 8, nos. 5–7: 293–309.

Sorabji, Richard. 1995. *Animal Minds and Human Morals: The Origins of the Western Debate*. Ithaca, NY: Cornell University Press.

Spielman, Fran. 2021. "Aldermen Vote to Close Loophole in Chicago's Puppy Mill Ordinance." *Chicago Sun-Times*, April 12.

Stevens, Blair. 2020. "Even Years After Blackfish, SeaWorld Still Has Orcas." 8forty, June%10. https://8forty.ca/2020/06/10/even-years-after-blackfish-seaworld-still-has-orcas/.

Sunstein, Cass R. 1999. "Standing for Animals." University of Chicago Law School, Public Law and Legal Theory, Working Paper No. 06.

———. 2000. "Standing for Animals (With Notes on Animal Rights) A Tribute to Kenneth L. Karst." *UCLA Law Review* 47: 1333–68.

Swanson, Sady. 2019. "Survival Story: Colorado Runner's 'Worst Fears Confirmed' When Mountain Lion Attacked." *Coloradoan*, February 14.

Swift, Jonathan. (1726) 2005. *Gulliver's Travels*. 5th ed. Oxford, UK: Oxford University Press.

Thorpe, William. 1956. *Learning and Instinct in Animals*. Cambridge, MA: Harvard University Press.

Townley, Cynthia. 2011. "Animals as Friends." *Between the Species* 13, no. 10: 45–59.

Tye, Michael. 2016. "Are Insects Sentient? Commentary on Klein & Barron on Insect Experience." *Animal Sentience* 9, no. 5.

———. 2017. *Tense Bees and Shell-Shocked Crabs: Are Animals Conscious?* New York: Oxford University Press.

Ul Haq, Mahbub. 1990. *Human Development Report 1990*. New York: United Nations Development Programme.

United States v. Moon Lake Electric Association, 45 F.Supp.2d. 1070 (D. Colo. 1999).

Van Doren, Benjamin M., et al. 2017. "High-Intensity Urban Light Installation Dramatically Alters Nocturnal Bird Migration." *PNAS* 114, no. 42 (October 2): 11175–80.

Victor, Daniel. 2019. "Dead Whale Found with 88 Pounds of Plastic Inside Body in the Philippines." *New York Times*, March 18.

Walzer, Michael. 1973. "Political Action and the Problem of Dirty Hands." *Philosophy and Public Affairs* 2, no. 2: 160–80.

Watkins, Frances, and Sam Truelove. 2021. "Fungie the Dolphin 'Spotted Off Irish Coast' Six Months After Vanishing from Home." *Mirror*, April 11.

Whaling in the Antarctic (Australia v. Japan: New Zealand intervening) (Int'l Ct. 2014). https://www.icj-cij.org/en/case/148.

White, Thomas. 2007. *In Defense of Dolphins: The New Moral Frontier*. Hoboken, NJ: Wiley-Blackwell.

———. 2015. "Whales, Dolphins and Ethics: A Primer." In *Dolphin Communication & Cognition: Past, Present, Future*, edited by Denise L. Herzing and Christine M. Johnson. Cambridge, MA: MIT Press.

Whitehead, Hal, and Luke Rendell. 2015. *The Cultural Lives of Whales and Dolphins*. Chicago: University of Chicago Press.

Wild Free-Roaming Horses and Burros Act, The (WFHBA), 16 U.S.C. § 1331 et seq (1971).

Williams, Bernard. 1983. *Problems of the Self*. Cambridge, UK: Cambridge University Press.

Wise, Steven M. 2000. *Rattling the Cage: Toward Legal Rights for Animals*. New York: Perseus Books.

Wodehouse, P. G. (1935) 2008. "Pig-Hoo-o-o-o-ey!" In *Blandings Castle*. London: Penguin.

———. (1952) 2008. *Pigs Have Wings*. New York: Random House.

Wolff, Jonathan, and Avner de-Shalit. 2007. *Disadvantage*. New York: Oxford University Press.

World Animal Protection. 2020. *World Animal Protection Index 2020*. https://api .worldanimalprotection.org/.

Zamir, Tzachi. 2007. *Ethics and the Beast: A Speciesist Argument for Animal Liberation*. Princeton, NJ: Princeton University Press.

Notes

INTRODUCTION

1. Throughout this book I often follow the common practice, among animal supporters, of using "animals" to mean "non-human animals," though from time to time I remind readers that this is a shorthand, as in my third sentence in the text. Human beings are also animals, but to say "non-human" everywhere would be cumbersome, and I hope my meaning is clear throughout.

2. See World Wide Fund for Nature's report on biodiversity: https://wwf.panda .org/discover/our_focus/biodiversity/biodiversity/.

3. This study by the Animal Welfare Institute, based on the classifications used in the US Endangered Species Act, gives a complete list of the species currently listed as endangered or threatened: https://awionline.org/content/list-endan gered-species.

4. Platt (2021).

5. BirdLife International (2017), https://www.birdlife.org/news/2017/01/24/10 -amazing-birds-have-gone-extinct/.

6. Nuwer (2019).

7. See Godfrey-Smith (2016, pp. 68–69, 73–74).

8. Poole (1997).

9. This behavior has been described many times, but for an especially fine description see Moss (1988).

10. A notorious case was that of a group of elephants from Swaziland, illegally airlifted to the US. I'll describe the case in chapter 10.

11. Whitehead and Rendell (2015).

12. See Victor (2019). The whale was not a humpback, but a Cuvier's beaked whale.

However, humpback whales are also affected by plastic ingestion, as are virtually all species of whale.

13. Wodehouse ([1935] 2008, pp. 60–86).

14. Shapiro (2007).

15. For more discussion, see chapter 12.

16. See Rollin (1995), a fundamental study on this topic.

17. For pictures, see Leonard (2020).

18. You can hear this on the Cornell Lab of Ornithology's site: https://www.all aboutbirds.org/guide/House_Finch/sounds.

19. Pitcher (1995). I discuss Lupa and her human friends further in chapter 11.

20. I draw on these articles in chapters 3, 11, and 12. We presented four of them at the annual meetings of the Human Development and Capability Association (HDCA), an international group of researchers, mainly economists and philosophers, working on global poverty and inequality, of which Nobel Prize–winning economist Amartya Sen and I are the two Founding Presidents.

21. The approach is used by the entire organization, Friends of Animals, where Rachel worked. Her boss, Michael Harris, recently published an op-ed about it, intervening in the case of a deprived elephant in captivity. See Harris (2021). I also intervened in the case, writing an amicus brief and appearing on a local news program. See Lee (2021).

1. BRUTALITY AND NEGLECT: INJUSTICE IN ANIMAL LIVES

1. I owe this argument to Christine Korsgaard, whose defense of this (basically Kantian) idea I discuss later. On this point, she and I are in complete agreement.

2. *Natural Resources Defense Council v. Pritzker*, 828 F.3d 1125 (9th Cir. 2016).

3. Many workplaces and even resorts have eliminated single-use plastic, in favor of recyclable cans and water in people's own bottles.

4. A leading thinker about wonder is Jeremy Bendik-Keymer. Three representative recent publications are: Bendik-Keymer (2017); Bendik-Keymer (2021a); Bendik-Keymer (2021b). See also his website: https://sites.google.com/case.edu /bendikkeymer/.

5. Aristotle, *Parts of Animals*, I.5.

6. See Nussbaum (2001, ch. 1).

7. See the discussion of "Fancy" in Nussbaum (1996).

8. See a similar conclusion in Nussbaum (2006, ch. 6).

9. See Nussbaum (2001, ch. 6).

10. See Nussbaum (1978), based on my doctoral dissertation.

11. Batson (2011).

12. See Nussbaum (2016a). For a shorter version of the same argument, see also Nussbaum (2018a).

2. THE *SCALA NATURAE* AND THE "SO LIKE US" APPROACH

1. Nussbaum (2006).
2. *Nair v. Union of India*, Kerala High Court, no. 155/1999, June 2000.
3. Sorabji (1995).
4. See the dissertation on this topic by Comay del Junco (2020).
5. Nussbaum (1978).
6. There are dissident strands in both, and there is a form of the Kaddish, or prayer for the dead, that includes a prayer for dead animals.
7. For example, see Kraut (2010, pp. 250, 256). Kraut uses the chasm to justify doing medical experiments on animals, but not on humans. See also my reply to Kraut in Nussbaum (2010c, pp. 463, 467).
8. Sextus Empiricus, *Outlines of Pyrrhonism*.
9. See Plutarch, *Life of Pompey*, LII.4; Pliny the Elder, *Natural History*, VIII.7.20.
10. Sorabji (1993) (quoting Pliny).
11. Ibid., p. 124, n.21 (quoting Pliny). See also Seneca, *De Brevitate Vitae* 13; Cassius Dio XXXIX.38, who says that the elephants raised their trunks as if imploring the heavens to avenge the wrong.
12. Sorabji (1993, pp. 124–25) (quoting Cicero, *Epistulae ad Familiares* [Letters to Friends] VII.1).
13. See White (2007, pp. 219–20).
14. Genesis 7 actually gives two different accounts: in the first there are seven pairs of each of the "clean" animals and of each type of bird, but only one pair of the "unclean" animals; later tradition interprets this as allowing for sacrifice. The second version, right after the first, mentions only a single pair of each type of animal, both clean and unclean, and of birds.
15. Genesis 9:12; Alter (2004).
16. Genesis 1:26–8 (verses 29 and 30).
17. Scully (2002).
18. Scruton (1999).
19. This nationally famous trial pitted two of the nation's most famous lawyers against one another: the crusading liberal Clarence Darrow, and the ex-politician, three-times-failed presidential candidate, William Jennings Bryan. The defendant, schoolteacher John T. Scopes, was charged with teaching evolution in violation of the state law. National attention was riveted on the trial, which seemed to pit religion against evolution. Because so much was made of the evolutionary claim that humans descend from "a lower order of animals," it was known as the "Monkey Trial." In the end, Scopes was convicted, but fined only $100. The fine was later set aside on a legal technicality, but attempts to have the Butler Act declared unconstitutional on free speech and religious establishment grounds failed— until 1968, when a similar statute in Arkansas was declared unconstitutional by

the US Supreme Court under the Establishment Clause of the First Amendment. The Scopes Trial was memorably dramatized in the 1955 play *Inherit the Wind*, by Jerome Lawrence and Robert E. Lee, later made into a film starring Fredric March as Bryan and Spencer Tracy as Darrow (1960).

20. Other activists working with primates, like Jane Goodall, seem to hold a similar view.
21. Wise (2000).
22. *Unlocking the Cage* (2016).
23. Wise (2000).
24. *Unlocking the Cage* (2016).
25. Ibid.
26. Ibid.
27. See generally Schneewind (1998), providing the history of the idea of autonomy in Western philosophy, and Dworkin (1988), the leading philosophical account in terms of higher-order desires.
28. Wise (2000); *Unlocking the Cage* (2016).
29. *Unlocking the Cage* (2016).
30. Ibid.
31. Ibid.
32. Ibid.
33. Ibid.
34. *Unlocking the Cage* (2016); Wise (2000).
35. *Unlocking the Cage* (2016).
36. Ibid.
37. See Whitehead and Rendell (2015, pp. 120–21).
38. Swift ([1726] 2005, pp. 135–84).
39. See generally Nussbaum (2004).
40. See generally ibid.
41. See ibid. See generally Nussbaum (2010a). See also Hasan, Huq, Nussbaum, and Verma (2018).
42. *Unlocking the Cage* (2016).
43. See Whitehead and Rendell (2015).
44. See de Waal (1996).
45. *Unlocking the Cage* (2016).
46. See ibid.
47. Brulliard (2018).
48. White (2007).
49. The "mirror test" tests an animal's ability to recognize its own image in a mirror by painting a dark mark on the back of the animal's head, visible only in the mirror, and also a sham mark, felt by the animal but not visible in the mirror. The animal's subsequent behavior—scrubbing its head to remove the dark mark—shows

that it has seen the mark in the mirror and connected it to its own head, and that it was not the tactile sensation of the mark that led to the scrubbing behavior. This test is connected closely to a sense of self, though people dispute whether it is a necessary condition for self-awareness, or only a sufficient condition.

50. Wise does not talk much about emotions, although he does draw attention to a striking example of appropriate empathetic emotional response. White, by contrast, has a lot to say about both human and dolphin emotional capacities, their neural basis, and their variety.

51. This last element is not theoretically emphasized by White, but many of his examples seem to use it. It is a bit unclear whether this "appropriate" treatment of other persons ought to be a necessary condition of personhood for White, who constantly emphasizes that humans generally fail to recognize dolphins despite the fact that they are actually persons, and who also draws attention to human aggressiveness toward other humans, by contrast to dolphins' nonaggressive behavior.

52. White (2007, p. 47).

53. Ibid., pp. 166–67.

54. Ibid., p. 8n.

55. Ibid.

56. Ibid., p. 176.

57. Throughout the book White conflates several different meanings of the idea of "individualism": in one meaning, "individualism" means that each and every separate creature counts, is a being with dignity, to be treated as an end and not as a thing or piece of property. In that meaning of the term, dolphins and humans are both individuals, and so (I think) are all other sentient animals. A second meaning of "individualism" is solitary self-sufficiency: the creature can do just fine without others. This is where White asserts that there's a big difference between dolphins and humans: they are profoundly enmeshed in their social group, whereas we are solitaries. But he says this, I think, mistakenly. Finally, White also uses "individualism" to mean "egoism," "selfishness," and suggests that humans are more personally selfish than are dolphins, for whom the group is of critical importance. This is an interesting claim, but hard to test. He does provide evidence that dolphins are very unaggressive by comparison to humans, apparently never lethally aggressive. But is that really altruism and control of selfish tendencies? It's hard to say. At any rate, to the extent that egoism is central to human life, White should either revise his criteria for personhood (not including the "appropriate recognition and treatment of other persons" as a necessary condition), or he should be more skeptical about whether human beings are persons!

58. White (2007, p. 182).

59. Ibid., pp. 188–200.

3. THE UTILITARIANS: PLEASURE AND PAIN

1. Singer (1975).
2. Bentham notoriously leaves the move from "is" to "ought" undefended.
3. Bentham ([1780] 1948).
4. Ibid., pp. 310–11.
5. Ibid.
6. Ibid.
7. Ibid.
8. For the sources of these and other anecdotes, see Campos Boralevi (1984, p. 166).
9. See the dissertation on this topic by Lee (2003).
10. See the free e-book at Bentham (2013), https://www.gutenberg.org/ebooks /42984.
11. Korsgaard (2021, p. 159) (quoting Singer).
12. On adaptive preferences, see Elster (1983). Amartya Sen develops this concept in many articles; the essential references are in Nussbaum (2000b, ch. 2).
13. Nozick (1974, pp. 42–45). In *Anarchy*, wanting to be active is the reason against plugging in that Nozick stresses most. In later versions, he also emphasizes an interest in being in touch with reality, not living in a dreamworld.
14. Of course, one might invent a special pleasure and call it the pleasure of agency; Mill appears to do this. But unless this pleasure is understood to be qualitatively, not just quantitatively, different from other pleasures, it will be difficult to capture the intuition contained in the example. Mill understood this point, and his view is not vulnerable to my critique.
15. Sidgwick ([1907] 1981).
16. For Sidgwick's life and political activities, see Schultz (2004).
17. See de Lazari-Radek and Singer (2014).
18. For example, he has addressed Korsgaard's "container" argument. His response is complex. See Korsgaard (2018b, p. 159) for his assertion of the container view, but elsewhere, apparently responding to her critique, he articulates it in a more limited form: "[I]n some circumstances—when animals lead pleasant lives, are killed painlessly, their deaths do not cause suffering to other animals and the killing of one animal makes possible its replacement by another that would not otherwise have lived—the killing of animals without self-awareness is not wrong." Singer (2011, p. 108). We should note that Singer thinks most animals lack "self-awareness."
19. Singer (1975).
20. Singer (2011, p. 101).
21. In *The Point of View of the Universe*, de Lazari-Radek and Singer do mention another aspect of Nozick's scenario (2014, p. 257). The objective view of pleasure taken in that book does make Singer more vulnerable to Nozick's arguments,

but he suggests that our preference for being in touch with reality is the result of status quo bias.

22. He traces the change in his views to Sidgwick's arguments, and he has further articulated his new view in the book co-authored with de Lazari-Radek. This shift separates Singer from economic Utilitarians, with whom he was formerly allied, since they think of welfare in terms of the satisfaction of preferences. But the change makes little difference to his views about animal treatment, or the objections to those views.

23. University College London offered degrees and fellowships to atheists from 1826, but it was not until 1836 that it secured legal recognition as a college within the University of London, and this was presumably too late for the self-educated but degreeless Mill, who had already started working for pay for the British East India Company in 1823, and he continued in the company until 1858.

24. See Nussbaum ([2004] 2005) and Nussbaum (2010b). A fine overall treatment of Mill, with whose interpretations I largely agree, is Brink (2013).

25. Mill (1963, vol. XVI, p. 1414).

26. Mill (1963, vol. X, p. 223).

27. Ibid.

4. CHRISTINE KORSGAARD'S KANTIAN APPROACH

1. Kant does at times make objectionably racist remarks, which have been justly criticized.

2. Kant read the Stoics (in Latin, since he did not know Greek), and was obviously influenced by them. Bentham did not pay much attention to the history of philosophy, and Mill charged him with failure to "derive light from other minds."

3. Kant ([1798] 1974, 8:27).

4. J. S. Mill, fond of German philosophy, probably did know Kant, and he does appear to avoid the errors of both, see chs. 3 and 5.

5. Korsgaard (2004).

6. Korsgaard (2018b).

7. Korsgaard (1981). John Rawls was the chair of her dissertation committee, and I was the second reader.

8. Kant shows no detailed knowledge of Aristotle, and his cursory references are not accurate.

9. Kant ([1788] 1955); Akad., p. 5.161.

10. Kant ([1798] 1974, 8:27).

11. Kant ([1785] 2012).

12. Korsgaard (1996a).

13. Akad., p. 429.

14. Kant's fourth example, a prohibition on suicide, has been controversial among

Kantians, and some very distinguished Kantians have invoked the Kantian idea of autonomy to argue in favor of physician-assisted suicide.

15. Of course, this is happening right now to the children of immigrants, but it has occasioned widespread outrage.

16. See Korsgaard (2018b, p. 99), who quotes a longer section of the text. Obviously, this passage is the source of her book title.

17. There appears to be a clear correlation between cruel treatment of animals and bad behavior toward humans, but it is difficult to tell whether the relationship is causal, or whether the two are related aspects of a warped psychology.

18. See Korsgaard (2018b, pp. 99–101) (referencing Kant's *Lectures on Ethics*).

19. Ibid., pp. 100–101.

20. Ibid., p. 103 (quoting Kant's *Lectures on Ethics*).

21. *Fellow Creatures* is dedicated to Korsgaard's cats.

22. Korsgaard would object that I am already relying too much on intuitions, as she charges Aristotelians with doing in Korsgaard (1996b).

23. Korsgaard (2018b, p. 27).

24. Ibid., p. 31.

25. Ibid., p. 14.

26. Ibid., p. 145.

27. Ibid., p. 77.

28. Ibid., p. 139.

29. Ibid., p. 146.

30. Ibid., p. 237.

31. Ibid., p. 43.

32. Ibid., p. 40.

33. Ibid., p. 48.

34. Ibid., p. 47.

35. Ibid., pp. 48–50.

36. Ibid., p. 50.

37. The deaths of elephants on Indian railroad tracks, where trains rarely obey their speed limit, is a woefully common occurrence, as a random internet search will show, and the group of adult females typically tries to shield the babies from harm, even at lethal costs to themselves. See de Waal (1996), which discusses elephant self-sacrifice.

38. Observed on a safari in Botswana in 2012.

39. See de Waal (1996); de Waal (2006).

40. See de Waal (1989); de Waal (1996); de Waal (2006).

41. Maestripieri and Mateo (2009).

42. Whitehead and Rendell (2015).

43. Safina (2020).

44. Korsgaard (2006).
45. See Smuts (2001). See also de Waal (2019).

5. THE CAPABILITIES APPROACH: FORMS OF LIFE AND RESPECTING THE CREATURES WHO LIVE THEM

1. I already extended the CA to animals in chapter 6 of Nussbaum (2006). The approach in this chapter (and subsequent chapters) is similar, but far more detailed.
2. The approach is also called the Human Development Approach, but for obvious reasons I have stopped using that name and have tried to convince others not to use it. See my remarks in Nussbaum (2019).
3. I develop my version of the CA in three books: Nussbaum (2000b); Nussbaum (2006); and Nussbaum (2012). The last of these also has an extensive bibliography of relevant other publications by both Sen and me on the topic. Because it deals with the work of many theorists, not just my own, I use the "Human Development" subtitle, though I myself am not fond of it.
4. See the Human Development and Capability Association: https://hd-ca.org.
5. Ul Haq (1990).
6. Nussbaum (2000b, ch. 2).
7. See the free e-book at Dickens ([1854] 2021, ch. IX), https://www.gutenberg.org/ebooks/786.
8. As I discuss in Nussbaum (2012), internal capabilities correspond to what are called "capabilities" in the Human Capital approach, as for example in the work of James Heckman (discussed in an appendix in that book).
9. Wolff and de-Shalit (2007).
10. Strictly speaking, they should say "fertile capability," but the alliteration was too tempting.
11. This is my view, not Sen's. He uses the idea of capabilities for comparative purposes only.
12. See Nussbaum (2012) and Nussbaum (2008).
13. Nussbaum (2000b, ch. 2).
14. Rawls (1986). Rawls is clear that the overlapping consensus may take time to achieve, and he offers a persuasive account of how, over time, people might move toward it.
15. This example was given by French philosopher Jacques Maritain, one of the framers of the Universal Declaration of Human Rights, describing how the framers, from Egypt, China, and other nations and traditions, sought an ethical language that could win a consensus. See Maritain (1951, ch. 4).
16. See further in Nussbaum (2011).
17. People interested in philosophical typologies (and please skip this note if you

are not!) often ask whether my version of the CA is *deontological* or *consequentialist*: does it, that is, recognize as central a set of ethical duties, or does it strive, in the manner of Utilitarianism, for a good set of consequences? Since these are schoolbook classifications, not subtle philosophical positions, it should come as no surprise that my answer to this question is complicated. There is a strong deontological component to the view, in the sense that promoting each of the capabilities up to the specified threshold level is *required* of a nation, on pain of being judged to have failed in minimal justice; and individuals are ethically required to try to attain that justice. However, the capabilities are an interlocking set of ends, just as in human life people strive for interlocking ends. People are teleological (end-directed) creatures, and the capabilities are envisaged as bases for their effective striving toward whatever mode of flourishing life they select. (In a way, people's own activity is the end, and the capabilities are only bases for that; but in political terms, the end or goal is to secure the capabilities: what comes after that is left up to people's own choices.) Consequentialism sometimes takes the form of promoting a static state, such as satisfaction or pleasure. I have criticized this type of consequentialism. But there are forms of consequentialism that view activities or the opportunity for activities as intrinsically valuable ends. As I suggested in chapter 3, it seems that the Utilitarianism of John Stuart Mill was of this sort. Mill also insisted that the ends were plural, differing in quality and not simply quantity. And he counted respect for dignity as among the important hallmarks of an adequate set of ends. Mill did think of his Utilitarianism as a comprehensive political (and personal) doctrine that ought to replace other such doctrines, especially religious ones. That is a large difference between my CA and Mill's views. But in other respects my view and Mill's are similar. Amartya Sen, too, has long emphasized that consequentialism can have plural ends, qualitatively distinct from one another.

18. This word is frequently preferred in the disability-rights literature, as more suggestive of joint activity than the word "guardian."

19. Poole et al. (2021), https://www.elephantvoices.org/elephant-ethogram.html. See also Angier (2021).

20. See Nussbaum (2018b).

21. Sen (1983).

22. See Smuts (2001).

23. See Gordon (2020). A possible citing of Fungie has been reported by an animal welfare group recently, see Watkins and Truelove (2021).

24. For the relationship, see Nussbaum (2012).

25. As I did in the amicus brief mentioned in the introduction, on behalf of Happy the elephant: Wise, fully aware of my differences with his approach, invited me to contribute the brief, highlighting the CA. And on Thomas White's recent embrace of the CA, see the conclusion.

26. See also Korsgaard (2018b, pp. 191–214).
27. See ibid., pp. 204–6.
28. Korsgaard (2018a); Korsgaard (2013).
29. Korsgaard formulates this idea using a strong distinction between instinct and will that I have rejected; but I accept her basic idea.
30. Bradshaw (2020).
31. *Natural Resources Defense Council, Inc. v. Pritzker*, 828 F.3d 1125 (9th Cir. 2016).
32. See ibid., at 1142. See generally Horwitz (2015), describing the sonar program in detail.
33. Marine Mammal Protection Act (MMPA), 16 U.S.C. § 1361 et seq (1972). Chapter 12 will describe the statute further.
34. *Pritzker*, 828 F.3d at 1142.
35. Ibid., at 1130–31.
36. Judge Gould practiced law in Seattle for twenty-five years before his nomination to the bench by President Clinton, and has also served as an adjunct professor at the University of Washington School of Law, also in Seattle, a school whose curriculum includes a wide range of offerings pertinent to animals, including "Coastal Law" and "Law of the Sea." Rachel Nussbaum got a first-class education in animal law there, preparing her for her subsequent career as an advocate for wild animals.

6. SENTIENCE AND STRIVING: A WORKING BOUNDARY

1. Aristotle, *On the Movement of Animals*, ch. 7, 701a33-36.
2. Not surprisingly, philosophers defend several different views; I present here a common view and one that I myself find the most convincing.
3. Tye, (2017, pp. 67–68).
4. See the free e-book at James ([1897] 2021, preface), https://www.gutenberg.org/ebooks/7118.
5. One example is Gowdy (1999), a portrayal of the lives of elephants from an elephant viewpoint. It is of course linguistic, but based on her outstanding grasp of research about how elephants live and think.
6. Tye (2017, pp. 86–88).
7. See also Tye (2016).
8. Nussbaum (1978, ch. 7).
9. Balcombe (2016, p. 72).
10. Wodehouse ([1952] 2008, p. 248).
11. Nussbaum (1978, ch. 7).
12. Dawkins (2012, p. 92); see also Tye (2017, p. 85).
13. Hilary Putnam and I used a similar example to illustrate the Aristotelian point that explanations on the formal level are frequently preferable, as explanations, to those that seek the ultimate level of matter, in Nussbaum and Rorty (1992).

14. See Balcombe (2016, p. 72).

15. Some animal advocates use "fishes" as the plural of "fish," thinking that the plural "fish" implies that these creatures are not individuals. They seem wrong linguistically: English contains such irregular plurals. "Sheep" is another such case, and I don't know of anyone who thinks that the use of the plural "sheep" implies that each one is not an individual.

16. Rose et al. (2013).

17. Braithwaite (2010).

18. Ibid., ch. 3; see also Balcombe (2016, pp. 78–80).

19. Braithwaite (2010, pp. 103–4).

20. Ibid., p. 104.

21. de Waal (2019). Other important studies of animal emotions are Bekoff (2008) and Safina (2015).

22. Lazarus (1991). See Nussbaum (2001, ch. 2).

23. de Waal (2019, p. 205).

24. Damasio (1994). I discuss his findings and those of quite a few other neuroscientists and cognitive psychologists in Nussbaum (2001, ch. 2).

25. Damasio (1994, ch. xv).

26. Ibid.

27. Ibid., p. 36.

28. Ibid., pp. 44–45.

29. See ibid., pp. 46–51, where Elliot is put through a battery of decision-making tests, which require only analysis and not a personal decision, and does very well. He produced an abundance of options for action. "'And after all this,' said Elliot to Damasio, 'I still wouldn't know what to do!'"

30. Nussbaum (1978, ch. 7).

31. Tye (2017, ch. 9).

32. Braithwaite (2010, pp. 92–94). She describes complex experiments in which fish, faced with choices about how to position themselves in relation to potential rivals, clearly use this thought pattern.

33. See Balcombe (2016, pp. 25–39); Tye (2017, p. 114). See generally Tye (2017, ch. 6).

34. Braithwaite (2010, p. 113).

35. The actual taxonomy is more complex: the two major groups are Osteichthyes, bony fish, of which the teleosts are by far the largest subgroup, and the Chondrichthyes, cartilaginous fish, of which the elasmobranchs are the largest subgroup; a third major group comprises the jawless fish, Agnatha.

36. Tye (2017, p. 102).

37. Ibid., p. 103.

38. Ackerman (2016, p. 55) (quoting Harvey Karten).

39. Emery (2016, p. 8).

40. Ibid.

41. Ibid., p. 11 (quoting Thorpe [1956]).

42. Ackerman (2016, p. 58) (summarizing the research of Erich Jarvis).

43. Ibid., ch. 3 (summarizes this research).

44. Pepperberg (2008).

45. Ackerman (2016, p. 40); Ackerman (2016, ch. 5); Emery (2016, pp. 77–87, 174–75).

46. Ackerman (2016, ch. 4), and see a remarkable photo of a bowerbird's edifice in Emery (2016, p. 77).

47. Tye (2017, pp. 127–28) describes experiments in which, when chicks were made uncomfortable by air ruffling their feathers, the mother birds exhibited physical signs of stress, and began clucking toward their chicks reassuringly. Many experiments have shown that corvids and parrots are capable of taking up the perspective of another bird, often for purposes of deception. Other experiments show that ravens respond with pleasure and play to the happy playful displays of another raven, and also react negatively to distress in others: see Ackerman (2020, p. 162), and Emery (2016, pp. 158–59), who finds evidence for empathy in consolatory behavior after a fight. See also Safina (2015) and Safina (2020) for an extensive account of the capacities of parrots.

48. Ackerman (2016, ch. 7) summarizes the research.

49. Tye (2017, pp. 131–33).

50. Godfrey-Smith (2016); Braithwaite (2010, pp. 122, 134).

51. Godfrey-Smith (2016, p. 9).

52. Braithwaite (2010, p. 122).

53. See ibid., pp. 122–29. Related experiments were conducted on shrimp. See also Tye (2017, pp. 156–58).

54. See Tye (2016) and Tye (2017, pp. 141–56).

55. Tye (2017, p. 144).

56. Ibid., p. 188.

57. See "Jagadish Chandra Bose," at https://www.famousscientists.org/jagadish-chandra-bose/.

58. See references in Tye (2017, p. 189).

59. See ibid., p. 189. See also Karpinski et al. (1999, p. 657).

60. Tye (2017, p. 189).

7. THE HARM OF DEATH

1. I investigated this Epicurean argument in Nussbaum (1994, ch. 6) (quoting Epicurus's *Letter to Menoiceus*), and later, with a somewhat changed position in Nussbaum (2013).

2. See Nagel (1979, pp. 1–10). Similar examples have been developed in important articles by John Martin Fischer, to which my Nussbaum (2013) is a dialogical

response. For full references to Fischer's articles, see that article. He also edited the valuable collection Fischer (1993). His latest summary of his position is in Fischer (2019).

3. Here I am responding directly to Fischer, who creates such an example.

4. Furley (1986); McMahan (2002).

5. See Nussbaum (2013) for more on these two false consolers.

6. See "The Makropulos Case: Reflections on the Tedium of Immortality" in Williams (1983, pp. 82–100).

7. See Nussbaum (1994).

8. Actually, Bentham restricts killing to important human purposes, ruling out "wanton" killings, i.e., just for amusement or pleasure. He thought eating animals was permissible if practices are humane, and he continued to eat meat throughout his life—unlike many contemporaries, who rejected meat eating.

9. But see my qualifications about Singer in chapter 3.

10. Lupo (2019).

11. Hare (1999, ch. 11). Originally published in Hare's *Essays on Bioethics*, but the reply by Singer is included only in the Jamieson volume.

12. Braithwaite (2010), p. 182, and https://urldefense.com/v3/__https://www.psu.edu /news/research/story/touch-withvictoria-braithwaite/__;!!CxwJSw!J9hVaQVFU 9Z6znRFtNTS8Ak0N_0GJ2lq9BVPI8MOgZumc2TgCKwAI4SUTKT6G2KhP -m8WwC4tysvAtKFgTzCc2BobjW9Dhm_$.

13. However, Balcombe has never offered a counterargument to my argument about the harm of death, first published in Nussbaum (2013), nor to related arguments made by Hare and accepted by Singer.

14. For a defense of a pure vegan diet, see Colb (2013).

8. TRAGIC CONFLICTS AND HOW TO MOVE BEYOND THEM

1. The hereditary curse on the house that caused the dilemma was not his fault, nor did the Greeks think it was. Tragic dilemmas are prominent in other world cultures—in the Indian epic *Mahabharata*, for example, a tale of civil war.

2. See Nussbaum (2000a). The Agamemnon example was used by Bernard Williams in his important article "Ethical Consistency" in Williams (1983). See also Nussbaum (1986, ch. 2). In terms of how to model these dilemmas logically, some favor abandoning "ought implies can," while Williams suggests denying that "I ought to do A" and "I ought to do B" entails "I ought to do A and B."

3. An important treatment of this question is Walzer (1973).

4. Crawley (2006).

5. The "3Rs" originated in Russell and Burch (2012).

6. Nuffield Council on Bioethics (2005), https://www.nuffieldbioethics.org/assets /pdfs/The-ethics-of-research-involving-animals-full-report.pdf.

7. Including Beauchamp and DeGrazia (2020).

8. Akhtar (2015).
9. Ibid.; Rowan (2015).
10. See Kitcher (2015).
11. Beauchamp and DeGrazia (2020). This valuable book includes critical assessments of Beauchamp and DeGrazia's proposed principles from a wide range of scientists and ethicists.
12. Ibid., p. 15.
13. Ibid., p. 66.
14. Guaranteed Rate Field (the Chicago White Sox) offers vegetarian chili and veggie burgers; Coors Field in Denver offers vegan pizza, veggie burgers, and veggie dogs.
15. In this section I draw heavily on two articles: Holland and Linch (2017) and Nussbaum (Wichert) and Nussbaum (2017a).
16. Holland and Linch (2017, p. 322).
17. Ibid.
18. These two cases are taken from Holland and Linch (2017), who give further sources for them.
19. For a full treatment of this case, see Nussbaum (Wichert) and Nussbaum (2017a) with reference to various sources on the controversy. The quoted sentence giving the exemption is actually from a predecessor law of 1931, but the current Convention (1946) is very similar.
20. See Whitehead and Rendell (2015, ch. 2), investigating all of the prominent contenders.
21. See Narayan (1997).
22. See Benhabib (1995, pp. 235–55).
23. One might compare the contention by communitarian political theorists Dan M. Kahan and Tracey L. Meares that the Fourth Amendment rights against unwarranted search and seizure should be waived whenever the local African American community (meaning whoever shows up at a meeting) votes so to suspend them: see Kahan and Meares (2014).
24. Scully (2002, pp. 175–76).
25. Ibid.
26. Ibid.
27. See Nussbaum (2000b, ch. 1).
28. Devlin (1959).
29. D'Amato and Chopra (1991, p. 59).
30. Holland and Linch (2017, pp. 322–36).
31. Lear (2008).
32. See Burkert (1966).
33. One of the most successful recent operas is Jake Heggie's *Moby-Dick*, which shows how contemporary media make brutality to whales available for stage representation.

34. See Connor (2021).
35. See Delon (2021).
36. See Bever (2019).
37. See Swanson (2019).
38. One group that is promoting such a complex solution is GroupElephant, which works with both elephants and rhinos in Africa, and at the same time with rural villages. See groupelephant.com.
39. Sen (1996).

9. ANIMALS WHO LIVE WITH US

1. The 2019–20 National Pet Owners Survey, conducted by the American Pet Products Association.
2. See Rollin (2018). This number is up from 56 percent in 1988.
3. Although this is a poetic fiction, it depicts animal-human relationships that seem to have been common in the Greek world.
4. Homer, *Odyssey*, Book XVII, pp. 290–327.
5. See generally Homer, *Odyssey*, Book XVII.
6. See Rollin (2018). I'll discuss this article further below. See also Katz (2004).
7. Donaldson and Kymlicka (2011).
8. For important philosophical work on asymmetrical dependency, see Kittay (1999).
9. Francione (2008); Francione and Charlton (2015). For other critiques of his approach, see Donaldson and Kymlicka (2011) and Zamir (2007).
10. And of course, a piece of property cannot have property rights. And yet, surprisingly, animals have some property rights under current law: see my discussion of Karen Bradshaw's book in chapter 5.
11. The word "collaborator" is used in the disability rights movement, and valuably transferred by Donaldson and Kymlicka (2011, ch. 2) to the human-animal relationship.
12. Sunstein (2000, pp. 1333, 1342, 1363–64, 1366).
13. Cole (2014).
14. Beam (2009).
15. Burgess-Jackson (1998).
16. Thanks to Rory Hanlon for this information.
17. See "Should the Tail Wag the Dog?" in Orlans et al. (1988, ch. 15, pp. 273–87).
18. Here is a useful summary from the ASPCA of the situation of dogs and cats in shelters: https://www.aspca.org/animal-homelessness/shelter-intake-and-surrender/pet-statistics.
19. Aguirre (2019).
20. Piscopo (2004), https://thehorse.com/16147/injuries-associated-with-steeple chase-racing/.

21. See Donaldson and Kymlicka (2011, p. 139).
22. Ibid.
23. Ibid., p. 136.
24. Ibid.
25. See ibid. (discussing Farm Sanctuary).

10. THE "WILD" AND HUMAN RESPONSIBILITY

1. I showed a draft of this chapter to my daughter, Rachel, before her final illness, when she was still working at Friends of Animals in Denver as a Government Affairs attorney. She said that she agreed with my approach, but a lot of other people would not!
2. This section overlaps with a section of Nussbaum (2006, ch. 6), though I now put the contention in even stronger terms.
3. See ibid. (discussion of Botkin [1996]).
4. See Bradshaw (2020).
5. See Van Doren et al. (2017), for example.
6. See chapter 12 for discussion.
7. Feingold (2019).
8. See, for example, Renkl (2021). A good example of an organization in my own city that gives such advice is Flint Creek Wildlife Rehabilitation at https://flint creekwildlife.org/.
9. Chicago Zoological Society (2021), https://www.czs.org/Chicago-Zoological -Society/About/Press-room/2021-Press-Releases/Update-on-Amur-Tiger's -Second-Surgery-at-Brookfield.
10. See "Veterinarians in Wildlife and Ecosystem Health" in National Research Council (2013, ch. 7).
11. Beauchamp and DeGrazia (2020).
12. See Siebert (2019a). See also Siebert (2019b).
13. Siebert (2019a, p. 42).
14. Ibid., pp. 26–33, 42, 45. The article discusses alternative, and viable, proposals that were made to address the environmental stress the herd was under, and also makes it clear that a conservation group, GroupElephant, had offered to pay all the expenses to transfer the elephants to a wildlife reserve in South Africa.
15. *Blackfish* (2013).
16. See discussion in Nussbaum (Wichert) and Nussbaum (2019).
17. Stevens (2020), https://8forty.ca/2020/06/10/even-years-after-blackfish-seaworld -still-has-orcas/.
18. See Whitehead and Rendell (2015).
19. Ibid.
20. White (2007, pp. 198–215).

21. Berger (2020), https://www.buckettripper.com/snorkeling-and-diving-with -dolphins-in-eilat-israel/.

22. This example was given by the Bronx Zoo; however, I can no longer find the source online.

23. See generally: https://animals.sandiegozoo.org/animals/leopard.

24. McMahan (2010). Given the brevity and the speculative nature of this piece, it seems unfair to credit McMahan with a philosophical theory on this topic.

25. For an excellent example of new philosophical research on these questions, see Delon (2021).

11. THE CAPABILITIES OF FRIENDSHIP

1. This paper is partially based on Nussbaum (Wichert) and Nussbaum (2021). See also other articles from this symposium: Bendik-Keymer (2021b), Delon (2021), and Linch (2021).

2. Pitcher (1995, p. 20).

3. See Smuts (2001).

4. Pitcher (1995).

5. Pitcher (1995, p. 20).

6. Ibid., p. 32.

7. Pitcher never names the relationship in the book, partly because it was written in a still-closeted time, partly because it was intended for families. But there was no concealment in their life.

8. Pitcher (1995, pp. 30–31).

9. Ibid., pp. 160–61.

10. Ibid., p. 161.

11. Ibid., p. 162.

12. Ibid., pp. 46–47.

13. Ibid., p. 53.

14. Ibid.

15. Smuts (2001).

16. Ibid., p. 295.

17. Ibid.

18. Ibid.

19. Ibid., p. 299.

20. Ibid., p. 300.

21. Ibid., p. 301.

22. See Poole (1996).

23. Ibid., p. 275.

24. Ibid., p. 270.

25. Ibid., p. 276. Both male and female African elephants have these secretions.

26. Ibid.

27. Townley (2011).

28. A salient case was the 1951 movie *Bedtime for Bonzo*, in which a psychology professor (played by Ronald Reagan) tried to teach a chimpanzee human morality, proving the superiority of nurture over nature. Nobody associated with this movie seems to have had any interest in the real moral lives of chimpanzees in their own group.

29. See Whitehead and Rendell (2015).

30. Amos (2015).

31. See NineMSN (2017) (summarizing the views of activists against the zoo's adoption of Knut), https://web archive org/web/20070701010523/http://news .ninemsn.com.au/article.aspx?id=255770.

32. de Waal (2019).

33. Ibid., p. 20

34. Ibid., p. 13. Van Hooff, born in 1936, is still living.

35. Pepperberg (2008). For more scientific detail see Pepperberg (1999).

36. See Bekoff (2008).

12. THE ROLE OF LAW

1. See Sen (2009). I reply to Sen in Nussbaum (2016b).

2. In this section I am indebted to Sunstein (2000). The page references are to the working paper version, Sunstein (1999).

3. Sunstein (1999, pp. 5–6).

4. Animal Welfare Act (AWA), 7 U.S.C. § 2131 et seq (1966).

5. Ibid.

6. Ibid.

7. Ibid.

8. *Anti-Vivisection Society v. United States Department of Agriculture*, 946 F.3d 615 (D.C. Cir. 2020). Recently, the appellate court granted standing to the plaintiffs and denied the USDA's motion to dismiss.

9. Endangered Species Act (ESA), 16 U.S.C. § 1531 et seq (1973).

10. The Wild Free-Roaming Horses and Burros Act (WFHBA), 16 U.S.C. § 1331 et seq (1971).

11. Ibid.

12. Marine Mammal Protection Act (MMPA), 16 U.S.C. § 1361 et seq (1972).

13. Ibid.

14. Ibid.

15. Migratory Bird Treaty Act (MBTA), 16 U.S.C. § 703 et seq (1918).

16. Ibid.

17. For the current list of protected birds, see "List of Migratory Birds," 50 C.F.R. 10.13 (2000), https://www.govinfo.gov/app/details/CFR-2000-title50-vol1/CFR -2000-title50-vol1-sec10-13.

18. *North Slope Borough v. Andrus*, 486 F.Supp. 332, 361-2 (D.C. Cir. 1980).

19. *United States v. Moon Lake Elec. Association*, 45 F.Supp.2d. 1070, 1074 (D. Colo. 1999). Subsequently, other energy companies entered plea agreements to avoid trial on the same issue.

20. *Newton County Wildlife Association v. United States*, 113 F.3d 110, 115 (8th Cir. 1997).

21. *Seattle Audubon Soc. v. Evans*, 952 F.2d 297, 302 (9th Cir. 1991).

22. See Friedman (2021); Friedman and Einhorn (2021).

23. See "Regulations Governing Take of Migratory Birds," 50 C.F.R. 10 (2021), https://www.govinfo.gov/app/details/FR-2021-01-07/2021-00054.

24. *Hollingsworth v. Perry*, 570 U.S. 693 (2013).

25. *Elk Grove Unified School District v. Newdow*, 542 U.S. 1 (2004).

26. *Lujan v. Defenders of Wildlife*, 504 U.S. 555 (1992).

27. *Nair v. Union of India*, Kerala High Court, no. 155/1999, June 2000. For subsequent cases, including a 2014 Supreme Court case, coming to the same conclusion, see Shah (2019), https://www.nonhumanrights.org/blog/punjab-haryana-animal-rights/.

28. Sunstein (1999); Sunstein (2000).

29. *Animal Legal Defense Fund, Inc. v. Espy*, 23 F.3d 496 (D.C. Cir. 1994).

30. I omit "competitive injuries," briefly treated by Sunstein and found unpromising.

31. *Lujan v. Defenders of Wildlife*, 504 U.S. 555 (1992); *Sierra Club v. Morton*, 405 U.S. 727 (1972); *Humane Society of the United States v. Babbitt*, 46 F.3d 93 (D.C. Cir. 1995).

32. *Japan Whaling Association v. American Cetacean Society*, 478 U.S. 221 (1986).

33. *Animal Legal Defense Fund v. Glickman*, 154 F. 3d 426 (1998).

34. Ibid., at 429.

35. *Sierra Club v. Morton*, 405 U.S. 727 (1972).

36. Ibid., at 752 (Douglas, dissenting).

37. Ibid., at 745 (Douglas, dissenting).

38. Ibid., at 752 (Douglas, dissenting).

39. *Cetacean Community v. Bush*, 386 F.3d. 1169 (9th Cir. 2004).

40. Ibid., at 1175.

41. *Palila v. Hawaii Department of Land and Natural Resources*, 639 F.2d 495 (9th Cir. 1981).

42. For this suggestion I am indebted to Jared B. Mayer. After I drafted this chapter, I got to know the related work of David Favre in Favre (2000) and Favre (2010). Favre's work is internal to the legal system as it is, giving fiduciary rights and a type of standing only to animals who are someone's property. Thus, it assumes, at least for the sake of making concrete progress, that it is permissible to hold animals as "living property." I, of course, deny this. And it offers legal progress

only for a limited class of animals, primarily companion animals. Nonetheless, it is very good work, and it is interesting to see how far protections can go through an approach rooted in current law, with all its defects.

43. See Scott and Chen (2019, pp. 227, 229).

44. Mayer (2020).

45. For the most recent: https://www.humanesociety.org/sites/default/files/docs /2020-Horrible-Hundred.pdf.

46. Brulliard and Wan (2019).

47. See SourceWatch: https://www.sourcewatch.org/index.php/Missouri_puppy mills.

48. Holman (2020).

49. Municipal Code of Chicago, § 4-384-015 (2014).

50. *Part Pet Shop v. City of Chicago*, 872 F.3d 495 (7th Cir. 2017).

51. Associated Press (2020), https://apnews.com/article/8f5dada41cb7a4afc25403d4 c93365f5.

52. Spielman (2021).

53. See PAWS: https://www.paws.org/resources/puppy-mills/.

54. For a comprehensive overview of this issue by the Animal Legal Defense Fund, with a map showing how things stand in the states at present, see: https://aldf .org/issue/ag-gag/.

55. Pachirat (2011).

56. See the European Convention's website for discussion of food safety: https:// ec.europa.eu/food/sites/food/files/animals/docs/aw_european_convention _protection_animals_en.pdf.

57. European Parliament and Council Regulation No. 2008/20/EC, L47/5 (2018).

58. See the World Animal Protection's "Animal Protection Index" (2020), https:// api.worldanimalprotection.org/.

59. In this section I draw extensively on three articles co-authored by me and the late Rachel Nussbaum Wichert. Most of the legal analysis and discussion of the International Convention for the Regulation of Whaling and the International Whaling Commission is hers. These articles contain extensive references to the legal literature that I do not attempt to reproduce here. See Nussbaum (Wichert) and Nussbaum (2017a); Nussbaum (Wichert) and Nussbaum (2017b); Nussbaum (Wichert) and Nussbaum (2019).

60. *Sonic Sea* (2016).

61. A comprehensive account of the treaty and its history can be found in Fitzmaurice (2017), https://legal.un.org/avl/pdf/ha/icrw/icrw_e.pdf. See also her book Fitzmaurice (2015). See also Dorsey (2014).

62. *Whaling in the Antarctic (Australia v. Japan: New Zealand intervening)* (Int'l Ct. 2014), https://www.icj-cij.org/en/case/148.

63. Fujise (2020).

64. *Institute of Cetacean Research v. Sea Shepherd Conservation Society*, 725 F.3d 940 (9th Cir. 2013).
65. See my detailed account of Kozinski's resignation as a result of sexual harassment allegations, in Nussbaum (2021).
66. Gillespie (2005, pp. 218–19) (quoting New Zealand representative to the IWC).
67. See: http://us.whales.org/issues/aboriginal-subsistence-whaling.
68. Ibid.
69. Especially remarkable is Rebecca Giggs (2020). With her vivid and passionate writing, Giggs powerfully makes the case that whales are not only important in their own right, but also a test of the depth and insight of our humanity.
70. At the time, however, New Zealand was not fully independent of Britain, and there were other provinces that also granted women the vote early.
71. See my chapter on pride in Nussbaum (2021).

CONCLUSION

1. See White (2015). He specifically cites my earlier work in Nussbaum (2006).
2. See chapter 3 for this and other examples of Bentham's love for animals.
3. I discuss this emotion at greater length in the final chapter of Nussbaum (2018a).
4. Rott (2021).
5. Harvey (2021).
6. Animal Legal Defense Fund (2021), https://aldf.org/article/animals-recog nized-as-legal-persons-for-the-first-time-in-u-s-court/. For the opinion, see *Community of Hippopotamuses Living in the Magdalena River v. Ministerio de Ambiente y Desarrollo Sostenible*, 1:21MC00023 (S.D. Ohio 2021).
7. As discussed in chapter 12, Indian courts have given animals standing as persons since 2000 (in Kerala), since 2014 (in the nation as a whole). A judge in Argentina ruled in 2016 that Cecilia, a chimp, whom her ruling transferred to a sanctuary in Brazil, was a person with legal standing: see Samuels (2016). And Kaavan, an elephant in Pakistan who won transfer to a sanctuary in Cambodia in 2020, was also given personhood and standing. His story is the subject of the recently released documentary *Cher and the Loneliest Elephant*, chronicling the role of actor Cher, along with various animal welfare groups, in his release. According to the Nonhuman Rights Project (email correspondence), these (and the news from Colombia) are the only examples of animal personhood so far.
8. Osborne (2021).
9. Levenson (2021).
10. Carrington (2020).

Index

About the Author

MARTHA C. NUSSBAUM is the Ernst Freund Distinguished Service Professor of Law and Ethics, appointed in the Philosophy Department and the Law School of the University of Chicago. She gave the 2017 Jefferson Lecture for the National Endowment for the Humanities and has received the 2016 Kyoto Prize in Arts and Philosophy, the 2018 Berggruen Prize in Philosophy and Culture, the 2021 Holberg Prize, and the 2022 Balzan Prize in Moral Philosophy. She has written more than twenty-two books, including *Upheavals of Thought: The Intelligence of Emotions*; *Anger and Forgiveness: Resentment, Generosity, Justice*; *Not for Profit: Why Democracy Needs the Humanities*; and many more.